Olcayto Eryüksel
Suadiye Pembegül Sok. Gülpalas
Ap. D. 14 Istanbul-Turkey
Tel. 359 08 52

TURKEY 1972

Main texts written by
NÖEL CALEF

Contributors

BARBARA SHUEY
IDA TURNER DONNAT
SUSAN AKERS GEORGE

Color Photographs by SONIA HALLIDAY
Drawings by W. RONDAS
Black and white maps by RAYMOND XHARDEZ
Color fold-out map by KULTURA, Budapest
Black and white photographs by SONIA HALLIDAY (16),
Turkish Ministry of Tourism (4), Club Méditerranée (1)

fodor's

TURKEY 1972

Illustrated edition with color map and city plans

EUGENE FODOR
WILLIAM CURTIS
Editors

ROBERT C. FISHER
BETTY GLAUERT
Associate Editors

PETER SHELDON
Area Editor

DAVID McKAY COMPANY, INC.-NEW YORK

Travel Books Edited by Eugene Fodor

1936 ON THE CONTINENT
1937 IN EUROPE
EUROPE IN 1938
MEN'S GUIDE TO EUROPE
WOMAN'S GUIDE TO EUROPE
FODOR–SHELL TRAVEL GUIDES, U.S.A.
    (8 volumes)

1972 Area Guides, Revised Yearly

GUIDE TO EUROPE
JAPAN AND EAST ASIA
CARIBBEAN, BAHAMAS AND BERMUDA
SOUTH AMERICA
INDIA
MEXICO

1972 Country Guides, Revised Yearly

AUSTRIA
BELGIUM AND LUXEMBOURG
CZECHOSLOVAKIA
FRANCE
GERMANY
GREAT BRITAIN
GREECE
HAWAII
HOLLAND
HUNGARY
IRELAND
ISRAEL
ITALY
MOROCCO
PORTUGAL
SCANDINAVIA
SPAIN
SWITZERLAND
TURKEY
YUGOSLAVIA

Printed and bound in the Netherlands
by Dynamic Inc. Maarn

EDITORS' FOREWORD

A recent addition to the expanding list of titles in the Fodor series, *Turkey* represents a challenge to the reader, and the preparation of this book was a formidable task for authors and editors alike. Our task was monumental—how could we hope to compress into a few hundred pages the fantastic opportunities Turkey offers the traveler? How, indeed, could we be selective about the abundance of magnificent beaches, exciting historical sites, treasure troves of art and the myriad of exotic mosques? Surely, we thought, we should include them all. Include them we did, at the risk occasionally of being terse in our comments, for no one can discard a single element that goes to make up this touristic paradise, this land called Turkey.

It's hard to talk about Turkey without talking in contrary terms. At one and the same time, it's among the newest and the oldest countries in Europe (and geographically, it's not *all* in Europe, anyhow). Guardian of the Bosphorus, it is the eastern anchor of the North Atlantic Treaty Organization, yet it maintains a strong presence in the Middle East and is on increasingly friendly terms with neighboring communist nations. At one and the same time, it straddles Europe and Asia—that is, the Turkish giant stands with one toe in Europe and a huge body in Asia (this country's 296,000 square miles make it bigger than France, and even, perish the thought, bigger than Texas!).

Scenically, it offers everything from snow-crowned mountains to tropical beaches (the latter but a few hours' travel from the former). In Turkey, thanks to its history of four energetic cultures, you can span 20 centuries just by crossing the street. Culminating a glorious history of Hittite, Hellenistic, Byzantine and Turkish accomplishments, this nation today is the free world's most fantastic experiment in bringing 31,000,000 people overnight from the Middle Ages to the 20th (or even the 21st) century.

Turkey is the New Frontier for the tourist. Comparatively undeveloped with respect to hotels and other facilities (as opposed to Spain or Switzerland), it is also uncrowded. The empty beaches will afford you privacy, the uncrowded roads relatively carefree travel. Above all, you will experience the thrill of being on the receiving end of traditional Turkish hospitality, especially in the smaller towns and in the countryside. Eager to meet with foreign visitors (especially if you have taken the trouble to learn a few phrases in Turkish), the Turks will, given the chance, overwhelm you with kindness. The nation is on the verge of great expansion in the tourist plant, so if you want to reap the benefits of a friendly welcome without too much competition from other travelers, get to Turkey as fast as you can!

★ ★ ★

Among the many people, Turkish and non-Turkish, who have helped us to produce this book, we owe a special debt to:
The members of the Ministry of Tourism, in particular Mr. Nihad Kürsad, former Minister of Tourism; Mr. Munci Giz, Deputy Undersecretary of the Ministry; Mr. Umit H. Demiriz, Director-General of Information in the former Ministry of Tourism and Information, and his assistant, Mr. Erdogan Icen; Mr. T. Karacabey, Director of the Turkish Tourist Office in London; Mr. Okyay Camlibel and Mr. Yusuf Mardin, former directors of the London office; Mr. Zeyyat Gören, Director of the Turkish Tourism Office in New York; Mr. Edwin Ryžy of the Ministry; and Mr. Ali K. Aknil and Miss Ömür İnanli of the Istanbul office.

★ ★ ★

In a book of this size, a few errors are bound to creep in, and when a hotel closes down suddenly, or a restaurant's chef produces an inferior meal, our comments seem suddenly out of place. Let us know, and we will redouble our efforts to investigate the establishment and the complaint. Your letters will help our correspondents throughout Europe to pinpoint trouble spots, and may help them in evaluating the results of their own research.

As faithful readers of the Fodor series know, merely listing an establishment in one of our books is sufficient recommendation. Needless to say, establishments will not know if they are listed, or dropped, until the book is published.

We accept advertising from a few firms representing the cream of the travel industry, but there is absolutely no connection between the advertising and the editors' recommendations. We have advertising for two good reasons, namely (1) the advertisements partially defray the high cost of yearly republication, including revising the books thoroughly, something which we are the only guide book series in the world to do; and (2) the advertisements themselves carry useful information to readers, frequently showing photographs of the establishments or containing other information which we cannot include in our own text.

CONTENTS

THE TURKISH SCENE

THE FACE OF TURKEY

AN INITIATION TO TURKEY

Europe's Window on the East

People take to Turkey, or they do not. The boundless tracts of barren land filled the French author Benoist-Méchin with awe. "A huge plain, an empty space lost in the back of beyond; a sea of low-lying grass, rippling in the wind, dry in summer, but renewed each spring into fresh green, giving off the very smell of life under the trampling of the wild horses; a deep wide sky, too big for the earth, holding, or so it seems, the fate of a continent."

Lawrence of Arabia was struck by the unthinking obedience of the Turkish soldier. "This quite hopeless lack of initative made of them the most dependable, tireless, and tractable soldiers in the world ..."

André Gide came back from Konya, sickened. "The land is farmed, but where are the farmers? As far as one can see, and from far back, not a living being, not a village, not even a lonely hut ... the country, the whole people, in its backwardness and formlessness, is beyond understanding or hope ..."

Yet the self-assurance of the Turkish country-dweller in all his poverty is astonishing. He and his betters, says Lord Kinross, have "above all, that lack of an inferiority complex which may derive from centuries of running an empire".

All four men are right.

One of our collaborators wrote, "No sooner have we left behind us, on the highway, an austere Bulgaria, whose huge red star shines far out from the top of the border watchtower, than we have the feeling of having crossed the line that divides the west from the eastern wonderland of our youthful dreamings." Another traveler put it differently: "No sooner have we crossed the eastern border into what is, after all, the poorest part of Turkey, that skirts Iran, than we at once have the feeling of home, of being back again in the western world."

Again, both men are right, each in his own way.

The Turks are a mixed nation, made one by a common will. They are a people formed by an eastern culture and religion, who have undertaken to raise the level of living by way of western reforms, giving up many age-old customs which were the source of their strength at one time. Like the hands on the face of a clock, the traveler is too late or too early for the perfect point in time and place, pointing east or west alternatively as he traverses the country.

Religion's Heavy Influence

The will to bring the country up to date and on a par with the western world, a task undertaken by Mustafa Kemal and carried on by his followers, could not be made universal overnight in a country whose peasants make up 80 percent of the people. If western Europeans and Americans imagine they have remained a Christian culture, Turkey, long untouched by the forward movement of the western world, is all the more firmly founded on an unmoving base, that of Islam. That being so, religion here has remained a living force, stronger than the individual man, and shaping both his private and public life, where the westerner has long been free to act according to his own lights.

Within that set religious framework, Kemal introduced an idea, of long standing in the west, but revolutionary in the east: that of separation between religion and state. Until the republic which Atatürk founded, the sultan was also the caliph; that is to say, the king was also pope. With a fully justified ruthlessness, modern Turkey's great man laid a hot iron to the open sore. To say that he healed the ill, or that he failed to heal it, would be going too far; the outcome was somewhere in between. Until his time, the state of affairs had never been questioned. Even those who felt no need for religious reforms felt the need to back their leader, his countrymen's hero. Those who mistakenly wished, once Kemal Atatürk was dead, to go back to the past, found they had nowhere to go.

That today's government gives a token freedom to the die-hard conservatives to go back to the old ways; that the wearing of the turban is allowed in the countryside; that the priests are here and there getting back a hold on society; that many women go on wearing a veil—none of that can any longer stop the Turk from knowing that the ruling of a country and the ruling of souls are two different things, and that it is possible to keep them apart. If some *ulemas* may, at the opening of a sermon, speak to their Moslem brothers before addressing them as brother Turks; if the call to prayer can again be chanted by the *muezzin* in Arabic, the sacred language, and not in Turkish, as Kemal had ordered, the progressive elements look on these small steps backward as so many harmless, old-fashioned revivals. Kemal has been a miracle-worker for the Turkish people, and not the least of his miracles has been to show his countrymen that they could fit into the life of the modern world without giving up the faith. Nowadays, any Turk will tell you that the Gazi Mustafa Kemal was never against religion, but against the political power of the priesthood.

The Turk believes in God. God is Allah and Mohammed is his prophet. But his eyes, from now on, look to the west, even if his body and soul are bent in prayer towards the southeast.

Peasants, Poets and Politicians

The evolution of the countryside is slow, and its dead weight, slowing down the forward drive of the towns, is often a drag on the state. Of course, the canvassing of votes has often led the would-be deputy to support the peasant in the "good old ways" to which the latter was attached. Kemal alone, the idol of the masses, could afford to undertake unthinkable changes.

Who and what are these peasants? A Turkish writer, Mahmut Makal, himself of peasant stock, describes them: "Brave, rooted in old customs, long-suffering, simple yet cunning, the town-dwellers' new ways have not touched them. Religion has shaped them and stopped the clock, and passing events come and go without leaving a trace." This trait, together with the power to withstand hardship, to be contented with a bare living, strength of body and an ingrained fatalism of the mind, have made of the Anatolian peasant the best soldier in the world.

The western European countryside is fast losing its land-workers as industry attracts manpower to the cities. In Turkey, the uprooted peasant finds himself at a loss in the towns, and barely keeps alive on odd jobs. The newborn industries cannot find jobs for five million new workers. Once in Ankara, Istanbul or Izmir, the young people who have left the family farm find nothing better, if they are lucky, than part-time work as a *hamal* —porters or dockhands—or as *boyaci*—shoe-shiners.

The feudal spirit is still strong among the wealthy landowners, or *ağas*, and among the former ruling classes and the rich business-men. The peasant remains in their power—by long force of habit, by training, by unthinking acceptance of the established order, he shoulders without question his forefather's load.

Mustafa Kemal did not have time to do it all. He died too young.

And the city intellectuals? Socially speaking, the young stu-dents come for the most part from the middle class. The rich also send their sons to the university; but the boys tend to take courses with openings into well-paid jobs. The workman is clearly under a handicap. On an ideological level, the new generation has been educated in the principles of Atatürk: secularization and nationalism.

There has always been a certain provincialism in the Turkish character, and it still holds true. (If you ask a man what he is, he will not answer "I am a Turk"; he will say, "I come from the Black Sea".) The country is still divided into distinct regions that the native-born look on as homelands. A merger that usually takes a very long time here took place within a few years, and for two reasons: first, the unifying effect of the war of indepen-dence. Second, modern times had brought far-flung places to-gether by modern means—the press and the radio. In 1923, Atatürk found himself in a divided country. By 1933, he had united it.

The building of roads and the new railways and cross-country buses had helped, of course. In the old days, a man from Erzurum had never seen a woman from Edirne in his own town; today, marriages between young people from far-flung places is a common practice. Added to that, there is an inland movement of emigrants; also, meeting with foreigners of all kinds, though seemingly irrelevant to the unification of the Turk, has worked towards it by broadening his outlook, while strengthening his common front against altogether alien cultures.

Effects of Working Abroad

Turks now go to Germany, to France, to Switzerland, to Belgium; even to Australia and to Canada. And they marry Christians; the workman comes home with a German or Belgian bride. She is made welcome by his closed Moslem family, doubtless with misgivings; but such a thing, unheard-of in father's time, is no longer considered unacceptable.

In 1971, give or take a few numbers, there was talk of 500,000 Turks working on two- or three-year contracts in foreign lands. These men, and sometimes women, who have crossed the border and known other ways of life, come home and conform to family custom, but bring new ideas with them. First of all, who goes abroad? Up to now, it was (and then, rarely) a student taking a course in a foreign university. Nowadays, it is the Anatolian farmer, the peasant, who leaves. He comes back, well dressed, with hat and umbrella: a European. With money also, which is all to the good! For the rest of his life, he will be giving lessons to the village—for he comes home to his village with his fine suitcases and, if he struck it rich, a car.

So much for appearances. Inwardly, what has become of him? On setting out, he is a Turk on his passport, a Moslem on his identity card, if maybe less so in practice. From time to time, he used to go to the mosque, for form's sake more than from faith. No sooner has he crossed the border than this lukewarm soul becomes a single-minded patriot and a devout zealot, and thereby so much clay in the hands of ideologists. Humanly speaking, he brings back with him a broadened cultural outlook and some professional skill. He buys a bit of land, and builds a house on the western plan. While the men are away, the villages are left to the women. Such a change in Islam—a woman who fends for herself! A change whose outcome it is difficult to foresee, beyond the present fact that the evolution of Turkey is well under way.

What does the westerner make of it, and above all the foreigner visiting in Turkey? Loosely the following: the Turk seeks no more than his own well-being. Only the truly evolved Turk among the elite of the big cities has changed his outlook together with his way of life.

Hospitality as a Way of Life

However brief his stay in the country, the traveler will above all remember the open-handed generosity of the Turks, whose inborn hospitality cannot fail to touch him. A word to the wise: form no opinion on Turkey in Istanbul alone.

During your travels, try stopping, just for the sake of experience, in a small Turkish village. You will at once be surrounded by the nicest kind of attention—the poorest peasant will feel bound to offer you something, if only a chair to sit on. Remember, you are never a tourist in Turkey—you are a *misafir*, a guest, to whom all regards are due. There will always be somebody, a boy smarter than the rest, who can garble a smattering of foreign words. Coffee? Tea? A cigarette? A glass of water? Somebody will run to bring it from the fountain. A circle will form. You will all talk together through a makeshift spokesman, or with your hands. In less time than it takes to tell, you will feel lost in the pages of a travel book of the 19th century, or even earlier. The poor in Turkey may not be clean, as modern standards go, but they are delightful, with an age-old charm whose loss we instinctively feel. Accept the *çay* (tea)—it will give them pleasure; accept the *kahve* (coffee)—so sickly with sugar in your honor that you will have to make an effort to swallow it.

Unlike most Mediterranean countries, Turkey, even in the most crowded and lively ports, is not noisy. The women hang the washing at the windows, but they do not call out loudly to each other across the street. The Turk speaks quietly and acts slowly, with an almost priestly dignity. He is pleasant and well-mannered, and his speech is flowery. It is worthy of note that he treats his animals well. By nature and by upbringing, he is an easy-going man, a grave optimist.

A farmer's wife at Kütahya, near Iznik
Photo: Sonia Halliday

The Turk has no ill-feeling, let alone an anti-colonial complex, towards the great powers who, over the centuries, obtained enormous privileges by treaties, called *capitulations*. These were a form of mortgage by which several European countries signed a paid agreement with the government, the terms of which freed the nationals of each from any law or tax but that of his own country, down to the very postage stamps. Of this lowest ebb in his history, the Turk seems to have lost even the memory, as he has of his past greatness and power. All that matters to him is the present. The past, if he knows of it at all, is over; the future is in the hands of Allah.

When he gladly boasts, at times, thumping his chest like Tarzan: "I am a Turk!", he is not only priding himself on the feats of his forebears— his pride is a matter of present fact, that of belonging to a community; to him, that is joy enough. He has imported cars, but no complexes, from abroad.

The key-word, no less strong for being unspoken, is *sabır*, patience. The whole Middle East is conditioned, by its history, its religion, and its very climate, to a patience that breeds its own quiet wisdom.

Remember that talk between well-mannered people, if it turns on politics, is full of taboos. The last days of the Caliphate may be summed up in two words: horror and abomination. You will be spared the details, offensive to foreigners, who did not always behave like gentlemen. The educated Turk will also take care not to remind you that his country, for 400 years, held sway over a quarter of Europe.

Dignity in the Towns

In both the town and the country dweller, in spite of the republic's leveling policy, class distinctions are still very marked, as is the poor's eagerness to serve the rich. Birth, position, money —all play a strong part. However, the seeming servility of the lower orders is not without its dignity, and is moreover quite free of the hostility elsewhere common between classes. There is often an innate honesty—a powder-room attendant will offer a lady a towel, eau-de-cologne, a comb, but refuse a tip because "The gentleman has already given me". You will also find that the worker is loyal to his employer, and that together they form a sort of family.

Bodrum (ancient Halicarnassus) seen from the Crusaders' Castle
Photo: Sonia Halliday

This being so, the shining of shoes is looked on by the servants as a demeaning task, as unwelcome a job as in America—you will nearly always find the shoes you left outside your door as dusty in the morning as on the eve before. Is it a hint from the shoe-shiners' union? In some hotels, an agreement has been made with a "specialist", who takes care of the work; in any case, the shine will be charged on your bill.

Be that as it may, the city streets are full of *boyaci*. In his hands, the small, shining, painted or brass-plated box, with its brushes, its rags, and its shoe polish, becomes the tool of a skilled workman, to be handed down from father to son. A far cry, indeed, from his Italian or Spanish counterpart, who juggles with the brushes and puts more spit than polish— he should see the Turk at work! The *boyaci* will not merely smear your shoes with black or brown; he mixes the polish from both tins to most nearly match the shade of the leather, with the care of a painter, and like a painter he fixes the color with a high varnish. When he is through, you walk away in works of art. The artist looks at his disappearing handiwork through narrowed eyes, then, with a wave of the hand of the utmost *grandezza*, he summons a nearby errandboy and orders a well-earned glass of tea.

The difference between town and country is striking. To give a rough idea, the three big cities (Istanbul, Ankara and Izmir) have three-fourths of the doctors in all Turkey, over three-fourths of car number plates, and almost as many radio sets.

The big centers are a hodge-podge of humanity: Turks, foreigners, and the resident minorities. These last—Sephardim Jews, Armenians and Greeks—are mostly grouped together in Istanbul. Though often working side by side, they live apart. These colonies have dwindled in size, but play an important part in the life of the city; fluent in foreign languages, the men are given many jobs that deal with tourists. That is why the Turk, at every mishap that befalls the traveler, is apt to shrug off all responsibility: "It's the fault of the minorities", as indeed it is, and none of his business.

For the town dweller, outside of the very rich who live in palaces, and the very poor (whose lot we shall go into later), the housing is not unlike that of western Europe, but on a simpler scale. It gets, to be sure, simpler and simpler, as we travel eastward. A high-ranking official in a ministry, with an important job, has a small four-room apartment for a family of four to five people, in what looks to the European like a workman's housing unit. The rent is fairly low, paid for monthly. In summer, the rooms are bearable; they all have cross-ventilation, as indeed they must. But the winters! It is in winter that a country's poverty is plainly shown. And at that, our high-ranking official belongs to a privileged class; he earns something like TL 2,000 ($ 134 or £ 56) a month.

Big businessmen and manufacturers, of course, earn more. But by far the greater part of the people can never make such a sum. The average white-collar worker is paid TL 1,000 ($ 67 or £ 28) a month, the workman even less. For the odd-job man or the unemployed, there are no lodgings but the *gecekondu*, not really a slum, but well on the way to becoming one. It's an old Turkish custom—a house built in one night, the roof on by dawn, on unowned land, belongs to the builder. He has squatter's rights, and cannot be moved out. Of course, if a night-watchman happens to catch him before the roof is on, he will have to begin all over again. This side-line of the law has become a commonplace in Turkey since the republic has lured more and more peasants towards the towns, so much so that there is talk of giving the squatters legal rights of ownership.

The Villagers' Existence

Poor as they are, the makeshift huts of the *gecekondu* have become the villagers' dream by comparison with the village. On the country roads, the traveler is often dismayed by the nameless villages, poverty-stricken and sun-baked, with a huddle of broken-down walls, patched up with the clay bricks that are set out to dry.

In the eastern provinces, the harsh winters make for a dire poverty unknown to western man. The peasant buries his house halfway into the hillside. Unlike the cave-dwellers, he does not settle into a natural hole, open to all weathers; he digs himself a dwelling-place into the rock, one room, rarely two. Odd as it may seem, this den is clean. The peasant sits on the floor of beaten earth, and sleeps on a hand-woven carpet, the *kilim*.

Outside, at the entrance, is a three-legged stand, over a fire made of cowdung: *tezek*. It burns well, without flame, but with a good red heat; the smell is awful. Another drawback, it has to be blown on ceaselessly. The pot hangs from the crotch of the stand, and so much for the wretched soup-kitchen.

Where there are trees, the houses, of course, are made of wood —not logs, but planks, with wooden tiles for the inner roof. The overhanging roof is made of clay poured onto laths and thatched with straw, which keeps out the heat in summer and the cold in winter. The more skillful builders make openings for windows. Those who have the means buy glass panes; the others cover the gaps with animal skins or bladders, through which seeps a meagre light. The names of villages often recall a color: *boz*, grey, or *sarı*, yellow. It is the shade of the earth that gives the settlers' dwelling-place its character and its name.

The *yurts*, or cone-shaped leather tent of the Mongolians, is not often seen, being cold and easily upset by the wind. As a rule, it belongs to the nomads, or *yürük*, above all in the Taurus, to the south.

The food is barely enough to keep the peasant alive. He lives on his own produce; the *Shiite* Muslim of the east eats neither rabbit nor pork—for that matter, meat is seldom seen on his table, when he has a table. His daily fare is bread, made of wheat or corn; on feast days, he may have a fowl or mutton roasted on the spit, *kebab*. But it will more likely be a cheaper meat: *pastırma*, a kind of sausage made of dried beef pounded with plenty of garlic.

In a bad harvest year, there is nothing to fall back on. In those parts, a time of hunger begins with a time of feasting—the peasant kills and eats the animals he can no longer feed. After that, there is nothing but to wait for Allah to have mercy on the painfully empty belly. (Of late, the U.S.A. has helped through the harsh winters with speedy shipments of wheat.)

If you happen to pass through a middling-sized village, take a walk through the market. The tradespeople are not ready for the tourist trade—all they have on display is for the local shopper. You will see objects on sale that nobody back home would think of making or selling, let alone buying. And the buyer? You have not, as yet, measured the depth of his poverty. Not that you are lacking in feeling, but that he himself seems not to feel it. His acceptance of his lot, his fatalism, while not joyful, are neither sad nor indifferent. He is, after all, alive, and the Turk loves life above all.

In these empty plains which cover nearly one-third of the country, any form of entertainment is scarcer still than in the coastal west. Most small towns have movie houses, but the cafés, of course, are everywhere. That does not mean that the men who sit at the tables always order coffee or tea—it is more often a glass of water with a spoonful of raspberry or rose jam (often on the house) and a well-thumbed newspaper. Between work, men spend the day there, while the women keep busy at home. The café owner has no hard feelings towards his many unprofitable guests —he has chairs, and what are chairs for if not to sit upon? Talk is free for all, and the owner himself, more often than not, pulls up a chair to take part in it. It is the very center of village life and gossip. Where there are several cafés, the men talk across the road, or get up to change tables—they can hail a waiter from either one and order a glass of tea. They are on good terms with both owners, who would not think of taking offense. Anyway, the business works out the same all round, in the end.

Things are different, of course, in the west of Turkey and even more so in the big towns copying foreign ways. Even so, the presence of a Turkish woman is frowned upon—she is supposed to meet her friends in her or their home. Cafés are for the men.

To the western mind, the Turk sells his wares with a naiveté that lacks all commercial sense. He is, for reasons that spring from a living religion, altogether honest in his dealings: it is written that you shall not harm your neighbor. Theft is almost unknown. It happens, of course, that in shops that cater to foreigners (and even to Turks) the bill is sometimes slightly upped, and not always by "the minorities". That is called progress. Little by little, the younger generation is conforming to international usage, and the time will soon come when the Turk can take care of himself as well as the next man.

As a buyer, the Turk is no better than as a salesman. For the most part, he shops only for his strictest needs, and stays within his means. There is no flood of advertisements to make him want things he can well do without—only the big firms go in for publicity. Out of ten advertisements, five or six are given over to the banks. The traveler is at a loss to understand why, but the reason is simple. The banks, mostly state-owned, cannot exist without making a bid for the people's small earnings. A man can open an account with as little as TL 150 (about $10). All means are good that catch a client—the number of every bank account is dropped into a lottery, drawn from once to four times a year; apartments and even (why not?) nice fat sums of cash fall to the lot of the lucky winners.

Nightlife

The houris of the Moslem heaven, the odalisques of the Moslem harem, of whom 18th- and 19th-century romanticists used to dream, live only in the pages of old-fashioned novels. There are nightclubs catering to the local Turks as well as the tourist trade, with rather sterile belly-dancing. If the traveler wishes to see where the lower-class local citizens go for their belly-dancing, he must go the Sirkeci quarter, near the rail station. He will come into a big hall crowded with tables, and with people eating and drinking. The women in such places are frankly bawds. On the stage, an orchestra makes up in noise for all the Turks' quiet daily manner. The violin, the *saz* (a sort of mandolin) and even the tambourine, let alone the voice of the singer, are amplified by loudspeakers. The devilish din let loose by the music covers the shrill voices, the guffaws, and the overall uproar. On the fingers of the dancing-girls are the *kaşık* —a sort of castanet, like a metal spoon—which add to the hubbub. One dancer follows another, all in a state of sleazy undress. The show is always the same—a few lewd shakes that have nothing to do with art, belly-dancing, or even eroticism. The clapping is barely over when the ear-splitting music breaks out again, another dancer comes on stage, and the whole dreary round begins all over. (In the fashionable nightclubs, the show is the same, if less coarse.)

In the old days, the dancing-girl would "honor" the guest by shaking in front of him. He was then bound to place a gold coin on the forehead of the backward-swaying odalisque, whose task was to go on twisting without letting the coin fall. In this age of paper money, the fans walk up to the stage and slip a banknote into the girl's bra, or, if they are more daring, into the top of the panties. Nowadays, the fun is rough and ready. Where, the romanticist might ask, is the eastern refinement of old?

The answer to this question is, of course, that democracy has killed refinement in belly-dancing. Dancing kept on the level of an art for the chosen few is one thing—a show put on for the masses and for gullible foreigners is another. It is the unbridgeable gap between quality and quantity. To make matters worse, good Turkish dancers are signed up abroad, where they make better money; they put in only a few appearances at home, when on holiday. Both reasons explain the cheapening of an art which, long kept to a high standard by a knowledgeable few, has lowered itself to the undemanding tastes of the crowd.

Leisure and Culture

Not Friday (Islam's sabbath), but Sunday, is the day of rest in Turkey. The women are always busy around the house. The men are at the sidewalk cafés. Some play *tavla*, a game that travelers of old brought back to the west under the name of backgammon. Sometimes, families go on a picnic to the Çamlık, a wood on the outskirts of town; the older people rest in the shade of the trees, while the children play. In the richer towns, the Çamlık has a swimming-pool; it often has a café, and a restaurant where you can bring your own food. In the villages, the few spare hours are spent even more simply—sitting on the doorstep or gossiping.

There is no nationwide television, though a network has recently been set up, and men trained in its use. On the other hand, people make what can only be called immoderate use of the radio, even more so since transistors have flooded the market. Unluckily, the Turks, who have a rich folklore and a remarkable musical background, are now in the throes of the modern age's growing-pains, pop music being heard everywhere.

There is a fairly flourishing movie industry here. As a rule, the Turkish movie is a melodrama, a pistol-packing eastern, so to speak, of the war of independence, or a song-and-dance story. The output is high, perhaps fourth-greatest in the world, but foreign films are imported, mainly from the U.S.A., Italy and England.

There are concerts and opera, of course, in the big towns. Istanbul has a number of enterprising theatrical companies, *tiyatro* that sometimes put on foreign avant-garde plays. During the season, festivals, both of music and theater, take place amid historic ruins. The spell of sound, of lighting, and of old stones can make the onlooker forget that he is seeing a play about Italy, written in English and spoken in Turkish, in a Greek setting.

The age-old tradition of the shadow-play is fast dying out. The main character, *Karagöz*, is (or *was*, it may almost be said) an unmannerly puppet, a poor boob who settles all his quarrels with blows, a good guy always fooled but coming out the winner in his endless sparring with swindlers, ruffians and bawds. The farce, meant for both children and grown-ups, often went far beyond western European bounds of seemliness.

There are quite a few Turkish magazines—as more people learn to read, the old story-teller is disappearing. Most of the old tales dealt with the most popular character in the Near East, Nasreddin Hoca. Renowned for his wisdom and his wit, he seems to have lived sometime in the 14th century, though his so-called sayings and doings would have filled up more than a lifetime.

The Place of Women

A few women, in the big towns, have taken to the letter the law of Atatürk, who put women on the same legal footing as men. Some have even sued for divorce in court, and won against the husband. By far the greater number, however, are still following older traditions.

The middle-class town-dwellers dress western fashion. In the countryside, the *şalvar*, or long baggy bloomers, are fast disappearing, as is the bodice. Nowadays, country women wear straight linen slacks, western style, which they call a pyjama, and a sweater.

In Anatolia, if she has not yet taken to western ways, a woman always wears a shawl or a scarf on her head. When a man passes by, she still draws a corner of it over the lower part of her face. In old-fashioned towns, like Konya or Kayseri, most of the women are veiled. Atatürk, in his war against old customs, made the wearing of a fez punishable by prison; but while asking the women to drop the veil, he left them to do as they pleased. (To discourage wearing of the veil by respectable women, Atatürk ordered prostitutes to wear it constantly!)

Women are "tolerated" in the mosque. Nothing forbids them

from going, beyond an unwritten law. It is simply expected that they pray at home. The mosque, being a public place, is meant for men only.

To offset these drawbacks, the ladies have charming names—*Melâhat*, "beauty", for example. As a matter of fact, so do the men —*Demir*, "iron", and *Aslan*, "lion". In Turkey, the men and women are sometimes called after the flowers, the fruits, and the dew of a beautiful countryside.

We have spoken in passing of family life, with a word of pity for the woman. She seldom, however, pities herself. She knows no other life, and hers is not without advantages. Fully taken in charge by her husband, she is not asked to share his worries. On the other hand, she alone rules the household, thereby earning the unquestioned respect of her children. She can also look forward to the day when she passes all her burdens on to her daughter-in-law—old age, which begins early, has also earned the right to unquestioned respect. Last, but not least, her needs, however humble, are taken care of by her husband.

Of course we are talking of the country. In the towns, the women, more modernized, look more and more up-to-date. But outside of the towns, in spite of all the government's efforts and the most progressive laws, the Turkish woman, on the whole, remains backward. Luckily, commonsense tells us that she will not long remain veiled and in shadow, when her childhood friends are living in the light of day.

The Last Word

On saying good-bye to the *misafir*, the guest, the Turk says: *güle-güle*. Word for word, that means: laughing-laughing. The true meaning is "Go with a smile". Hopefully, your trip to Turkey will also end with the greeting: "güle-güle!"

Illustration at head of this chapter: A general view of Istanbul.

FACTS AT YOUR FINGERTIPS

FACTS AT YOUR FINGERTIPS

Additional practical hints about hotels, restaurants, transportation, etc., of a regional and local character, not contained in this section, will be found throughout the book.

A KEY TO HISTORICAL SITES

The modern Turkish place-names for many historical sites may be unfamiliar to the reader looking for places of which he has read in classical studies. The historic names are given in the left column below, the modern place-names (or nearest town today) in the right. See color map at end of book for additional historical place-names.

Classical Name	Modern Name
Aesani	Cavdarhisar
Alexandria	Troas
Amisos	Samsun
Adrianople	Edirne
Ancyra	Ankara
Antioch	Antakya
Antioch of Pisidia	Yalvaç
Antiphellus	Kaş
Aphrodisias	Geyre, nr. Karacasu
Aspendos	Belkıs
Assitawandas' Palace	Karatepe
Assos	Behramkale
Attaleia	Antalya
Brusa	Bursa
Claudiconium	Konya
Claudiopolis	Mut
Cnidos	Datça
Colophon	Değırmendere
Commagenes	Nemrut Dağı
Constantinople	Istanbul
Cybira	Horzum
Daphne	Harbiye
Didyma	Yenihisar
Edessa	Urfa
Ephesus	Efes, nr. Selçuk
Filyos	Hisarönü
Flaviopolis	Kadirli
Gallipoli	Gelibolu
Gordion	Yassihüyük
Halicarnassus	Bodrum
Hattuşaş	Boğazköy
Heraklea	Ereğli
Hierapolis	Pamukkale
Issos	Dörtyol
Kanes	Kültepe
Karasu	Giresun
Lampsacus	Lapseki
Laodicea	Denizli
Magnesia ad Sipylus	Manisa

Classical Name	*Modern Name*
Magnesia ad Maeander	Söke
Midas	Yazılıkaya
Milidia	Nr. Arslantepe
Miletus	Balat
Mylasa	Milas
Myra	Demre
Neocaesarea	Niksar
Nicaea	İznik
Nicomedia	İzmit
Nyssa	Sultanhisar
Olba-Diocaesarea	Uzuncaburç
Pergamum	Bergama
Perge	Aksu
Philadelphia	Alaşehir
Philomenion	Akşehir
Phocea	Foça
Phoenicus	Finike
Pompeiopolis (I)	Viranşehir
Pompeiopolis (II)	Taşköprü
Priene	Güllübahçe
Sardis	Sart, nr. Salihli
Segalossos	Ağlasun
Seleucia	Silifke
Selimye	Side
Smyrna	Izmir
Sylleum	Yanköy
Telmessos	Fethiye
Termessos	Güllük
Theodosiopolis	Erzurum
Thyatira	Akhisar
Trebizond	Trabzon
Tripolis	Buldan
Troy	Truva
Xanthos	Kınık

Konyaalti Beach, near Antalya, on the Turquoise Coast
Photo: Sonia Halliday

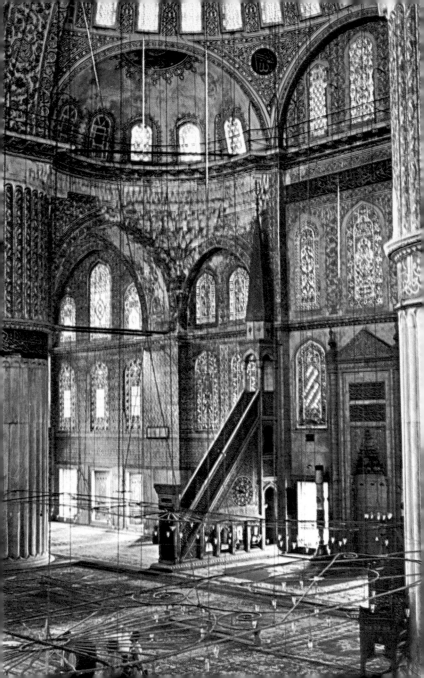

PLANNING YOUR TRIP

WHEN TO GO? In Turkey, the tourist season lasts from the beginning of April to the end of October, and is at its height in July and August. The best time of the year is from April to June and in September and October. Some parts of the country, like the Aegean and the Mediterranean, attract visitors the year round. Istanbul is very pleasant in autumn.

Temperatures.
Average for 24 hrs given first, then average early afternoon temperature, Fahrenheit. (See "*Staying in Turkey*" for more information.)

	Jan.	Feb.	Mar.	Apr.	May	Jun.	Jul.	Aug.	Sep.	Oct.	Nov.	Dec.
Ankara	31	34	41	51	61	65	73	73	65	57	47	36
	39	42	51	63	73	78	86	87	78	69	57	43
Istanbul	41	42	45	53	61	69	73	73	68	61	53	46
	45	47	52	61	68	77	81	81	75	67	59	51

CALENDAR OF EVENTS

In **February,** at Uludağ, Burse, international ski championships. Also at Kayseri, Erzurum and other sites.

March 18 is ANZAC Day at Çanakkale, but it is a local Victory Day, of course.

April, from the 18th to the 26th, Spring Festival in Manisa. The 23rd, National Sovereignty and Children's Day, is celebrated throughout the country with programs of sporting and cultural events. On the same day, Tulip Festival at Emiğan (Bosphorus) near Istanbul. Horseracing all month at Izmir.

The 1st of **May,** for the Turks as for the English countryside, is May Day, the feast of spring, and not Labor Day, as in western Europe. The month of May sees the first of the many theater, music, and folklore festivals of the year: those of Ephesus, with theater in the ancient ruins, and of Aspendos, with its many artistic events, among which are the classical plays put on by the Turkish National Theater. Festival of Pergamum in late May. The Festival of Pamukkale (Hierapolis), near Denizli, with folk songs and dances, plays in the antique theater, lasts 4 days during the second half of May (variable dates), followed by the Theater and Music Festival at Antalya, and the Festival of Istanbul. The Black Sea Fair in Samsun lasts from the 19th of May to the 10th of June. The 19th of May is dedicated throughout the country to Youth and Sport; among the more noteworthy events are an Art Exhibition, and a display of athletic games and gymnastics by school and university students in the Ankara Stadium. Horseracing May 1–June 30 at Ankara.

In the second half of **June,** the Turkish wrestling matches of Kırkpınar in Edirne, last 3 days. Concerts by Mehter Military Band in Istanbul (until August). On the 27th, Constitution Day (1960) is celebrated throughout the country with parades, military bands, fireworks. In late June or early July, St. Peter's feast day is celebrated at Antakya, with religious ceremonies in St. Peter's Grotto.

Inside the Blue Mosque, Istanbul
Photo: Sonia Halliday

July 1st is the Day of the Sea, with boat races in all Turkish ports. From the 5th to the 10th of July, the Festival of Nasreddin Hoca is held in Akşehir. Follows the Bursa Sword and Shield Festival, from the 7th to the 12th. The Istanbul Theater Festival begins on the 5th of July and lasts until the 15th of September, with a program of both Turkish and foreign companies.

From the 11th to the 18th of **August** is the Festival of Troy. The biggest Christian event of the year is held on the Sunday after the Assumption, in the "House of the Virgin Mary" on Mount Aladağ near Ephesus. Thousands of pilgrims throng to the spot, and the Archbishop of Izmir says Mass. From the 20th of August to the 20th of September an International Fair, the biggest commercial event of the Near East, is held in Izmir. The 30th of August is Victory Day, with a big military parade in the Ankara Hippodrome for the President of the Republic. The Gaziantep and Mersin Festivals are also held in August.

More festivals in **September:** from the 5th to the 8th in Manisa; Festival of Aphrodisias; from the 19th to the 20th in Pamukkale, with folklore dances, among which the famous shield dance of Bursa. Also: Congress of Sivas and Aydin Festival; Iznik Festival; Cappadocia Festival. Izmir Liberation Day is September 9th.

On the 1st of **October,** the opera season opens in Ankara and in Istanbul. From the 1st to the 10th of October, both a festival and a fair take place in Antalya. Festival of Trabzon, 25th. The 29th is the anniversary of the Turkish Republic, with big youth and army parades in the Ankara Hippodrome for the president, as well as in Taksim Square in Istanbul for the governor.

In **December,** an interesting event: the Rites of the Whirling Dervishes, in Konya, from the 7th to the 17th. Best book your tickets well in advance through a travel agency.

Note   Some events have variable dates from year to year, so check in advance of your trip.

THE HIGHLIGHTS OF TURKEY. The art of travel, like all arts, is to know what to leave out. You cannot see, in one visit, all of Turkey, a country as big as France, Belgium, Switzerland, Denmark and Portugal put together. Air travel, of course, allows you to cover great distances in a short time, and the Turkish inland airlines are well run; but it gives you at best a very fleeting knowledge of the country, the people, and their way of life. By car, you are kept within the bounds of good highways, by train to a few main railway lines, and passenger ships on a cruise, as a rule, only dock in Istanbul and Izmir.

Most drivers enter Turkey through *Edirne.* The first look at the Selimiye mosque, and the street life, is unforgettable. Of course, no traveler would think of going to Turkey without a long stay in *Istanbul.* The old town, its countless Mosques and palaces and museums, the network of its streets, the modern town overlooking the Bosphorus, one of the most beautiful waterways in the world, and the Golden Horn, form a whole that delights the most hardened globe-trotter.

Bursa is worth a day's outing for its monuments, its atmosphere, and its position at the foot of Mount Uludağ, the Olympus of Bithynia. It is within easy reach of Istanbul, as are the beaches of Kilyos and of Şile on the Black

Sea, the Princes' Islands, Çanakkale (by boat from Istanbul), and the ruins of Troy for lovers of antiquity. Historic *Nicaea* (Iznik) is also nearby.

Towards *Ankara*, Abant and its lake, via Bolu. Ankara itself is a green oasis in a near-desert landscape, with its modern architecture and its Hittite museum, the last an indispensable preparation for sightseeing in Boğazköy.

On the west coast of the Mediterranean, *Izmir* is the best starting point for excursions to the ancient Greek towns of *Pergamum*, *Ephesus*, *Dydima*, *Priene*, and so on. The whole region is full of interest to art lovers. *Pamukkale*, near Denizli, has one of the wonders of nature: its splendid petrified waterfalls. On the southern coast, *Antalya* is a magnificent holiday resort: beaches and mountains as far as Alanya, and mild weather even in winter.

To the south and southeast of Ankara, the Turkish art towns of *Konya* and *Kayseri*, and the extraordinary stone outcroppings of *Göreme* and *Ürgüp*, are part of a separate itinerary. The region of *Antakya* (the old Antioch) and of *Adana* and *Iskenderun*, on the way to Syria and Lebanon, is mostly of historical interest.

To the northeast, on the *Black Sea*, the coastline from Sinop to Trabzon is just being discovered. Best see it by boat, a 6-day cruise leaving from Istanbul.

The east of Turkey is touristically little developed. It is the way to Iran (the detour by Samsun and Trabzon, along the coast, is recommended). To the southeast of Erzurum, the Lake Van region is stark and beautiful, and has some interesting ruins. Archeologists will find the valley of the Euphrates (Fırat in Turkish) of great interest, together with the astonishing necropolis of the Commagenes.

Some of the most renowned *Christian sites* are in Turkey, such as the Virgin Mary's house in Ephesus, St. Peter's cave in Antakya (the old Antioch), the Basilica of St. John at Ephesus, and at Demre, the church of St. Nicholas (near Kaş). Going back to Bible times, some 40 place-names in the New Testament alone are now within the Turkish border. The "Seven Churches of Asia" on the scene of St. Paul's momentous journeys, are all here.

For a first journey, it is best to limit yourself to Istanbul, Izmir and environs, with, perhaps, a trip to Ankara, and a well-earned rest in Antalya.

WHERE TO GO? Even more than in other countries, it is not easy to plan a trip through Turkey. There is too much to see at one time, too many things to be taken into account:—whether you are going to sightsee, to rest, or just to travel around; whether you are willing or not to put up with discomfort and bad roads. As of now, there are two planned tours, along good roads, with good hotels, and within fairly close range of the more interesting sites.

The short tour takes you from Istanbul to Yalova – Bursa – Manisa – Izmir – Ephesus – Izmir – Pergamum – Troy – Çanakkale: about 620 miles in 5 or 6 days.

The grand tour takes you from Istanbul to Bursa – Troy – Pergamum – Izmir – Ephesus – Kuşadası – Pamukkale – Burdur – Antalya – Alanya – Silifke – Konya – Göreme – Ankara – Istanbul: about 1,680 miles in about 2 weeks.

If you have no car, and want to spare yourself the trouble of train travel and booking hotel rooms, take a steamer from Istanbul for a cruise along the Aegean, Mediterranean, or Black Sea coasts, with stopovers at the main ports. You can make the trip last longer, from 6 to 12 days, by changing boats.

If you have time to spare, a good car for bad roads, and are sufficiently adventurous not to mind varying degrees of discomfort and language difficulties, you can undertake the devotee's tour of Turkey, nearly 3,730 miles, in a month, as follows: Istanbul – Ankara – Boğazköy – Amasya – Tokat – Sivas – Malatya – Adiyaman – (Nemrut Dağı) – Gaziantep – Adana – Kayseri – Cappadoccia – (valley of Göreme – Ürgüp – Nevşehir) – Konya – Beyşehir – Antalya – Burdur – Pamukkale – Aydın – Ephesus – Kuşadasi – (Priene – Miletus – Dydima) – Izmir – Pergamum – Edremit – Troy – Bursa – Istanbul.

 HOW TO GO? When you have decided where you want to go, your next step is to consult a good travel agent. If you haven't one, the *American Society of Travel Agents*, 360 Lexington Ave., New York, 10017, or the *Association of British Travel Agents*, 50–57 Newman St., London, W1P 4AH, will advise you. Whether you select *Maupintour*, *American Express*, *Cook's*, or one of the smaller organizations, is a matter of preference.

They all have branch offices or correspondents in the larger cities. The *American Automobile Association* also arranges numerous escorted tours abroad. There are good reasons why you should engage an agent.

Travel abroad today, although it is steadily becoming easier and more comfortable, is also growing more complex in its details. As the choice of things to do, places to visit, and ways of getting there, increases, so does the problem of *knowing* about all these questions. A reputable, experienced travel agent is a specialist in details, and because of his importance to the success of your trip, you should inquire in your community to find out which organization has the finest reputation.

If you wish your agent to book you on a package tour, reserve your transportation and even your first overnight hotel accommodation, his services should cost you nothing. Most carriers and tour operators grant him a fixed commission for saving them the expense of having to open individual offices in every town and city.

If, on the other hand, you wish him to plan for you an individual itinerary and make all arrangements down to hotel reservations and transfers to and from rail and air terminals, you are drawing upon his skill and knowledge of travel as well as asking him to shoulder a great mass of correspondence and detail. His commissions from carriers won't come close to covering his expenses, and thus he will make a service charge on the total cost of your planned itinerary. This charge may amount to 10 or 15 percent, but it will more than likely *save* you money on balance. A good travel agent can help you avoid costly mistakes due to inexperience. He can help you take advantage of special reductions in rail fares and the like that you would not otherwise know about. Most important, he can save you *time* by making it unnecessary for you to waste precious days abroad trying to get tickets and reservations. Thanks to his work, you are able to see and do more.

There are four principal ways of traveling:

The *group tour*, in which you travel with others, following a pre-arranged itinerary hitting all the high spots, and paying a single all-inclusive price that covers everything—transportation, meals, lodging, sight-seeing tours, guides. And here your travel agent can book you with a *special interest* group; thus you needn't spend a high proportion of your tour trotting round museums if you would much rather be wandering round botanical gardens, and you will be among people with similar interests to your own.

The *prearranged individual tour,* following a set itinerary planned for you by the travel agent, with all costs paid in advance.

The *individual tour,* where you work out the itinerary for yourself, according to your own interests, but have your agent make transportation and hotel reservations, transfers, and sightseeing plans.

The *free lance tour,* in which you pay as you go, change your mind if you want to, and do your own planning. You'll still find a travel agent handy to make your initial transport reservation and book you for any special event where long advance booking is essential.

TURKISH TOURISM AND INFORMATION OFFICES

500 Fifth Avenue, New York, N.Y. 100036	Tel. LO4-5990
49 Conduit Street, London W.1	Tel. 734-8681
56 Piazza della Repubblica, Rome	Tel. 46-29-57
Rue Hamra, Beirut (Lebanon)	Tel. 23-48-89
Press Attaché, Turkish Embassy, 20 Philhellinon, Athens (18)	Tel. 23-80-50
Turkish Embassy, Khiyabani Ferdowsi, Teheran (Iran)	Tel. 25-351

TRAVEL AGENTS SPECIALIZING IN TOURS TO TURKEY

In the United States:

Amarican Express, 65 Broadway, New York 10006.
Berry World Travel, 91st & State Line Rd., Kansas City, Missouri.
Global Tours, 230 Park Ave., New York 10017.
Maupintour Associates, 270 Park Ave., New York 10017.
Travcoa, 111 N. Wabash, Chicago 60602, Ill.

In Great Britain:

Academy Travel Ltd., 10 Bloomsbury Way, London WC1A 2SJ.
Aegina Club Ltd., 25a Hills Road, Cambridge.
Erna Low Travel Service, 47 Old Brompton Road, London SW7.
Horizon Holidays, Ltd., 17 Hanover Street, London W1.
Lord Brothers, 9 Grosvenor Street, London W 1.
Lunn-Poly Holidays & Travel, 36 Edgware Road, London W2.
Oceanways, 23 Haymarket, London SW 1.
Thos. Cook & Son, Ltd., Berkeley Street, London W 1.
Wings Ltd., 124 Finchley Road, London NW3.

171.5
13.0
201.0
―――――
385.5
―――――

WHAT WILL IT COST? To date, travel in Turkey is still relatively inexpensive. Outside of the big towns, the cost of living is downright cheap, but hotels are not up to western standards. Hotel prices are approved routinely by the Ministry of Tourism.

The hotel industry being, by and large, in its infancy, the traveler (unless he is camping) will be better off in the few hotels of European standing: at least Category 2 in the official hotel guides (and in this book). Motels are built and equipped on western lines, all rooms with showers, restaurants; they are rated category 2. There are a few big luxury hotels, like the *Hilton* in Istanbul, the *Büyük Ankara* in Ankara, and the *Büyük Efes* in Izmir, where a room with two beds, bathroom, telephone and airconditioning costs about 170–250 TL (for the last two) or 250–320 TL (for the first). *For exchange rates, see p. 39.*

Of course, you can get by very well on a limited budget; auto fuel is not expensive; neither are trains, and buses and shared taxis or dolmuş even less so; the inland airlines are reasonably priced.

The traveler who wants to avoid dull meals in hotels or international-style restaurants should go to Turkish restaurants; he will eat better and pay less, and it will cost him hardly more than to pay board at his hotel.

Of course, each traveler spends according to his needs and means. But to have a general idea of the cost of travel, see the range of prices in the organized tours. For instance, a 15-day return journey (round-trip) by air from London, all costs included, costs about $240 (£100), while an 8-day trip could be about $300 (£125) if you stay exclusively at deluxe hotels.

Cruises in the area, some touching Turkey too briefly, operate by air from New York to a Mediterranean port, then, for example, 12 days on a ship touching Greek, Turkish and Cypriot ports, and return to New York by plane. Average cost: $750 to $1100.

The free lance traveler who scorns organized tourism still needs to make a rough estimate of his holiday expenses. Here are a few prices of hotel rooms (single with bath or shower):

At *super deluxe* establishments (*Hilton* in Istanbul, for example), $15 to $20 (£6.25 to £8.34);

At *deluxe* hotels, $10 to $13 (£4.17 to £5.42);

At *first-class* hotels, $8 to $10 (£3.34 to £4.17);

At *moderate* hotels, $6 to $8 (£2.50 to £3.35);

At *inexpensive* hotels, $4 to $7 (£1.65 to £2.90);

And at *rock-bottom* hotels, $3 to $6 (£1.25 to £2.50).

Your meals will cost: Breakfast in a hotel, 5 to 10 TL (except the *Hilton*); Lunch or dinner in a *deluxe* restaurant in Istanbul, Ankara or Izmir, 30 to 60 TL, in more *modest* Istanbul establishments only 15–25 TL. In *all other places* in Turkey, you can expect to pay about 10–20 TL. (Table d'hote only, wines, etc. not included in figure.)

A Turkish coffee costs from 1 to 1.35 TL, a glass of beer to take out, 1.70 TL, in restaurants, 2.75 TL. A pack of 20 Turkish cigarettes costs 1.80 TL (*Bafra*), 4.50 TL (*Yeni Harman* or *Samsun*). A pack of English or American cigarettes costs 8–10 TL. A man's haircut is 4 TL, a woman's shampoo and set 25 TL, a manicure 5 TL. A ticket for the opera is 9–25 TL. A drink in a nightclub is from 25 to 58 TL, depending on the place.

TYPICAL FIRST-CLASS BUDGET FOR ONE DAY
(around Istanbul)

(*Exchange rate: $1 = 15 TL, £1 = 36 TL, approximately.*)

Room in a first-class hotel	130 TL
Breakfast	10 ,,
Lunch and dinner in a modest Turkish restaurant, with half a bottle of local wine and Turkish coffee	60 ,,
Transportation (dolmuş, ferry)	10 ,,
Outing	20 ,,
Cigarettes	10 ,,
Extras	10 ,,
or approximately $16.65 or £6.94	250 TL

You will notice the relatively high cost of the hotel room as compared to the price of meals, for whereas you lodge "western style", you will do better, in every way, to eat "Turkish style". On the other hand, the shared taxi or dolmuş is well organized, and often spares you the expense of a private taxi.

Throughout the Istanbul region, the cost of hotel rooms is fairly high, as the demand is still far ahead of the supply. Elsewhere in the country, prices are lower, and in Edirne as in Bursa, you can find a decent room with 2 beds, bath or shower, for around 70 TL.

DEVALUATION OR INFLATION?

Devaluation in some European countries, with consequent rising taxes and costs throughout, and possible inflationary trends to come, make accurate budgeting in advance an impossibility in any country.

Prices mentioned throughout this title are indicative only of costs at time of going to press. Check with your travel agent near the time of your trip for latest details.

 WHAT TO TAKE? The first principle is to travel light, and fortunately for the present-day traveler, this is really possible, due to the manufacture of strong, lightweight luggage, and drip-dry, crease-resistant fabrics for clothing. If you plan to fly, you have a real incentive to stay below the first-class transatlantic limit of 66 pounds and economy limit of 44 pounds; each pound overweight costs extra money. Moreover, most bus lines as well as some of the crack international trains place limits on luggage weight (usually 55 pounds) or bulk.

Even if you are traveling by ship, resist the temptation to take more than two suitcases per person in your party, or to select luggage larger than you can carry yourself. Porters are increasingly scarce in these days of European prosperity, and you will face delays every time you change trains (or hotels), go through customs, or otherwise try to move about with the freedom that today's travelers enjoy. Motorists need to be frugal, too. You should limit your luggage to what can be locked into the trunk or boot of your car when you make daytime stops. At night, everything should be removed to your hotel room.

Clothing. If you are wisely limiting yourself to two average-size suitcases, it's obvious that your clothes must be carefully selected. The first considerations are the season of the year and the countries you plan to visit. You must also bear in mind the altitude at which you plan to stay. Sea level resorts may be fine for summer wear, but warmer evening clothes are essential for places only a few miles inland at a higher altitude.

Travelers checks are the best way to safeguard travel funds. They are sold by various banks and companies in terms of American and Canadian dollars and pounds sterling. Most universally accepted are those of *American Express*, while those issued by *First National Bank of New York* and *Bank of America* are also widely used. Best known and easily exchanged British travelers checks are those issued by *Thos. Cook & Son* and these banks: *Barclays*, *Lloyds*, *Midland*, and *National Westminster*.

Women. The present vogue for mix-and-match separates minimizes travel problems: two or three skirts of varying texture, with four or five types of blouses or sweaters will ring the changes through any number of days. Drip-dry and non-crushable fabrics will make for easy laundering. Pack a warm sweater or two, or a knitted jacket, and a light wool or fur stole for evening. Underwear should be the minimum of easily washed nylon, and a light nightrobe that could double as a beach robe is useful. Lightweight rainwear is also advisable.

Practical, low-heeled shoes may seem less attractive than open-toed or stiletto models, but they are much more comfortable for the hours of walking over cobbled or dusty streets that you are likely to do. A pair of soft, sleek slippers is useful for long plane or bus journeys, as well as in the hotel bedroom.

Men. Apart from a business suit for evening wear and a lightweight suit, a sports jacket to mix with two or three pairs of slacks, a light raincoat or overcoat should complete your outerwear requirements for several weeks. Shirts and underwear are best of drip-dry variety, and whether the shirts are of the standard or colourful style will depend on the country you are to visit. Socks and pyjamas are also best when in drip-dry fabric. A lightweight dressing gown that will double as a beach robe is also useful.

If you are visiting a number of countries during your trip, consider leaving your electric razor at home and take a battery-operated razor.

Generally. Tissue handkerchiefs, such as Kleenex, are useful when traveling, and they are usually much more expensive abroad. Toilet rolls never come amiss, especially in the country districts; these, of course, can be bought en route in the larger towns. Although towels are usually supplied in European hotels, soap is very often not, so bring a tablet or two to last you until you can stock up in the shops. Remedies for headaches, constipation, seasickness, etc., are best brought with you because, though readily available, they may not suit you so well as the ones you are used to. Prescriptions for special medicines and for spectacles should always be carried.

Americans and Britons can arrange with one of the travel credit organizations for a European charge account that enables them to sign for hotel and restaurant bills, car rentals, purchases, and so forth, and pay the resulting total at one time on a monthly bill. This is particularly advantageous for businessmen traveling on an expense account or on business trips whose cost is deductible for income tax. Offering this service are the *American Express*, with branch offices in all major cities, *The Diners Club*, 10 Columbus Circle, New York, *Carte Blanche*, 3460 Wilshire Blvd., Los Angeles, *Eurocard*, 48 Blvd. Adolphe Max, Brussels I, Belgium, and others.

Special recommendations for Turkey. The country can be sizzling in summer and chilly in winter, although neither extreme will likely be as great as transatlantic visitors might be inclined to expect. Turkey is a Moslem country, and while bikinis and too brief beachwear may pass in the major international resorts, don't offend local susceptibilities by walking in the street of a small, provincial town in "undress". Women should not enter religious establishments or mosques in slacks, shorts, or attire exposing too much of the body. Show the same respect you would in a cathedral or synagogue.

 PASSPORTS AND VISAS. Passports, but no visas, are required for citizens of the following countries desiring to visit Turkey for a stay of up to three months: United States, United Kingdom, Irish Republic, Australia, Canada, New Zealand, Japan and most west European countries.

Getting a passport should have priority in your plans. **U.S. residents** must apply in person to the U.S. Passport Agency in New York, Chicago, Boston, Miami, New Orleans, San Francisco, Los Angeles, Washington, D.C., or the local court-house. Take with you a proof of citizenship, birth certificate, two recent photographs, $2\frac{1}{2}$ inches square, and \$12.

If you are not an American citizen, but are leaving from the United States, you must have a Treasury Sailing Permit, Form 1040D, certifying that all Federal taxes have been paid; your travel agent, steamship company, or airline can tell you where to get it. To return to the United States, you need a re-entry permit. Apply for it at least six weeks before departure in person at the nearest office of the Immigration and Naturalization Service, or by mail to the Immigration and Naturalization Service, Washington, D.C. Residents holding an Alien Registration Card ("green card"), while they do need the Treasury Sailing Permit, do not need any other papers if they go abroad intending to stay less than one year. If they expect to stay abroad over one year, then they need the re-entry permit, which can only be obtained in the United States. This permit entitles the non-citizen resident to stay abroad a total of two years. (Naturalized American citizens may now stay abroad an unlimited length of time, even in the country of their origin.)

British subjects must apply for passports on special forms obtainable from their local Ministry of Employment and Productivity, or a travel agent. The application should be sent to the Passport Office according to residential area (as indicated on the guidance form) or taken to the nearest employment exchange. Apply at least 3 weeks before the passport is required. The regional Passport Offices are located in London, Liverpool, Peterborough, Glasgow, Newport (Mon.) and Belfast. The application must be countersigned by your bank manager or by a solicitor, barrister, doctor, clergyman or justice of the peace who knows you personally. You will need two photos. The fee is £ 5: passport valid for 10 years. The *British Visitor's Passport* is *not* valid for Turkey.

Note: Train passengers need a passport (but no visa) to go through Yugoslavia and Greece, a passport *and* transit visa through Hungary and Bulgaria.

Health Certificates. Not required for entry into Turkey, but both the *United States* and *Canada* require that citizens and alien residents alike present a certificate of vaccination against smallpox that is not older than 3 years prior to the re-entry date. The simplest way is to be vaccinated before you leave. Have your doctor fill in the standard form which comes with your passport, or obtain one from a steamship company, airline, or travel agent. Take the form with you to present on re-entering. If you put off vaccination until your return to the States, remember to allow time for the reaction that checks the efficacy of the vaccination. Not required for re-entry to *Britain*.

Medical treatment in Turkey. The *International Association for Medical Assistance to Travelers Inc.* (I.A.M.A.T.), makes available to travelers, at no charge, a list of general practitioners and specialists in main centers. The doctors participating are all English-speaking, and have had training in the U.S., Canada or Gt. Britain. Whether you are a sufferer from a chronic ailment for which special medicine or treatment is required, or whether you need the services of a doctor through sudden illness abroad, the membership (*free*) is highly recommended.

Once a member, you are provided with a membership card listing centers in 50 countries, including Turkey. On telephoning the center listed, you will be given a choice of doctors on the day's rota. The fee charged by a general practitioner is regulated by the association. (Office call is about $ 8).

For membership write: I.A.M.A.T., 745 Fifth Avenue, New York 10022; or 1268 St. Clair Ave. West, Toronto.

In return for this free service, I.A.M.A.T., a division of the Foundation for the Support of International Medical Training, and recognized by the American Medical Association, hope you will send a tax-deductible contribution to them. Your gift will further their work in raising the level of health in developing countries through scholarships, local medical education, etc. Some of the money will be used, in addition, to continuing the monitoring activities of I.A.M.A.T. over its list of doctors and hospitals throughout the world, the better to serve the traveler in need of medical care.

A similar service to travelers, but charging $ 5 per membership, is offered by *Intermedic*, 777 Third Avenue, New York.

Getting to Turkey

FROM NORTH AMERICA AND BRITAIN

BY PLANE. Istanbul and Ankara are connected by plane to most of the big cities of America and Europe. Only one airline links Turkey directly with New York—*Pan American*, with daily flights. From London, through flights are operated by *THY* (*Turkish Airlines*) (twice weekly), *BEA* (four times weekly), *Pakistan International Airways* (four times weekly) and *Iran Air* (twice weekly).

For tourists from Britain who intend to take advantage of stopovers on the Continent before proceeding to Turkey (see below), several European airlines can provide routings from London. *Swissair*, for example, can take you on its DC–9 jets to Geneva or Zurich, thence on to Istanbul. An outstanding feature of *Swissair* is its fine food and thorough service.

Turkish Airlines (*THY*, *Türk Hava Yolları*), connects, among others, Amsterdam, Brussels, Munich, Frankfurt, Zurich and Rome with Istanbul. *THY* also have a run between Athens and Izmir, Tel Aviv and Istanbul, Beirut and Adana, Brussels-Zurich and Izmir.

Roundtrip air fare, economy class, from New York to Istanbul is $884 (off-season, $784). A 29-45-day excursion fare, roundtrip, available during certain periods, is only $410, higher at weekends and peak periods.

Return air fares from London are £140 ($336) economy class, £186 ($446) first class. Day-flight tourist return fare (summer) is £105.30 ($253).

Note: Air fares are expected to rise, so consult your travel agent or airline office.

Air-car service. Your airline or your travel agent will take care of all the formalities, and a car, with or without a driver, will be waiting for you at the airport.

BONUS STOPOVERS

From North America

A wide variety of stopovers is available at no extra fare to travelers bound from North America to Turkey. The airlines allow you 6,010 miles each way to complete the trip from New York to Istanbul, permitting considerable flexibility in your itinerary. Stopovers, of course, are entirely optional. You can fly on the same aircraft throughout if you prefer.

Leaving New York, you can be routed first to Copenhagen, via Glasgow. The Scottish city can be used as a sightseeing base before winging across the North Sea to Denmark. Although Scotland is far north of Turkey, this routing is the same as the direct fare.

Between Copenhagen and Istanbul it's possible, without extra cost also, to travel into Eastern Europe, stopping at Warsaw and then visiting Budapest and Belgrade. An intermediate stopover at Athens between Belgrade and Istanbul also is in order. Another possibility is to fly from the Danish capital to Prague and Vienna before stopping at Budapest and picking up the original routing.

Copenhagen also may be used as a gateway for itineraries featuring Germany en route to the Turkish city. There are a number of possible routings. One takes the traveler to Hamburg, Bremen, Hanover and Frankfurt. Continuing south to Istanbul, stopovers also can be made at Nuremberg or Stuttgart and Zurich before arriving at Munich. Another choice of routings is available between Munich and Belgrade. You can visit Vienna and Budapest or land at Zagreb.

Numerous other routing possibilities exist between New York and Istanbul. After visiting Glasgow, you may travel via Edinburgh or Manchester to London.

Another way of reaching London is to fly via Ireland. It costs not a penny more to land at Shannon and Dublin en route. You may continue from Dublin to London nonstop or via Liverpool, Manchester and Birmingham.

Crossing the Channel on the next stage of your trip to Turkey, you have a wide choice of onward routings. You can fly first to Paris and then to Geneva and Nice, thus enabling you to add a many other areas of interest.

Next comes Rome and Athens before arriving in Istanbul. What about alternate routes on the Paris/Istanbul portion of the trip? If you prefer, you can also visit Basel and Zurich before arriving in Geneva. Between Geneva and Rome, you can substitute Milan for Nice if you prefer. Still another possibility is to travel from Zurich to Milan direct.

Instead of turning South from Zurich to Italy, it is also possible to travel from Zurich to Germany, Austria, Eastern Europe, Yugoslavia and Greece. One routing extends from the Swiss city to Munich and then continues to Zagreb, Belgrade, Athens and Istanbul. Another takes you to Vienna and into Eastern Europe at Budapest before arriving in Belgrade.

Portugal and Spain also can be included in an Istanbul itinerary. Leaving New York for Europe, you land first at Lisbon, and then continue to Madrid and Barcelona before crossing into France at Nice. Additional stops at Rome and Athens are in order before arrival in the Turkish city.

Geneva may also be added after visiting Spain and Portugal on some New York/Istanbul itineraries.

Basic economy roundtrip fare, New York/Istanbul is $784, available for one year; first class is $1224 but check with your travel agent for details of many less expensive excursion fares available for shorter periods.

From Britain

British tourists flying from London to Istanbul pay £140 return (roundtrip) tourist fare, but there are other, lower, one-month fares.

A wide variety of free stopovers is offered passengers from Britain. One example permits you to fly via Paris, Geneva, Nice, Rome and Athens. Another allows travel via Cologne, Frankfurt, Vienna, Budapest, Belgrade, Sofia and Athens.

From the Commonwealth

Australian and South African tourists may visit Istanbul en route to or from the U.K. at no extra fare. There are many varied routings. A passenger originating in Johannesburg, for instance, can fly to Istanbul via Tehran, then continue through Europe.

BY PLANE. See *By plane from North America and Britain*, p. 43.

BY TRAIN. Two *main* railways connect Turkey to the chief cities of western Europe. To the north, trains from Holland and Belgium pass through Germany and Austria towards Yugoslavia. To the south, trains from France and Switzerland pass through the north of Italy towards Yugoslavia. All trains have sleeping cars, second-class berths, and a dining-car. The following are the fastest and best connections for Turkey:

Orient Express: London-Paris-Lausanne-Milan-Trieste-Ljubljana-Zagreb-Belgrade-Sofia-Istanbul. Time of journey: 67 hours.

Tauern and *Tauern-Orient Express:* London-Brussels-Cologne-Munich (change)-Salzburg-Ljubljana-Zagreb-Belgrade-Sofia-Istanbul. Time of journey: 67 hours.

The prices of a few fares (subject to change):
London-Istanbul, round trip, 1st class   £79.75 ($190)
London-Istanbul, round trip, 2nd class   £52.80 ($127)
Extra charge for sleeping-berth and meals.

BY BUS. A good way to travel is by motor coach, which allows the traveler a close view of the Balkans. A fascinating tour can also be had through *Wings Ltd.*, 124 Finchley Rd., London N.W. 3, who organize adventure trek holidays in Land Rovers to remote eastern Turkey from £76 ($182). *Varol Tourism*, 32 Allen Rd., London N.16, have a weekly coach service from London to Istanbul. The journey takes 5 days. Roundtrip, £35 ($84).

Penn Tours, operating its big airconditioned coaches through Turkey en route to India, will take passengers for Turkey only if space is available, but naturally gives priority to India-bound travelers. The longer trip is fascinating, and includes 10 days within Turkey (Istanbul, Ankara, Göreme, Adana, Antioch). Cost of trip to India one way £133 ($380). Penn Tours, 122 Knightsbridge, London SWI.

Garrow-Fisher Tours, 37 Fife Road, Kingston-on-Thames, Surrey, operates a tour similar to Penn's.

ORIENTBUS connects Brussels to Istanbul from the beginning of April to mid-September of every year. This service is run by the *Generalcar* travel agency, 10 rue de la Montagne, Brussels 1. Departure: every Saturday. Price from London, including rail and boat connections from England to Brussels, and hotels and meals en route to Istanbul, is only $146.40 (£61) round trip.

One of the many *Europabus* lines connects Munich to Istanbul year round. Journey takes 3 days from Munich. Fare of £33.65 ($82) round trip includes overnight accommodation. Departure and bookings: *Touring-Bureau*, Starnberger Bahnhof (railway station) in Munich, or Victoria Coach Station, London.

Olcayto Eryüksel
Suadiye Pembegül Sok. Gülpalas
Ap. D. 14 Istanbul-Turkey
Tel. 359 08 52

BY SHIP. There are many boat runs between Turkey and Europe, besides the *Turkish Maritime Lines* (*Denizyolları*), whose many up-to-date and remarkably well-run liners (*Akdeniz, Karadeniz, Samsun*, etc.) make the round trip from Marseilles or Venice to Istanbul, with ports of call: 4 days there and 3 days back. The *Truva* car ferry transports passengers and 100 cars from Venice and Brindisi to Izmir in 3 days; the *Istanbul* from the same ports to Istanbul. Fare ranges from $45 (£18.75) to $85 (£35.45) per passenger and vehicles from $21 (£8.75) to $40 (£16.70) one way, from Venice. Fares from Brindisi are less, of course. London agents: *Walford Lines*, St. Mary Axe House, London E.C. 3.

The *San Marco* and the *San Giorgio* of the Adriatica Company shuttle between Trieste-Venice-Piraeus-Istanbul all the year round. The French liners have no regular run to Turkey but sometimes organize cruises, with stopovers, to Istanbul, Izmir, and other ports (spring cruises of the *France* and the *Renaissance*). Italian and Greek liners, *Atlantica, Franca, Olympos, Mykonos*, etc., do likewise.

If you wish to travel on a Russian boat, the M/S *Litva* sails once a month from Marseilles to Odessa on the Black Sea; ports of call are Genoa, Naples, Piraeus, and Istanbul.

A few airline companies, like *Sabena*, organize air-and-sea cruises, the ships leaving from Venice or Piraeus.

Pleasure craft. The Turkish government has set up customs houses in the following ports (arranged from west to east) for travelers on private yachts:

Istanbul	Çeşme	Fethiye	Alanya
Çanakkale	Kuşadası	Kaş	Mersin
Dikili	Bodrum	Finike	Tarsus
Izmir	Marmaris	Antalya	Iskenderun

 BY CAR. From Paris, Brussels, or Geneva, you must count on an average of 4 to 5 days, depending on your hurry or the speed of your car, to cover the 1,860 miles to Istanbul, and to this add London-Paris driving time if appropriate.

(1) Starting from Paris, the best road passes through Châlons-sur-Marne, Metz, and Saarbrücken, where you join the network of German highways, on through Mannheim and Karlsruhe, branch off towards Stuttgart and Munich, Salzburg, Graz, Maribor, Zagreb.

The Maribor-Zagreb road is not bad, but narrow and winding. At Zagreb, you link up with the highway (*autoput*) to Belgrade. It is straight, monotonous, bumpy, and crowded with trucks (mostly by night). It has only two lanes.

Still bypassing Bulgaria, you drive from Niš to Skopje and on to the Greek border on the fine highway, sometimes cut through rock. In Greece, turn left on entering Salonika towards Kavalla, Komotini, Alexandroupolis, and branch right heading for the Ipsala Bridge (Turkish frontier), Tekirdağ and Istanbul. The detour around Bulgaria is about 280 miles, but through delightful country.

(2) An alternative route after Salzburg takes you through Vienna to Hegyeshalom, the Hungarian border town.

To drive through Hungary, you need a 48-hour transit visa. It can be issued at the border or in advance at the Hungarian Legation, 2437 15th St. N.W., Washington, D.C. or the Hungarian Embassy, 35 Eaton Place, London W.1. You can also obtain it through a travel agency, or if need be, the Hungarian Embassy in Vienna. Since 1967, the border police in Hegyeshalom will stamp the Hungarian transit visa on your passport, but this will slow you down, though you will have to wait for your car insurance anyhow—about 30 forints and 15 minutes, if all goes well.

Then on to Budapest and Szeged, the Yugoslav border, Subotica, Belgrade, the highway to Niš, the road to Sofia, Dimitrovgrad and the Bulgarian border. No visa needed if you stay *more* than 24 hours. Otherwise, a transit visa can be obtained at the border or beforehand, at the Bulgarian Embassy, 2100 16th St. N.W., Washington, D.C. or the Bulgarian Legation, 12 Queen's Gate Gardens, London S.W.7. Car insurance for 72 hours issued at the border costs 7 levas.

On to Sofia, Plovdiv, Haskovo, Svilengrad, and the Turkish border; another car insurance fee for Turkey (50 TL), and then on to Edirne and Istanbul.

(3) Drivers starting out from Brussels will go by Loncin, Cologne, and Frankfurt. Better branch off to the Nuremberg highway (*autobahn*), less crowded, and rejoin the main highway at Munich.

(4) Starting out from Geneva, the shortest way passes through Berne, Zurich, and Kreuzlingen. Enter Germany at Konstanz, take the ferry (15 minutes) to Meersburg, and drive along the road to Ulm, where you will link up to the main highway (see above) before Munich. If you do not wish to traverse Bulgaria, you can drive down from Salzburg towards Graz and the Yugoslav border—Yugoslavia requires no visa.

The above highways have the advantage of being more or less flat, and without mountain passes. On the other hand, they are sometimes monotonous (across Hungary and the Zagreb-Belgrade road, especially).

(5) Starting out from Geneva, another road passes through one of the tunnels of the Alps (Mont Blanc or Grand St. Bernard) to the Val d'Aosta (very crowded in summer, 4-lane highway under construction); take the Italian highways near Turin towards Milan and Venice, then at Mestre, a good road towards Trieste and the Yugoslav border. At Trieste, cold war of signposts: don't look for the road to "Rijeka", because it's marked "Fiume" by the Italians. From Rijeka to Karlovac, a good road leads back to the highway at Zagreb. From Switzerland, you can also drive, from Milan onwards, on the Autostrada del Sole (toll) down to Salerno, then, on a good road, to Brindisi; ferryboat to Greece, Igoumenitsa, Larissa, and Salonika, where you link up with the road that bypasses Bulgaria, or direct from Brindisi to Istanbul or Izmir.

(6) A little used, and therefore uncrowded, road is that which leads from Budapest to the Romanian border on Route 4 (at Püspökladány, turn right on Route 4a); border town is Borş. Transit visa required, but no insurance. On to Oradea, Cluj, and Bucharest, to the Bulgarian border bridge of Giurgiu-Russe; insurance. On to Tarnovo, the picturesque former capital of Bulgaria, then to Haskovo, where you link up with the first highway (see 2, above). Expect, however, a good long wait at the Romanian and Bulgarian borders.

(7) If you have time to spare you may, at Rijeka, take the magnificent Adriatic coastal road (*magistrala*) far beyond Dubrovnik, drive inland towards Titograd, and link up with the road through Bulgaria at Niş or the road through Greece at Skopje (for the former through Titovo, Uzice, and Kragujevac, for the latter through Peş, Kosovska Mitrovica, and Priştina). The roads are all under repair, and their state is such that you will have to slow down to nearly 20 miles an hour.

All these roads are unavoidably crowded in places. At the height of the season, best drive through Hungary, for after a mini-jam at the Hungarian border, you can drive on fairly fast. There are filling stations all along the way. Beware of Sundays and nightfall; in the east, most filling stations have an early closing time. Fill up your tank at every possible occasion.

There are yet other variations to the road to Istanbul, such as Munich-Salzburg-Bad Gastein, the Tauern Tunnel (car-ferry train), Mallnitz, Villach, and Yugoslavia; or else the Greek ferryboat at Brindisi to Piraeus, and on and up towards Salonika and Istanbul; but that takes time.

Road maps. Most of the official tourist organizations, whether Hungarian, Yugoslav, Bulgarian, etc., give free road maps, sketchy but enough to go on. For an overall map of the Paris, Brussels, or Geneva to Istanbul journey, the Swiss cartographers, Kümmerly & Frey, put out a map (*Balkans*) which gives you the detailed network of roads from Germany to Turkey, listed above.

By car-ferry train or by car-ferry ship. If you do not wish to drive all the way there are car-trains with sleepers: Paris-Milan, Brussels-Milan, and Brussels-Villach in Austria, from where you link up, either through the Wurzenpass or through the Loibl (Ljubelj) tunnel, with the Yugoslav highway which connects Ljubljana to Zagreb, Belgrade, and beyond.

The *Turkish Maritime Line* (*Denizlolari*) plies twice weekly from Venice via Brindisi: the *Istanbul* to Istanbul, the *Truva* to Izmir. Each takes 100 cars and over 400 passengers. Airconditioning, swimming pool; shower and toilet in every cabin. See "*By Ship*" section, earlier.

Driving license. The international driving license is compulsory in Turkey. En route, for all countries except Greece, the national driving license is enough. The *green insurance card* is only valid, as a rule, for European Turkey (Thrace). In fact, you will have to take out a new insurance for all of Turkey.

Arriving in Turkey

CUSTOMS. Turkish custom officials are very lenient with travelers and rarely look through their luggage. You are allowed your personal belongings, sporting, camping, and photographic equipment, and a bottle of alcohol, but only 50 cigarettes. On the way out, you have the right to souvenirs and gifts, silver and carpets up to 2,000 TL; beyond that, you must have an exchange slip to prove such objects were acquired with foreign currency. There is no duty, however, going out.

EXCHANGE. Banknotes and travelers cheques, whether in American dollars or English pounds, are allowed up to any sum. The rate of exchange of the Turkish pound (TL) is now app. 15 TL for 1 U.S. dollar, app. 36 TL for 1 English pound. Two major banks for all kinds of transactions: *T.C. Ziraat Bankasi*, with 700 branches in Turkey, and *Türk Ticaret Bankasi*, with over 100 branches.

You are allowed to bring in (and take out) only 100 TL. You can change your money at authorized hotels and at banks, at the official rate of exchange.

There are banknotes of 1000, 500, 100, 50, 10 and 5 TL, and coins of 1 TL and 50, 25, 10 and 5 kuruş.

Staying in Turkey

THE WEATHER. The climate in Turkey varies a good deal according to time and place. On the Anatolian plain, summer is hot and dry (up to 102° Fahrenheit) and winter snowy and cold (down to 2° F below zero). The Black Sea coast is mild and damp, with a rainfall of 90 inches a year, while the Mediterranean coast has a moderate climate the year round, with an average of 75° F. In winter, on the Black Sea and the Mediterranean coastlines, a rainy season makes the earth green and renews the precious water supply; but there are days in Iskenderun and Antalya when it is warm enough to bathe. The long summer can be burning hot, but even so the mountain nights are fairly cool, and the coastline is freshened by a sea breeze. When spring is over, most of the sun-parched landscape takes on a pale brown color, except on the sea shore. Maximum and minimum temperatures in a few main cities are as follows:

	January	*July*
Ankara	38°–14° Fahr.	95°–60° Fahr.
Antalya	60°–44°	92°–73°
Bursa	50°–35°	88°–64°
Istanbul	50°–37°	90°–67°
Izmir	57°–42°	94°–71°
Trabzon	52°–42°	78°–68°

HOTELS. The official Turkish classification starts with an *L* (luxurious) and then descends steeply from *1* (first class) to *4* (rock bottom). *M* stands for motel, *P* for pension, *O* for an inn. Luxury hotels are to be found only in and around big cities like Ankara, Istanbul, and Izmir, and so far they are few; a room with 2 beds and bath costs between 170 and 320 TL, not including service and tax. There are not many first-class hotels either, and the price of a room with bath for 2 people is between 100 and 180 TL. Moderate and even occasional inexpensive hotels possess modern comforts, but plumbing is almost universally a weak point, in western- and eastern-style bathrooms alike. Pleasing decorations hardly compensate for this basic fault.

Roughly, we have equated the official categories with our own designations, keeping in mind that what is "first-class" in Turkey is relatively modest by American standards, particularly with respect to bathing and toilet facilities:

Luxurious	Official category: luxurious
First-class	Category (1)
Moderate	Category (2)
Inexpensive	Category (3)
Rock-bottom	Category (4)

Motels are usually in the moderate or inexpensive category. For details, see "*Camping*" below, and regional chapters.

Off the tourist beat, there are places where you will not find one hotel up to western standards. These unclassified and unclassifiable establishments are not necessarily unclean or badly run, but they have none of the comforts we now take for granted: the plumbing is often out of order, there is no hot water, the walls are thin and let through every sound. Of course the price, except in and around Istanbul, is very much lower. See "*What Will it Cost?*", earlier.

Good boarding houses, marked P (for "Pension"), are only to be found in Istanbul, Izmir, or Ankara. Beware of the boarding house ads on the roads leading from the Bulgarian or Greek borders to Istanbul. What passes for "modern comfort" in Turkey will dismay the average westerner.

In a few places, far from everywhere, the only lodgings available are in the private homes of leading townsmen, who give the traveler a warm welcome as a guest, and are not to be offended by an offer of payment. It has to be experienced to be believed. If you happen to be such a lucky guest, remember to send a letter and a small gift—not of money—in thanks for the friendly hospitality, unhappily fast disappearing as the business world takes over greeting the tourist.

Taking into account the scarcity of good hotels, you must, if you are going during the season, book your rooms well in advance through a travel agency.

 HOLIDAY CAMPS. These group settlements, set up for foreign tourists, are made for organized holidays, the cost of which includes roundtrip air travel and lodging in a two-bed bungalow. Private beaches, dance orchestras, planned entertainment, organized outings, yachting, skin-diving and fishing, and so on. Of these holiday camps, the best known are:

FOÇA, near ancient Phocaea, from where the Greeks of Asia Minor sailed to found the port of Marseilles. Restaurant, nightclub, amphitheater. 250 concrete bungalows, each with separate rooms and washrooms—showers, wash basins and toilets. The cabins are grouped in 2 small hamlets, one on the hill, the other in the olive grove. Skin-diving, fishing, etc. An 18-day stay, including round trip air fare from New York, costs from about $550 to $675.

Information at the *Club Méditerranée,* 516 Fifth Ave., New York 10036; 530 W. 6th St., Los Angeles 90014; 40 Conduit St., London W. 1; or 8 rue de la Bourse, Paris (2e), France.

KUŞADASI, near Ephesus, on the Aegean Sea, on a secluded olive-clad promontory and between 2 beaches of fine sand. Bungalows for 800 people, also with washrooms. Bar, outdoor theater, nightclub with record library, small port for sailing craft, bathyscape, very rich sea-depths. Two-week holidays, including air fare to and from Paris, about $300 (£125).

Information: *C.E.T.* (*Club Européen de Tourisme*), 29 rue des Pyramides, Paris (1er), France.

Closer to Kuşadasi village is the much less elaborate *Kuş Tur Village,* which accepts local bookings.

STUDENT TRAVEL AND YOUTH HOSTELS. Young people, more specifically students and scholars, traveling in groups or alone, can lodge at one of the 50-odd student homes and youth hostels in Turkey. If they are listed as "student" or "teacher" on their passport, or if they are bearers of an international Youth Hostel card, they have right of entry to these establishments, whose prices vary from 6 to 9 TL for students and from 7 to 10 TL for teachers. Students may also obtain a card from the Turkish National Student Federation entitling them to reductions up to 50 percent on domestic transport and even certain reductions in fares to Turkey from within points in Europe. Cost: 10 TL.

For detailed information and for booking, write to the *Tourist Department of the TMTF* (National Federation of Turkish Students), Babiali Cad. 40, Cağaloğlu, Istanbul; or to the *Tourist Department of the TMGT* (Turkish National Youth Organization), Tünel, Istiklâl Cad. 471/2, Istanbul.

These departments also arrange excursions for the young in Istanbul and throughout Turkey. Sample tour: 5 days to Bursa, Troy, Pergamum, Izmir and Ephesus: $30 (£12.50). The Turkish National Tourist Office in your country will be pleased to give you all needed information.

It is also worth contacting the travel department of your National Students Union.

Working holidays in Turkey. Students may enlist in the international youth labor camps, engaged on building-yards and social service work, around Istanbul and on the Mediterranean coast. Volunteers are housed and fed, but not paid. They can write to the *Association for the Promotion of Labor Camps in Turkey,* Aşiyan Cad. 4, Bebek-Istanbul.

RESTAURANTS. Avoid the international-style restaurants where the food is indifferent—to please all comers, no doubt—thereby pleasing nobody; go to Turkish restaurants, where you will be served tasty and healthy meals. You will pay far less, and be made welcome by a restaurant-keeper honored by your presence. They are frequented by Turkish men only, but a foreigner can go in with a woman. The bill of fare is, of course, written in Turkish, but you can point out your chosen dish, either among those on display behind glass or by going into the kitchen to choose among those simmering on the stove—except in deluxe restaurants, or those so-called, you are welcome to go into the kitchen and choose your own food. You will find the names of a few standard dishes in the chapter, *Food and Drink*. The service is among the fastest in the world. Leave a 10 percent tip for the waiter and something for the boy who brings the wine, even if service is included in the bill. In some Turkish restaurants, you will find damp scented towels in the washroom to freshen up with; put a small tip of 50 to 100 kuruş in the plate.

In the small towns, you will only find simple restaurants (*lokanta*); these are not always much to look at, but though the food is simple, it is often quite tasty, and absurdly cheap. Nevertheless, check your bill; the country people are honest, but not strong on arithmetic.

In Istanbul, Ankara and Izmir, you will pay from 40 to 80 TL for a several-course meal in a deluxe or first-class restaurant, from 20 to 40 TL in a middling restaurant, and from 15 to 20 TL in a *lokanta*. In the provinces, a meal will cost about 15 to 30 TL.

TIPS. In hotels which cater mostly to Turks, a tip of 10 or 15 percent of the bill will be gratefully received. Most of the good hotels include a percentage for service on the bill, but it is un-likely to find its way to the right pocket; better give a tip, even small (you can round out the sum on the bill) straight to those who took care of you—it is a small price to pay for such smiling willingness to please. About 3 to 5 TL per day to the chambermaid. Waiters expect a 10 percent tip.

Taxi drivers, whose pleasant good manners are unknown among their kind in western Europe, do not expect a tip, but they tend to overcharge foreigners, so agree on a price before setting out. You may then round out the fare asked—the meter is often just for looks. At the movies or at the theater, 50 kuruş to the usher is enough. At the barbershop, men tip 1 TL or 20 percent; at the hairdresser's, women tip 2.50 TL or 10 percent. Porters expect 2 TL per bag, washroom attendants 1 TL, bellboys, 2 TL.

CAMPING. In Turkey, during the last few years, camping is in full boom. Organized camping grounds are mostly in the west near Istanbul and the highway from Greece or Bulgaria. The Ministry of Information and Tourism issues a multilingual folder, *Camping-Turkey*, with all you need to know: time of year when open, location, equipment, and so on. The big oil companies, BP in particular, own well-organized camping grounds (*Mocamp*) with electricity, running water, and sometimes a swimming pool, near some filling stations. As yet, there is no folder listing *all* the camping grounds, and they do not all have the same rules, but by and large they are run there as elsewhere. You will find the list of the main camping grounds in this book, in the chapters dealing with each region.

Mocamp rates (subject to change): 6 TL per person per night, plus 2½ TL per car, plus 2½ TL per tent. Rental of tents at some Mocamps: 15 TL per single tent, 25TL for double, per night. For more details, write *Kervansary Co.*, PO Box 211, Şişli, Istanbul.

HUNTING AND SHOOTING. In Turkey, almost all the countryside is still open to sportsmen. Foreign travelers can hunt or shoot in Turkey after having obtained a license from the local authorities or the *Kaymakam* (district government); it is valid in that region for a year, or at any rate until the beginning of the following budget year: 1st of March. You can bring your own firearms (2), so long as you declare them at the customs (duty free) coming and going, and 500 cartridges per rifle.

It is open season the year round for wolf, lynx, and wild boar. The last is found almost everywhere, in the countryside around Tarsus (in southern Turkey), around Balıkesir (south of the Sea of Marmara), around Muğla and Marmaris (to the southwest). The season for other game, such as wildcat, fox, hare, rabbit, wild duck, partridge, woodcock and quail, is closed between March 1st and July 31st. It is forbidden, in all seasons, to hunt stag, deer, and fawn, together with wild sheep and other grazing animals, or to shoot certain kinds of bird. Here are a few clubs that will be of use to you: Adana: *Avcılık ve Atıcılık Klübü*; Balıkesir: *Avcılık ve Atıcılık Klübü*, Yeşilli Cad. 6; Muğla: *Avcılar Klübü*, Şükran Kahvesi; Mersin: *Atıcılık, Avcılık Ihtisas Spor Klübü*, Eski Ziya Paşa Gazinosu Karşisi, Ankara: *Türkiye Avcılar ve Atıcılar Klübü*, Tuna Cad., Yenişehir.

Two travel agencies—*Van der Zee*, Cumhuriyet Caddesi 16, and *Cem*, Harbiye Halaskar Gazi Cad. 68—both in Istanbul, organize hunting or shooting parties for small groups.

FISHING. Not organized. So far, no license needed. You can pass your fishing tackle through the customs duty free.

SHOPPING. For those used to price-tag shopping, Turkish bazaars have a somewhat disconcerting way of doing business. If you are nonetheless willing to undertake the endless bargaining (*Pazarlık*), try matching your wits against the charming shopkeepers of Istanbul's renowned covered bazaar; they will do their best to show you that the price they ask is more reasonable all round than the price you offer. Of course, you must keep in mind that it is both bad manners and bad business to grossly underbid.

A bid of half the price asked is fair enough; the haggling can begin around that sum, within reason, sometimes over a cup of coffee on the house, if it's a big item. Old as it is, the trick of not seeming to care what or whether you buy still works. Whether you have plenty of money to spend or not, there is such a wide range of Turkish handicraft—the best buy, of course, is carpets—that nobody need leave empty-handed.

CLOSING HOURS AND DAYS. The day of rest in Turkey, as in most countries, is Sunday. The following are legal holidays: the 1st of January; April 23, Children's Day; May 1st; the 19th of May, Youth Day; the 27th of May, anniversary of the Revolution; the 30th of August, Army Day; October 29, anniversary of the Republic; November 10, anniversary of Atatürk's death. A few shops stay open through the holidyas. As a rule, banks are open from 9 a.m. to 12 and from 1:30 to 5 p.m., and most of the shops from 8 a.m. to 7 p.m. (The latter close for lunch, however.) The great Islamic feasts *Seker Bayram* (3 days) and *Kurban Bayram* (4 days) vary every year, according to the Moslem calendar.

POSTAL SERVICE. The sign "PTT" means "Post, Telephone and Telegraph". Rates for abroad: letters under 1 ounce, 100 kuruş; postcards up to 5 words, 50 kuruş; over 5 words, 60 kuruş. Stamps for Turkey: letters up to an ounce, 50 kuruş (airmail, 60 kuruş); postcards up to 5 words, 10 kuruş; over 5 words, 30 kuruş. Airmail tax for every half ounce or postcard: to Europe 30 kuruş, to Canada and the U.S.A. 120 kuruş. (Prices due to rise in 1972.)

Poste Restante (General Delivery). In the big post offices, letters addressed to the traveler "Poste Restante" (*Post-Restan* in Turkish) is registered in ledgers, and listed by alphabetical order and date of arrival. As a rule, you will be given the ledger to find your own name, on showing your passport or any other identification paper. Ask those who write to you to indicate your name clearly, better still to print your surname, for it sometimes happens that the letter may be listed by mistake under your first name. There is a small fee to pay for withdrawing your mail. The biggest post offices are the following: *Istanbul*, Central Post Office, Yeni Postane Caddesi, Sirkeci; *Ankara*, Central Post Office, Atatürk Bulvari, Ulus; *Izmir*, Atatürk Caddesi. In the small towns where the clerks don't understand English, ask: *Bana mektup var mı?* ("Any mail for me?") or just say simply: *postrestan.*

Telephone. You can phone from tourist offices, hotels, and cafés. In the big towns, the telephones are automatic. Calls are cheap, but sometimes it takes a long time to get through.

PHOTOGRAPHY. Turkey, beautiful and strange, is a photographer's paradise. However, country people are camera shy, and unposed snapshots will turn out better than planned pictures. Besides, never lose sight of the fact that you are in an Islamic country, where the age-old taboo against portraying a human image still lingers, especially in out of the way places.
All big towns sell foreign brands of film, but it is very expensive.

ELECTRIC CURRENT. In European Istanbul, 110 volts (except the *Hilton*, where it is 220); in all of Asia Minor, 220 volts.

DRINKING WATER. You can safely drink water anywhere in Turkey, except in the farther regions of Central Anatolia, where it may give you a slight loosening of the bowels. All cities chlorinate their water now. If you like neither wine nor beer, ask for the very good (non-fizzy) mineral water of Kizilay.

INTERPRETER GUIDES. The Information Offices of the Ministry of Tourism, as well as travel agencies, have professional interpreter-guides to show travelers around. In large cities like Ankara, Istanbul, and Izmir, guides for small groups are paid from 26 to 30 TL an hour. Special *Tourist Police*, speaking English, French and/or German, are on duty in Istanbul, Ankara and Izmir.

Getting Around in Turkey

BY PLANE. Turkey is a big country. Distances are made yet greater by the mountain ranges. That being so, the plane is by far the fastest means of travel, and low flying often gives the most wonderful bird's-eye view. The *THY* (*Türk Hava Yolları*), *Turkish Airlines*, measures up to the standards of international airlines, and connects the country's biggest towns with its DC–9 jets, Viscount and Fokker F-27's. Most flights take off 2 or 3 times a week, all the year round. THY fares are among the lowest in Europe. For instance, one-way tourist class:

Ankara-Adana	215 TL	Istanbul-Ankara	175 TL
Ankara-Trabzon	215 TL	Istanbul-Antalya	160 TL

Children from 2 to 12 pay only half fare. Students have a 10 percent discount, journalists 50 percent. Passengers are allowed 44 pounds of luggage.

BY TRAIN. Turkish railways are state-owned. Great strides have been made lately, thanks to new rolling stock and fast diesel trains (*motorlü tren*). Nonetheless, train travel is fairly slow because of the winding railroad tracks, so planned to stop at the widely-scattered towns or to bypass mountainous ground. For instance, the train journey from Istanbul to Ankara takes a full day (360 miles as against 282 miles on the highway). There are straight runs from Istanbul/Haydarpaşa to Kars, via Ankara and Kayseri; to Adana and Syria (Alep); and to Baghdad. The train from Istanbul to Izmir follows the sea coast up to Bandırma. There are whole regions, like Antalya, without railroads. East of Ankara, parts of the railroad, such as bridges and tunnels, are masterpieces of civil engineering.

There are still 3 classes on the trains. The foreign traveler, unless he is young enough to rough it, or has the writer's wish to get down to the bone, or is just simply on a shoestring, would do better to travel in first or second class. The fare varies according to the type of train (slow, fast, or diesel), and there is a 20 percent discount on a roundtrip ticket. Cost of a one-way ticket from Istanbul to Ankara: 1st class, 52 TL; 2nd class, 37 TL; 3rd class, 26 TL; for ordinary trains. For fast trains: 1st class, 63 TL; 2nd class, 44 TL; 3rd class, 32 TL. If you are part of an organized group, or have "journalist" or "student" written on your passport or other papers, you have the right to a discount on a one-way fare.

Avoid traveling by night, unless you go by sleeper. The best diesel trains (second-class) usually run by day.

BY SHIP. Though poor in railroads, all of the Black Sea coast can be reached by ship, as can the Mediterranean shore around Antalya. The *Turkish Maritime Lines (Denizyolları)*, owned by the Denizcilik Bankası, has two lines. The first or Black Sea *(Karadeniz)* line sails from Istanbul to Hopa, near the Soviet border, a fast run that touches the main ports of Zonguldak, Sinop, Ordu, Giresun, Trabzon and Rize; and a slow run that puts into the small ports, whose only means of communication it sometimes is.

The second or Mediterranean *(Akdeniz)* line sails from Istanbul to Çanakkale, Izmir, Bodrum, Fethiye, Finike, Antalya, Mersin and Iskenderun (Alexandretta). A few runs have common ports of call, such as Kuşadası and Marmaris. 13-day cruises from Istanbul cost from $30 to $90 (£12.50 to £37.50).

There are many local runs, notably in the Sea of Marmara, to Mudanya and Gemlik, to Çanakkale and the islands of Imroz and Bozcaada. A ferryboat loads cars from Çanakkale to Eceabat; 10 or more round-trip crossings daily.

The ships on the fast lines are well equipped, with cabins, saloon and dining room, first and tourist class, and moderate fares. A company folder will give you all the needed information. In fine weather, it is by far the best way to travel, though, of course, fairly slow. The fast Black Sea ship takes 49 hours from Istanbul to Trabzon. On the other line, the Mediterranean line ship leaves Istanbul on Friday and touches port at Antalya the following Tuesday, with stopovers at Izmir and other ports of call.

Teachers, students, children, press, and others have a discount of 10 to 25 percent, according to class. Children under 4 travel free of charge; under 12, half fare. Round-trip tickets get a 10 percent reduction.

Special tourist discount: A 50% reduction is made, both on single and return (round-trip) tickets, on internal services for tourists arriving in Turkey on a *Turkish Maritime Line* vessel from abroad.

BY TAXI. You will have no trouble finding a taxi. The Turks use a form of taxi unknown to the westerner: the *dolmuş*. The word comes from the verb *dolmak*, to stuff (vine-leaves stuffed with rice are called *dolma*). The dolmuş is a collective taxi with a fixed route and fares, and starts only when stuffed full of passengers. They look like other taxis, but have a yellow stripe (instead of checkers). Just the same, most taxis, sign or no, go in for the dolmuş business, even during rush hours. At the day's end, you can hardly fight your way through the throng of people crowding around the countless taxis, while the drivers call out the routes and the customers shout to be taken. You think that no policeman can untangle such a traffic jam, but in time all is back in order. The dolmuş fares are cheap, often no more than 1 TL, but in Istanbul (at least) foreigners are sometimes charged a multiple of the fare.

BY CAR. Driving is to the right of the road, and according to traffic rules cars are overtaken on the left, but in the towns, and above all in Istanbul, best be on the lookout: you will be by-passed on both sides in a kind of vehicular slalom, cars cutting across from left to right to stop dead in front of you; but as nobody drives very fast, you are given time to slam on the brakes. Chief responsibility for the chaotic traffic lies with the shared-taxis (dolmuş) that stop on every street corner to let off a passenger. The dolmuş keep close to the curb, so better drive in the middle of the street if its width allows.

In the big Turkish cities, drivers may not always follow western rules, but drive none the worse for that. There are no crazy dashes from one red light to the next, or tearing through tunnels at 55 miles an hour. There are few traffic lights and many policemen who, however helpless they may seem at first glance, succeed somehow in directing traffic with shrill whistle blasts. Traffic jams, though very frequent, rarely last long, and no tempers are lost.

You park where you can, sometimes on the pavement. Watch out for the many small one-way streets; in Istanbul it is safer to drive along the big modern thoroughfares: even if longer, you will find your way more easily and lose less time in the long run.

On the open road, driving becomes more troublesome; the Turkish driver still seems to feel that the road belongs to him alone. He hardly ever uses his dimmer switch. You will find yourself overtaken on a curve or on the top of a rise, or will suddenly meet a big truck head on. If you overtake a car, give a long hoot in warning and a short hoot in thanks as you pass; he will hoot back in acknowledgment. It is a way of filling with sound the long stretches of road through a lonely landscape, mostly empty unless close to Istanbul and Ankara. You will often come across carts, driven on the left to see better the coming cars; also bicycles.

On the main highways, you will occasionally meet a file of military vehicles. These files are often endless and are a real danger, insofar as cars trying to over-take them drive to the left of the road, leaving no room for you if you happen to be coming towards them; slow down and stop as near to the edge of the ditch as you safely can.

You will sometimes meet flocks of animals: sheep, goats, geese, etc. The sheepdogs in the countryside are still not used to cars, and run barking in front; slow down and drive with care, for many dogs are killed on the road, and the death of a sheepdog is a heavy loss to a poor shepherd. At night, watch out for peasant carts; a small flickering lantern is the only tail light, when there is one at all. You will also meet with picturesque sights, such as a mule leading on a rope a troop of haughty camels who lurch slowly on, scorning to draw aside for a car.

Not that Turkey is chock full of risks for the western driver. On the contrary, you will, in a few days' time, be more relaxed than on a German highway, where you are always unnerved by reckless drivers speeding by at 75 miles an hour. On the other hand, remember that Turkey has one of the highest accident rates proportionate to the number of cars.

State of the roads. The big highways are fast becoming excellent. They are mostly in rough asphalt, giving a good grip to the tires. The highway through Bulgaria and then on to Edirne – Istanbul – Bolu – Ankara – to Adana and the Syrian frontier is good; so is the spectacular coastal road round the Sea of Marmara taking in Bursa and then along the Aegean Sea till Kuşadasi, inland to Denizli and Burdu, meeting the Mediterranean again at Antalya for the sublime scenery to Mersin and the junction with the Adana highway. But maintenance is not always up to western European standards. As to road repairs, there are warning signs, but they are as a rule placed too late: so, by night as by day, watch out.

As for roads where building is under way, or secondary roads, you will have a harder time. It sometimes means miles of dirt road and pebbles, where you will flounder in dust in summer and in mud during the rainy season. As repairs are undertaken the whole width of the road, you will have to slow down to 15 miles an hour or less ... The sight of a bulldozer clearing the way will at least be a sign of better driving to come.

The secondary roads marked on maps as "stabilized (unsurfaced) roads" are best avoided, unless you have good springs, a high-slung car, shatterproof glass against the flying stones, and windows that shut tight against the dust.

Road signs. The latest road maps give a list of road signs not unlike the standard European kind. However, apart from one or two granting right of way or signaling a curve, there are in fact very few. There are a few Turkish signs of American inspiration, in two kinds: a white rectangle with a sign inside a red circle, or a yellow diamond. We shall merely point out the "no through" sign: a black arrow barred with red in a red circle on a white ground; and the "slow down" sign (watch out for it at the risk of falling into a pothole or a road repair ditch): a yellow diamond with the one word: *YAVAŞ*, meaning "slow". *DUR* means "stop", and stop at once ... *DIKKAT* in a white rectangle means "watch out", drive with care. Forewarning signals are very few, except for milestones, every 10 kilometers (6.2 miles). Entry and exit in the four big cities is not easy; signposts outside even the smallest town indicate beside the name, the population (nüfus) and altitude (rakim). A clearly discernible and comprehensible distinction is between the blue signs for place names and yellow for historical places.

Repairs. No need to worry about a breakdown and getting stuck in the back of beyond; Turkish mechanics will always manage to get you going again, at least until you reach a big city for full repairs.

In larger cities, particularly in Istanbul, there are whole streets given over to car repairs. In one of these, the Dolapdere Caddesi, well placed near the tourist centers, one shop repairs radiators, another electric fittings, another steering wheels, yet another brakes. Each workshop is run by an expert with a team of young boys. The prices are not high. Give the boy a small tip. If you are not in the workshop during the repairs, usually done while you wait, don't leave the car papers in the car. These workshops are open even on Sundays and holidays, and have no closing hours. That being so, a possible breakdown and all the trouble it entails elsewhere is nothing but a passing mishap in Turkey.

Road maps. You should have a detailed map showing the state of the roads in Turkey. Some maps are like clocks: they are fast and show as "finished" lengths of roadbeds still under repair, while other maps are behind the times. A new Highway map is issued by the Ministry of Tourism every 2 or 3 years. Most up to date are the maps put out by BP and SHELL, free for the asking at the Turkish border stations of Kapikule and Pazarkule.

TABLE OF ROAD DISTANCES (IN MILES)

	Adana	Afyon	Ankara	Antalya	Balikesir	Bursa	Denizli	Diyarbakir	Edirne	Erzurum	Eskisehir	Istanbul	Izmir	Kastamonu	Kayseri	Konya	Malatya	Sarnsun	Sivas	Trabzon
Afyon	363																			
Ankara	305	198																		
Antalya	122	485	426																	
Balikesir	354	183	381	475																
Bursa	627	280	350	749	423															
Denizli	527	180	251	649	350	100														
Diyarbakir	488	139	336	610	251	181	241													
Edirne	346	710	587	331	700	610	830	316												
Erzurum	726	426	421	848	597	331	287	835	1009											
Eskisehir	539	822	624	523	893	965	865	495	301	992										
Istanbul	433	111	156	554	282	194	277	960	301	736	779									
Izmir	588	281	277	704	452	243	452	242	340	242	848	196								
Kastamonu	643	289	457	765	337	132	232	413	155	736	144	301	375							
Kayseri	462	320	160	584	503	434	333	458	232	340	990	356	317	566						
Konya	211	383	203	333	464	546	446	507	458	621	144	356	305	480	321					
Malatya	19	151	162	341	226	308	270	565	385	572	461	1082	572	467	221	238				
Sarnsun	267	566	424	251	621	655	705	163	705	268	467	701	856	425	459	321	459			
Sivas	82	463	265	610	646	586	602	525	614	430	422	470	718	198	221	330	427	362		
Trabzon	332	473	303	400	586	629	615	310	700	346	435	556	736	311	121	359	154	216	282	
Van	615	689	492	620	868	812	828	402	840	203	648	696	944	424	404	642	367	226	106	693
	594	931	789	577	947	1122	1070	254	1210	264	927	1222	822	586	810		362	467		

First aid. Remember that first aid stations, ambulances, hospitals, nursing homes, and so on, do not have the red cross, but a red *crescent* on a white ground.

Spare parts. They are hard to find outside the big towns. Best take a spare-part kit along. Most of the big makes of cars have agents in the main cities of Turkey. For the addresses of foreign car representatives, ask your car salesman for the booklet *After-sales service in Europe*.

Car hire. A hired car can be waiting for you in Istanbul at the airport, the railway station, or the dock. The cost of hire covers all forms of insurance; it varies from about $7 (£2.90) for a small 4-seater to $12 (£5) for a Chevrolet per day. Apply to: *Hertz*, Mete Cad. 26/4, or to *Bayram Tours*, Cumhuriyet Cad. 191, both in Istanbul. Minimum mileage requirements make selfdrive cars expensive.

Car hire with a driver (usually American cars): about 25¢ (10p) a mile, daily minimum 125 miles. Food and lodging for the driver will cost you about $10 (£4.20) a day. Apply to *Bayram Tours*, 191 Cumhuriyet Caddesi or to the *Vanderzee Travel Service*, Cumhuriyet Caddesi 16, both in Istanbul; Atatürk Bulvari 68/B, in Ankara; Atatürk Caddesi 134, in Izmir.

Petrol or gasolene. The big oil companies are all represented in Turkey, and each has its filling stations. Gas costs from 1.90 to 2.10 TL per liter (1.76 pints) for super grade, 1.45 to 1.60 per liter for regular, depending on the distance from main distribution centers. Oil is fairly expensive. In towns, there are few filling stations, and they are often fitted into house fronts and easy to overlook. On the main highways there are more, often advertised a few miles in advance by billboards. The big companies such as BP, Shell and Mobil edit road maps showing the location of their filling stations throughout the country. They are usually open from 6 a.m. to 10 p.m. Distilled water is hard to come by; best carry your own and service your own battery when needed.

Car transportation from the Turkish coast to the Greek islands. Drivers starting out from Istanbul can shorten or vary the return home by using the small boats that ply between the Turkish coast and the Greek islands, just opposite. These boats are not up to date, but they manage to make room for a few cars. The main crossings are: (1) Çeşme to the island of Chios (Sakız in Turkish); (2) Dikili (road from Izmir to Istanbul, to Mytilene (ancient Lesbos), (Midilli in Turkish); (3) Marmaris, southwest of Muğla, towards Rhodes. Modern ferry boats take cars and passengers from each of the above islands to the Greek port of Piraeus, outside Athens.

There is another short cut to be had by taking the Çanakkale-Eceabat (Dardanelles) ferry; at least 6 crossings a day in season.

Leaving Turkey

CUSTOMS GOING HOME. If you propose to take on your holiday any *foreign-made* articles, such as cameras, binoculars, expensive time-pieces, and the like it is wise to put with your travel documents the receipt from the retailer or some other evidence that the item was bought in your home country. If you bought the article on a previous holiday abroad and have already paid duty on it, carry with you the receipt for this. Otherwise, on returning home, you may be charged duty (for British residents, purchase tax as well).

Americans who are out of the United States at least 48 hours and have claimed no exemption during the previous 30 days are entitled to bring in duty-free up to $100 worth of articles for bona fide gifts or for their own personal use. The value of each item is determined by the price actually paid (so save your receipts). Every member of a family is entitled to this same exemption, regardless of age, and the allowance can be pooled.

Not more than 100 cigars may be imported duty-free per person, nor more than a quart of wine or liquor (none at all if your passport indicates you are from a "dry" state, or if you are under 21 years of age).

Do not bring home foreign meats, fruits, plants, soil, or other agricultural items when you return to the United States. To do so will delay you at the port of entry. It is illegal to bring in foreign agricultural items without permission, because they can spread destructive plant or animal pests and diseases. For more information, read the pamphlet "Customs Hints", or write to: "Quarantines", U.S. Department of Agriculture, Washington, D.C. 20250.

Antiques are defined, for customs purposes, as articles manufactured over 100 years ago and are admitted duty-free. If there's any question of age, you may be asked to supply proof.

Small gifts may be mailed to friends, but not more than one package to any one address and none to your own home. Notation on the package should be "Gift, value less than $10". Tobacco, liquor, and perfume are not permitted to be mailed.

If your purchases exceed your exemption, list the items that are subject to the highest rates of duty under your exemption and pay duty on the items with the lowest rates. Any article you fail to declare cannot later be claimed under your exemption. To facilitate the actual customs examination, it's convenient to pack all your purchases in one suitcase.

Purchases intended for your duty-free quota can no longer be sent home separately—they must accompany your personal baggage.

British subjects, except those under the age of 17 years, may import duty free one-half pound (250 grams) of tobacco or cigarettes, one-sixth gallon (1 bottle) of spirits or liqueur, one-sixth gallon (1 bottle) of wine, and one-half pint of perfume and toilet water, of which no more than half may be perfume. Also 1 cigarette lighter and £10 worth of souvenirs. If you go over these limits, you can expect to pay duty on the *excess quantity* (or on the *whole* amount if this is more than double the import allowance).

Note well. Exporting antiquities is strictly prohibited, and the penalties for attempting to do so without prior authorization are severe!

You are allowed to take jewels, works of art, carpets, etc., out of the country duty free up to value of 2,000 TL; after that amount, exchange receipts must be shown—keep *all* your receipts! (See *Customs* section, prior.)

 NUISANCE TAX. Unfortunately, Turkey, like most other European countries, makes you pay a ransom to fly out of the country. This nuisance tax, so often demanded of the unsuspecting traveler just after he has triumphantly spent his last bit of local currency and is congratulating himself on his careful budgeting, amounts to 15 TL at the airport.

TURKEY: FACTS AND FIGURES

A BIT ABOUT GEOGRAPHY. The very features that make Turkey such an interesting place—its greatly diversified terrain and the wide variety of its climate—also make it difficult to give a simple and concise geographical description of the country.

Turkey's overall features are as follows: Asia Minor is a high plateau (Anatolia) separated on the north from the Black Sea by a mountain range that is 2,000 feet high on the west and over 10,000 feet high on the east, the Pontic chain. Anatolia's southern boundary consists of a second mountain range parallel with the other, the Taurus chain, of which the highest peak, Erciyaş Dağı near the center of the country, in Cappadocia, soars to a lofty 12,848 feet. These two mountain systems merge to form an imposing complex, the topmost point of which is Mt. Ararat (16,945 feet), supposedly the spot where Noah safely brought his Ark to rest on dry land after the Deluge. The surrounding countryside is volcanic and plagued by earthquakes of frequent occurrence. Vast plains stretch southward from this mountainous group: among other things, they contain Lake Van with its salt waters (2,256 sq. miles). Beyond lies a mountain barrier, extending into Iran and Iraq, its peaks occasionally rising to 13,000 feet.

The western part of Turkey is particularly variegated, alternating between moderately high mountains and deep valleys covered with river deposits and uneven ground, sloping down to a sharply indented coastline facing out to the innumerable Greek islands that dot the Aegean Sea. The northwestern edge of Anatolia ends at the famed Dardanelles Straits and the Bosporus, which form the southern and northern gateways to the Sea of Marmara, noted for a distinctive phenomenon: the fresh waters of the Black Sea are drained southwards by a surface current, while far below an undercurrent keeps the salty depths of the Aegean flowing in the opposite direction.

The portion of Turkey that lies in Europe, Eastern Thrace, begins on the far side of the Straits. It makes up only slightly over three percent of Turkish territory, or some 9,068 sq. miles out of a total 296,185 sq. miles. Thrace is bounded by Greece and Bulgaria. Further on, in a clockwise direction, there are the Black Sea to the north, the U.S.S.R. (Georgia and Armenia) and Iran to the east, Iraq, Syria, and the Mediterranean on the south, and the Aegean Sea on the west.

The sources of the Tigris (Dicle) and the Euphrates (Firat) rivers emerge in the eastern part, near Elazığ and Erzurum, respectively. The Tigris flows first into Syria and continues on to merge with the Euphrates, which flows directly into Iraq. The area watered by these two great rivers, later combined into one, is fabled Mesopotamia, now lying mostly in Iraq. Because of the Taurus mountains, only a very few rivers finally reach the Mediterranean: they are swiftly rushing streams, but their deltas form an invaluable asset to agriculture. Four main rivers empty into the Aegean: they are streams with abundant deposits that have gradually blocked up the estuaries and spelled the doom of ancient Greek settlements like Milet and Ephesus. These rivers include the Maeander (Büyük Menderes) and the Hermos (Gediz). Turkey's principal rivers flow into the Black Sea, after wending their tortuous way through the Pontic Mountains, where countless gorges punctuate the landscape. The latter rivers include the Halys of the ancients, called the Kızıl Irmak today (this is Turkey's longest, 715 miles), and Yeşil Irmak, and the Sakarya, none of which is navigable.

CLIMATE, FLORA AND FAUNA. Turkey is blessed with four different types of climate: oceanic, Mediterranean, continental, and mountainous. The Black Sea coastal area is a temperate zone (same latitude as Rome), with a mean winter temperature of 43° F., rising to 68 and 77° F. in the summertime. It has abundant year round rainfall. This area is renowned for its forests of leafbearing and coniferous trees, and for the apples, pears, cherries, hazelnuts, mandarin oranges, and tea that are grown there.

The Straits area marks a transition from the Mediterranean climate that prevails along most of the Aegean coast; here, there is plenty of rain, particularly at the end of autumn, and the region enjoys mild winters and hot summers (in Izmir, the temperature can drop to 48° F. in January and range up to the low 80's in summer). The well-irrigated plains produce a variety of crops, including corn, tobacco, cotton, wheat, grapes and figs.

Along the Mediterranean shores, summer can be sweltering

(sometimes above 100° F.), but the temperature seldom dips below 50° F. in winter. The Taurus mountains, which at one time in history used to sheer sharply down to the water's edge, now slope gently out beyond, providing warm, moist, fertile alluvial plains for the coastal area: two such are Pamphylia, at the mouth of the Antalya Gulf, and Cilicia, stretching out to Iskenderun (Alexandretta). The local vegetation is tropical, with iflourshing banana trees, palm trees, citrus trees, sugar cane and cotton.

The enchanting climes described above, occasionally referred to as the "Turkish Riviera", or the "Turquoise Coast" are swimming resorts from 1 April to 30 October. They present a sharp contrast with the central plateau of Anatolia, where the altitude seldom descends below 2,640 feet, and where the scattered valleys lying to the north and south are barely passable. The land to the west has variegated relief. Mountains shoot up abruptly above the water's edge, and are divided by deep clefts that allow the balmy Aegean breezes to blow in toward the interior of the mountain chain. Central Anatolia is a region of plateaux and depressions, with occasional bodies of water, including Lake Tuz Gölü, the water of which is said to be saltier than that of the Dead Sea. Its climate is affected by its remoteness from the sea, and offers many contrasts: it is dry and salubrious, and can be torrid in summer, but becomes freezing in winter. Although there is a certain amount of humidity near the mountains, which allows the forests (coniferous trees, oak, beech and junipers), to thrive the remainder of the plateau is more reminiscent of a subdesert or a steppe.

The mountain air becomes progressively colder going in an eastward direction and is accompanied by frequent rainfall. North of Mt. Ararat, near the Russian border, mean winter temperatures are below 50° F. and snow is plentiful. However, even in these continental regions, winter in the valleys is severe, with extremely hot summers. The latter foster a Mediterranean type of vegetation wherever enough water is available.

Turkey is the habitat of the same animals as are found in the European countries, plus camels (which are becoming ever scarcer) and buffaloes. There is no shortage of sheep and goats, nor of cattle. Sportsmen will find wild boar roving in abundance, as well as bears, lynx, all species of rodents, and even leopard.

POPULATION. Modern Turkey, as it was conceived by Atatürk, is in active evolution. It is literally a developing country in every sense of the term. Its founder took the Western world for his model, thereby setting off what was to be a prodigious revolution from every standpoint for the people of Turkey.

The idea of reform had been uppermost in forward-looking people's minds for nearly a century, and Turkey made the change virtually without transition from an autocratic, selfish regime to a democracy designed to provide its people with material advantages and a decent living-standard.

Moreover, the annual rate of population growth (three percent) is less than the increase in national income (six percent). While this is satisfactory, the chief concern of Turkish authorities at present is to raise the income even higher.

Turkish demography is powerful, and average life expectancy at birth is quite good, because of the vastly improved public health conditions. Since the revolution, Turkey's population has virtually trebled, and now numbers around 35 million.

As a result, agriculture, which is the basis of the Turkish economy, is being required to put forth an enormous effort to fulfill its primary role of feeding the Turks themselves, and, secondly, to produce enough to export. With the setting up of the republic, agriculture was in a sorry plight. A segment of the population was still nomadic, estates were the property of a few great private landowners, and prevailing farming methods were nothing short of antediluvian.

The nomads (*yürük*, "those who wander") were finding it increasingly difficult to rent winter pasture-lands from the regularly settled peasants in the coastal areas, or even to find mountain grazing lands in summer (the latter were in ever shorter supply because of the constant expansion of cultivated areas). Consequently, the nomadic peoples tended to settle. However, even today there are still entire families who migrate with the seasons, although their numbers have dwindled substantially. Brand-new farming villages were created to accommodate the *muhacir*, or refugees, from the dismembered Ottoman Empire, from Russia and from Central Asia. (The most recent arrivals are from Sinkiang, or Chinese Turkestan.)

Turkey is also transforming its outward appearance by giving a "new look" to the overall territory: pasture-lands are yielding to crop plantations, and reforestation is proceeding apace. Land is likewise being reclaimed in the steppes. In 1939, planted areas (both sown and lying fallow, which is the method still prevailing today) accounted for only 17 percent of the country's total area, as against over 30 percent today. During this same period, the percentage of surface area assigned to meadow lands, pasturage, and steppes declined from 55 percent to around 35 percent, and the amount of land planted with vineyards, vegetables, fruit orchards, and olive trees rose from 1.7 percent to 3 percent. In summary, since the founding of the republic, the total cultivated area has increased from about 25,000 sq. miles to about 142,000 sq. miles.

However, many years of frustrating and heartbreaking efforts were required before the government subsidies to farmers produced any positive results. Since World War II, the output of wheat, a basic foodstuff, has increased fourfold, and in a good year it reaches eight million metric tons. Other cereals include barley, corn, and oats. Fruit is in plentiful supply, and Turkey is a major exporter of raisins and hazelnuts. The other fruits—mainly citrus—grown in the southern part of the country serve primarily to fill domestic needs. The latter also absorb the country's potatoes and other vegetable crops. An important source of foreign exchange lies in the exporting of cotton and tobacco. However, new possibilities have been explored, with the result that Turkey now is busy with sugar beet and olive oil refineries.

Traditional Turkish methods of livestock raising were anything but efficient, and provided only a meagre yield. New procedures had to be introduced, and it was necessary to cut down the number of goats, which, although they furnish mohair wool, also cause considerable damage to plant life by their habit of uprooting rather than nibbling at, the vegetation. To counterbalance this, the flocks of sheep were increased: Turkey remains a major wool producer. There is no lack of cattle or other farm livestock, including horses, donkeys, buffaloes and camels.

INDUSTRY. Agriculture continues to present the major sector of the Turkish economy, accounting for 40 percent of the national income. However, this percentage is declining in favor of public and private services, and industry. The latter now accounts for probably one-fourth of the country's national income, with the various services representing another 35 percent

But, during the period immediately following the founding of the republic, when the country was still reeling from the shock of change, industry had a hard time getting off the ground. Note should be taken of the government's years of vain attempts to inculcate a spirit of enterprise, to impart technical know-how, and to provide capital at a time when the country was still depleted, barely emerging from the last convulsions of the Ottoman Empire.

Industrialization didn't really get under way until 1933, with the introduction of the first Five Year Plan and the creation of the Sümerbank. The latter's task was to set up all kinds of factories with government funding, while mines, electrical power, and commercial companies were the responsibility of the Etibank, created in 1935. Lastly, the Agricultural Bank was reorganized. These assorted agencies were coordinated in 1938 by a decree authorizing the state to supplement private initiative wherever the latter was lacking, and converting the three banks listed above into government economic agencies. Other institutions likewise became state agencies, including various local authorities for the exploitation of the soil, for mechanical and chemical industries, for railways, and for postal and communications services.

These various government agencies operate with state funds, although somewhat in the manner of private companies, and with considerable leeway in their decisions and activities. In theory, the scope of their activities is restricted to the creating of enterprises and to the eventual handing over of the latter to establishments with limited liability, subordinate to them. In addition, there are various forms of association between public and private enterprises, plus, of course, companies whose capital is entirely private (sometimes derived from foreign sources).

Industrialization has been pushed forward concomitantly with the development of mining resources, which are limited. A few oil wells are being worked with the assistance of foreign concerns. The presence of iron deposits and domestic coal deposits has facilitated the creation of metallurgical industries. The availability of cotton, wool, and silk have fostered the expansion of the textile industry, plus the traditional rug-making industry. Paper-pulp and cellulose, cement, fertilizers, food products, refining, and distilling are other features of contemporary Turkish industry, the most highly developed branches of which are the assembly of trucks and buses, the processing of chemicals, etc. This necessarily brief survey should also mention the development of electrical plants and power: capacity has now risen to well over three million kilowatt-hours.

COMMUNICATIONS, COMMERCE, AND ECONOMY.

The communications systems inherited from the Ottoman Empire were, to say the least, rudimentary: they consisted of a primitive road network and a bare 800 miles of railways. By now, there are more than 60,000 miles of roads (including some 16,000 miles of well-paved highways) and nearly 5,000 miles of railways. Truck and bus traffic is heavy, but the national average for private car ownership is one automobile for every 200 inhabitants. Turkish airlines are a government monopoly: the T.H.Y. (Türk Hava Yolları) operates flights between the country's major localities (there are around 30 airports), and also schedules a numbers of runs to foreign countries.

Despite development effort in every field, Turkey's balance of payments shows a deficit. This is understandable, considering that equipment has to be bought abroad and that the exports, mainly agricultural, do not make up for these foreign purchases. Turkey imports machinery, electrical equipment, vehicles, mineral oils, iron, steel, raw materials for textiles, wood, fertilizers, and pharmaceutical and chemical products. Its exports are, as stated above, in addition to copper and chromium, primarily agricultural products. Turkey's closest business relationships are maintained with the United States and the Common Market countries. (It has had an association agreement with the latter since 1963.)

It would not be repetitious to end this section by recalling that Turkey's real problem resides in its population explosion. The fact that some 150,000 Turkish workers have gone to work in the Common Market countries bears eloquent witness to this situation. Turkish officials, acutely aware of their country's problems, drew up the new 1961 constitution around their prime objective, i.e., the support of the state's democratic functioning by economic strength. The constitution's declaration of goals states that "Turkey is an under-developed country; the demands of our epoch make it imperative to improve the social and economic structures of the nation, which lay neglected for centuries. The state must provide for this necessity through economic, social, and cultural recovery." This was the guiding spirit under which the 1963–67 Five Year Plan was worked out, the purpose of which was "the achievement and the maintaining of the optimum rate of economic growth along with the promotion of social justice within the framework of a democratic regime".

HOW THE STATE FUNCTIONS. Present-day Turkish institutions are the result of two revolutions: the setting up of Atatürk's republic in 1923, and the 1960 reformation. After restoring the country's independence, Mustafa Kemal completely eradicated all traces of the past and adopted a whole set of reforms: abolition of the caliphate, proclamation of a republic, replacement of Islamic law by civil law, recognition of the equality of the sexes in all domains, substitution of the Roman alphabet for the Arabic characters, instituting of the international systems of calendar and time, adoption of the metric system of measurements, purifying of the Turkish language by the deleting of Arabic and Persian elements, abolition of the fez and discouragement of the veil, abolition of the *medrese* (schools whose courses of instruction were based exclusively on theology), and the creation of modern universities and technical institutes—in other words, the Westernization of Turkey.

The parliamentary system set up included a single assembly, called the Grand National Assembly, and a single party. In 1945, additional political parties were authorized. The Democratic Party gained the majority in 1950. However, its rule stirred up so much opposition that the army, supported by the élite, took over in 1960. Another new constitution was adopted in 1961, approved by popular referendum. It provides for two houses of congress: although the parliament continues to be designated as the Grand National Assembly, it is now composed of an upper and a lower house, the latter corresponding to a house of representatives.

The spirit of the new constitution might be summed up in four words: the state is democratic, secular, social, and national. It is based on the rights of the individual, to whom it grants not only the traditional privileges of citizenship but also the social rights that the citizen pledges himself to protect and promote. The constitution defines the principles of the limits of the legislative branch's authority, in order to prevent the latter from conflicting with the constitution, as had occurred under the First Republic. It recognizes parties as indispensable to overall democracy. The president is elected for seven years by the two houses, but is not eligible for a second term. *Signs of the times:* An army coup (quite bloodless) in early 1971 brought about a change in government, but the generals have promised a free election by early 1972.

THE TURKISH LANGUAGE. The Turkish language is a branch of the Ural-Altaic group, and therefore does not belong to the Indo-European tongues. It is a distant relative of Finnish, Hungarian and Mongolian. The earliest known examples of a written Turkish language are inscriptions carved on two stone tablets discovered in Northern Mongolia near the Orkhon River; a few other examples have been found in the area of the Upper Yenissey. They date from the eight century A.D., and the characters used are similar to those of a Semitic alphabet that gradually spread out over Asia, getting itself transformed in various ways in the process. The dialect of these ancient texts is the Uygur.

From the above evidence, it can be deduced that Turkish was indeed used in Northern Asia. In addition to having left its imprint on Eastern Europe and in the Balkans, this language can be found all over Asia in the form of a multitude of different dialects, which reveal numerous similarities. In addition to the 35 million Turks themselves, there are 29 million Soviet citizens, 18 million Chinese, and eight million Iranians and Afghans who speak Turkish (in the broadest sense of the term).

The Turkish language appeared in Asia Minor as early as the 11th century with the Seljuk and Ottoman invaders. After the latter had risen to ascendancy, the name of their first sultan, Osman, was given to the language that is spoken in Turkey today: Osmanli. This particular language closely resembles those spoken in Azerbaijan and Turkmenistan. Together, they constitute the Turcoman sub-group.

However, even prior to settling in Asia Minor, the Turkish tribes came in contact with the Moslem religion, of which they were to become zealous followers, and managed to introduce a fair admixture of Arabic into their own language. The rich religious, moral, scientific, and artistic resources of Islam, in short, of Arabic civilization, could not fail to rub off to a certain extent on these wandering hordes, still on the look-out for new kingdoms to conquer. Toward the 12th century, the Persian tongue in its turn contributed to the enrichment of the Turkish language, which developed into a majestic form of speech (perhaps overly so for the ordinary people, who continued to speak their own native dialects among themselves). This situation, incidentally, gave rise to two parallel developments in literature (see below). The Turko-Arabic-Persian language was used by persons in the imperial court, in the government, and by the élite, all of whom accounted for under ten percent, combined, of the total population.

The throwing open of Turkey to Western ideas led to a certain simplification of the language, which had become "inflated" and at the same time added a substantial number of new words. It was immediately apparent that the Arabic characters that had been used for writing Turkish were scarcely suitable for the conveying of subtle distinctions in pronunciation. (Arabic contains only three vowel sounds, whereas Turkish has eight.) One of Atatürk's basic reform ideas was to go back to a purified national language, one that would be close to its original sources. He consequently decreed the use of the Roman alphabet, infinitely more suited to rendering the written language accurately. He also founded the Turkish Linguistic Society, assigned the task of ridding Turkish of its foreign words and replacing them by typical Turkish equivalents, or by words based on the morphology peculiar to the language. Despite the fact that since 1960 the authorities have been refraining from any attempts to further reform the language, the Turks themselves are now tending wherever possible to replace Arabic or Persian terms by indigenous expressions. Still, it is a noteworthy fact that the Westernization of Turkey has in itself entailed the adoption of certain European words. The truth is that although the Turks have successfully managed the return to original linguistic sources, they have also made of their language a flexible instrument that is readily adaptable to the requirements of modern living, while remaining a vehicle of art and culture.

THE ALPHABET. English ranks first, before German and French, but outside the three main towns, foreign languages are not widely spoken. In travel agencies and the better-class hotels, however, there will be somebody who speaks at least one, and often all three. It is unlikely that you will pick up Turkish during your stay, but a smattering of a few key words will be a great help, especially when driving through the countryside. Look up the words you need at the back of the book, under *Tourist Vocabulary*.

The alphabet, a few letters of which have diacritic marks modifying the sound to suit Turkish phonetics, has done a great deal to establish contact between Turkey and the western world. Though the older people still read Arabic, the young, by and large, know only the Latin characters. The Turkish alphabet is very simple, as each letter always keeps the same sound, whatever its place in the word.

Beginning with the vowels, *a* is pronounced u as in ugly; *e* is pronounced as in egg; *i* is pronounced e as in evil; *ı*—without a dot—is like o in seldom or e in master; *ö* is pronounced er and *u* is pronounced oo; *ü* is the sharp French vowel, unknown in English, and to be learned by ear as best you can. The *e* is always sounded, and every vowel is separate, *ay* being pronounced like i—(as in line)—e (as in evil). The downbeat always comes at the end of the word: Ul*u*, or marks the split in compound words or names: Büyük*d*ere, Kad*ı*köy.

The consonants have the same sound as in English, except for the following: *c* is like j in Jack; for instance *canlı*, "lively", is said "janli"; *ç* is like tch—for instance, *çay* (tea) is said "tchai"; *g* is always hard, as in got; *ğ* is like h in hot, drawling out the preceding vowel—Tekirdağ becomes "Tekirdaah"; *s* is always soft, as in silk; *ş* is like sh—*paşa* is pronounced "pasha".

There is no *x* in Turkish; it is written ks. Also, there is no merging of consonants—*ph* is not pronounced f, but as two distinct letters—Tophane is pronounced "Top-hane". There are no *g* nor *w*, either.

LITERATURE.

Until the 19th-century reform, Turkish writers almost without exception used poetry as their sole mode of expression. Men of letters tended to view prose as devoid of artistic potentialities. The earliest-known Turkish text, the carved stone Orkhon inscriptions, is also the first recognized example of Turkish literature. This text is remarkable for the vivid and elegant style in which it recounts the epic of the Turkish people up to the time of their liberation from the yoke of Chinese domination.

The outstanding literary work written in Turkish before the language became invaded by Arabic and Persian words was the *Treatise and Dictionary of the Turkish Language* compiled by

Mahmud Kashgari. This work, written in Bagdad in 1074, still remains today *the* standard reference both for the language itself (in which all the poetic genres are to be found) and as a source of information on the daily lives of the people in Turkestan. At about the same time, and in the same area, there also appeared the first Islamized work, printed in Arabic characters and metrics, the *Kutadghu Bilig*, or *Science of Happiness*, a long didactic poem by Yusuf Has Hadjib.

The poet Mevlâna (1207–1273) enriched Turkish literature with his *Divan–el–Kebir*, an impressive collection of poems containing over 40,000 couplets. Then, too, there was Nasreddin Hoca, the storyteller and philosopher *par excellence*, a superior mind far above the considerations of this crass material world, who poked gentle fun at the prevailing stupidity all around him. This 14th-century author draws the freshness of his inspiration from simple common sense, as well as from the wisdom of the ages. His reputation has spread far beyond the confines of Turkey itself. Under the name of Goha, he is beloved in Egypt and North Africa. The Sephardic Jews in the Mediterranean basin appreciate him as the inimitable Djoha. His writings are also justly famed among the Kurds (in Iran) and in Russia.

Turkish literature followed two separate and distinct patterns: while one part of it remained loyal to traditional and popular modes of expression, another branch underwent Arabic and Persian influences, and became increasingly refined and flowery. The gap grew ever wider between the "man in the street" and the court poetry, with which was associated all that was fine and noble. In the attempt to adapt Arab-Persian poetry patterns to their native tongue, Turkish poets devised an increasingly subtle and esoteric manner of speech, which by the time of the post-classical period at the end of the 18th century had declined into sheer estheticism, abstraction, symbolism, and decadence.

It should be noted here that the rules of the game obliged the court poets to avoid at all costs stating things baldly. They were expected to enshroud their sentiments or messages in outlandishly elaborate and contrived forms. It was only in metaphors that they were able to find a certain escape beyond the confines of imperial absolutism. On occasion, failure to conform to these rules could prove fatal. Although their minds might be free, their tongues were, so to speak, shackled by the weight of gilded chains. In the 14th and 15th centuries, the Persian linguistic influence became all-powerful. Nevertheless, the outstanding poet of this period was a mystic named Yunus Emre, who expressed himself in the people's language.

With the Turks established in Istanbul (the former Byzantium) by the mid-15th century, the classical period of Ottoman literature began. The Persian language became completely assimilated, and was no longer slavishly imitated. The poets were better able to cope with a more personal mode of linguistic expression. But there was a complete schism between court language and that spoken by the common people. Certain names are to be noted in this connection: Ahmed Pasha, who made an invaluable contribution to the improvement of poetic techniques; Necati, a lyric poet who exerted a considerable influence; and, above all, Fuzuli and Baki in the 16th century. Fuzuli was the complete opposite of a court poet, leading a poverty-stricken existence in Bagdad, but he was gifted with the ability to sing beautifully of love. Baki, the "prince of poets", is a perfect example of the sumptuousness of the Divan, or court. Nefi was another 17th-century poet, a dignitary noted for his biting satires and an explosive personality which contrasted drastically with those of the obsequiousness courtiers. He quite literally lost his head after overdoing matters in his attacks against some of the V.I.P.'s of the time. Nabi, who lived in the 18th century, was a more intellectual poet, although equally renowned for his sarcastic wit. Naili was melancholy and delicate in temperament: his style is prized for its freshness and its power of evocation.

The classical period also yielded a few prose works written in the language of the people, the most celebrated of these being the *Chronicles*. Some prose writing was also done in the court language, but its style was far less mannered than that of the poets.

The post-classical period is represented by Nedim, who typified the decadence of the Era of the Tulips, during which the concern with refinement attained the farthest limits of preciousness. Classical popular poetry had an illustrious representative in Karacaoglan, who sang of the lives of the common people in the 17th century.

But reform was looming up on the horizon. In 1839, Sultan

Abdulmedjid introduced the first Western ideas into the Ottoman Empire. It was inevitable that these ideas should influence both the form and content of literature. In fact, literature became an arm against despotism, a weapon wielded by the espousers of the romantic cause of freedom. Poetry was no longer the sole literary form, yielding ground to prose, and transforming itself into a means of expression for ardent patriots. The fomenters of this particular revolution were Namık Kemal and Abdülhak Hamit.

But the language was still heavily overburdened with Persian elements. Although the movement had received its initial impetus from earlier leaders, it was mainly under the aegis of Ziya Gökalp that literature became definitely oriented toward themes inspired by national and traditional sentiments set down in a language that sought to return more and more closely to the original Turkish. Two poets in particular had a strong influence in this respect: Yahya Kemal and Mehmed Akif.

Atatürk's decrees aimed at purifying the language thus served only to consecrate and to expand on a national scale the reformist movement and to give it the force of law. The Turkish language is still continuing to evolve and to adapt itself even today. Contemporary poets, who have left no themes unexplored, have consistently experimented with new techniques. New literary genres had begun budding forth immediately after the *tanzimat* (the reforms of 1839). With the founding of the republic came the introduction of the short story featuring social, descriptive, and autobiographical themes, as well as the novel, long neglected in Turkey. It would be painstaking here to list all the names of the many Turkish novelists. But particularly deserving of mention are Yaşar Kemal (author of *Memed, My Hawk*, which has been translated into 15 languages), Yakup Kadri, Kemal Tahir, Halit Ziya Uşakhpil, Halide Edip Adıvar, Reşat Nuri Güntekin, Yakup Kadri Karaosmanoglu, and Mahmut Makal (born in 1930), whose *Bizim Köy* is a vivid account of life in an Anatolian village (this last-mentioned book has gained a considerable reputation for its author).

CULTURAL LIFE. Turkey's cultural reputation has been spread abroad through its literature and its theater. However, the earliest Turkish play written and performed in accordance with

European traditions dates only from 1859, and can be traced to the influence of visiting foreign theatrical troupes. At about the same time, Turkish musicians became acquainted with Western music through the Italian composer Donizetti, who founded the Turkish Imperial Orchestra.

The theater was so strongly permeated with the concept of freedom (this was the period of the Young Turks) that the wild enthusiasm aroused by the first important Turkish play, entitled *The Fatherland*, by Namık Kemal, wound up with the playwright's getting himself exiled. For some time thereafter, Turkish actors confined themselves to the performance of foreign plays only, until the best writers returned from exile subsequent to the promulgation of the new constitution of 1908. Just before 1914, André Antoine, the founder of the Free Theatre, established the Istanbul Municipal Conservatory. After the war this became the Istanbul Municipal Theater. Modern Turkish theater asserted itself, and Istanbul now boasts four municipal and 13 private theaters, which also stage opera and ballet.

Among better-known playwrights are Orhan Asena (*Seed and Earth*), Turhan Oflazaoğlu (*The Mad Sultan*), Gungor Dilmen Kalyoncu (*The Living Monkey Restaurant*), and Hidayet Sayin (*Pink Woman*).

Dame Ninette de Valois founded the State Opera classical ballet company, which now composes 50 dancers. It is so successful that several of its best men and women have been lured away to more famous groups in Europe and America. (Some claim Rudolf Nureyev to be of Turkish origin, after all!) Performances can be seen in Ankara, in the same opera house where foreign and Turkish operas are staged. Among the latter, *Nasreddin Hoca*, by Sabahattin Kalender, and *Van Gogh*, by Nevit Kodalli, are perhaps best-known.

Ankara acquired a new conservatory in the late 1930's, and this led in 1948 to the establishment of the National Theater, with departments of both opera and drama, and the capital now has six public and five private theaters. The current trend is toward decentralization, along the lines of the National Theatres established in Izmir and Bursa. The National Theater has made a reputation for itself on its foreign tours, including notable appearances in Paris in 1960 and in Athens in 1961. Every summer, Istanbul is host to the International Youth Festival, in which many amateur groups from all over Europe participate.

EDUCATION. The Five Year Plan mentioned above applied to all levels of activity, including education. The goal here is to ensure elementary schooling for all children by the mid-1970's. Presently, about 65–75 % attend elementary schools. One of the plan's other aims is to develop higher and graduate education on a fuller scale, with the emphasis on technical training. The turning out of scientists, researchers, technicians, and qualified specialists is one of the foremost objectives of the plan.

THE PRESS. The press in Turkey has really been "free" only since the adoption of the new 1961 constitution. However, members of the press must comply with an ethical code, and all offenses are judged by a court of honor, whose decisions are given wide publicity (hence moral pressure), and can lead to the offending newspaper being deprived of official recognition (hence economic pressure). The Istanbul papers with the largest circulation are the *Hürriyet, Milliyet, Tercüman, Aksam,* and *Cumhuriyet;* in Ankara, they are the *Adalet* and *Ulus.* In early 1968 Turkey inaugurated limited television broadcasting services.

MANNERS AND CUSTOMS IN TURKEY. Your enjoyment of Turkey will depend somewhat on your contacts with its people. You will be well advised to bear in mind the Turk's psychology, the dualism of his Eastern and Moslem traditions on the one hand, his pride in being a citizen of a country with modern Western structures on the other. It behooves you to maintain a comprehensive attitude toward the various customs and attitudes that are a direct legacy from Islam, but don't try too hard to detect Eastern mysteries in certain realms that public laws and popular good will are striving to rationalize, secularize and Westernize.

And now that the above premises have been postulated, don't let yourself be dismayed by their apparent complexity. Generally speaking, since Turkey has, after all, *had* its revolution, people will appreciate your observance of the rules of Western courtesy, and will understand your own approach. To the Turkish mind, the term "European Turkey" has no particular meaning: the country *is* European, and has European partnerships. For one thing, refrain from referring to places by their ancient names: to do so would be like retreating five, ten, or so centuries into the past. Say "Istanbul", not "Constantinople"; Izmir", not "Smyrna"; and "Anatolia", not Asia Minor. Turkey these days is nationalistic in the best sense of the word.

With the above considerations duly noted, you will be finding yourself inside mosques in which people are at prayer. Although you run absolutely no risk of meeting up with any religious fanaticism, you will encounter the truly living image of faith. Respect it: remove your shoes at the entrance (you can put on the slippers that are for rent near the doorway), and remember to observe silence and discretion. For example, don't stand gaping and staring at the prostrations of the faithful, although you will be allowed in at the hours of worship. (In contrast with the practice that prevails in other Moslem countries, Turkish mosques tolerate the presence of the "infidel" at prayer-time.)

Another thing: the Turkish mind has not become totally emancipated in these past 50 years. There is no reason to be surprised at this, nor especially to make fun of it. Although the wearing of the veil is "no longer recommended" by law, you may quite possibly see women who have not been able to bring themselves to comply with this secular provision. Don't deliberately focus your camera on such rare examples it would be inconsiderate to display obvious curiosity about this survival of past customs. Generally speaking, women have not yet quite managed to shed all the conventions. The mere fact that a girl goes out alone with a man, even when she is unmarried, might compromise her. It is therefore only fitting that Western women behave and dress with corresponding appropriate decorum.

And here are two more items for your consideration in connection with Turkish manners: Firstly, people use the first name to address each other properly. The name is followed by "Bey" (or, for women, by "Hanim"). Secondly, the coffee ritual—a cup is usually served to guests—involves your emptying your cup down to the last drop, except for the dregs.

You will soon realize that in Turkey there is no point in rushing, or in asking anyone else to hurry up. This state of affairs by no means indicates a prevalence of congenital national sloth. The underlying reason for this attitude is more likely a philosophy of existence called keyif, the same philosophy that was being cultivated by our Roman ancestors when they advised mankind to take advantage of the fleeting moment, and quoted Horace's "Carpe diem". Let yourself revel in the finest kind of epicurianism —in the pleasurable, delicate, and not too recondite science of enjoying the passing hour. All the elements conspire to ensure relaxation: the limpidity of the air, the caressing breezes that waft away the heat, good food, a delicious drink, congenial company, the soft lapping of waves against the sides of a boat, the heady perfume of flowers and orchards, a landscape glimpsed through a mist . . . You can accept such things as they come or you may deliberately seek them out. Either way, you will achieve satisfaction.

If you are lucky enough to be out for an idle stroll on a balmy spring evening, with the evening sky deepening from blue into black, while the muezzin's far-off voice calls the faithful to prayer against the background murmur of the Bosporus lazily foaming up along the shore, let yourself be lulled by the sweetness of the moment; then you will know what keyif really is. It is a state of utter bliss, imparting languor to the senses while at the same time sharpening the mind. It will provide the perfect touch to your stay in Turkey.

RELIGION ("Submission to God's Will") is the name of the Moslem religion, which claims to be a revelation of God in the world through His Prophet, Mohammed. It is very like Judaism, and, to a lesser extent, Christianity; the Old Testament prophets and Jesus himself are viewed as moral leaders of mankind, but are looked on only as forerunners of Mohammed, the greatest of all.

The sacred book of the Moslems is the Koran, a summing-up of the old Gospels, which offers the faithful a set of moral rules whereby they may better the good that dwells in every man. All Moslem law, all social and political institutions of the Ottoman Empire were taken from the Koran. As in Christianity, heresies and schisms from the supreme power of the religious ruler, the Caliph, have split the Moslem religion into sects. In Islam, the one-ness of God ("there is no God but God") is a sharp contrast to the Christian concept of the Holy Trinity.

Mohammed was born in Mecca around 570 A.D. Banished for his belief in one God, he went to Medina in the year 622, the year of the *Hegira*, the flight which marks the beginning of the Islamic calendar. He returned in 630 to conquer his native town, where he died two years later.

THE TURKISH SCENE

A GLIMPSE AT TURKISH HISTORY

Crossroads of Occident and Orient

Asia Minor's destiny was cut out for it by the facts of its geographical situation—its vocation has been to serve as the turntable for the sundry migrations of mankind. Over the centuries, Asia Minor has been the springboard for the conquest of both Europe and Asia, and it is only natural that it should have become the favorite battlefield for a succession of conquerors bent on gaining a foothold on one or the other of the two continents.

It is generally recognized that life began in the east and gradually evolved westward, trailing in its wake all the weapons of warfare and other slightly more embryonic ingredients of civilization. During this remote period, Europe was constantly in the throes of anarchy and barbarism. The first known European culture was Cretan, followed by that of Greece, with Rome entering the picture some time later. The energies of Greek expansion enabled it to span the Aegean, entering Asia Minor. In many instances the Hellenes found local settlements more or less firmly in place. Some were simply wiped out, while others underwent a process of gradual absorption.

The year 1,000 A.D. was an outstanding turning-point in history. By then, Christianity had become unshakeably established in the minds and hearts of a large segment of the world's people, and Islam had been consolidated by the admixture of a new force —the Seljuk Turks and the Ottoman Turks. The "giants" were bound to clash with each other for centuries to come—through the Crusades (10th to 14th centuries), the Balkan occupation (14th century), and the Spanish Reconquest (15th century).

As the Seljuk Turks slashed their swath through Persia (10th century) in the course of their headlong westward rush, they absorbed a new religious influence, the Moslem faith, and by the time they reached Asia Minor, they had been fully converted to Islam. In all likelihood, without the benefit of this interlude, the Seljuks would simply have borrowed some sort of para-Christian culture from the Byzantines, and would not have bothered to develop their own. Europe brought their successors, the Ottoman Turks, to a halt on land at the gates of Vienna (1579 and 1683) and on the waters in front of Lepanto (1571). There is good reason to believe the Ottomans at that particular point were perhaps more highly refined than western Europe itself.

What had been happening in Anatolia prior to the arrival of the Seljuk Turks? First of all, there had been the prehistoric period—man's presence in the Mediterranean area during the paleolithic era (unpolished stone) is attested to by multiple evidences, among which the Karain Cave, near Antalya, is noteworthy. Neolithic and chalcolithic vestiges (up to the sixth millenium B.C.) have been brought to light at Konya (Çatalhöyük) and at Burdur (Hacilar). Two thousand years later, southern Anatolia fell under the influence of Syria—this was the Tell Halaf civilization. From as far back as the third century B.C., east-west exchanges had been going on. In the second half of the third century B.C., a new people, the Hittites, arrived on the scene, and concomitantly, the bronze age was ushered in. During this entire period, men driven by the vicissitudes of war and by natural phenomena kept crisscrossing Anatolia in every direction. Inevitably, certain of the migratory hordes settled in conquered territory.

The first wholly successful and lasting exploit of this kind was accomplished by the Proto-Hittites, who founded their first kingdom towards the beginning of the second millenium B.C. (1600–1400 B.C.). Their successors continued to be known as

Hittites, although in the process they had assimilated part of the Assyrian culture. Under their impetus, the kingdom expanded to Syria and became an empire. This expansion did not fail to arouse the vigilance of the Egyptian rulers, who were carrying on exchanges with the north and east via Palestine, Syria and Anatolia.

The Hittite empire slowly but surely asserted itself and gained an ascendancy, reaching its heyday under an extremely dynamic sovereign, Suppiluliuma. Egypt's king in those days was Ramses II, likewise a highly ambitious ruler. Their two armies clashed in 1286 B.C. at Kadeş, on the Oronte River, and the result was a tie. The two kings reached an agreement for a pacific coexistence, which lasted only as long they both lived. The decline of Egypt's glory is a familiar part of history. The Hittite empire was invaded by warriors known as the Sea People, more specifically as the Phrygians, who filled the vacuum left by the Hittites.

In the meantime, things hadn't been idle in the west. The Achaeans and the Aeolians, presumably from the Balkans, sailed across the Aegean and founded colonies on the coast. The Achaeans also waged a certain famous war against the Anatolians in Troy (c. 1200 B.C.), later immortalized by Homer in *The Iliad*. After their victory at Troy, not all the Achaeans rushed straight back home. Parts of their troops scattered throughout Asia, founding enclaves, colonies and cities—this was the Greek period in the areas that today constitute Turkey. These settlers co-existed with the Phrygians, and also with the Cimmerians, who had established themselves after invading the land in the seventh century, B.C. During the sixth century B.C., another empire, Persia, was in the throes of expansion. The Persians ruthlessly swept everything out of their path in a precipitate dash to attack Europe. They were stopped by the Greeks and firmly ushered out. There ensued a long and bloody struggle for the suzerainty of the former kingdoms and confederations of Hellenic cities.

At last it came to be the turn of the west once again. In the fourth century B.C., another storm—this time a Macedonian tempest—unleashed its fury under Alexander, whom nothing and no one was to resist. Crossing the Dardanelles in the spring of 334 B.C., Alexander by early summer had routed the Persians on the Granicus, near the site of modern-day Biga. He then pushed on to Gordion, near Ankara, and there severed the famous Gordian knot, an act which the oracle had predicted would open up Asia to him. After conquering all the Aegean settlements, Alexander liberated Cilicia (the Mediterranean coast). By the end of 333 B.C., at Issos, not far from Iskenderun (Alexandretta), he had inflicted a second defeat on the Persians. His army then overran Egypt and Mesopotamia, and within a short time he had reached the banks of the Indus. Ten years later, Alexander died at the age of 33.

His generals divided up the empire, but instead of enjoying their good fortune peacefully, Seleucus, Lysimachus and Antigonus quarrelled over parcels of territory. The descendants of the first-mentioned, the Seleucids, continued to wage war against Pergamum, which had fallen to Eumenes and subsequently to Attalus.

The second century B.C. ushered in a new rival, Rome. The Roman Legions established a strong bridgehead by winning a resounding victory over the Seleucid king, Antiochus III, at Magnesia on the Sipylus (present-day Manisa). Over the period of a halfcentury, by dint of alternating the use of the sword with a judicious admixture of diplomacy, Rome moved in for good. When the last king of Pergamum, Attalus III, died in 133 B.C., he left a will bequeathing his kingdom to the Roman Senate. Needless to say, his testament was hotly contested by various factions. Naturally, Rome took possession of the inheritance *manu militari*. The Pontic kingdom on the Black Sea was the only one to put up a show of resistance, but its rulers, Mithridates and Pharnaces, were duly put in their place by a few Roman generals named Sylla, Lucullus, Pompey and Julius Cesar. Rome also subjugated Armenia into the bargain.

(The origin of the word *Rumi* presumably lies in the name of Rome. The feeling of hostility engendered by Roman "enlightened paternalism" had become so strong that this nickname has survived to this day as a term applied to all outsiders, but mainly to Christians.)

Meanwhile, a highly significant event had occurred in nearby Palestine, in a little town called Bethlehem. Until the fourth century A.D., the Asian provinces of the Roman Empire were in comparative ignorance of it and of its portent.

The Byzantine Empire

It wasn't until 324 A.D. that the somnolent Gateway to the East was finally jerked out of its apathy by the assumption of complete power by a Roman emperor favorable to Christianity. Constantine the Great (288?–337) made the faith legal, and in place of the clandestine symbol of the fish, adopted the Cross, the symbol of the Redemption. All this would still have had but little meaning for Asia if, very soon afterward, Constantine hadn't transferred his seat of empire to the shores of the Bosphorus, at a safe distance from the ever-more-ominous Barbarian incursions. Thus Byzantium became Constantinople, and Constantine's successors went even further, by dividing up the former Roman possessions into the Western Empire, with Rome as its capital, and the Eastern Empire, whose capital remained Constantinople. One of the sequels to this activity, notably the Barbarian conquest of Rome, which put a full stop to the Western Roman Empire, doesn't enter into this survey of Turkey's history.

Byzantium was thereafter the single great spiritual power. For a while, it, too, enjoyed the might that it had inherited from Rome. The center of gravity of the known world had shifted eastward, and inexorably the few remaining vestiges of Rome and of Latinity were replaced by elements of the Hellenic heritage. (The word Byzantine, by the way, means "Easternized Greek".)

Byzantium reached its zenith under Justinian (527–563), an emperor who both could and did hold off the Sassanids. At the time, Persia was still deploying tireless efforts to thrust its way westward. A new religious belief arose in the seventh century, generating fresh energy in men—Mohammed created Islam and hoisted the green banner of Holy War. By 634, Byzantium had been forced to abandon Palestine, and two years later, the Arabs were at the gates of Antioch. And, as the history of Istanbul shows, the Moslems reached the Bosphorus in 663.

Byzantium-Constantinople was shaken by the endless strife of the "War of the Icons". Actually, the iconoclasts had been on the rampage since the sixth century. The interdiction against representing the human form, specifically that of sacred personages, was basically an Eastern concept, and can be noted in both Judaism and Mohammedanism. Leo the Isaurian got an anti-icon concept approved by a council held in Constantinople in 730. As a result, precious artistic treasures were destroyed in the name of the respect that had to be shown to God. The shatterers of images were not formally condemned until the councils of 787 and 842, and their intransigent spirit continued to flare up with every revival of later puritan fanaticism—with the Waldenses, the Albigensians, the Hussites, and, much later, with the Reformists.

In 867, after perpetrating the assassination of Michael III (The Drunkard), Basil the Macedonian ascended to the throne. Under his rule, the state recovered its authority and prestige, and the flood of Arab invasions was stemmed. Government by this energetic dynasty continued through the year 1056.

After the extinction of the Macedonian dynasty with the much-married Empresses Zoë and Theodora, Asia Minor was overrun by new invaders, the Turks themselves, until Alexis I, founder of the Comnenes, temporarily succeeded in containing them.

The Seljuks

The Seljuks hailed from Mongolia, a vast and vague place periodically sending forth hordes. But the only point of resemblance between the Seljuks and the Mongolians was that both were tough and ambitious. The Seljuks were descended from the T'u-Kin people, whose eastern branch held sway over the steppes in the sixth century. When the uygurs returned from their various expeditions, they brought back assorted scraps of civilization. (*Uygur* meant "member of the group", those subject to its laws and customs, as opposed to *khazak*, meaning an independent individual, strictly out for himself, a free-lance.) Sheer anarchy prevailed until the hordes eventually became organized under Genghis Khan, in the 13th century—before then, their manner of existence and their language were the only ties between tribes.

In the beginning, the T'u-Kin—a Chinese name that underwent a series of deformations to finally resolve itself into Turk—were a rather insignificant group. However, they were reputed for their physical prowess, an attribute which has survived until today. In addition, the tribe had become so populous that its name gradually came to designate all the nomads who spoke the same language. Sometime around the tenth century they had grown powerful enough to effect a foray into Persia, where they learned about the Islam religion, which attracted them by its combative spirit.

An uygur prince from the Aral Sea region named Seljuk, the son of Ukak (Iron Bow), gave his name to these invaders of Asia Minor. As a matter of fact, they had already been infiltrating for some time, their incursions consisting mainly of raids by isolated groups who made a quick strike and fled with their loot. But the newcomers were efficiently organized and had a strong military structure. For their invasion of the western frontiers of Persia, they had an able leader, Togrul Beg (1038–1063), who made Isfahan his capital and pushed his troops farther and farther westward. Among the big attractions was the grass that grew on the steppes of Asia Minor. Not only did it provide excellent cattle fodder, but it was also supposed to make a "fermented drink that rendered women fecund and men invincible". According to another version, a single drop of this magic potion had the power to "lave the warriors' hearts of the world's grime". So, the Seljuks decided to settle right there without further ado.

The Arab Caliph of Baghdad, who was threatened by insurrections, appealed to his new neighbor for assistance. Togrul Beg was only too eager to help—he could ill afford to miss such a fine chance to get one foot in the doorway beyond his own new frontiers. Later on, Byzantium was to commit the same mistake, but for the time being it was delighted with the fate of the upstart Armenian kingdom, which was taking all the beatings. When Constantinople's Emperor Romanus IV (also called Diogenes) realized, too late, the invaders' intention to occupy the territory they had conquered, he determined to have it out with them. The result was a crushing defeat for him at Malazgirt, in 1071. Togrul's successor, Alp Arslan (1063–1072), managed to capture his opponent alive. According to one (probably apocryphal) version of the event, the Seljuk leader asked the Byzantine ruler how the latter would have treated him if fate had reversed their roles, whereupon Romanus answered: "I would have run you through with my sword". Arslan smiled softly and replied: "I would not be guilty of such a cruel act, one so contrary to what your Lord Jesus Christ would have recommended". He then set Romanus free, "with all due civility". However, this didn't get the latter very far, for in the meantime Michael had seized Romanus's throne. Upon his return, the usurper simply had Romanus's eyes put out, a dastardly deed that not only forestalled bickering over the throne, but also caused its victim's death.

When the Turks first laid eyes on the plateaus of Anatolia, they felt right at home. They recognized here the sky, the climate, and the mountains of their native Turkestan. Thus the foundations were laid for the union of a land and a people, a base that was to be cemented centuries later by Kemal Atatürk. Indeed, beginning in the 11th century, this union proved so binding that thenceforth the Anatolian Seljuks and the Iranian Seljuks pursued their separate destinies. In Persia, they became completely absorbed by the civilization around them. In Anatolia, they imposed their own Turkish culture.

By 1078 the Seljuks had spread out to Kayseri, Konya, Erzurum, Nicaea, and the shores of the Bosphorus; Lydia and Ionia had also capitulated to them. However, Constantinople was a tougher nut to crack, and besides, events had taken an unexpected turn—the Crusaders were now knocking at the gateway to Asia Minor.

When Malik Shah (reigned 1072–1092) succeeded Alp Arslan, he followed his predecessor's path. But, as often happens, his heirs wrangled over the spoils and divided the pieces among them, thereby weakening the empire. In 1097, when the Seljuks were defeated by Godfrey of Bouillon's First Crusade at Dorylaion, near Eskişehir, Byzantium took advantage of the situation, and in the wake of the Crusaders, recaptured many territories. The Second and Third Crusades were repelled by the Turks at Amasya and Ereğli. Having been betrayed itself, Byzantium went so far as to betray the Crusaders, for the benefit of the Seljuks. The situation was a hopeless muddle, and neither Conrad III nor Louis VII of France was able to get through to the Holy Land. Frederick Barbarossa had better luck in crossing Anatolia and reaching the Mediterranean, only to meet his death by drowning in the Göksu River (Calycadnos), whereupon his army scattered.

The Seljuks had grandstand seats for the Fourth Crusade, but all they could afford was the luxury of looking on and cheering. The Crusaders and the Venetians took Constantinople in 1204 and founded there an ephemeral Latin Empire. The remainder of the Byzantine Empire broke up into independent states, one of them being the Nicaean Empire. The Genoese, who considered that they had been cheated out of their rights, delivered the Crusaders' Constantinople into the hands of the Nicaean Emperor, Michael VIII in 1261. In exchange, they received certain commercial privileges and exemptions. In the meantime, the Seljuks had consolidated their own positions. The great ruler Alâeddin Keykubat (1219–1236) even found time to be a patron of the arts, including architecture. But there were also a few setbacks. In 1243, Genghis Khan and his Mongols appeared on the scene and dealt a nasty blow to Keykavus II (1237–1245), near Erzincan. The empire disintegrated into a scattering of more or less independent, half-Turkish, half-Mongolian emirates. The emirate of the Osmanli family was soon called upon to play a catalyzing role. One of the last of the Turkish invading tribes, the Osmanlis had Söğüt as their capital. Their ruler, Ertogrul, was well on the way to building a glorious reputation for himself. His son Osman (1281–1326) was to bequeath a lasting name to the world in the form of the adjective "Osmanli," which the Western world perpetuated as "Ottoman". The last, tragic, rulers of Constantinople reigned under the name of the Palaeologus family (1261–1453). Byzantium had managed to hold out, although it was being bled white by a thousand wounds inflicted by restless Slavs, to the west, and to the east, the hardly less active Turks. Worst of all were the domestic quarrels that undermined it from within, the cupidity of its Italian neighbors at next-door Galata.

The Ottomans

The Turks were steadily making progress. Osman's son, Orhan, captured Bursa (Brusa) in 1326, before going on to take Nicomedia (Izmit) and Nicaea (Iznik). Thirty years later, in 1357, the Turks had established a foothold in Europe, following the fall of Gallipoli (Gelibolu). Byzantium, in innocent unawareness of what it was doing—ignorance was already bliss in those far-off-days—called on him for help in fighting the Serbs. (John VI even married off his daughter to the sultan.) Murat I (1359–1389) arrived in the Balkans in 1362, after capturing Andrinople (Edirne). From 1371 on, he levied a tribute on Byzantium. He also founded the Janissaries (*Yeni-Ceri*, "new troops"), who quickly gained fame as an emblem of Turkish power. Fatally wounded but victorious, Murat died in 1389 after totally routing the Serbs at Kossovo. (The Bulgars had been brought to their knees the previous year.)

Murat's successor, Bayezit (1389–1403), enjoyed an enviable reputation that earned him the sobriquet of *Yıldırım*, "The Thunderbolt". (Among other security precautions, in order to ensure the safety of his backland territories, he ordered the strangling of his own brother.) By 1391 he had succeeded in blockading Byzantium, whose sovereignty was thus confined within its own walls. Manuel Palaeologus, feeling uneasy, stopped cooperating—disappointed by the Crescent, he began looking toward the Cross. This time he called Sigismund of Hungary to the rescue. The latter, sensing the need for caution, or perhaps just anxious to get rid of the Turkish peril once and for all, proposed a crusade. The king of France dispatched his cousin, John of Nevers, with 2,000 noblemen, and the finest flower of Christendom got itself hacked to pieces at Nicopolis, in Bulgaria (1396), by Bayezit, who, now that his steam was up, invaded Morea (the Peloponnesus) and prepared to besiege Constantinople.

Byzantium's outlook for the 15th century couldn't have been more bleak. When it beseeched the heavens to send succor, who should appear on the scene but that perpetrator of dire deeds, Tamerlane, in person. The Mongols seeped in again, and the Turks did an about-face to meet them. What happened exactly? Actually, if the two Asias represented by Bayerit and Tamerlane had united—which would have been logical—Europe probably would have ceased to exist. The official legend is that Tamerlane sent a friendly envoy to Bayezit, who proceeded to receive him most haughtily. So the two conquerors fought it out in Central Anatolia, in front of Ancyra (Ankara). It seems that the two war machines were, above all, eager to size each other up, mostly just to see who would come out on top. Tamerlane won and promptly returned to his native steppes. Turkish impetus suffered a slight setback from this thrashing, and matters remained stationary for exactly half a century.

Following Bayezit's demise, the sultanate fell prey to sundry rivalries, including those of the emirs of Karaman. For ten years

the bickering went on over who should have the right to en-
sconce himself in the *divan*, or cabinet chamber. In 1413, Mehmet
I got the upper hand over his brothers, although not for long.
His son, Murat II, succeeded him in 1421, and immediately
launched into a series of brilliant campaigns. He wrested Thes-
salonica from the Venetians, got Morea securely under his thumb,
and broke through all the way to Wallachia. But there were setbacks. Constantinople contrived to hold out against him in 1422,
and he lost Wallachia (now part of Romania) as the result of a
coalition between Albania, Serbia, and Hungary (the Treaty of
Szeged).

Let's pause for a moment to contemplate the backlashes of
fate. From their expeditions, the Turks had been bringing back
plunder that included kidnapped slaves. The most promising
young male specimens were forcibly converted to Islam and
enrolled in the Janissaries' military establishment. This was the
treatment meted out to, among others, George Castriota, the
son of the prince of Albania. George displayed such precocious
gifts as a warrior that honors and glory were heaped upon him,
and he was dubbed Skander Beg, or the Bey of Alexander. When
the day came for him to take arms against his own countrymen,
he rebelled. Abruptly, in the heat of the battle of Morava in 1443,
he defected, switching over to the other side and devastating the
ranks of his erstwhile comrades-at-arms. He was finally overcome,
but not before he had been converted to Christianity and become
a legendary hero. In the course of his amazing career, he organized and led the coalition that drove Murat into accepting the
compromise of Szeged. This was a catastrophe for Murat, in
addition to which there was the failure of his campaign against
the regent of Hungary, John Hunyadi. At Murat's death in 1451,
the throne devolved upon Mehmet II, who was to reign until
1481.

The Turkish Empire

With the accession of Mehmet II, the Turkish empire assumed
the role of a leading European power. He soon became known as
Fatih, the Conqueror. He entered Constantinople on May 29th,
1453, and in 1458, the city became his capital. During his probings
into central Europe, he suffered a few minor rebuffs at the hands

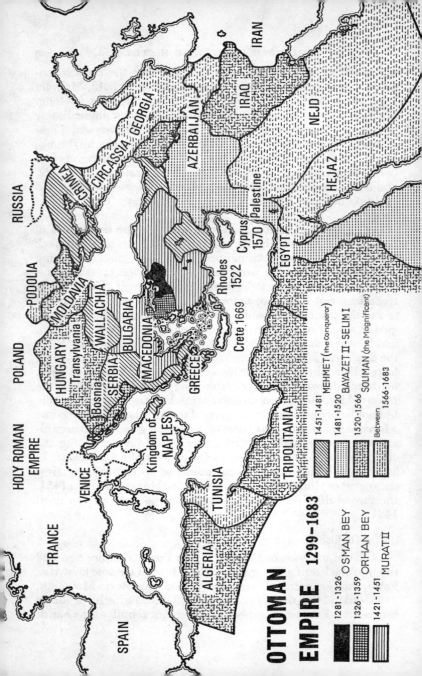

OTTOMAN EMPIRE 1299–1683

1281–1326 OSMAN BEY	1451–1481 MEHMET (the Conqueror)
1326–1359 ORHAN BEY	1481–1520 BAYAZET II – SELIM I
1421–1451 MURAT II	1520–1566 SOLIMAN (the Magnificent)
	Between 1566–1683

RUSSIA

IRAN

CRIMEA

CIRCASSIA GEORGIA

AZERBAIJAN

IRAQ

NEJD

PODOLIA

HEJAZ

Palestine

POLAND

MOLDAVIA

Cyprus
1570

EGYPT

HOLY ROMAN EMPIRE

HUNGARY

Transylvania

WALLACHIA

BULGARIA

Bosnia

SERBIA

MACEDONIA

Rhodes
1522

Crete 1669

GREECE

VENICE

FRANCE

Kingdom of
NAPLES

TRIPOLITANIA

TUNISIA

SPAIN

ALGERIA

of Matthias Corvin, the king of Hungary. Blessed with an attractive personality, Mehmet II, in addition to being a great patron of the arts and fluent in six languages, also had a talent for organization that made the government of his empire outstanding among his contemporaries. Serbia and Bosnia bowed to the yoke, as did the Venetian concessions, which he forced to pay tribute. Moldavia, Wallachia, and the Crimea were vassalized. The Italian enclaves in Greece found themselves threatened, as did Italy itself, when the Turks occupied Otranto in 1480.

The reign of Mehmet II's successor, Bayezit II (1481–1512), got off to a bad start. First, his brother Cem (pron. Jem) turned out to be an incorrigible trouble-maker. Then, the Mameluks from Egypt invaded the area around Adana, but were successfully evicted. Looking for outlets in Europe, he set upon Albania again; the Venetians sued for peace. But Bayezit II lacked the verve of his predecessors. A lover of the arts, an avid reader (particularly addicted to the works of the Moslem philosopher, Averoës), he was also given to pleasantries of a sort, and found it amusing to send Pope Innocent VII the lance blade that had pierced Christ's heart. The pope saw no harm in this offering, and turned it over to the sculptor Pollaiulo, who was then working on a statue of the sovereign pontiff. The sculptor was obviously even more of a joker, and visitors to St. Peter's in Rome can see the statue of the pope grasping in one hand the weapon that transfixed the flesh of the Redeemer. Bayezit's son Selim eventually plotted with the Janissaries, whose word was law in and around the seraglio, and the hapless sultan found himself deposed in 1512.

In order to consolidate and secure his possessions in Asia and Africa, Selim I (1512–1520) somewhat neglected Europe. His ambitions extended to Persia, Syria, Egypt and Arabia. Although he revealed himself to be a brilliant administrator with a fine sense of justice, he was merciless when it came to passing judgment, and within eight years he had eight of his grand vizirs put to death. One especially significant event marked his reign— Selim I added the title of caliph to that of sultan. Thenceforth, the rulers who sat on the throne of Constantinople were also the spiritual heads of state, the supreme religious leaders of the Moslem faith. Thus, Islam's highest spiritual authority reigned over both Asia and Europe until the time of Kemal Atatürk.

Under Suleiman I, the Magnificent, the Turkish empire saw its greatest territorial expansion. From 1520 to 1566, it continued to thrust forward its frontiers and to reinforce its possessions. In many instances, the carefully selected regional governors enjoyed a certain popularity among the Christians of the subjugated areas. Ghislain de Busbeck, who was then the Holy Roman Empire's envoy to the government of the Sublime Porte, left the following commentary: "With the Turks, honors and important appointments are awarded in recognition of talent and diligence, of assiduity and devotion. A dishonest or clumsy individual is doomed to stay at the lowest rung of the ladder as an object of scorn and contempt . . . . This explains the Turks' success in their undertakings, their domination over other peoples, and the continuous expansion of their empire."

The sultan intervened in the Christian disputes that were rending the western world asunder, and also dabbled in European politics. Francis I of France sought an alliance with the Turkish sultan against Emperor Charles V of Germany. The sultan's admiral, Hayreddin, who was none other than the formidable Barbarossa (his fortress still stands at Kuşadasi on the shores of the Aegean) went so far as to set up a naval base at Toulon, from which he made his forays along the Spanish and Italian coasts, attacking the installations of the emperor-king who claimed that the sun never set on his empire. Belgrade fell in 1521, and Hungary knuckled under to the Turks in 1526, at Mohács. In 1529, the Turks were fighting beneath the walls of Vienna. This was the end of the trail for them, but for centuries yet to come, the Balkans, southeastern Europe, and North Africa were to remain under Turkish domination. Turkey's possessions stretched out, curved like the Prophet's crescent around the eastern Mediterranean. But, just as the Arabs before them had failed to effect any real breach in the wall of Christendom, the Turks never got into central Europe: their empire was too farflung and too heterogeneous, and the Occident was already in its ascendancy.

The very institutions that had contributed to the strength of the Ottoman empire also carried in them the seeds of its destruction. The centralization of powers made for efficiency as long as those powers were in strong and resolute hands, but it also provoked wrangling and rivalries, which were all the more numerous

The image of Turkey as an exotic land will remain so long as mosques such as Istanbul's Süleymaniye stand.
Photo by Sonia Halliday

The magnificence of Byzantium can be appreciated in churches throughout Turkey, but the frescoes are nowhere more beautiful than in Istanbul's Kariye Museum.
Photo by Sonia Halliday

because of the prevailing polygamy that swelled the ranks of the pretenders. The subjugated peoples were governed by Turkish dignitaries who relied increasingly on the good will of the people whom we call nowadays, "collaborators".

There was also considerable pride, a bad omen. Since it looked as if Allah had aided the caliph's plans for conquest, the sultans concluded that divine aid was a sure thing. The letters written by Suleiman the Magnificent began with the words "I, the Sultan of Sultans, the Sovereign of Sovereigns, the dispenser of sceptres and the shadow of Allah on the earth . . .". In response to overtures from Francis I, he deigned to reply with the barest civility, merely to "acknowledge receipt of the request for assistance that had been submitted to the foot of the Imperial Throne, the refuge of humanity". He continued by urging the king of France to be of stout heart: "Night and day, our horse is saddled and our sword is girded". (Upon receiving this letter, Francis I is reported to have exclaimed: "And when, oh Turk, do you procreate?")

There was worse to come. Somewhat in the manner of the Spaniards who, at the sight of the gold from the New World, tended to believe that the source could never dry up, the Turks seldom condescended to engage in crass commerce and trade. The empire's economy was in the hands of the Jews (notably of Sephardic Jews who had been expelled from Spain in 1492), Armenians, Levantines, and some French and Italians among the Europeans. The *divan* granted the privilege of operating a business, thereby perpetuating the fatal error of Byzantium, which had allowed the Genoese to establish themselves in Galata. The French, governed by the strict discipline of the chamber of commerce in Marseille, assumed the succession. This step marked the beginning of the Capitulations. The first one, conceded to Francis I in 1535, was an authorization for ships flying French flags to navigate in Turkish ports, and to underake the protection of holy sites in Palestine, and also for disputes among French nationals to be settled by the French consul. In 1579, England obtained the same advantages, followed by Holland in 1612, Austria in 1615, and Russia in 1711. As Marcel Clerget described it: "Within a short time, to all intents and purposes, the Porte was no longer the lord of its own domains. The Turkish markets were flooded with European merchandise."

After Suleiman had been stopped short at Vienna, he waged campaigns in Asia, Persia, Azerbaijan, and Mesopotamia. His death at the age of 72, during the siege of Szigetvár in Hungary, brought an end to a reign that had lasted exactly 46 years and 46 days. The grand vizir contrived to keep the news of Suleiman's demise secret until the arrival of the great man's successor, Selim II, who remained in power until 1574. When Selim II captured the island of Cyprus in 1570, an aroused Christendom decided that matters had gone too far. A fleet made up mainly of Spanish and Venetian ships was hastily assembled by the pope and placed under the command of a young military genius, Don Juan of Austria, a bastard son of Charles V. The Ottoman fleet took a terrific beating at Lepanto in 1571, and this disaster put a definitive damper on Turkey's aspirations. Yet the country still remained a sought after ally—Queen Elizabeth of England offered Turkey a friendship pact "against the idolaters," i.e., against Catholic Spain.

Decadence

The Barbaresques, or Berbers, who were the North African tributaries of the Turks, had now begun to cultivate a taste for independence. Endless intrigues were woven at the court in Constantinople. The sultans acquired a new enemy—Russia, who not content with mere fighting along her frontiers, was fomenting revolts among the slavic peoples in the Balkans. Inside Turkey, the Janissaries drove hard bargains in return for favors, and they had full say as to who the next sovereign would be. Soon after they deposed and assassinated Osman II in 1622, Europe took the offensive and recaptured Transylvania. The old giant still had some fight left in him, however—in 1667, Crete fell under Turkish domination, but Kara Mustafa met with a new rebuff in 1683 at Vienna. The Ottomans subsequently lost Hungary, Dalmatia, and Morea to a coalition of Austria, Poland, Venice, and Russia. Rivalries, disorder, and anarchy gradually undermined the firm structure that had constituted the empire's strength. At the end of the 17th century, Persia recaptured Azerbaijan and Peter the Great snatched the Crimea away from "the infidels".

As the result of an attempt to recoup under Ahmet III (1703–1730), Turkey retrieved a few territories, without being able to hold on to them. Succeeding rulers—Mahmut I (1730–1754), Mustafa III (1757–1774), Abdul Hamid I (1774–1789) and Selim III (1789–1807)—wore themselves out just trying to keep things patched together. The Turkish empire, already in the throes of agony, was mercilessly battered by Russia. The Czarina declared herself protectress of the Orthodox Christians in the Ottoman Empire. (Her noble attitude offered obvious advantages and several discerning nations followed suit.)

What occurred next was a temporary reprieve in the process of downfall. The French Revolution was keeping Turkey's traditional enemies busy, and when Napoleon launched his Egyptian campaign, England hastened to shut France off from a route that might have led to India. Better still, a provisional alliance was concluded between the two irreconcilables, Russia and Turkey.

The Janissaries clung unswervingly to their traditions—in 1807 they perpetrated the assassination of Selim III, an enlightened monarch who was attempting to put an end to their power and to the corruption within the government. Chaos thenceforth prevailed in Constantinople until the accession of Mahmut II (1809–1839), a realist who managed to check the headlong rush to ruin. Under the terms of the treaty of Bucharest in 1812, he ceded Bessarabia to Russia in order to enable Czar Alexander I to face Napoleon. In 1826, Mahmut II finally dissolved the corps of Janissaries, those incessant fomenters of unrest; when they rebelled, he simply ordered his artillery to fire its cannons on them.

In the 19th century, despite various efforts to endow the Turkish empire with modern structures, the final agony inexorably set in. Both Austria and Russia redoubled their attacks. England discovered that it had extensive interests in that part of the world. The Romanians, Bulgarians, and Serbians developed a thirst for freedom. Greece liberated itself after years of fighting (London Conference in 1830). The Serbians staged an uprising in their turn, of which the only immediate outcome was a temporarily privileged status.

By now discord was rampant in the Turkish camp. Mehmet Ali, the Egyptian pasha, marched on Constantinople in 1833. At the time, the sultan fortunately was able to rely on his good neighbor, the Czar, who willingly lent him a hand in exchange for a privilege—the use of the Bosphorus Straits in time of war. France, under Louis Philippe, supported Egypt. Meanwhile, England, Austria, and Prussia were blockading the Egyptian ports. Mehmet Ali eventually had to yield, and the great powers granted him hereditary power in Egypt. Abdul Mecit (1839–61), who succeeded his father to the Turkish throne at the age of 17, had only to affix his signature.

The Sick Man of Europe

The big powers were already quarrelling in anticipation over the spoils of a Turkish Empire that as yet had not been completely brought to its knees. The youthful sultan and his eminent prime minister, Mustapha Rashid, attempted to put through internal reforms, but the latter were defeated by the corruption of the regime. As the sequel to a quarrel between the Catholics and the Orthodox Christians concerning the holy places in Palestine, Czar Nicholas I demanded tutelary authority over the ten million Orthodox Christians living in Turkish possessions. The sultan bristled indignantly and war broke out in 1853. The initial Russian victories goaded the French and British, who forthwith formed an alliance to intervene in the Crimea. The treaty of Paris in 1856 imposed ... the status quo! After they had done their best to hasten his death by every conceivable means, the good doctors were now outdoing themselves to ensure the survival of "the sick man of Europe". The final blow had been postponed *sine die*. Naturally, the victories of Sebastopol and Malakoff had somewhat improved the plight of the Eastern Christians, who were henceforth to enjoy the same rights as the Moslems.

French diplomacy was now part of the councils of the Divan. Under Napoleon III France proposed domestic reforms in Turkey. But the faction of the "Old Turks" clung fiercely to established traditions, and the European part of the declining empire was in a perpetual state of insurrection. The big powers stood by as referees, chalking up the blows and picking up the pieces. Montenegro repulsed the Turks, Romania shook off the yoke, and Lebanon, through French intervention, acquired a privileged status.

As a consolation, the "Old Turks" set about creating an organ-ization, called the "New Ottomans", clandestine at its inception. This provided the basis for the movement eventually known as the "Young Turks". The latter promoted the concept of a Tur-kish *nation*, an idea that was revolutionary at the time precisely because the Ottoman Empire was made up of so many diverse nationalities. Under the circumstances, the joint uprising staged by Bulgaria and Bosnia set off a real political upheaval.

Midhat Pasha succeeded in convincing the cabinet ministers that only a constitutional regime could save the country. Abdul Aziz, who had come to power in 1861, was deposed. His nephew, Murat V, lasted less than a year on the throne. Abdul Hamid II acted as the liquidator between 1876 and 1909. The independence of Serbia, Romania, and Bulgaria was recognized at San Stefano and at Berlin in 1878. Austria-Hungary got control of Bosnia and Herzegovina; Russia kept Kars and Ardahan; England set itself up on Cyprus; and Greece occupied Thessaly. The Turkish treasury was scraping the bottom of the barrel, and Abdul Hamid offered his monopolies for hire to foreign capital. There was an "empire for sale" . . .

At the beginning of the 20th century, the Committee for Union and Progress imposed a constitution. Abdul Hamid yielded at first, then withdrew his consent. Haunted by fear of assassination, his usual reaction to any threat was to have his opponents sum-marily executed at the first sign of anything resembling disloyal conduct.

In the midst of this sordid atmosphere, there were two men quietly pursuing their separate way, two men destined to change Turkey's destiny: Enver Pasha and Mustafa Kemal. Completely different personalities, they inevitably became rivals. For many years, it was thought that the former had succeeded and that the latter had failed. In the end, Enver Pasha became the forgotten man, and his rival survived, generally remembered by his three full names, Mustafa Kemal Atatürk.

Meanwhile, in 1909, Abdul Hamid had abdicated under pressure by the Young Turks. Mehmet V (who reigned until the end of World War I) agreed to a constitutional government, but soon began veering off in the direction of a military dictatorship. Enver Pasha, clever, adaptable, and versatile, threw himself in the thick of the political fray. (Mustafa Kemal, a fierce, uncommunicative, and violent man, was too young at the time.) Whereas his rival, Enver, sought to "Turkify" the miscellaneous nationalities that made up Turkey, Kemal advocated Westernization within the framework of an aroused nationalism. On the diplomatic scene, Enver was entering into an increasingly closer relationship with Germany, whose Kaiser was loudly proclaiming his cry of "Drang nach Osten"! ("Drive to the East"). With good reason, Kemal was beset with misgivings about the avidity of such an ally. However, for the time being, no one could foresee the turn of events, and the future Ataturk could only continue champing at the bit.

The various dependencies of the crumbling empire were getting restless. Both the Arabs and the Christians rejected Turkification. In 1911 war broke out with Italy over Tripolitania. When it became necessary for the Turkish army to get ready to fight, the people at the top suddenly remembered a certain gifted and devoted officer surnamed Kemal. A Balkan war in 1912, against a Serbo-Greco-Bulgarian coalition, inflicted a severe defeat on Turkey. The second Balkan war, in 1913, turned Serbs, Greeks and Romanians against their former ally over the distribution of the rich spoils. The ensuing crushing defeat of Bulgaria allowed Turkey to reoccupy Eastern Thrace.

The Young Turks committed a supreme blunder by siding with Germany in World War I. The French and British forces met with failure in their attempt to land at Gallipoli, which was being defended by Mustafa Kemal and the German General Liman von Sanders. But—and there were plenty of "but's"—the Russians were occupying Van, Erzurum, and Trebizond, and the British were moving up from Egypt and the Persian Gulf, making their way northward along the Mediterranean coast. In 1917, they had reached Baghdad; by 1918, they were in Jerusalem, and the French were occupying Syria.

Renaissance

On October 30th, 1918, the sultan capitulated and signed the Armistice of Mudros. Kemal had at last been appointed commander-in-chief on one of the fronts, and when the time came to lay down arms, he rebelled against the conditions of the armistice, which were tantamount to a dismemberment of Turkey. He launched an appeal to his followers and comrades in arms, who joined him in a congress at Sivas, where they decided to defend Eastern Anatolia at any cost, and to expel the Greek army which had been brought into Smyrna-Izmir by the combined French, British, and American fleets. Kemal's committee quickly assumed the form of a counter-government. In order to understand the conflict that was besetting the minds of high-ranking Turkish officers, it must be remembered that their sultan was also their caliph. It made no difference that Mehmet VI was merely a puppet in the hands of the Allied diplomats. They were rebelling not only against temporal authority but also against the highest spiritual authority of Islam, and for some of them the decision was an agonizing one.

In 1920, a great "national assembly" convened in Ankara, while the constitutional government in Constantinople was calmly continuing to sell out the country. In a provincial town out on the steppe, the illegitimate heirs of the "sick man of Europe" were bracing themselves to challenge the testament of the dying patient, who lay hemmed in by businessmen. The Treaty of Sèvres, in August 1920, confirmed the direst apprehensions— Turkey was about to be dismembered. Greece, not even waiting for the treaty to be ratified, dispatched troops inland from Smyrna. To the east, the Armenians were getting ready to proclaim the republic that the treaty had provided for them. Kemal boldly faced up to both these fronts. General Kazim Karabekir went off to cope with the insurgent Armenians, even recapturing Kars from the Russians. On the Western front, General Ismet Pasha held the Greek troops, and eventually defeated them twice, at Inönü, near Afyon Karahisar. (His name has gone down in history as Ismet Inönü.)

The fact can never be overemphasized that, on the Turkish side, a people exhausted by four years of war and privations was fighting in response to the call of its national hero. Their arms were pitifully inadequate, with no one standing by to offer assistance. Their ranks decimated by sacrifices, they had just about reached the end of the rope. What spurred them on was their national pride, which was about all they had to sustain them. A new battle began that lasted 20 full days. On September

13th, 1921, a laconic communiqué announced that not a single Greek had been left alive east of the Sakarya River.

The Ankara assembly awarded Kemal the title of Ghazi, the conqueror. He was also confirmed as commander-in-chief, winning a final and decisive victory at Dumlupinar at the end of August 1922. The Greeks dispersed in a disorderly retreat toward Izmir. The Turks made a triumphant entry into the recaptured port city, while the British phlegmatically re-embarked their defeated allies. Most of the rejoicing was at the expense of the Greek shopkeepers. A gigantic fire, started by saboteurs or by some other means, got out of control and destroyed a great part of the city.

Theoretically it was all over, and the Allies refrained from intervening. The chapter "Around the Sea of Marmara", in this guidebook, describes the single encounter between Turkish and British troops and its outcome. Finally, on October 11th, 1922 (Izmir had been captured on September 19th), the Mudanya armistice removed the scar left by the Treaty of Sèvres. The existence of Turkey was assured.

Even now, Kemal didn't pause, for at last his real work was about to begin. By November 1st—only three weeks later—he was busy rounding up support by every means, including threats and promises, in order to achieve his aims, which he knew were sound. Elections took place and the sultanate was abolished. The caliphate remained temporarily—the time wasn't yet ripe to dispose of it. And Kemal eventually settled the fate of the religious body that had influenced the country's policies for so many centuries. On October 29th, 1923, the republic was proclaimed and Kemal was elected president.

Now he could roll up his sleeves and set to work. His cherished goal was to modernize Turkey along Western patterns. The main hurdle was the country's deeply-rooted attachment to the religious past, but by March 23rd, 1924, this prodigious man had had the caliphate abolished by the Assembly. The final dissolution of the religious orders was brought about in the following year when the calendar based on the Hegira was replaced by the Gregorian calendar. The year 1926 saw the introduction of legal reforms: Turkey adopted the Swiss civil code, the Italian penal code, and the German commercial code. By 1928 Islam had ceased to be the official religion, and the Roman alphabet, which is far more adapted to the sounds of the Turkish language, had replaced Arabic script. Furthermore, the muezzins were no longer allowed to use Arabic, the language of religion, to call the people to prayer. The metric system came into force in 1931. Women acquired the right to vote in 1934. The fez was outlawed for men, and women were recommended not to wear the veil. Under the extraordinary impetus of this unusual leader, Turkey had, in a few years, practically filled in the gap of centuries.

Kemal Atatürk died on November 10th, 1938. Obviously, all his sweeping reforms hadn't been accepted without a murmur, but he remains the cherished son of his people. A quick glance at today's Turkey will make you realize the superhuman effort of this exceptional man, who shook a resigned populace out of its apathy, who overcame the opposition of those clinging tenaciously to their feudal privileges, who soothed the antagonisms of his companions when the various religions issues were raised.

The testimonies of all who knew Kemal Atatürk, the biographies and history books—with the obvious exception of those that have been written with a sentimental veneer—agree in describing this "father of Turkey" as a man endowed with a superhuman capacity for work.

How can a foreigner assess the full scope and weight of the enormous past that Kemal Atatürk had to eradicate in order to pursue his duty as he saw it? Who can truly know what he himself had suffered earlier, when on all sides he met only with humiliation and isolation? Would it have been humanly possible to achieve what he achieved if he hadn't kept his mind resolutely set on the goal to be attained, with the iron hand in the iron gauntlet? His mission was to fill in the gap of the centuries of backwardness accumulated by his country. In his very starkness, he may well be one of the most touching and attractive characters that the 20th century has produced. He is undeniably one of its most important historical figures.

Second in importance only to Kemal Atatürk himself is the fact of Turkey's neutrality during World War II. Its symbolic declaration of war on Germany and Japan, dated February 23rd, 1945, was more a diplomatic gesture than a political act.

The first Turkish republican governments were the creation

of some of Kemal's co-workers, chiefly under the direction of his faithful long-time comrade, Ismet Inönü. Celal Bayar, who founded the Democratic Party in 1946 and took over the reins of power in 1950, was also one of the "veterans of the past". But few of his successors possessed Atatürk's prestige or presence, his manner or bearing. The unshakable sovereignty of the *agas* (big landowners) did more than doom the agrarian reform to failure, it exerted extreme electoral pressure on the Assembly by turning the peasant vote (accounting for some 80 percent of the electorate) into a personal matter. The opposition had only one recourse, that of seizing power through a *coup d'état*. In 1960, the army overthrew the government and dissolved the Democratic Party, which was replaced by the Justice Party. The latter won the elections in 1965 and again in 1969, but in 1970 a right wing democratic party was again formed.

Disturbed by continuous unrest and violence, the army again overthrew the government in early 1971 in a very quiet and bloodless *coup d'état*, but promised faithfully to hold free general elections "within 12 months". Having kept their promise to do so in the last *coup*, it is quite likely they will do so again, and that parliamentary democracy will be fully restored to Turkey by the spring of 1972.

Illustration at head of this chapter: Suleiman the Magnificent among his soldiers (from a 16th-century miniature in Topkapi Palace).

ART AND ARCHITECTURE

Four Epochs of Vigor and Grace

The jutting peninsula that Asia throws out towards Europe has always been a meeting place for Orient and Occident. Peoples coming from the West or the East occupied it again and again. Some managed only to create an ephemeral sovereignty with no developed cultural tradition; others used it as a base for powerful empires or dominated it from outside. When these nations reached the height of their political supremacy and the full flowering of their art, they left an indelible imprint on Anatolia.

Anatolia's artistic past is marked by four great epochs: The Hittite period, the Greek and Roman colonization, the Byzantine Empire, and the reign of the Turks, whether Seljuk or Ottoman.

Hittite Art

The high Anatolian plateaux were the scene of a brilliant civilization which lasted for 2,000 years and whose influence spread as far as Upper Syria. From 3000 B.C. until a thousand years before our era, the Hittites built thick-walled palaces and temples and powerful fortifications. Their buildings were as massive as the surroundings scenery, but their metal workers were capable of sculpting delicate statuettes.

The burial ground of Alaca Höyük to the east of Ankara has proved literally a gold mine. Turkish archeologists have uncovered a multitude of gold and copper vases, jewelry fashioned with cornaline and rock crystal, statuettes of bulls and stags, the latter with slender bodies and hooves and extraordinarily developed antlers, plus many decorative pierced metal plaques with geometric designs. Most of these objects held religious significance— the statuettes and plaques, for instance, were often equipped with sockets so they could be attached to staffs and held aloft during ceremonial processions. Unfortunately we know very little about these rites held 5,000 years ago. The best of these funerary objects—belonging to the so-called proto-Hittite period—are on view in the Ankara museum.

More Hittite art of this period has been discovered at Kültepe near Kayseri. Here the motifs were obviously influenced by Sumer and Babylon—there are highly stylized female idols, engraved cylindrical seals, goddesses with animals, the struggle of Gilgamesh and the bull, and lions and stags crossed like X's among the themes. The Ankara Museum also has some long-mouthed, large-handled vases made by the potters of Kültepe.

The principal Hittite period begins with the new empire in about 1450 B.C.; its showcase is the empire's capital city, Hattusas. The site has been only partially excavated, but it is evident to the most unpracticed eye that the Hittites here were preoccupied with defense and with power. Hattusas was built on a rocky spur in the heart of Anatolia, high above a ravine which has given its name to the present village of Boğazköy, or "village of the gorge". The floorplan of several buildings is visible on the ground, and one may make out angular corridors leading to the halls, and the paved courtyards of palaces and shrines. A double wall of irregular but well-fitted stone blocks protected the capital on the plateau side, and the ravine formed a natural rampart on the other. The vaulted gates are defended by porches surrounded by bastions, and on each side of these gates, Hittite artists carved animal or human guardians. Two panels with lions have been left on the site. They are not statues added as decoration after construction of the edifice as in Mesopotamia, but wrought directly from the mass of rock. The lions seem to leap out from the walls, but are imprisoned in the stone at their waists; and it is evident that the artist was less interested in imitating nature than in giving his creation the most terrifying appearance possible. The paws are thick, the mane suggested symbolically by short locks chiseled on the muscled body, the jaws are open and threatening.

Hittite sculpture is more forceful than graceful, with a few notable exceptions. One, at Alaca Höyük, is a sphinx whose feminine face has a sort of Mona Lisa smile; some will prefer her to her sister from Hattusas, now in Istanbul, whose countenance, in spite of damage, gives a good idea of what ideal feminine beauty must have been for the Hittites.

The best example of relief sculpture is probably the "king" who guarded one of the gates of Hattusas and who now may be seen in Ankara's museum. He is actually the great god Teshub, but the confusion is understandable since he is dressed and armed like a royal Hittite. His head is sculptured in profile while the torso is seen from the front; and like most statues of men of the period, he wears a short tunic whose wide belt secures a curved dagger with a large grip. The left arm is folded back towards the body, its closed fist ready to strike; while the right hand grasps a hatchet of a type still frequently seen in Luristan (a present-day province of Iran). The god wears the up-turned pointed shoes typical of all personages in reliefs of this style, and looks as though he were ready to set off on a march. The head conveys the general impression of strength—a heavy jaw, thick lips, massive nose, and a far-from-pleasant look in the eye. Teshub wears a conical helmet with a lock of his hair hanging down from the top of it.

Hittite sculpture is much the same everywhere and it would be useless to look for an evolution in the style or for differences among "schools". However, the choice of locations and the ways of treating groups of figures vary and from this point of view, the Yazilikaya friezes, near Boğazköy, are quite remarkable.

Here are relief sculptures alive with figures measuring anywhere from two and a half to seven feet tall. They parade along the rocky walls of two galleries— in the great gallery is the whole roster of Hittite deities, men on one side, women on the other. The two ranks converge towards a central panel at the end; it depicts the mystical union between the god Teshub and the goddess Hepatu.

The members of this pantheon all have the same stiff hieratic attitude, and can only be distinguished by their size, costume, and particular godly attributes. The male divinities wear short tunic around their hips and pointed headdresses. The goddesses, like women everywhere, are more ornamental, with their long pleated skirts, cylindrical tiaras, earrings and bracelets, Some in the procession stand aloft on symbolic animals in the Assyrian style, while others stand beneath ideograms somewhat like Egyptian hieroglyphics. In spite of their static appearance and their rather stereotyped decoration, the friezes of the great gallery constitute without a doubt an original work of art both as to style and technique.

One of the bas-reliefs in the small gallery is more cosmopolitan and exemplifies a number of influences which Hittite art managed to synthesize. It shows a sword whose handle is fashioned of a human head placed above two horizontal lions "resting" and two more lions lying head downwards along the edges of the blade. Is this a stone copy of some king's fabulous sword? Experts say it is more likely a god itself, and cite examples of "hoplolatry" (weapon-worship) ranging from Sumerian and Assyrian daggers through Syrian hatchets to a whole range of objects from Crete and the Aegean world. Recalling how much the Hittites admired force, one is hardly surprised at this example of the cult of arms.

Hittite sculptors chiselled busily for hundreds of years on any number of rocky walls in Anatolia. Another example of their work can be seen at Ivriz (or in Istanbul's Archeological Museum, where there is a cast of these reliefs).

The new empire inaugurated grandeur in sculpture, but its official business also kept the gem cutters busy producing seals and signets, and several Turkish museums have fine collections of these. The Hittites at this point stopped copying their Mesopotamian counterparts, and began producing seals with original designs—usually a god or animal in the center, with braid and scrolls around the edges. The style reminds one generally of that of the reliefs.

About 3,000 years ago, the cultural and political influence of the Hattusan Hittite Empire began to wane, with a few die-hard outposts remaining here and there. The tablets from Karatepe in the Ankara Museum tell a tale of long-forgotten feasts and festivities at the palace of the Hittite kings of Cilicia (Southern Turkey) who reigned until the eight century B.C. In Upper Syria around Kargamiş and Zincirli, the Hittite tradition persists until about the seventh century, but the sculpture deteriorates, and instead of conveying strength, begins to look merely heavy. The Mesopotamian influence, vanquished for a few centuries, returns to the fore. The Hittite tunic gives way to the Babylonian robe, the typical Assyrian beard seems to grow on every face and the turned-up toes of Hittite shoes are rarely seen. When Hittite politics could no longer impose a culture, they simply went out of style.

Greek and Roman Art in Anatolia

The Greeks who fled from the Dorian invasions around 1100 B.C. took refuge on friendlier shores of the Aegean in Anatolia. Here they set up confederations and leagues of cities which did much to keep the cultural and ethnic traditions of these immigrants alive. Aeolians settled north of the Gulf of Smyrna, Acheans colonized the valley of the Caîque, and Ionians founded a confederation of 12 cities around Ephesus and Miletus whose influence was to determine in large measure the art, literature and philosophy of the western world. The Dorians themselves crossed the Aegean a little later and settled in the south, above and below the Cnidus peninsula. These cities in turn established colonies and trade centers on the shores of the Propontis (the Sea of Marmara) and the Pontus Euxinus (Black Sea). The sea lanes between all these centers were crowded with ships carrying not only wares and riches, but in another sense, art and culture.

The states of the interior of Anatolia also welcomed Greek civilization whose traditions blended easily with their own. One might say that nobody missed the Hittites, for a number of other peoples came to fill the rôle they had left vacant. Between the 13th and the eighth centuries, the Phrygians built up a powerful state; several archeological discoveries serve to acquaint us with their civilization. A sculpture of a temple façade carved on a rock at Midas Şehri ("City of Midas"—the same one whose touch turned everything to gold) near Eskişehir gives a good idea of Phrygian sacred architecture. The French archeologist Albert Gabriel made an important find nearby—the remains of a foundry, which confirms legends that these people were not only accomplished metal workers, but metal worshippers as well. At the ancient site of Gordion, about 60 miles southwest of Ankara, an American team has uncovered pavements and mosaics which prove the existence of vast palaces and shrines.

While the Phrygians were busy in the north, the Lydians in central Anatolia and the Carians in the south (near Hallicarnassus) were creating their own civilizations. Both peoples were in constant contact with the coastal Greeks and their art shows this influence. In the rough country of the southwest (near Fethiye), in Lycia, a French archeological mission is working on the sites of Xanthos and other coastal cities. They have found tombs dug out of the rock with façades resembling Greek temples, and others, less Greek, which seem to imitate in stone the wooden beams of houses or even the keels of ships.

Inside Anatolia, local tradition and Greek culture mingled to create original forms, but on the coast the works of art are indistinguishable from those of Greece itself. There are remnants from the archaic period onward, and if there is not too much evidence to go on, it can be blamed on Anatolia's particularly lively history and not on the lack of artists.

The Byzantines pillaged and destroyed the Temple of Athena at Assos, built in the sixth century B.C. There are still a few handsome Doric capitals on columns of the Acropolis high above the entry of the Gulf of Edremit, but the delightful archaic friezes are now in the Louvre—the result of a princely gift from Sultan Mahmud II to France in the 19th century. Istanbul has, however, its share of the remains of the temple. In its Archeological Museum, you will find other vestiges of Anatolia's archaic Greek art—red vases decorated in black, terra cotta sarcophagi, ancient coins, and memorial stones to the dead. These few objects are all the more precious since they pre-date the Persian occupation, which considerably hindered the development of Greek art in Anatolia. One notable exception—it was here that the Ionian order (columns with scroll capitals) was first created; it soon replaced the more severe Dorian throughout the Greek world.

Alexander the Great and the Macedonian conquest changed not only the face of history, but the face of art. Artists and achitects could now count not only on their own talent but on the

Spanning the Golden Horn, Istanbul's Galata Bridge connects the old city with the new.

*Istanbul's Covered Bazaar, rebuilt after a fire in
1954, is paradise for those who love shopping.*
Foto by Sonia Halliday

enormous financial means placed at their disposal by ambitious oriental potentates who wanted buildings splendid enough to further their own prestige. Among the many kingdoms patched together out of the débris of the Macedonian Empire was that of the Attalids; its capital, Pergamum (now Bergama) is the most typical representative of the Hellenistic style.

In another of history's changes of course, Rome soon established her supremacy in Asia Minor. But instead of disrupting society or art, the arrival of the Romans strengthened both by vastly improving the commercial and economic affairs of the new province. The result was the wealthiest epoch in Anatolia's long history.

Very recent excavations under the direction of Dr. Erim on a *National Geographic Society* grant have unearthed an incredible number of archeological treasures at Aphrodisias, 95 miles southeast of Izmir. This is a Greco-Roman city which flourished for several hundred years from the first century B.C. and so rich in finds that marble heads literally fall out of old walls. Digging has only been undertaken since 1961, and already a theater, concert hall, agora, acropolis, and baths have been unearthed with probably much more to come. The Romans kept everything that the Greeks had built, and added the marks of their own genius.

The same principle holds true at Didyma, where the huge temple of Apollo, begun by the Greeks, was finished by the Romans in much the same style. And, as everywhere in the empire, they improved general conditions in the country with roads, bridges and aqueducts, while adding baths to the amenities of the cities at municipal or private expense, plus temples built to the glory of their emperors. Augustus' temple at Ankara is embellished by his last will and testament, engraved on one of its walls.

There are of course some stylistic changes—Roman architects used the arch to a far greater degree, and certain types of edifices like the basilica and the triumphal arch make their appearance for the first time. Hadrian's Arch at Antalya is decorated with acanthus leaves, scrolls, carved ox-skulls and lion heads.

Wealth and power have their disadvantages. One of them in architecture is the desire for the colossal—and what was best in the Hellenistic style soon tended to exaggeration. Corinthian capitals, richer but less graceful than the Ionian, came to be used almost exclusively. Cities like Ephesus were graced with wide streets, bordered with colonnades. At Miletus, a 25,000-seat theater rose from the ground. The southern coast of Anatolia between Antalya and Mersin is literally covered with Roman buildings, and almost every hill is the site of some ruin or other. But quality does not always run with quantity, and most of these vestiges lack the subtlety and grace of Hellenistic art.

Byzantine Art

Christianity sowed its first seeds in Anatolia in the fourth century, and from these seeds grew a rich harvest of churches and monasteries throughout the land. Some were built in groups; the most remarkable of these is certainly the cluster of religious shrines at Bin Bir Kilise Deresi (The Valley of a Thousand and One Churches) near Karaman, which is largely intact. In this neighborhood, most of the churches date from about the tenth century. Some are built on the classic lines of a basilica with three parallel naves or a single one; others follow the plan of the cross. Near Ürgüp in Cappadocia there is a multitude of churches hollowed out of volcanic stone. But it was only natural that the handsomest shrines were built in Byzantium itself.

Rome had been the inventor of the basilica with parallel naves, but the Byzantine architects developed it in their own style, building on Roman tradition with oriental techniques and splendor. The dome came into common use, and some churches also had a narthex or vestibule preceding the sanctuary itself, as in Romanesque architecture in Europe later on. Saint Irene in Istanbul, built during the reign of Justinian in the sixth century, is a fine example of a basilica with three naves, a dome and a narthex.

Emperor Justinian's reign also witnessed the construction of one of the world's biggest religious edifices—the great Saint Sophia Basilica. A narthex 195 feet long and 39 feet wide precedes the long central nave, which is surmounted by a dome 100 feet in diameter. The dome is flanked by two half domes and supported by four gigantic pillars; the great arches of two half domes and four pendentives (or triangular vaults) serving as intermediaries between the circular dome and the square floorplan outlined by the pillars. The side naves have galleries high above the floor which look out onto the central nave. The group of domes is supported outside by thick buttresses, giving Saint Sophia a heavy silhouette; inside, however, the soaring domes and the play of light on the slender columns of the galleries give a feeling of lightness, space and freedom.

Justinian ordered the great church to be covered with mosaics on a background of gold, but the ones now decorating the basilica are of a later date. On the tympanum above a door in the vestibule is a fine Virgin and Child with Emperors Justinian and Constantine on either side. The arch of the narthex is covered with gold mosaic with geometric designs in color. The royal door leading from the narthex to the nave is guarded by a severe-looking Christ enthroned, while the walls of the nave are covered with beautifully-veined marble plaques.

There is no other example that matches the Byzantine grandeur of Saint Sophia, for shortly after its construction, tastes changed and architects came to prefer more intimate sanctuaries and less solemn decoration. A new and charming style came into being after the ninth century, of which the Kariye Cami (formerly the conventual church of Holy Saviour-in-Chora), with its mosaics and paintings, is a particularly attractive specimen.

Very little remains of Byzantine palace architecture, though not far from Saint Sophia, one may see some murals and pavements of the sacred palace maintained in their original location. These scenes, dating from the sixth century, depict hunting parties and aspects of everyday life in the palace. The walls of Constantine Porphyrogenitus' palace, with their fine arched-lintel windows are still standing near Kariye Cami, but of two other once-imposing palaces of Byzantium—Justinian's and Alexis Comnenus' at Blachernae—there is nothing left but a few stones.

Byzantine military architecture ranks far below that of medieval Europe for quality and inventiveness. The walls of Constantinople may be long, but they are poorly put together of inferior materials. The only monumental gateway worth looking at is the Golden Portal, which is now part of the castle of Yedikule. It was designed in the fifth century, more for prestige than for defense. Other fortresses, like those of Miletus or Assos, will only make the true art lover sad, for their rough walls were hastily thrown together with stone stolen from fine classical monuments.

Turkish Art: Seljuk and Ottoman

Anatolia had already played host to just about every people possible in the ancient world, but her historical ups and downs were not yet finished. In 1071, the Seljuk sultan, Alp Arslan, defeated and captured the Byzantine emperor, Roman Diogenes, at Malazgirt, and thereby opened the gates of Asia Minor to the Turks. The tribes came streaming down from upper Asia and found what has been called a "new Turkestan".

From the tenth to the 13th century, Turkey was very prosperous, thanks to its location on the caravan routes linking the Orient to the Occident. As usual, wealth fostered art, and the new ease in communications brought not only goods but artists from Persia and the Far East to the Seljuk capital at Konya. Here they met the artisans and architects who had come in on the first Turkish wave, and between them they created an entirely new style. The Turks did not abandon their traditions, but with the help of these new outside influences, they adapted them intelligently to local conditions. With the Seljuk dynasty, Turkey witnesses for the first time a number of architectural features commonly used in Asia— tall gateways with niches, triangular vaults decorated with stalactites and prisms, ogival archways, and ceramic tiling.

Most of these features, combined with Byzantine building techniques, were later taken over by the Ottomans, who brought Turkish art to its zenith, but the Seljuks must be credited with making the transition from the art of nomadic tribesmen to the delicate and refined products of their Ottoman successors. There are few examples of Seljuk palace architecture extant (except for the ruins of the Beyşehir palace), but many public, religious and funerary monuments are still standing.

The mosque—which is in many Moslem countries an elegant and graceful affair—in Anatolia had to contend with the rigorous climate while respecting sacred tradition. Both help to explain the austerity of such mosques as the Alâeddin (built in 1220 at Konya), whose almost blank façade is pierced with narrow windows at the top. Inside however, the colonnaded prayer hall is reminiscent of its Syrian counterparts. At Erzurum, in the far northeast, the altitude is 6,500 feet, and the high plateau almost reminds one of Tibet. Here the Great Mosque (Ulu Cami), with its thick walls and only occasional arched door or small square window, looks more like a fortress than a place of worship. Next door, the *medrese* (Koranic school) looks less threatening. Its grey stone gateway is flanked by two square bases, from which rise two fluted minarets covered with enameled brick. Carved bands of scrolls and stylised palm leaves adorn the gateway, while the vault is honey-combed and embellished with stalactities, as will also be the case with the Ottoman style. The interior is designed along the traditional lines of all *medreses* or *imarets* (hospitals or alms-houses) —the courtyard is bordered on two sides by short, thick columns supporting broken arches. Two large broken cylindrical arches cut the colonnade in half. The cells must have been uncomfortable with no light and low ceilings. A high nave, now in ruins, once prolonged the courtyard.

Part of the severity of Erzurum is due to its grey building stone. At Konya, the stone used is black and white marble, which gives a much more inviting aspect to monuments like the Karatay *medrese*. The two colors are alternated on its façade, which is further adorned with scrolls and intertwined bands, plus three chiselled cabochons on the upper part. We find some of the same motifs, including the cabochons, on the façade of Ince Minare Cami ("the mosque with the slim minaret"), not far away. This mosque is also decorated with wide stone ribbons, and if these carvings seem odd, it is because they are a sculptured transposition of the fancy work on saddles and bridles, of which Turkish nomadic horsemen were so fond.

The memories of tribal days on the steppes are still strong in Seljuk funerary architecture. Their mausoleums, called *türbes* or *kümbets*, look exactly like *yurts*, or Turkish tents, which were fashioned of circular wooden slats, then covered with felt. One of the most famous *türbes* in Turkey is the Döner Kümbet ("Turning Mausoleum") of Kayseri, which owes its name to a legend claiming that its conical roof will turn at the slightest touch; and looking at the graceful roof poised on the slender shaft of the tower, one can believe the tale.

Turkish tribes arrived on the scene between the end of the 11th and the end of the 13th centuries. The House of Osman, one of the many tribes that arrived, became the masters of the land. The fabulous Ottoman Empire chose Bursa as its capital from 1325 until 1453, and even today, Bursa boasts 188 mosques, many of which date back to the beginnings of the Ottomans. The biggest of these is Ulu Cami, which took 36 years to complete (1379–1415), and whose floorplan of four parallel naves is reminiscent of the first Seljuk mosques. Ulu Cami is roofed by 25 little cupolas, with a shaft in the center for the light to pour through. The Orhan Mosque (1304–1417) is far more like a Byzantine church, but its decoration of scrolls and arabesques, its gateway and its *mihrap* (the niche that indicates the direction of Mecca) with stalactites and honey-combing are pure Turkish.

The Green Mosque (1415–1424) exemplifies Ottoman art at the height of its glory. The plan is one often found in Bursa—an upside down "T": two long halls, one after the other, and two smaller ones opening off the sides of the first. The walls are covered up to eye level with green ceramic tile accented in blue, and the motifs on the marble that outlines the windows are far more refined than comparable Seljuk work.

Even non-historians recall the magic date of 1453, which marks the fall of Constantinople, the death in battle of the last of the Constantines, and the end of Byzantine civilization. What had been Byzantium, then Constantinople, became Istanbul—the new capital of the Ottoman Empire. Ottoman rulers lost no time in transforming the churches into mosques and in beginning construction of other shrines worthy of their captured prize. Saint Sophia with its majestic dome impressed the Turks, and in 1506 Beyazit II, the son of the conqueror, ordered that a mosque bearing his name be built along the same lines. This mosque, with its dome supported by four pillars and its side naves, not only adapts intelligently the style of the Byzantine basilica but also ushers in the golden age of Ottoman architecture. The 16th century witnessed the zenith of the empire's political power, the height of its religious fervor, and the full splendor of its art. This is the era of Suleiman the Magnificent, who commissioned Sinan, the greatest of Turkish architects, to build his splendid mosque, one of the masterworks of Ottoman art. Turkish architecture comes into its own, freed from all influence of Byzantium. The elegant ascent of the cupolas towards the great dome, and the soaring minarets give the mosque an outline which is both slender and majestic. This classic Ottoman art continued to flourish throughout the 17th century, one proof being the mosque of

Ahmet I, better known as the Blue Mosque because of its extraordinary ceramic interior decoration.

Did the Turks then lose confidence in themselves and in the uniqueness of their own style? Perhaps so, for the 18th century is stamped with increasingly foreign influences from Europe or Persia. For a while, under Ahmed III (1703–1730), the tulip becomes almost an obsession with Turkish artists, this flower replacing all other decorative motifs. Later in the century, the baroque movement, born elsewhere and imported into Turkey by foreign craftsmen, was in vogue, as evidenced in the Nuuri Osmaniye Mosque of 1757.

This decadence, once begun, became predominant in the 19th century. The Dolmabahçe Palace (1840), on the Bosphorus, is a strange hybrid—a cross between a Moorish castle, Italian baroque palazzo, and a Hindu shrine. If it were not for such minor arts as ceramics and carpets, the best in Turkish tradition would have died out altogether.

The most impressive architectural work of the contemporary republican period is without a doubt the mausoleum of Mustafa Kemal in Ankara. Its severe and majestic lines lend support to the hope that we are witnessing the dawn of a new era in Turkish art.

Of modern artists, those known internationally include Aliye Berger, Ihsan Cemal Karaburcak, Bedri Rahmi, and Metin and Nazmiye Nigar.

Illustration at head of this chapter: Metal object found at Alacahöyük (proto-Hittite period, c. 2100 B.C.). Ankara, Archeological Museum.

FOOD AND DRINK

A Medley of Turkish Delights

As long as the Turks were nomads, their food was necessarily extremely limited, but when they settled they soon adopted the national dishes of the conquered, to whom the culinary gifts were eventually returned after centuries of refinement in the great palaces of Istanbul. This accounts for a certain uniformity of taste throughout the vast expanse of the former Turkish empire. From the Balkans, the Crimea and the Russian coast of the Black Sea down to Egypt and Tunisia, you will come across Turkish dishes, and at once know them by the taste, if not always by the name.

The kebabs and other mutton dishes and smoked meats have a long history, deriving from the Turks' days on the Central Asian plateaux of their forefathers. Many vegetable dishes, especially those served stuffed with rice, onions, pinenuts and currants, are creations of Seljuk courts at Isfahan and Khurasan (in modern Iran). Vegetable dishes cooked in oil and served when cold are, however, an Ottoman inspiration.

Of course, Turkish food is at its best in Turkey. In the restaurants of the big hotels you may find native cuisine, or you may be served a so-called French dinner. In Turkey as elsewhere, the latter may be the trademark of tasteless dishes, served with a great deal of fuss by a crowd of waiters. Unless you prefer show to a good meal, it is often not worth the cost. When in Turkey, you might, therefore, wish to eat as the Turks do. The cooking is done both with butter, for warm dishes, and with oil, for cold dishes. No need to worry—the oil has none of the strong taste and smell that puts the squeamish traveler off, as in Spain and Portugal, though a change of diet may sometimes play havoc with his insides. Furthermore, it is the eastern country where spices are used with the lightest hand. It would need a whole book to give the reader an idea of the range of Turkish cooking. Indeed, such cook-books, written in English or French, are on sale in the bookshops of Istanbul, Ankara and Izmir.

(One note: we suggest you take breakfast in your hotel under any circumstances. An American or European breakfast is virtually unobtainable elsewhere.)

In many Turkish restaurants the dishes are on display, behind glass in the better ones, on a counter in the others. You may even be called into the kitchen to lift the lid off the pots and pans, and have a look inside—a pleasant and practical way of choosing for foreigners who neither know the name of a dish nor how to say it if they did. However, here is a list of dishes, in alphabetical order, for those who have to deal with a bill of fare.

Aşure: a kind of pudding of boiled wheat, figs, and hazelnuts, for dessert.

Ayran: buttermilk (actually, beaten yoghurt).

Baklava: layers of strudel pastry with ground walnuts and syrup, for dessert.

Biber Dolması: green peppers stuffed with rice and pinenuts and cooked in olive oil.

Boza: a drink made of fermented wheat.

Bülbülyuvası: "nightingale's nest", somewhat like baklava, shaped like a nest, made with pistachios.

Cacık: cucumber salad with yoghurt and olive oil dressing, and a touch of garlic.

Çerkez Tavuğu: boiled chicken Circassian style, with a sauce of crushed walnuts and red pepper.

Döner Kebab: leg of lamb broiled on an upright spit. Try it with rice, yoghurt or tomato sauce.

Düğün Çorbasi: "marriage soup" of meat broth, eggs, and lemon juice.

Fasulye Piyazi: salad of white beans with onions, hard-boiled eggs, and an olive oil dressing.

Güllaç: waffles with almonds ground in milk, a dessert.

Hamsi Tavasi: fried anchovies, perhaps for an appetizer.

Hünkâr Beğendi: "His Majesty liked it", stewed lamb with chopped eggplant.

İç Pilâv: fried rice cooked in broth with raisins, pinenuts, and spices.

Imam Bayıldı: "The priest fainted" with joy on tasting the fried eggplant slices with layers of onion and tomato cooked in olive oil, and served cold.

İşkembe Çorbası: soup of tripe and eggs, on the heavy side.

Kabak Tatlısı: pumpkin cooked with sugar and ground nuts.

Kadın Budu: "woman's thigh", fried rice and meat balls.

Kadın Göbeği: "woman's navel", not bad at all ... for a dessert.

Kahve: Turkish coffee.

Kavun: melon.

Kiliç Şiş: bits of swordfish wrapped in bay-leaves and broiled on a spit. Strange-tasting.

Lâkerda: slices of fish preserved in salt.

Kuzu Dolması: baked lamb, stuffed with *pilâv* rice.

Midye Dolması: mussels stuffed with rice and pinenuts and spices, and cooked in olive oil.

Şira: grape juice.

Su Böreği: waffles stuffed with minced meat or with ewe cheese.

Şiş Kebabi: the Turkish dish, known all over the world—pieces of lamb and tomato, skewered on a spit and broiled over charcoal.

Turşu: a many-vegetabled pickle.

Yoğurt: made of fermented milk and known to all; in Turkey it is used as a sauce in many dishes, as we use sour cream. *Ayran* or buttermilk is yogurt in its drinking form.

Zerde: rice pudding with saffron.

Zeytin Yağlı Patlıcan Dolması: eggplant stuffed with rice and spices and cooked in olive oil.

A big meal starts best with a glass of *rakı*, a colorless grape brandy flavored with aniseed and served iced. It is usual to add water, which turns it a cloudy white. Rakı is always accompanied

by *meze*, small snacks, and sometimes by *hors d'oeuvres*. This is
followed by the main course. Meat is usually eaten alone, as it
often is in southern countries; salad is served apart. Last come
the pastry and a coffee.

Here are two meals you would do well to try:

(1) Begin with the typical *dolmas*. *Dolmak* means "to stuff",
and the *yalancı dolma* is a vine-leaf stuffed with rice and herbs and
cooked in oil. Then, order chicken, hot or cold—for instance, the
çerkez tavuğu on our list. After that, a salad—*fasulye piyazi*, maybe.
For dessert, a *baklava* and a Turkish coffee.

(2) The light soups are vegetable broths, and very good. If
you are very hungry try the *düğün corbasi*. For the main dish, taste
the real Turkish *şiş kebab*, together with eggplant, *imam bayıldı*.
For dessert, a *zerde* and, if you still have room, a *kavun* or melon,
the best in the world.

It will all be a great change to the dull meals served in the so-
called international restaurant. If you wish to taste real Turkish
cooking, go to one of the few restaurants recommended in this
book or to one of the obscure cheaper places, the ordinary *lokanta*.

To drink, you have water in capped bottles or Turkish beer,
which is very good. You may order Turkish wine, red (*Kırmızı
şarap*) or white (*beyaz şarap*), whether from Tekirdağ, from around
Izmir or from Anatolia—they are all good. A few names:
Kulüp, *Doluca*, *Kavaklidere*, *Trakya* (dry, from Thrace, Tekirdağ),
Marmara, and *Buzbağ* (full, red). Soft drinks include *Fruko*, a kind
of bitter lemon, and the ubiquitous Coca-Cola and Pepsi-Cola.

Everybody has heard of Turkish coffee, or *kahve*, finely pow-
dered, mixed with sugar and water, and boiled to a froth in a
brass pot. It is ordered to taste: a lot of sugar, *şekerli* (westerner,
beware!); a little sugar, *az şekerli*; *orta şekerli*, medium; without
sugar, *sade*. It is drunk in small sips, between gulps of water, and
never to the end; the bottom of the cup is thickly coated with
dregs. According to an old saying, a cup of coffee is worth 40 years
of friendship. (Whether this is an appraisal of coffee or of friendship is a matter of opinion.)

During the last war, tea bushes were planted on the Black
Sea coast, where there is both hot sun and plenty of rain. Tea,
or *çay*, is everywhere served in glasses, with sugar and sometimes
with lemon, never with milk. In Turkish-style hotels, tea is served

for breakfast. On ferryboats, tea, being cheaper, is more often served than Turkish coffee.

As for local alcohol, we recommend *rakı* (87° proof), *votka* and brandy. Since tonic water is hard to find in Turkey, we suggest *Fruko* with your vodka or gin for long, cool drinks. Local liqueurs of note include a rosé, made from rose petals (about 50° proof), and *Mersin*, a clear liqueur made from oranges (about 70° proof).

Illustration at head of this chapter: A chef carving slices of lamb for döner kebab.

THE FACE OF TURKEY

ISTANBUL

Oldest Crossroads of the World

Once upon a time, this city was a rival of Rome. As if hanging on a heavenly balance, the star of one city fell as the other rose on the ever-changing map of the sky. The oldest crossroads in the world, Byzantium was the key to the gateways between east and west. A meetingplace for many peoples, it did not, oddly enough, become a melting pot—if different nationalities met, and often mingled, they never merged. And when, as is bound to happen, a few did, they begot Levantines, who, far from forming a new people, strengthened the warring strains of Europe and Asia.

Stripped of her political power, modern Istanbul still holds her own. The Turkish nation is healing its wounds, renewing its blood, and throwing in its lot with the development of Anatolia. Istanbul still boasts of being part of the European continent and opens her doors to her old lovers' children, today's travelers, who still go out of their way to have a look at her faded beauty. She welcomes them all, every one in his own language, and with much of her old charm. She may be a ruin, but what lovely remains! The well-mannered guest will repay her welcome by not looking too closely in those parts of her house which are not meant for his eyes. The western European or American, feeling his part of the guilt for this state of affairs, has coined a face-saving word—"picturesque".

Turkish Street Life

There are countless ways of visiting Istanbul, all good. Whichever way you look, something will catch your eye and slow down your step. It is almost impossible to stick to a plan—you stop on the way to admire a house, a mosque, a ruin, and forget the rest. You may even be held up by a dancing bear on late Sunday mornings, when the bear-tamers, each with his animal shambling behind on a leash, cross the Galata bridge to Beyoğlu, where the foreigners live. Or maybe you will stop to look at a wool-comber, squatting in an old courtyard above the gutted mattress he is busy repairing with a strange tool, made of a steel piano string drawn tight on a wooden bow. As he loosens the hard-packed wool, it flies up like snowflakes to the deep low sounds of the twanging string, like the harp of a new David playing to a sleepless Saul.

A thousand and one sights will catch your eager eye, and stir your curiosity. Why do the shoes upcurve at the tip—a leftover from the old Turkish slipper? And the street porters, how odd they look—not in the least "as strong as a Turk", poor things, but gaunt and puny, always bent double whether burdened or not, as if bearing the shadow of a load. Not a day passes that you will not meet with a huge headless bundle walking by on two spindly legs.

Another sight is the swarm of small boys hurrying to and fro with endless cups of Turkish coffee or glasses of tea on brass trays, swinging on chains. And why are almost all publicity posters and billboards given over to banks? Another puzzle.

The sellers of *simit*, a doughnut – shaped bread sprinkled with sesame seed, push through the crowds, followed by sweet peddlers. The wares look tasty, as they do on the makeshift stalls selling peanuts, pistachios, roasted marrow seed and chick-peas, almonds and hazelnuts—titbits dismissed by the squeamish as dusty and uneatable. The women buy the sweets, the men buy the *simit*, for, bad as sesame oil may be for the foreign liver, it is held to be very tasty to the Turkish palate.

All kinds of wares are for sale, on the two trays balanced by a pole on the peddler's neck. And there is the sherbet vendor, with his leather bottle wrought with brass, chrome and ironwork, who pours the iced fruit drink or *şerbet* (from which European languages obtained "sherbet" and "sorbet") over his shoulder into the glass he hands to the thirsty customer.

After school hours, the children run out into the streets, chattering and giggling, looking touchingly old-fashioned in black pinafores and white Peter Pan collars.

The very streetsigns afford entertainment. Foreign words are taken over bodily, if somewhat twisted to fit Turkish spelling—a woman will follow a *şampuan* at the beauty parlor with a *sandviç* in a *büfe*, while her husband has a *viski* in his *kulüp*.

At a bus-stop, shaded from the sun by an awning, a crowd waits patiently, straggling across the pavement like a string of ants. The *boyacis* go up and down among the men with bright-colored bowls of polish and rags (the shortest walk may make shoes unsightly with dust).

All in all, for a westerner not yet jaded by too much travel, the sights of Istanbul are as much in the streets as in the museums.

A Capsule History of Istanbul

On the landing beach of Lygos, whose origin is unknown, a Greek navigator called Byzas anchored his ship in the seventh century B.C., and founded the town which bears his name: Byzantium. Consulted about the site of the new colony, the Delphic oracle indicated "opposite the country of the blind", which Byzas rightly interpreted to mean the European entrance to the Bosphorus, opposite Chalcedon, whose earlier Greek settlers had been blinded by the fertility of the Asian shore. The splendid natural harbor of the Golden Horn brought about a far greater commercial prosperity, with its inevitable outcome: the greed of neighbours. The Persian king Darius having taken it by force of arms, the Spartan regent, Pausanias, "liberated" it in 478 B.C., an act which almost precipitated a war between Sparta and Athens. Independent once again, Byzantium held out against Philip of Macedonia—father of Alexander the Great—and against the Gauls.

The sign of the Crescent dates from these battles—it was the light of the moon that betrayed Philip's movements to the besieged townsmen.

As to the war with the wild Gallic hordes it ended in a commercial agreement—tribute from Byzantium, to be levied by payment for each crossing of the strait. This high-handed procedure did not at the time go by the respectable name of tolltax.

Weakened by unceasing warfare against invaders, Byzantium fell at last to the Roman legions. Here again, its craftiness came into play—making the best of a bad bargain, it threw in its lot with the conquering enemy. Though the city, with so powerful a backing, could well afford to overlook the baffled fury of its forsaken allies, it was soon to pay a bitter price for such doubtful protection. In the quarrel between Prescennius Niger and Septimus Severus, Byzantium was luckless enough to back the wrong horse. After a long and bloody siege, Niger's rebel town was taken by the forces of Severus, at the end of the second century.

The Birth of Constantinople

Severus, who prided himself on being a just man (once he had safely got rid of his enemies), rebuilt Byzantium, adding theaters, archways, and baths to mark his victory, as was the way of Roman conquerors. He even gave it a Latin name—Augusta Antonia. Later, in 324, when Constantine made of it the capital of the Empire, it became Nea Roma. Newly converted to Christianity, forewarned by his endless troubles with Barbarian forays into Italy, Constantine built strong new walls, together with palaces and churches (among them, St. Sophia).

For the most part, however, the people remained pagan, until forcibly enlisted into the new religion by Theodosius the Great (378–395), a Galician from Spain. In spite of this high-handed act, this ruler was renowned for his clemency. Two of his sayings are known to us: "Would God I had it in my power to raise the dead!"—a praiseworthy statement for a soldier—and another, giving his reasons for not punishing those who plotted against the king: ". . . if they act unthinkingly, they are to be scorned; if through madness, pitied; if through ill-will, forgiven".

The end of the fourth century saw the division of the Empire. Theodosius had two sons. Honorius and Arcadius, who split the heritage between them. The former went to Rome, to rule the western empire; the latter mounted the golden throne of the eastern empire, in the city to be known henceforth as Constantinople, the city of Constantine. During the reign of Theodosius II, named the Younger (408–450), a strange happening took place. In 421, the armed forces of Byzantium and Persia "were seeking each other out for battle". But, face to face at last, "they were both filled with fear and fled, each from the other".

The Barbarian invasions spared neither Rome nor Constantinople. Rome fell in 476, leaving Constantinople sole ruler of the Roman Empire. Yet neither the official use of Latin nor of Roman law deterred the people from cherishing its age-old Greek heritage. The emperor was called the *basileus*. Constantinople was, in fact if not in name, the capital of the Greek world. Ephemeral emperors and short-lived dynasties rose and fell from Theodosius II (408–450) to Justinian (527–565), the way to the throne often being cleared at sword's point. Throughout it all, the Barbarians came, laid waste, left, and came back.

The priesthood, embroiled in a web of theology and too busy splitting hairs, played a leading part in the troubles. In 513, one faction set fire to the city to spite the other. Forty years later, a civil war burned down the Senate and Constantine's St. Sophia. The city was saved from itself at last by a hard-headed union of blue blood and red—Justinian married the beautiful and ruthless Theodora, an actress and harlot. Between husband and wife, they put down the so-called Circus uprising. They also rebuilt the whole city, and St. Sophia as it stands today. They defeated the enemy—Vandals, Goths, and Persians. It was, however blood-stained, the golden era of Constantinople and of the Byzantine Empire.

Having reached the zenith attained by Justinian and Theodora, the power of Constantinople began to wane. It was harrassed relentlessly by hordes from the Urals, the Persians, and the Arabs. Moslem forces laid siege to the wicked city, but they were thrown back by a new weapon, Greek fire (with a petroleum base). It was later to be used in the clash between the Cross and the Crescent, Islam wielding it against Christianity. According to the singed Crusaders, it was a kind of firebrand that "burst into flames upon wetting"—whether in oil or molten wax we do not know.

During the ninth century, another Theodora ruled Constantinople as regent for her son Michael. She restored the cult of images. A chronicle of her time, listing her virtues and praising her piety, ends with the cold-blooded statement: "she ordered the hanging, decapitation, and burning of a hundred thousand Manicheans".

The second half of the ninth century witnessed a renewal of wealth and power under the rule of the Macedonian emperor, Basil I. Skillfully using religion as a tool for policy, he spread Christianity into the Balkans and into Russia. The next hundred years sees another golden age, under Constantine Porphyrogenitus. The far-flung renown of the extraordinary wealth, beauty, and pageantry of Constantinople became the waking dream of every adventurer. However, as often happens, the rise of the arts of peace was to lead to the weakening of ruling power.

The fruit was overripe, and ready to fall at the first onslaught, that of the Turks—the Seljuks. A misfortune never comes singly, and in mid 11th century the Patriarch, Michael Cerularius, brought on the schism of Christianity. The dogmatic dispute over the provenance of the Holy Ghost became overlaid with frivolous bickering. For form's sake, the eastern church accused the western church of eating meat on Wednesdays, eggs and cheese on Fridays; of shaving the priests' beards; of wearing a ring "like a married man" when a bishop; of one dip into water instead of three, at christenings. There was indeed something in all this, of the pettifoggery of the Byzantine priesthood, who set great store by such quibbles; but, outside of a few holy and hidebound old men, there was more spite than saintliness in the quarrel. The fact was, Constantinople could not bear to let Rome have religious supremacy, after having wrested political leadership. There followed an outbreak of excommunications, from west to east and from east to west. Where there had been two Empires, there were now two Churches.

For some time past, the rulers of Venice, Amalfi, and Genoa had asked for, and been granted, free port for trade in Constantinople. The gold rush was on, and the end of the 11th century saw the beginning of the Crusades. The first two went off fairly well, in spite of the cold war between the Greek and Latin churches. Both Louis VII the Pious, of France, and the German emperor, Frederick Barbarossa, would gladly have razed Constantinople to the ground; but the wish turned out to be simpler than the deed. As for the third Crusade, it got around the difficulty by by-passing the city of "the wily Greeks".

When the fourth Crusade was under way, a palace revolution overthrew the throne of the *basileus*. The emperors, at that time, belonged to the Angelus family. Alexis III deposed his brother Isaac and, for good measure, put out his eyes. The blind man's son, also named Alexis, called on the Crusaders for help. With noble hearts aflame and "the chink of gold coins as sweet to the ear as the call of a trumpet", the Latin knights came rushing to the rescue. Put back in power, Isaac and Alexis IV made their peace with the Pope of Rome; and the Greeks rose against them in a body. A great many corpses later, an Alexis, by then the Vth, was crowned emperor, and broke with Rome. The Crusaders saw red. Taking Constantinople in 1204, they mercilessly burnt and sacked the one great city in Christendom. Most of the city's priceless works of art were stolen or destroyed. As for the people, the soldiers of the Cross had no foolish pity—"man is as grass, and as grass he passeth away". Besides, wholesale slaughter had much to be said for it; for lack of Greeks, a Latin emperor, Baldwin, was put on the throne, and the empire itself split up into lots among the barons.

Not for long. In 1261, Michael VIII Paleologus recaptured Constantinople, or rather, what was left of it. The Venetians and the Genoese still shared a monopoly of all trade, which would not have mattered much had these blood brothers not also been at odds. War broke out again, Greeks against Latins, and Latins against Latins. Outside the walls of the city, the Seljuks had given way to the Ottomans, who laid siege to Constantinople. One way or the other, ancient Byzantium was destined to fall into the hands of the Turks.

Fate was to give the city a breathing-space. Tamerlane and his Mongolian hordes swept through the Middle East, and defeated the Turkish Sultan Bayezit in bloody battle, under the walls of Ankara. What followed is one of the unaccountable freaks of history; in a thunder of horses' hooves, he galloped with his men back to his barren plains, without troubling to exploit his victory. Both east and west breathed a sigh of relief.

Ottoman Capital

Under the leadership of Mehmet II, the Turks returned to attack. From 1453 on, Mehmet II bore the well-earned title of *Fatih*, the conqueror. He took Constantinople with 80,000 men, as against the 200,000 of the emperor Constantine XI Dragases. The Golden Horn being closed to shipping, the sultan ordered his men to carry his ships by land into the water! Furthermore, he was backed by powerful artillery, organized by a Hungarian gunner. On the evening of the 29th of May, Mehmet made a triumphant entry on horseback, in a city littered with the dead of both armies. Passing St. Sophia, the church of the infidels, Mehmet reined his steed, dazzled. Such noble beauty was made by man for the greater glory of the true God, Allah. The sultan lost no time. He ordered his men to take away the two-headed eagle, emblem of the empire, and to put in its place the Crescent of old Byzantium, to which he added his star, which had led him to glory. And so the old basilica became a mosque.

The town once taken, there was no killing. For many reasons, amongst which the law against the useless taking of life, Islam showed more mercy in victory than Christianity. The fallen townsmen were replaced by Moslems from Anatolia and many churches were made over into mosques; but a Greek Patriarch was named, and Galata was left to the Latins. It was the first of Concessions given to foreigners, whom the sultan did not wish to rule; they were later given the name of *capitulations*. The Jewish quarter of Balat was untouched, and Jews, Greeks, and Armenians were free to live and pray there as they pleased. For that reason, it later filled with Jews and Moors chased from Spain in 1492, as well as displaced persons from the provinces conquered by the Turks—Bulgarians, Serbians, Albanians, and Romanians.

Following the Turkish conquest, the story of Constantinople (now known as Istanbul) becomes that of the Ottoman Empire, whose capital it was, and at the same time, that of Islam, since the Sultan was also the Caliph, Commander of the Faithful.

The Sultanate was abolished in 1923 by the revolution of Kemal Atatürk, and the capital was moved to Ankara.

Practical Information for Istanbul

WHEN TO GO? Nothing can be more pleasant than to visit Istanbul in the spring or the beginning of summer. In April and May, when the weather is warm without being hot, the former capital is at its best—the beaches are not yet crowded, and the surrounding countryside is not yet parched by the scorching midsummer sun. Some may prefer the mellow mildness of October and early November. The sensible traveler will do well to avoid the torrid months of July and August, the peak of the tourist season. Every day, towards sundown, a breeze from the Black Sea cools the city. It is fairly cold in winter, but often sunny, in spite of rainy spells. (See Temperature chart on p. 33.)

HOW TO GET THERE? All aircraft lands at Yeşilköy. A bus service connects the airport with the terminal in Taksim, 40 minutes away. (Fare: about 10TL). A taxi from the airport to the big hotels in Beyoğlu costs about 80TL. Ships anchor in the Bosphorus, off Galata, to the south of the Dolmabahçe Palace. (Smaller ones may tie up at the pier.) Trains, by-passing the old Stamboul, stop at the Sirkeci Railway Station. Coming by car from Edirne on E97 and E5, the driver takes the avenue Millet Caddesi (E5) through the old ramparts. (See *How to Get There?* in *Facts at Your Fingertips* section earlier in this book).

WHAT TO SEE? The best way to see Istanbul is to stroll around at random, and to take some of the excellent sightseeing tours offered. Set yourself a few landmarks in old Stamboul, where nearly all the historic monuments are. Begin with the part bounded on the west by Atatürk Boulevard—one of the wide modern thoroughfares cutting north to south from the Golden Horn to the Sea of Marmara—and on the east by the Bosphorus. Within that scope you will find St. Sophia, the Mosque of Sultan Ahmed (or Blue Mosque), the Topkapı Palace, the Archeological Museum, the Hippodrome, the old cisterns, the covered bazaar. Towards the Atatürk Boulevard is the Süleymaniye Mosque, the biggest in town; and the Museum of Turco-Islamic Art nearby. Towards the Golden Horn are the Yeni and Rüstem Paşa Mosques.

Walk boldly through the small streets, however steep and badly cobbled. There is no way of giving street names—most of the signs seem to be somewhere out of sight—nor of following a given plan; but as the byways are fairly short and end in bigger thoroughfares, there is little risk of getting lost.

The new part of town (Beyoğlu) lacks character, but a walk in the neighborhood of the Dolmabahçe Palace, and the climb up one of the modern avenues towards Taksim Square, will open up wonderful views over the Bosphorus. Here, the paving is good, and you can go by car. Take a ferry boat, either at the Karaköy Bridge in Galata, or near Dolmabahçe Palace, at the Kabataş Wharf, and look at the city from the upper deck. Whatever the time of day, Istanbul's skyline is unforgettable. In the morning, the domes and minarets of the old city shine through the misty sunlight like a dream city; in the evening, the water pales to whiteness beneath the dark town, etched black against the sunset sky, and lighting up slowly as night falls.

The Golden Horn and the heights of Eyüp are worth a visit, but you will need a trained eye and a lot of imagination to enjoy the white mosque of Eyüp and the café that was once Pierre Loti's hangout, while overlooking the unsightly coal-barges that clutter the harbor and the warehouses that line, and spoil, the waterfront.

Pushing farther on, beyond the Atatürk Boulevard, you can end the outing with a walk through the old town, up to the ancient ramparts, and visit the Selim, Fatih and Mihrimah Mosques as well as the Kariye Museum near the ruins of the Byzantine palace (Tekfur Saray).

On the Asiatic shore is the Iskele Mosque (landing stage at Usküdar, the Beylerbey Palace, the Karacaahmet Cemetery, and the view from the top of Çamlıca Hill.

 HOTELS. Though numerous new hotels have opened in town as well as some motels on the Sea of Marmara, you will be wise to reserve well in advance, particularly during the high season. Most hotels in the first three categories, and all motels, have restaurants. The listed hotels have all rooms with bath or shower, except where otherwise stated. Water, however, flows only sporadically in summer, except in the bathrooms of the luxury category establishments. We grade hotels as we judge them, but give the official government categories (1, 2, 3, and 4) whenever appropriate.

(A Sheraton hotel is due to be constructed in Taksim Park by 1973, and an Intercontinental is planned.)

BEYOĞLU

This is the part of town in which are grouped most of the good hotels, all with a fine view.

Luxurious

HILTON, Cumhuriyet Caddesi, 418 rooms, some suites. The usual luxury town-within-a-town, with a Turkish touch. Nightclub, swimming pool, several restaurants, among which are the *Şadirvan*, the *Roof Grill* (excellent Turkish menu, but expensive), and so on.

First Class

DIVAN, Cumhuriyet Caddesi, 98 rooms, excellent service and elegant. Italian management.

PARK, Gümüşsuyu Caddesi, 208 rooms; an established reputation for excellent service and attention to every need.

PERA PALAS, Mesrutiyet Caddesi 98, the sole survivor of the opulent days of Abdul Hamid II, commands a splendid view over the old town. 113 rooms (90 with bath).

DILSON (89 rooms), **KEBAN** (84 rooms) and **KENNEDY** (60 rooms) are all in Siraserviler Caddesi, off Taksim Square. The *Keban* is rightly the most expensive, and the only one with a garage, while the others in this part of town dispose at best of some limited parking space.

The 184-room **MACKA** should be open early 1972.

Moderate (Category 2)

Gezi, Mete Cad. (51 rooms) and *Opera*, Ayazpaşa (67 rooms) are both close to Taksim Square. *King* (66 rooms) is also modern, but a little out of the way in Büyükdere Cad., Mecediyeköy.

Off Siraserviler Cad., the *Plaza* (32 rooms) and *Santral* (62 rooms) are also-rans.

Inexpensive (Category 3)

Deniz, Rihtim Cad., Rasimpasa, 30 rooms; *Imperator*, Balo Sok., Galatasaray, 52 rooms; *Kavak*, Meşrutiyet Cad., 42 rooms; *Konak*, Nisbet Sok., off Cumhuriyet Cad., 23 rooms. The *Yenişehir Palas*, Asmali Mescit, just makes the grade.

Rock Bottom (Category 4)

Alp, Mesrutiyet Cad., only one bath to 35 rooms, but a garage and restaurant; *Avrupa*, Topçular Cad., 23 rooms, no bath; *Metropol*, Asmali Mescit, 41 rooms (16 showers); *Truva*, Şehit Muhtar Cad., 26 rooms, are at least central. *Terminal*, 16 rooms, Iskender Cad., close to THY city terminal.

Berlin, 4 Levent, 36 rooms (11 showers) and *Tirol*, Samanyolu Sok., Şişli, 24 rooms, both have restaurants but are out of the way. So are the very similar pensions *Bonjur*, Ihlamur Cad., Nişantaşi, 33 rooms; and *Sibel*, Spor Cad., Beşiktaş, 14 rooms, none with bath; only the modern *Hayyam*, 20 rooms, is central, Cihangir Cad., Beyoğlu.

OLD STAMBOUL

Only the *Sözmen*, 74 rooms, belongs to category 2, Millet Cad., (the avenue leading to the airport and on to Europe), garage, restaurant. Just as comfortable is the *Kalyon* (3), on Florya Sahil Yolu, facing the Sea of Marmara, 42 rooms, restaurant. Also modern the *Kilim*, 25 rooms, on Aksaray Square, and nearby *Topkapi*, Oğuzhan Cad., 45 rooms; *Kent*, Ordu Cad. Lâleli, 42 rooms, 33 showers; in Beyazit, *Radar*, Tiyatro Cad., has 36 rooms, and *Teras*, Yeniçeriler Cad., 29 rooms; in Sircesi, *Ağan*, Saffettin Paşa Sok., 31 rooms, and *Güray*, Ibni Kemal Cad., 20 rooms.

Close to the noisy Sirkeci Station are also the *Ipek Palas*, 59 rooms (9 with bath), restaurant; *Şehir*, 40 rooms (10 with bath) and *Özipek Palas*, crowded into narrow Orhaniye Cad., as well as the *Eriş*, 35 rooms and *Hayyam*, 57 rooms, restaurant; all rock-bottom.

The only charm of the *Piyer Loti*, Dostlukyurdu Sok., lies in its name. 49 rooms (19 with bath), restaurant.

ÜSKÜDAR AND KADIKÖY

(Asian shore)

Inexpensive (Category 3)

Harem, at Selimiye, is near the car ferry. 100 rooms with shower.

Riviera is very well-placed in Kadıköy, with so-called showers in its 37 rooms; *Kordon*, 29 rooms (9 showers); *Idealtepe Motel*, 31 rooms, private beach.

BOSPHORUS

(European shore)

Probably the most enjoyable stay for the motorist is along this famous waterway, where bathing can be ideally combined with sightseeing from an ever-increasing number of hotels, all with restaurants.

Listed according to their distance from town, you meet first the *Çıragan*, inexpensive (78 rooms, most with bath), at Beşiktas.

Lido, at Ortaköy, is next, then the well situated *Bebek*, 45 rooms, at Bebek the small *Hisar* pension, rock-bottom, at Rumeli Hisar.

The **CARLTON** (1) is a hotel complex of some 200 rooms, swimming pool.

Boğaziçi (2), 34 rooms; *Turing* (41 rooms), at Emirgân, is newest.

Kara, moderate, is next (34 rooms), at Yeniköy.

TARABYA, 262 rooms, located furthest north, and finest of them all, is sumptuous, with excellent food and service. Outstanding reputation, perfect location. Luxury class, but moderately priced. Second only to *Hilton* in all Istanbul.

BLACK SEA

On the European coast, on the lovely sandy beach of Kilyos, the *Kilyos Motel* (2) has 109 rooms: for an invigorating stay even in the height of summer.

The holiday-maker in search of quiet, far from the madding crowds, will go still farther afield to Şile, also on the Black Sea, but on the Asian side. The moderate *Kumbaba Oberj* (Inn), 32 rooms (22 with bath), and the inexpensive *Değirmen*, 32 rooms, both with restaurants, and the rock-bottom *Deniz*.

SEA OF MARMARA

Closest to Istanbul on the European shore is the *Sultan* (4), 30 rooms at Bakirköy, followed by the *Ataköy Plaj*, 98 rooms.

ÇINAR is outstanding. Conveniently located at Yeşilköy (near airport and the sea), it boasts 150 deluxe rooms, restaurants, and a nightclub, among many other amenities. Fine beach and pool.

Along the highway west follows a string of modern motels; *Florya*, 24 rooms; the very comfortable *Baler*, 56 rooms, at Küçükçekmece; *Istanbul*, on a good beach at Güzelceköy, 82 rooms; *Solu*, 20 rooms, at Silivri; *Otel A*, 48 rooms, and *Kumburgaz*, 54 rooms.

On the Asian shore beginning with the *Cinardibi* (4), 22 rooms, at Suadiye; *Petek Pansiyon* (3), 41 rooms, at Fenerbahçe; *Baraz Pansiyon*, 32 rooms, at Maltepe; *Erdim Motel*, 52 rooms, private beach, and the cheaper *Marmara Beach*, 72 rooms, at Kartal; to the *Kare Motel*, 20 rooms, *Motel 212*, 28 rooms, and the very simple *Riyalto Pansiyon*, 24 rooms without shower, at Pendik.

PRINCES' ISLANDS

(ADALAR)

There are small boarding houses on all the inhabited islands, but the only real hotels are on the largest, Büyükada:

The new *Prens* (2) is now the best bet. Otherwise, try the *Villa Rifat* (Pension), or the *Splandit Palas*, rock-bottom (65 rooms, 12 with bath or shower), neither splendid nor a palace, but a pleasant place to be, away from it all. All three have restaurants.

OFFICIAL CAMPING GROUNDS. *Mocamp Kartaltepe*, 7 miles from Istanbul, is near the airport of Yeşilköy, has a pool; beach 2 miles away. *Küçükçekmece Dinlenme Kampı* is in Küçükçekmece, 14 miles from Istanbul. *Bakirköy Dinlenme Kampı* is in Bakirköy, near the Istanbul airport. On the Anatolian shore: *Fenerbahçe Dinlenme Kampı*, in Kadıköy.

RESTAURANTS. In Istanbul, as elsewhere, most hotels have restaurants, usually of the same class. In the big hotels, the food is for the most part international. It is far more entertaining to eat out, above all at night, when the townspeople are relaxing after the day's work. Many restaurants have a grill for the *kebabçı*, broiled on a spit within sight of the diner. Order Turkish dishes without misgivings: the cooking is tasty yet light, not oozing with oil as in Spain or heavy with starches as in Italy. However, it is best to go to the Turkish restaurants, the simplest but best of which are in old Stamboul. (The cost of a meal in Istanbul is based more on the setting and the service than on the quality of the food.) Try a well-kept *lokanta* (tavern) around Sirkeci, if adventurous.

BEYOĞLU

The *Hilton* provides in the Roof Grill not only a home away from home for the American palate, but also excellent authentic local dishes. Among other hotel dining rooms the *Divan* deserves to be mentioned for its good international cuisine and the *Pera Palace* for its period setting.

The *Oriental*, in Cumhuriyet Cad., next to the Divan and just as expensive, perhaps because of the orchestra, and the adjoining *007 Restaurant*, go in for fancy oriental dishes.

For genuine Turkish specialties try *Aziz*, Rumeli Han Pasaji, and *Façoli*, Cumhuriyet Cad.

The *Galata Tower* seasons its international menu with a staggering view over Stamboul.

Haci Salih, Sakizağazacı Sok., near Istiklâl Caddesi. Big restaurant, reasonable prices. (No alcoholic drinks.)

Liman Lokantasi, a waterfront restaurant near the bridge of Karaköy, in Galata. Excellent seafood specialties. Fine setting, lunch only. Fairly expensive.

Rejans, in Livo Lane. Turkish, Russian and French food. Moderate prices. The *China Restaurant*, Lamartin Caddesi 22, is mostly for Turks who want a taste of foreign cooking.

The *Ağa Lokantası*, if funds are running low; in Sakızağacı Sok., a street that cuts across Istiklâl Caddesi—a small mosque at the corner serves as landmark. The *Çardaş Lokantası*, also fairly cheap, is in the Nil Pasaji, near the "tünel" of the cable streetcar.

OLD STAMBOUL

All the Turkish restaurants listed below are to be recommended:

The *Konyalı*, at Sirkeci. Excellent traditional restaurant. (No drinks or wine served.) Reasonable prices.

A new *Konyalı*, right on the Topkapi Palace grounds, provides welcome light refreshment after strenuous sightseeing.

The *Pandeli*, in the old spice market, Mısır Çarsısı. Lunch only. Also Turkish, slightly "touristy".

The *Borsa* and the *Hacıbaba*, both in Bahçekapı, Sirkeci, are worth a try.

BOSPHORUS

(European shore)

Innumerable elegant, medium range and modest eating places are strung along the shore from south to north. Best-known are the *Motorest* at Beşiktaş, the *Batanay* and the *Lido* (with a small floorshow) in Ortaköy. In Arnavutköy, the *Kuyu*. In Bebek, the *Bebek*.

In Küçükbebek, *Gaskonyali Toma*. In Rumeli Hisar, the *Hisar*.

In Emirgân, the most famous Turkish restaurant: *Abdullah*, where you will do well to try the "shrimps diplomat" or the stuffed mussels, *midye dolmasi*. Fairly expensive. At *Nurettin* or the *Villa Zümrüt*, more reasonable prices.

In Yeniköy, the *Boğaziçi Lokantası*, with dancing at night; and the *Kulüp*. In Tarabya, the excellent *Fidan* is renowned; open all year. *Façyo* is new and excellent. In Büyükdere, seafood at the *Mardiros*, and unforgettable swordfish broiled on skewers, at the *Andon*.

In Sarıyer, in the upper Bosphorus, excellent dinner, with music, at the *Canlı Balık*.

Three restaurants worth noting: the *Ömür*, an excellent spot en route to the airport, whose *döner kebab* attracts lovers of good food. *Angelo* in Yeşilköy, and the *Beyti* in Küçük Çekmece.

PRINCES' ISLANDS

After a pleasant drive in an open carriage or *faeton*, you will enjoy some of the best cooking in Turkey at the *Akasya* restaurant, on the island of Büyükada. Also: *Kapri*, on the waterfront.

NIGHTCLUBS. If you expect a Thousand and One Nights' come true in Istanbul, you will be sorely disappointed. Outside of the *Kervansaray*, next to the Hilton, there is nothing like the floor shows in western Europe or America. As for what the leaflets grandly call "Turkish-style cabarets", promising bellydancers and stripteasers, the bait is bigger than the fish. Unless you enjoy sitting in a noisy crowd, deafened by the blare of a band, spearing titbits on a toothpick while looking at a rather repetitious display, better stay away. The drinks cost from 20 to 80 TL, according to the nightclub.

Kervansaray, Cumhuriyet Caddesi, Harbiye. Floor shows: eastern, western, and folklore.

Şardıvan Supper Club (dinner with dancing) and the *Marmara Roof Bar*, in the Hilton Hotel; eastern dances and western floor shows in an elegant setting.

The *Galata Tower*, dating from the 12th century, recently restored, boasts a good restaurant and a nightclub. Unforgettable view.

Foliberjer, Istiklal Caddesi in Beyoğlu. Floor shows: eastern, western, and folklore.

Winter headquarters for *Angelo's* of Yesilköy is at Bomouti, Sisli. Floor shows, eastern and western.

Çinar, in the Hotel Çinar, in Yeşilköy; dinner-dancing. Bellydance.

Pariziyen, Cumhuriyet Caddesi, near the Hilton. Striptease to the G-string.

Abidik Gubedik, *Dağ Klüp* and *Klüp A*, all in Rumeli Cad., Nişantaş, for simple dancing.

Reşat, Parmakkapi. Dinner and dancing.

Yeniköy Turizm Gazinosu, in Yeniköy, on the shore of the Bosphorus. Dinner, dancing, and floor shows.

In summer, try one of the many excellent nightclubs which move from town to the shores of the Bosphorus.

More like music-halls, no dancing, but a tableful of *meze*, Turkish appetizers: *Bebek Gazinosu*, in Bebek; *Cumhuriyet Gazinosu*, in Tepebaşı; *Kazablanca*, in Tepebaşı.

MUSEUMS. One rule of the Islamic religion, strictly observed until recently, forbids the representation of the living image. Some Ottoman rulers got around this law by inviting foreign artists, who were supposed to paint them by stealth, "without their knowledge". Mohammed II sent to Venice for Bellini who, among his portraits, made one of a Turkish artist at work—proof that the court encouraged clandestine painting, even among Turks. The delightful portrait of Mohammed II, sniffing a rose, has all the handmarks of Turkish art. However, most of these reportorial works of art are in museums abroad. Statuary, therefore, is limited mostly to Hittite and Greco-Roman antiquities or very recent works.

The difference between a mosque open to worship and a museum-mosque—like St. Sophia—is one of slippers: you need not leave your shoes outside a museum.

Here is a list of the principal museums of Istanbul (check the hours and days when open):

Museum of the Seraglio of Topkapı: dazzling display of the treasure of the Sultans, together with fine collections of glazed earthenware, china, old weapons and armor, enamels, miniatures, and the restored harem. 10 to 5. Closed on Tuesdays, October through May.

Museum of Ayasofya (St. Sophia). Originally a Christian church, it was destroyed by wars and fire and rebuilt almost entirely as it stands today by Justinian. Made over into a mosque by the Turks, it became a museum in the thirties. Remarkable sample of Byzantine art, awe-inspiring interior with its dome decorated in splendid mosaics and marbles. 9:30 to 5. Closed on Mondays.

Archeological Museum, in Gülhane Park, divided in two parts—Middle Eastern archeology (Mesopotamia and the Hittites), and Greek, Roman, and Byzantine archeology. Many fine statues. Renowned collection of old coins. 9:30 to 5. Closed on Mondays.

Church of the Holy Saviour in Chora (Kariye Mosque), near the Edirne Gate; Byzantine era. Fine mosaics and frescoes. 9:30 to 5. Closed on Tuesdays.

Museum of Turco-Islamic Art in the old kitchen of the Süleymaniye. Turkish religious art, miniatures, old copies of the Koran, old carpets—mostly prayer rugs. 10 to 5. Closed on Thursdays.

Museum of Mosaics in their original setting, the fourth-century palace of Constantine; mosaic pictures, architectural designs. 10 to 5. Closed on Wednesdays.

Atatürk Museum. Kemal Atatürk's house, unchanged, together with a display of souvenirs and documents dating from the birth of the Turkish Republic. 10 to 12, 2 to 5. Closed on Thursdays.

PALACES. The *Topkapı Sarayı*, the old seraglio where the Ottoman sultans once dwelt, is now a museum (see *Museums*). The *Dolmabahçe Sarayı* was built in 1854, in a Turkish-Indian-Baroque style worthy of *the Arabian Nights*. The imperial residence with fabulous reception rooms and halls, and 19th- and 20th-century paintings. (Open daily 9 to 11, 1:30 to 4, except Mon. and Tues., admission 15 TL.) The *Beylerbeyi Sarayı*, on the Asiatic coast of the Bosphorus, was built in 1865. The interior is magnificent, with its white marble walls and floors and its outsize Sevres vases. It once housed the Empress Eugenie, wife of Napoleon III. It has terraced gardens, a big artificial pond, and pavilions. Open daily except Mon. and Tues. The *Yildiz Saray* consists of a series of kiosks built during the last half of the nineteenth century. There is a workshop of glazed earthenware, and a park with beautiful trees, some five hundred years old. A wonderful view over the Bosphorus.

In the historical Tören, Malta and Çadir kiosks, connected by underground passages, Abdul Hamid II led his haunted life till his dethronement and confinement in Beylerbey. Visit only by a permit issued by the Tourist Office (see *"Useful Addresses"*).

SHOW BUSINESS. *Theater:* the season lasts from October to the beginning of June. Straight plays, being in Turkish, are apt to pall on the foreigner; but if he cares to try, the "City Theatre" is the best. *Opera and ballet:* luckily there is no need to understand Turkish to enjoy the State Opera; though its headquarters are in Ankara, it often comes to Istanbul for both opera and ballet. The magnificent new Opera House in Istanbul opened in 1969. Opera, ballet and plays are staged in spring, fall and winter. Tickets: from 9 to 25 TL. *Concerts:* the Musical Academy of Istanbul gives concerts of classical music, eastern and western, from October to May. Twice a month, concerts are given on Sundays, from eleven to one o'clock, in the *San* movie house in Pangalti. Tickets: from about 7 to 12 TL.

Cinemas: there are a great many movie houses in Istanbul, four of which show films in the original version. Tickets: around 3 to 5 TL.

SHOPPING. So far, there are few elegant shops and showy window displays as in the fashionable quarters of the larger European cities. As for bargains, the best are to be found in old Istanbul, at the great Covered Bazaar (Kapaliçarşı). Here, in a fascinating maze of crowded streets and alleys, you will find all your youthful dreams of the glamorous oriental market come true. Priceless jewels, junk and, of course, Turkish rugs of all kinds, from hand-woven masterpieces of the 18th century down to the less costly modern ones—even, unhappily, to machine-made imitations, made in Belgium. There are wares for all tastes and all purses, but it is best to be knowledgeable ... Women will like the Turkish house-wraps in colored silk, embroidered in silver or gold thread. The shops, to make things easier, are grouped together in kind. If you need information, the shopkeepers all speak a smattering of several languages.

Jewelry and carpets aside, the big bargain in Turkey is leather, very soft and beautifully worked, in all shapes and sizes. There is an endless choice of jackets, coats, and suits for both men and women, very cheap; one of the good shops is *Model-Konfeksiyon*, 75 Fesçiler Cad., where a pleasant salesman will welcome you in whichever one of a dozen languages you speak.

More shopping in Mısır Çarşısı (for food only) and on Istiklâl. The renowned sweet-shop, *Haci Bekir*, on Istiklâl, Beyoğlu, is *the* place to buy Turkish Delight: *lokum*. For the best in jewelry, go to *Adler*, in the Istanbul Hilton.

MOTORING IN ISTANBUL. By the end of one day, you will have learnt how to handle your car in the streets of Istanbul. Stroll on foot through the old town, but drive past the Golden Horn towards Taksim and Beyoğlu—look out for the road signs that seem to point away, but soon lead to new straight highways. Drive at 20 or 25 miles an hour, and keep calm. You will be by-passed on both sides, wherever there is room; cars will stop dead in front of you, and start off as suddenly. There *are* traffic lights, but almost no traffic rules beyond keeping an eye on other cars, jay walkers, and policemen. Traffic jams never last very long. An army of policemen keep order in the seeming lawlessness with sharp whistle blasts; they seem overwhelmed, but in fact do a very good job.

Parking is less of a problem than in western towns. The driver with a foreign license plate can park just about anywhere: the police will overlook it. Cars are not allowed to park in front of Sirkeci Railway Station, the space being kept open for taxis; but in fact the taxi-drivers themselves—very helpful and well-mannered in Turkey—make room for the foreigner, and guide him in and out. (If a small boy helps you, give him 50 kuruş.) Of course, there are paying parking lots. On the other hand, if you need to stop by a bank or a travel agency, and can find no place to leave your car, there will always be somebody to watch over it while you double-park. This, of course, in the crowded downtown streets; there is plenty of parking space elsewhere.

In Istanbul, filling-stations are carefully hidden in the ground floor of buildings; besides, there are few in town, and you will do well to fill up in the suburbs.

 TRANSPORTATION. If you have come to Istanbul without a car, or if you want to get around without it, the city bus system (imported Leyland vehicles) is good. Taxis usually wait at hotel entrances only; if you want to economize, do as the Turks, even well-off, do: take a shared taxi or *dolmuş*). At the Sirkeci Railway Station, a signpost shows the way to the dolmuş starting-place for Taksim; the cost of the fare is written on the stop sign, so there can be no mistake; you do not tip the driver. Nor do you talk to the other passengers, any more than on a town bus (even Turkish women use the dolmus). If you wish to get off before reaching the terminal, just say *dour*: stop. The driver will draw up at the first place allowed him—usually a bus or trolleycar stop—and you pay him the price of your fare.

There are several electric train routes of the Turkish Railways (TCDD) for the suburbs. Leaving from the Sirkeci Station, they take you to Ataköy and Florya, beaches on the Sea of Marmara. There are also many motorcoach tours of the town and outskirts, organized by travel agencies: all the needed information will be given you by a travel agent or the Turkish Tourist Office in the Hilton Hotel.

Besides the Sirkeci-Florya-Küçük Çekmece line, there is another suburban service that follows the Asian shore of the Marmara and its beaches: *Haydar-paşa* (Üsküdar)-Feneryolu-Erenköy-Suadiye-Maltepe-Kartal-Pendik.

Buses for the European shore of the Marmara set out from Taksim Square in Beyoğlu: No. 94 for Florya, No. 96 for Yeşilköy. For the European shore of the Bosphorus, up to Sariyer, No. 40 on Taksim Square.

For the Asian shore of the Marmara, the buses set out from the landing wharf in Kadiköy (Üsküdar). For the Asian shore of the Bosphorus up to Beykoz, they set out from Üsküdar. These buses are not numbered.

Dolmuş (cab ranks): Eminönü Meydani, the square opposite the Galata-Karaköy bridge, for Eyüp, the ancient ramparts of Edirne Kapı, and Topkapı. The square in front of Sirkeci Railway Station for the European shore of the Marmara and for Beyoğlu (Taksim). Taksim Square for the European shore of the Bosphorus. Landing-wharf in Üsküdar for the Asian shore of the Bosphorus. Landing-wharf of Kadiköy for the Asian shore of the Marmara.

The *bus-lines* for Ankara and the provinces all set out from Taksim Square and Sirkeci. Here are a few: *Jet-Turizm* (47–11–94); *Varan* (49–19–03); *Ulusoy* (44–12–71). Other stops near the Sirkeci Railway Station and Kadiköy.

OUTINGS. One of the most beautiful waterways of the world, the Bosphorus is an outing no traveler should miss. It is about 20 miles long, and from one-third of a mile to 2 miles wide. You can go up it by boat, leaving every hour from the Karaköy-Galata Bridge. All boats keep within the boom that closes the Bosphorus at the north-eastern outlet, leaving a fairly narrow passage for shipping. You can glimpse the Black Sea at a distance.

A highway runs the length of the European shore, passing through docks as well as residential quarters. It is plied in part by trolley cars, then by buses or by motor coaches. If you are a group, take a dolmuş. Another highway skirts the Asian shore, up to Beykoz.

The Princes' Islands, or Adalar, are four in number. They are 10 miles or so southeast of Istanbul in the Sea of Marmara. From the Karaköy-Galata Bridge, steamships and launches make a quick crossing (one-way fare between 2.25 to 2.75 TL). In the last island, Büyük Ada ("Big Island"), open carriages (*fayton*) drive you through the pine woods. Very good restaurants near the wharf.

Another half-day outing is the crossing of the Bosphorus by ferry boat, which leaves Kabataş for Üsküdar; climb up, on the Asian shore, on the hill of Çamlica, with its breathtaking view over Istanbul, the Sea of Marmara, and the Islands. Take a taxi or a dolmuş from Üsküdar.

A one-day outing to Bursa, capital of the Ottoman Empire in the 15th century, is by plane—a 20 minute flight (one-way fare about 56 TL, round trip 100 TL), 4 daily flights each way. The journey allows for a full day's stay in Bursa, but you have to board the plane at Yeşilköy, over 10 miles from Istanbul. By road, if you ferry your car at Kartal, you make a short cut of 93 miles; but at the height of the tourist season, you must make sure to arrive well ahead of departure times for the ferry boat, which leaves every other hour. The crossing takes about an hour and a half.

Yalova is a quite fine watering place on the Asian shore, 2 hours from Istanbul by a boat that sets out from the Karaköy-Galata Bridge. Healing springs, baths, and a European-style hotel, the *Termal*. There are also other hotels like *Güney*, *Büyük* and *Taş*, making a complex that is operated by the Turkish Maritime Bank.

Farther along the Black Sea, on the European side, a big beach, Kilyos; and on the Asian side, Şile. Both are reached by bus—those bound for Şile set out from Üsküdar, and those going to Kilyos stop at the small beaches all along the Bosphorus.

BOATS. Landing-wharfs for both shores of the Bosphorus, (there are three runs: European shore, Asian shore, and a to-and-fro ferry): for Üsküdar-Haydarpaşa-Salacak, to the right of the Galata-Karaköy bridge at Eminönü (on the Sirkeci side), looking towards Beyoğlu. For the Princes' Islands (Adalar) and Yalova, the slow run starts at the beginning of the bridge, the express run a little farther along the bridge, towards Beyoğlu. The landing-wharf for Kadiköy and Haydarpaşa is to the right of the bridge (towards the Bosphorus) on the Beyoğlu side, still facing Beyoğlu. The landing-wharf for all stops on the Golden Horn (Haliç) and beyond is to the left (on the Golden Horn side) at the Beyoğlu end of the bridge. The car-ferry Kabataş-Üsküdar comes in at the mouth of the Bosphorus, to the south of the Dolmabahçe Palace. This is the ferry to be taken if you stay at the Beyoğlu hotels. The Sirkeci-Üsküdar car-ferry docks to the right (towards the Bosphorus) of the Galata Bridge, beyond the wharves first mentioned above.

SPORTS. Whichever sporting club you choose, you are sure of a warm welcome. A few addresses: *tennis, fencing, and mountain-climbing:* Tenis Eskrim ve Dağcilik Klübü, Taksim *Tennis:* Taşlik Tenis Klübü, Maçka. Hilton Kortlari, Altinbakkal. *Water sports* (sailing, water-skiing, skin-diving, and so on): Istanbul Yelken Klübü, Fenerbahçe. Kalamış Yelken Klübü, Kalamış. Moda Deniz Klübü, Moda. Yüzme Ihtisas Klübü, Ortaköy. *Riding:* Atli Spor Klübü in Maslak. *Golf:* Golf Klübü, Büyükdere Caddesi, Levent.

You may, in season, see a football (soccer) match, though there are few big games. Stadiums: Mithatpaşa Stadyomu in Dolmabahçe; Fenerbahçe Stadyomu in Fenerbahçe. Indoor gymnasium (*Spor ve Sergi Sarayi*) near the Hotel Hilton. Season: Oct. through May.

BEACHES. On the Sea of Marmara, Florya can be reached by electric train, leaving the Sirkeci Railway Station. A fine beach. The same may be said of Ataköy: electric train to Bakirköy, then on by dolmus, taxi, or bus. Modern motels. On the Bosphorus, the beaches are small but plentiful. We list the names here, for outside of the places listed below you must *not* try to swim, because of the dangerously strong currents that cross the Bosphorus. On the European shore: Lido, Yeniköy, Tarabya, Bebek, near the castle of Rumeli Hisar, and Beyaz Park in Büyükdere. There are a few small beaches on the Asian shore, but only three of interest to foreigners—Moda, in Kadiköy, southeast of Istanbul, with yachting. Also Salacak, Küçüksu.

 USEFUL ADDRESSES. Travel information: *Tourist Information Office* at Hotel Hilton, tel. 46-70-50. *Türkiye Turizm Kurumu,* Istiklâl Cad., 186/2, tel. 44-98-42. *Danisma Bürosu* at Yesilköy Airport, tel. 73–82–40. *Turing ve Otomobil Kurumu* (Automobile Club), Şişli, tel. 48-71-27.

Consulates: *U.S.A.*: Meşrutiyet Cad., Tepebaşi 104-8. *Great Britain*: Tepebaşi, Meşrutiyet Cad., 34; *Bulgaria*: Mecidiyeköy, Garaj Sok. 4; *Iran*: Ankara Cad., Cagaloglu No: 1–2; *Iraq*: Ayazpaşa, Gümüşsuyu Palas Daire 4, *Lebanon*: Teşvikiye Cad., Saray Apt. 134/1–2; *U.S.S.R.*: Beyoğlu, İstiklâl Cad., 443.

Airlines: *THY* (*Turkish*), Terminal: Şişhane Sq., and Hilton Arcade; *TWA*, Hilton Arcade; *Air France*, Taksim Sq., Cumhuriyet Ave.; *Alitalia*, 135, Cumhuriyet Ave.; *BEA* and *BOAC*, 10, Cumhuriyet Ave.; *El Al* (*Israel*), 187, Cumhuriyet Ave.; *Iranair*, 39, Cumhuriyet Ave.; *Iraqi Airways*, 137, Cumhuriyet Ave.; *KLM*, Taksim Square: *Lufthansa*, 179, Cumhuriyet Ave.; *MEA*, 30, Cumhuriyet Ave.; *Olympic*, Cumhuriyet Ave.; *Pan American*, Hilton Arcade; *PIA* (*Pakistan*, 25, Cumhuriyet Ave.; *Sabena* (*Belgian*), Hilton Arcade; *SAS* (*Scandinavian*), Cumhuriyet Ave.; *Saudi Arabian Airlines*, Hilton Arcade; *Swissair*, Cumhuriyet Ave.

Shipping Lines: *Denizyollari* (*Turkish Maritime Lines*), Karaköy Customs; *Adriatica*, Karaköy Customs; *Bumerang* (*Russian Maritime Lines*), Tophane, Rıhtım Cad., Cıracı Sokak, Rehan, Kat 6.

Travel agencies: *Bayram Tours*, Cumhuriyet Caddesi 191 (opp. Hilton), takes a personal interest in the visitor to Turkey. It is headed by a multilingual young graduate of Harvard College, Kanık Arıcanlı, whose wife was also educated in America. *Türk Express*, at the entrance to the Hilton Hotel; *Van Der Zee Travel Service*, Cumhuriyet Caddesi 16; *Wagon-lits/Cook*, Cumhuriyet Caddesi 22; *Kontuar Turizm*, Cumhuriyet Caddesi 197.

American hospital: Admiral Bristol, Nişantaşi.

Churches: *Catholic*. Cathedral of the Holy Ghost, Altinbakkal in Harbiye, and St. Louis des Français, French Consulate, in Beyoğlu. *Dutch Protestant Chapel*. Postacilar Sok., Beyoğlu. *Union Church* (*Protestant*). At Dutch Chapel, address above. Jewish, Synagogue Beth Israël in Şişli.

Post Office, Yeni Posthane Caddesi in Eminönü.

Tourist Police (Turizm Polisi), Emniyet 5, Sube, tel. 44-98/4. Sirkeci Police Station, tel. 22-47-44.

Railroad information: *Sirkeci Railway Station* (Europe), tel. 22-30-79. *Haydarpasa Railway Station* (Asia), tel. 36-20-63.

Exploring Istanbul

You will find it difficult to fit sight-seeing into a timetable, as a passing glance at the map will show. Two-thirds of old Constantinople are in Europe: Old Stamboul (ancient Byzantium)—and Beyoğlu, across the river in Galata-Pera. Between them lies the Haliç, almost a backwater, crossed by the two bridges of Galata-Karaköy and of Atatürk. Incurably romantic, westerners named the Haliç the Golden Horn.

To go to Asia we must cross the Bosphorus, which connects the Sea of Marmara, to the south, with the Black Sea, to the north. The last third of Istanbul is on the Asian shore: parts of town called Üsküdar—the old Scutari—and Kadıköy, built on the site of old Phoenician and Greek settlements.

For the most part, places of historical and archeological interest are grouped together on the point that juts out between the Sea of Marmara and the Golden Horn: Old Stamboul. The old romantics are dead and forgotten, and today's young traveler wants above all to know why such a backwater was given the name of the Golden Horn. Well, here is the story. When the city fell to Mehmet the Conqueror, many things happened, among which the sinking of two ships "full of gold" in the Haliç. The thought of all that gold at the bottom of the water never left men's minds. In the nineteenth century, a German firm even offered to drag the strait and raise the ships; but the Sultan would not hear of it. As the shape of Stamboul on the map is something like a horn, the reason for the name becomes clear.

For a sweeping view over all Istanbul, you can also cross the Bosphorus; the countless ferry-boats that ply between both shores will take you over in a few minutes. The best view is from Çamlica, a name the traveler will come upon in many Turkish towns. The word simply means "copse", and as a place-name has come to mean "a leafy spot" for Sunday outings, with or without a picnic. Istanbul's Çamlica is in Asia, on a height, not far from the landing-wharf. The view over the Bosphorus and the city, above all at dusk and against the light, is unequaled.

Above the queues of cars cramming the huge square of Üsküdar rises the tall unbroken façade of the Iskele (Landing stage) Mosque, built by Sinan in 1547 for Mihrimah, daughter of Suleiman I.

ISTANBUL
(Not to scale)

1 Sultan Ahmet Mosque
2 St. Sophia (Museum)
3 Topkapi Palace &
   Archeological Museum
4 New Mosque (Yeni)
5 Suleymaniye
6 Fatih Mehmet Mosque
7 Oriental Museum &
   Museum of Turkish Art
8 Galatae Tower
9 Dolmabahçe Palace

Mosques

Ferry Terminals

Early in the morning, a soft mist shrouds the Bosphorus. If you have the good luck to have a room facing east, you will awaken to the cry of sea-gulls, the chirping of birds, the hoot of steamers, and the rising sun. The waterways are already crowded, and the big ferry-boats nose their way through the jostling *kayiks*. These are odd-looking craft: flat and wide, they taper inwards at both ends, the stern and stem turning sharply upwards: the gunwale almost forms a half-moon. Steered with oars or fitted with an engine, they become part of the landscape.

Adding to the noise and bustle, a crowd of fishermen throng around the harbor, picking up the flotsam thrown overboard to use as bait. The main catch in the Bosphorus is the striped tunny; gutted, boned, and left to soak in salt, it becomes the *lâkerda*, a dish much appreciated by lovers of good food. There is also plenty of mullet. The roe, dried, pressed, and preserved in a thin skin of wax, is held by many to be better than caviar.

At sundown, all the day's catch is spread out for sale on the wharf below the bridge of Galata, sometimes on an old newspaper, more often on the very stones. The bargaining begins; prices go down with the sun, and the poorer buyers wait patiently until the fish is within their means.

The Tower of Leander

In the middle of the Bosphorus stands a small island, and on that island stands a lighthouse—a long time ago, another stood here, surrounded by legend. Of legends, in fact, it had many, but the first gave it both its renown and its name—the Tower of Leander.

Once upon a time, there lived on the island a girl called Hero, "beautiful as the day is long", as in all fairy-tales. Though it is not in the story, she was probably shut away from sight by a jealous father, brother, or husband. Nonetheless, it so happened that a young man called Leander, a strong swimmer who daily braved the waters of the Bosphorus—then called the Hellespont —was washed up by a wave on the beach of her island prison. Fate brought the two together, and they fell in love. Hero, however, despaired: how would they meet again? But Leander swam back that very night, under cover of darkness, and stayed with her until dawn. Then, when "the lark, the herald of the morn", broke into song, he swam away. Night after night, the lovers met; until one dark night of storm Hero, waiting in fear for Leander's coming, saw daylight break on the becalmed sea, and the drowned body of her dead lover washed up for the last time on the shingled beach of her lonely island; and died of a broken heart.

The Bosphorus or Boğaziçi has a still older legend, as all crosswordpuzzle fans well know. When the gods of Greece were young, Zeus fell in love with a beautiful maiden, Io. Hera, on hearing of her husband's latest love and wishing, so we gather, to show what she thought of her rival turned Io into a cow. That not being punishment enough, Hera sent a gadfly to sting her. Goaded out of her blissful daisy-munching, the cow galloped without stop around the known world and over into Asia across the *Bosporus*, or "cow's ford".

The Pilgrimage of Eyüp

Breaking with the custom that begins the round of the mosques in the Eminönü district, we shall go first of all to Eyüp because it gives the foreigner a deeper understanding of what the faith means to a Moslem. The café where Pierre Loti—who captured the unique atmosphere of the declining imperial city in his novels —used to sit and gaze his fill, is higher up in Eyüp, to the northwest, following the southern shore of the Golden Horn. (It is not easy to find, in spite of the many signposts showing the way. Best put yourself into the hands of a taxi-driver or a guide, sooner than rely on your own bearings.)

The distant view is wonderful, though the surroundings are grim. The tangle of streets, houses, and hills is pierced by the sharp spires of countless minarets. Istanbul has from five to six hundred mosques, of which every one has from one to four minarets, sometimes six: at least a thousand needles pricking the unruffled blue sky.

The Arab Moslems, newly converted by Mohammed, had laid siege to Byzantium, and the standard-bearer and friend of the Prophet had fallen in battle, in 669. His name was Eyüp-ül-Ensari Halit bin Zeyd, and he was buried on the battlefield. Much later, during the siege of the city by Mehmet the Conqueror, the sultan had a dream. He told it to the scholar Ak-Şemseddin, who said that it revealed the site of the holy grave.

Mehmet at once gave orders to unearth it, and the dream was found true. The Conqueror then ordered a tomb and a mosque to be built over the burial-ground. It soon became, for all Islam, a place of worship and a pilgrimage on the way to Mecca.

Built in 1458, enlarged by Murat III towards the end of the 15th century, the mosque, shaken loose and cracked open by earthquakes, was torn down and rebuilt in 1800. Up to the present day, it is still a focus of Moslem piety. Here, the Commander of the Faithful came in great pomp to gird the sword of Osman, founder of the Osmanlı or Ottoman dynasty: a sword that was the symbol of the Caliphate.

The village of Eyüp has many old wooden houses, some with a pretty fretwork trim. At the door of the all-white mosque, you are offered water, held to be good for the health of body and soul. Inside is a vast paved courtyard, teeming with devout humanity. Unlike Christianity, the faith of Islam has not split apart and foundered under the weight of afterthoughts. It has remained whole, unquestionable and unquestioned, and in Eyüp this strikes the outsider as both natural and good—he suddenly sees a flash of pure truth which he will never see again. The Moslem, on going into this courtyard, washes himself altogether clean of the man he seems to be in the outside world. It is his bare soul and heart that he shows to his God.

Inside the second courtyard there is a huge tree, surrounded by an enormous railing. The inner walls are covered all around with magnificent glazed tiles, with red and sometimes yellowish designs on a blue ground. There are storks and pigeons. But what most catches the visitor's eye is the long row of faithful come to beg a favor at the tomb of Eyüp. One by one, they stop in front of the Window of Help where, strangely enough, the star of David stands out on the highly-worked brass lattice.

Under the archways, merchants sell their wares, and crowds of people come and go. But at the door, where visitors take off their shoes, all is quiet. A heavy curtain falls between the mosque and the outside world.

Inside, it is all white, with the usual writings of Koranic prayer. The prayer-rug is blue, worked in blue. Along the walls runs a design, also in mingled blues. Everywhere, withdrawn and open to God alone, men pray. There are many women, too, but they are together, in a corner. Once again, the rapt inwardness of the faithful strikes the outsider, who turns away, feeling awkward and an intruder.

The mosque is surrounded by small graveyards and lonely tombs or *türbes*, marking an underground maze of the dead. In front of the Window of Help, the crowd is as big as ever.

Whatever you do, don't miss Eyüp. If you do, you will lose your chance of understanding Islam.

Mosques and Museums

They say that Istanbul has from five to six hundred mosques. No need, of course, to see them all. The biggest and best are naturally grouped together in the old city, at Eminönü.

The mosque of Sultan Ahmet, better known as the Blue Mosque, is placed in the midst of interesting monuments. To the northeast lies St. Sophia, and, farther on, the Topkapı Palace, with the church of St. Irene between the two. To the southwest, Small Sophia: Küçük Ayasofya. To the west, the obelisk and the hippodrome; a little higher up, the water reservoirs of Yerebatan, the Sunken Palace. To the southeast, the Museum of Mosaics. It is therefore in this neighborhood that all sightseeing starts.

Alone of all mosques, the Blue Mosque boasts of six minarets. In spite of its immoderate size, its proportions are admirable. The architect was Mehmet Ağa, who built it by order of Sultan Ahmet I in seven years, beginning in 1616. The blue glazed tiles that cover the inside walls have given it its name. Many art critics place it higher than St. Sophia; it is certainly the masterpiece of Turkish architecture, together with the mosque of Sultan Selim in Edirne, and the Sülemaniye Mosque in Istanbul.

Formerly, people had to walk into the mosque in socks or stockings; nowadays, you are handed huge slippers to pull on over your shoes. Many foreigners seem to think that the shedding of shoes is a religious observance; but like many of Mohammed's laws, it is merely a measure of cleanliness, as the praying Moslem touches the ground with his head.

The middle dome (which is one hundred and nine feet wide, eight feet wider than that of St. Sophia), together with the smaller domes and half-domes which form the whole, rest on four massive pillars, 15 feet thick. The blue glazed tiles shine in the daylight, itself tinged with blue as it floods through the two hundred and sixty windows. On the floor, a very fine carpet, on which are scattered, here and there, old and remarkably beautiful praying-rugs.

Whatever the traveller may think of the inside—and in all likelihood he will be overawed—he will surely be deeply moved at the sight of the mosque seen from the Bosphorus. More than all other mosques, it gives the feeling of man's blind, upward reaching to the heavens.

St. Sophia

St. Sophia, or Ayasofya, is built on altogether different esthetic lines, in spite of the later minarets, being a Byzantine basilica open to the Christian cult in 360. Destroyed by the conflagration which devastated the entire district in the hippodrome riots of 532, St. Sophia was rebuilt in the following 30 years by Justinian. It is said that on seeing "his" finished cathedral, the overjoyed emperor cried out: "O Solomon, thou art vanquished!"

In 1453, Mehmet the Conqueror turned it into a mosque, and the renowned architect Sinan surrounded it with shrines. As the church had been built on the plans of a Christian basilica, there is no inner courtyard for ritual ablutions, as in mosques.

Just as Mehmet had wished to make a stand for Islam by turning St. Sophia into a mosque, so Kemal Pasha wanted to open a door to European ideas by making of it a museum for all, regardless of creed. To make his intention plain, the huge gilt disks engraved with the writings of the Koran and hanging all around the walls were taken down, leaving unsightly round stains. After the death of Atatürk, they were put back as part of the govenment's policy of religious tolerance. The Koran is back where it belongs, but Ayasofya is still a museum; Moslem rites are no longer celebrated and you can walk in with your shoes on (after buying a ticket).

The big middle dome rests on two half-domes; the whole is an amazing feat of architecture. The church was dedicated to the Virgin and not to the saint who bore the name of Sophia, the Greek word for wisdom. We, too, could speak of the *narthex*, but it seems simpler to say that the entrance has beautiful marblework and bronze doors, some of which still need cleaning. The mosaics above the door are well preserved—you can easily make out the two emperors, Constantine and Justinian, one offering his new city and the other his new basilica to the mother of Jesus.

Justinian was not a man to haggle over expense. He ordered marble from Egypt and from Turkey, from Asia and, mostly, from Ephesus. His worthy wife, Theodora, has her monogram on the capitals topping the columns. You will be shown the "weeping column", made of a porous stone that draws water up from the cistern below. The water that oozes out is said to work miracles, especially in curing eye diseases.

The objects in gold and silver: the throne, the altar table, the altar screens and the wall panels, all studded with jewels, are no longer part of St. Sophia's pomp and glory. All that is left is the description made by Paul of Silentium. As for the mosaics, they were defaced in the war against images. Later mosaics were plastered over by Mehmet the Conqueror, and to top it all an earthquake, in the nineteenth century, cracked open the walls, loosening the stonework. In 1932, a team of archeologists went to work to uncover and piece together the badly damaged pictures. Of the famous *Deisis* upstairs in the Women's Gallery (Gynecaeum), only the wonderfully expressive head of the Virgin, as well as parts of Christ and St. John the Baptist, remain. At the end of the gallery next to the great apsis, Christ stands between the Empress Zoë and Constantine Monomachos, the latter's likeness having been superimposed on Zoë's two previous husbands. The Virgin is surrounded by John II Comnene, Irene and Alexis (12th century), while a rare portrait of the Macedonian Emperor Alexander (10th century) came to light on a pillar of the north gallery.

When the Moslems turned the church into a mosque, they of course replaced the furnishings of the Christian cult by their own. The *mihrab* is in the apse. The *mimber* and the platform for the choristers were put in later, by Murat III, who also ordered from Ephesus the two great alabaster urns for ablutions. The baptistery became a *türbe*, and shelters the tomb of the sultans Mustafa I and Ibrahim. In the garden, among the fragments of columns, capitals, friezes and panels are the tombs of three more sultans— Murat III, Selim II and Mehmet III—as well as of several murdered princes.

Just behind St. Sophia, Mehmet II in 1478 constructed the Imperial Gate (*Bab-ı-Hümayun*), which leads to St. Irene, one of Byzantium's earliest churches, built over a temple of Aphrodite (Venus). Enlarged by Constantine the Great, it housed the Second Ecumenical Council in 381. Burnt in the great fire of 532, St. Irene, too, was rebuilt by Justinian, second in size only to St. Sophia, to which it was joined by a group of buildings. The three-naved basilica surmounted by a dome suffered badly in the earthquake of 740. Restored by Leo the Isaurian, it was transformed into an arsenal after the Turkish conquest, as it stood close to the parade ground of the Janissaries. The degradation of Divine Peace (Irene means "peace" in Greek) for purposes of war was not yet over, as the arsenal later became the Artillery Museum. Old cannons still lie in front of the sadly neglected brick building.

Between St. Sophia and Sultan Ahmet (the Blue Mosque), we cross the ancient Hippodrome, built in 203, today the At Meydanı. It holds a few monuments, of more historical than artistic interest. A fountain offered by the German Kaiser Wilhelm II to Abdul-Hamid, at the end of the last century. The obelisk of Thutmes III brought back from Egypt by Theodosius the Great; a monolith almost sixty-six feet high, it was topped by a metal ball that rolled off in the earthquake of 865. The bronze Serpent Column originally commemorated the Greek victory over the Persians, at Apollo's shrine in Delphi. Brought some 800 years later to his new capital by Constantine the Great, the three serpents' heads disappeared in the 18th century and it has been somewhat battered by time, from twenty-six down to sixteen feet. There is another obelisk, over ninety-seven feet high; now broken into bits, it was once, in the tenth century, covered with slabs of gilt metal, melted down by the Crusaders.

Küçük Ayasofya, the small St. Sophia, is beyond the Blue Mosque, on the southern shore of Istanbul. This church, dedicated to the saints Sergius and Bacchus, was built in 550 by order of Justinian. It experienced the same fate as its neighbors, and was converted into a mosque. The minaret added at the time has since been destroyed.

The Museum of Mosaics shelters a part of the floor of Constantine's Palace, the most import- and non-religious mosaics in town.

The small colored stones form pictures from mythology, nymphs and griffins and hunting-scenes, embellished with birds and fruit. Scholars are at odds over the age of this workmanship; some date it back to Theodosius or Justin, some to Tiberius or Justinian II: in other words, any time from the beginning of the fifth to the end of the seventh century.

Topkapı Sarayı (The Seraglio)

The promontory formed by the Bosphorus and the Golden Horn was the obvious site for Constantine's Sacred Palace, which remained unparalleled in Christendom for 800 years. But with the decline of the empire's fortune, the Comnenes became unable to maintain the splendor of earlier dynasties and withdrew to the much more modest Blachernae Palace, higher up the Golden Horn. Plundered by the Latins, the Sacred Palace and its no less magnificent dependencies were a sad ruin by the time of the Turkish conquest. Mehmet II chose for his first palace the site of the present university, but soon recognized the incomparable position of Topkapı ("The Gate of the Cannon", so named after the battery which fired the salute from Seraglio Point). He began to build in 1462, with the construction of a double rampart and the first kiosks, to which subsequent sultans added ever-more-elaborate architectural fantasies, till a bewildering conglomeration of buildings extended over four vast courtyards. Turkish conservatism perpetuated the tents of the nomadic past in stone and resisted the imperial tradition of huge palaces till the middle of the 19th century, when Dolmabahçe rose across the Golden Horn. Only once thereafter did a sultan return to the bloodstained Seraglio—in 1876, Abdul Aziz was detained in one of the pavilions before committing suicide.

We have already entered the vast Court of the Janissaries to see St. Irene, described earlier. Close by is the former Mint (Darphane); in the shade of the plane trees, the turbulent Janissaries prepared their meals and indicated their discontent by overturning the kettles, a dreaded protest followed several times by the murder of the then-reigning sultan.

A lane to the left descends to the Archeological Museum, one of the world's most important, with finds from Ephesus, Miletus, Sidon, Troy and numerous other ancient sites. Outstanding in the remarkable collection of sarcophagi is that of Alexander the Great, a perfectly preserved masterpiece of white marble, whose relief sculptures depict Alexander's hunt. Opposite is the Çinili Köşk, the Tiled Pavilion, the Conqueror's summer kiosk, covered with superb blue and green tiles. It now houses a museum dedicated to his memory.

Closer to the lower gate is the Museum of Oriental Antiquities, rich in Sumerian, Babylonian, and especially Hittite, treasures. The Gülhane Park extends to the *enceinte*, which is topped by a small pavilion from which the sultans could (without being seen) watch ambassadors and dignitaries entering the Sublime Porte (Bab-i-Ali), the name by which the Ottoman government was known for centuries. The rococo gate was until 1923 the entrance to the Grand Vizir's palace, which, though partly destroyed in 1911, now houses the provincial administration.

Back among the Janissaries' plane trees, the road stops at the ticket office in the Middle Gate (*Orta Kapı*), constructed by Suleiman the Magnificent (fourth sultan of Constantinople) in 1524 and which only the sultan was allowed to enter on horseback. From the towers on either side, state prisoners were led to execution beside the fountain in the first courtyard. The second is the Divan Court, dominated by the Divan. This restful-sounding word means, in Turkish, a place of hard work—the Assembly Room of the Council of State, presided over by the Grand Vizier or Prime Minister. The sultan might choose to be present, but behind a latticed window, hidden by a curtain. Nobody ever knew when he was listening in on the debate, though he sometimes pulled the hangings aside to put in a word. Adjoining the Divan is an exhibition of Turkish porcelains and a fine collection of arms. The Gate of the Dead on the left leads to the sumptuous imperial coaches in the former stables.

In the kitchens, opposite, meals were prepared for some 5,000 people. Now, they house a magnificent collection of 10th-century (T'ang) to 14th- and 15th-century (Ming) china (over 10,000 pieces), which the Chinese made to order for the palace. Some exquisite Japanese porcelain is also displayed. European glassware is on display in the old royal sweetmeat and pastry kitchen, lately restored. On the stone next to the Gate of Felicity (Bab-i-Saadet), the Prophet's standard was raised whenever

Holy War was declared, the last time being in 1914. In the third court, the quarters of the black and white eunuchs face Ahmet's II Audience Chamber (Arzodasi), where the sultans received foreign ambassadors. Just behind is the library of Ahmet III, containing priceless Arabic and Greek manuscripts. To the right, a portico of seven columns precedes the lodgings of the Seferlis, the corps of pages chosen for their beauty from among the boys of the Christian blood-tribute, who rivalled the occupants of the harem for the sultans' favor. In this wing are now shown the collection of miniatures and sultans' signatures, masterpieces of the dying art of handwriting, the foundation of Moslem decorative art. Imperial fashion, male of course, evolves slowly in the magnificent display of the sultans' robes, garments stiff with gold and silver thread and handworked linen, tooled leather, gold, silver, and jewels . . .

Yet even this splendor is but an introduction to the fabulous jewels of the Treasury, a true cave of Aladdin overspilling into four rooms. The breathtaking effect is, however, rather due to quantity than taste—there are emeralds weighing several pounds, every possible utensil and weapon encrusted with diamonds and pearls, no less than three thrones (including the Indian one, reputedly once belonging to Shah Ismail, and part of the spoil from Selim I's victorious Persian campaign), and the reliquary containing the arm and hand of St. John the Baptist. The famous emerald dagger, star of the film *Topkapi*, rests in Case 12 of the treasury's Room II.

There are trinkets, chalices, candelabra and medals, and jewels, jewels, jewels. Even so, it is but a trifling sample of the old Ottoman treasures. Gone is the gold paving on the floor of the royal reception room, gone are most of the painted panels and all of the silk hangings. But prominent in the showcases are the two uncut emeralds, weighing six and three pounds, which once hung from the ceiling like green lights. Yet firework displays of dragons and castles no longer light up the dark sky over the sultan's world-renowned tulip garden, where long-dead peacocks once unfurled their fans. (It is to the Turks that we owe the tulip (lâle), brought back to Louis XIV by the French ambassador to the Ottoman court.)

On the opposite side of the third court, behind the small

Ağalar Mosque, where the manuscripts from the palace's 17 libraries have been gathered, and the Hasoda Pavilion, where Turkish textiles are displayed, is the Harem, a bewildering maze of halls, terraces, rooms, wings and apartments grouped round the two large chambers of Suleiman the Magnificent and Murat III. Along the Golden Way, the favorite of the night entered the sultans' private quarters in the fourth and last court, in which small, elegant summer houses, mosques, fountains and pools are scattered through gardens on different levels. The grey granite Column of the Goths—one of many still commemorating Roman victories, but minus the original statue on top—celebrates the triumph of Claudius II over the Barbarians. The Pavilion of Circumcision faces the gilded bronze Baldachin of Sultan Ibrahim and the loveliest of the pavilions, the famed Baghdad Kiosk (covered with Iznik tiles), built by Murat IV after his conquest of Baghdad in 1638. The Erivan Kiosk was known as the Golden Cage, where the reigning sultan's closest relatives lived in strict confinement after the old custom of murdering all possible rivals at each accession had been softened in the 19th century. House arrest effectively kept the internal peace, but deprived the heirs to the throne of any chance to prepare themselves for the formidable task of ruling a great empire.

The picture-gallery has a somewhat scant showing. Besides the few portraits painted on the sly by artists invited to the court to do so—such as Bellini's famous portrait of Mehmet II—there are a few Turkish miniatures, very like the Persian in style: the same lack of perspective, but more brightly colored. Where the Persians painted love stories and legends in rose gardens, the Turks, more down to earth, painted peasants at harvest and soldiers in battle; when they did paint holy legends, you know it is Turkish by the sky, which in sacred art is always gold.

In the middle of the covered courtyard outside, bright with colored tiles, is a magnificent fountain, usually open to the public. A signboard in front of the room given over to religious relics asks visitors to speak in low voices and to "show respect". It is splendidly furnished with dark, richly-lined alcoves and low divans, against a background of beautiful tiles and fretwork windows. The Door of Confessions was brought from the Kaa'ba, in Mecca. The Prophet's Coat is kept there in the chest of a

Bursa's sword-and-shield dance is performed without musical instruments, but is nonetheless intensely rhythmical. It can be seen also, as here, in Istanbul.
Photo by Sonia Halliday

Alone of all Turkish mosques, Sultan Ahmet ("The Blue Mosque") boasts six minarets. It was built in seven years, unlike the fortress of Rumeli Hisar, hurriedly erected at the Bosphorus narrows one year before the fall of Constantinople.
Foto by Sonia Halliday

Thousand and One Nights made for Murat III, which holds a solid gold shrine within another gold shrine, a gift of Abdul-Aziz. Also on display are Mohammed's two swords, weapons of Allah with which Islam was able to conquer a great part of the world, and a bronze impression of the Prophet's foot print.

The marble-paved terrace gives on to one of the most beautiful views over the Golden Horn, Galata, and the Genoese Tower. All Istanbul is spread out beneath our gaze: the great mosques outlined against a sky spiked by minarets; Beyoğlu and its houses, Pera and its shops, and, beyond the Gate of Galata, a network of small streets and dwellings. Fishing-smacks, kayiks, islands, mosques, domes, crescents shining in the sun, fine houses and tumbledown shacks, boats and water: here is the Golden Horn, a wonderland as seen by Richard Burton, Pierre Loti, and a thousand other romantic nineteenth-century travelers; the Constantinople, at last, of our exotic dreams.

Water has always been a problem in Constantinople, and still is in summer, even in the most modern hotels. Constantine the Great began the construction of an aqueduct, which was finished in 378 by the Emperor Valens, whose name the impressive two storeys of arches across Atatürk Boulevard still bears. Constantine also excavated the Sunken Palace Cistern (*Yerebatan Sarayi*), which was enlarged by Justinian and connected to Valens' Aqueduct to provision the imperial palaces. West of St. Sophia, steps descend 39 feet into these ancient vaults, upheld by three hundred and thirty-six columns, topped by Corinthian capitals, and lapped around at the base by water.

The Cistern of A Thousand and One Columns (*Binbirdirek*), though actually possessing only 224 (in 12 rows), is south of the Divan Yolu Highway; it also dates from Justinian, and is equally impressive. In the prosperous days of the Macedonian dynasty, the palaces of the great nobles, as well as the monasteries, had their own private cisterns, which fell into disrepair after the conquest. But the public fountains were maintained and embellished. The most beautiful was reconstructed by Ahmet III in 1728 to the South of St. Sophia.

The Sülcymaniye Mosque was built in mid-16th century by the most gifted architect of the Turkish world—Sinan, who also built the beautiful mosque of Edirne, as well as many wings of

Topkapı and embellishments in St. Sophia. The Süleymaniye Camii is one of the few masterpieces of the world. Built on one of the seven hills of Constantinople, it bears the name of Suleiman the Magnificent, whose octogonal *türbe* (as well as that of his Sultana Roxelane) stands in the cemetery to the east. In spite of its wonderful glazed tiles, carpets, and stained glass, it has a striking look of bare austerity, the acme of artistic achievement. Under the rule of this sovereign, Turkey reached the heights of greatness and power, and this contrast of simplicity seems, therefore, all the more deliberate. The proportions are overwhelming —the middle dome is 181 feet high and 84 feet wide. The half-dome between the Mihrab and the Door of Mecca is one hundred and twenty-two feet high and seventy-six feet wide. Four massive columns uphold the whole. One hundred and thirty-eight openings, covered in stained glass, let through an eery light. If the four minarets have twice three and twice two balconies, it is to make the sum of ten: Suleiman the Magnificent, fourth sultan to reign over Constantinople, was the tenth ruler of the Ottoman Empire. The Museum of Turco-Islamic Art is in the old kitchens of the Süleymaniye. Korans, miniatures, and carpets are its most valuable treasures.

It is also to Sinan that we owe the mosque of Rüstem Paşa, son-in-law of Suleiman and Grand Vizier. Built in 1561, it has beautiful glazed tiles and remarkable designs of green, black, and brown marble. In 1571 Sinan built the mosque of Sokollu Mehmet Paşa, with its lone minaret and its undamaged glazed tiles; as well as that of Selim I, whose single dome above the austere prayer room rises from the portico of 18 columns which support 22 cupolas. Selim's *türbe* faces that of Abdul Mecit.

Outstanding among the innumerable mosques deserving a visit is that of Bayezit II, an important architectural link between the 15th-century Anatolian mosques and those of Sinan. The Moorish gate opposite leads to the university, which replaced the Conqueror's first palace. In the gardens stands the white marble tower of Bayezit, culminating in a curious roof.

Across the square is one of the numerous entrances to the Covered Bazaar (*Kapalı Çarşi*), partly rebuilt after the fire of 1954. It is a town in itself, covering over 2,000,000 square feet, its various sections given over to different trades.

Only the Royal Gate remains of the original Fatih Cami, built by the Conqueror on the site of the Church of the St. Apostles, burial ground of the Byzantine emperors on the fourth hill. Levelled by the destructive earthquake of 1667, the present Italianate edifice, whose four half-cupolas support the vast central dome, was finished a hundred years later by Mustafa III. Moslems cannot be buried inside mosques, so the Conqueror's *türbe* and that of his mother are in the garden.

The Zeyrek Cami, near Atatürk Boulevard, was originally the church of Christ Pantokrator, dating from the 12th century; its mosaics are in a fairly good state of repair. The "new" mosque, Yeni Cami, finished in 1663, was begun in 1597; here, the old-style architecture seems formalized in an unchanging pattern. It stands by the bridge of Galata, coming from Beyoğlu.

Once you are at the Yeni Cami, don't fail to have a look at the long, lead-roofed building with many cupolas, the Spice or Egyptian Bazaar (*Mısır Çarşisi*), so-called because most spices came from Egypt when the mother of Mehmet IV presented the Bazaar to the Yeni Cami in 1660.

The Bridge of Galata

Millions of people throughout the world mention it daily without knowing. It was long the only bridge between the old town, Istanbul, and Karaköy (Galata). The townspeople of Constantinople said simply, "the bridge". It so happened that two English families, each living on the opposite shore, had got into the habit of meeting most evenings for a game of cards of their own invention, a variation of whist. (In those days, entertainment was homemade.) However, nobody much liked crossing the bridge after nightfall, sometimes in the rain, always with the risk of hold-ups. To make matters even they took turns, saying: Tomorrow, it's your night to bridge." And so the word became the name of a card game.

Since the founding of the republic, a second bridge, that of Atatürk, crosses the Haliç or Golden Horn. But the Bridge of Galata has kept all its old charm. Both ends are thronged with street peddlars, small shops, cafés, and restaurants. At night, it opens to let the big ships pass. In daytime, the boats that ply the Asiatic shore or the islands lie nearby at anchor.

Between the bridge of Galata and Gülhane Park is the so-called low-life district of Sirkeci—or vinegar-makers—and the railway station of that name. The nightclubs here are said to be the hangouts of Turkish hoodlums, but in fact they are as harmless to outsiders as in New York's Greenwich Village or in London's Soho. On a wooden platform, in a deafening din heightened by microphones and loudspeakers, dancing-girls do sad turns, half belly-dance and half striptease, just about as sexy as mother taking off her girdle in the bathroom. The show, what there is of it, is mostly out among the spectators.

The Walls and Kariye Museum

You must have a passing look, if only through a car window, at Istanbul's Byzantine walls. About five miles long, they were badly shaken by the earthquake of 1894, though the inner rampart, 12 feet thick and 43 feet high, with 90 towers and seven monumental gates, is still the most imposing Byzantine monument. Begun by Theodosius II in 413, complemented by an outer wall and a moat connecting the Sea of Marmara with the Golden Horn, these walls, the strongest fortifications of the Middle Ages, were breached only twice—by the Latins in 1204 and the Turks in 1453.

On this itinerary, or any other, a "must" is the Kariye Museum. The church of the Monastery of Chora dating back to the reign of Theodosius II (408–450) was rebuilt by Justinian after the earthquake of 558. In the 12th century, it was again restored by order of Maria Dukas, a niece of Alexis Comnenus. There are remnants of mosaics belonging to that period, but the superb masterpieces whose fame has spread throughout the world date from the 14th century. Above the front door, you can still make out a kneeling Theodosius, offering Christ a model of the church. The whole story of the beginnings of Christianity is told on these walls, with a careful and even homely realism which brings it closer to western primitive art than to the formal Byzantine images of God in His glory, holy saints, and royal emperors. The Turks only converted the church of the Holy Savior in Chora into the Kariye mosque under the reign of Bayezit II (1481–1512). (The splendid mosaics were saved and restored with the help of the Byzantine Institute of America.)

Also close to the Edirne Gate, the best starting point for a walk along the top of the ramparts, are the romantic ruins of the so-called Palace of Constantine Porphyrogenitus (*Tekfur Sarayi*), two storeys of large rooms with rounded arches. Further along lie the sad remnants of the once magnificent Blachernae Palace, built by Alexis Comnenus, to which his son Manuel II transferred the imperial court in 1150. The Latin emperors resided there in unwonted luxury, as well as the Palaeologues in ever greater poverty, abandoning wing after wing till the bitter end in 1453, when the palace fell a victim because of its proximity to the walls.

On the other side of the bridge, Galata was once a Genoese settlement, a town apart from Byzantium, and powerful enough to remain neutral during the siege of its neighbor by the Turks. The name itself, Galata, was once in all likelihood an Italian word: *calata*, meaning a slope. The famous and sinister Tower of Galata, built in 1349, now houses a rooftop restaurant and night-club with a sweeping view over the town. To the north of Galata is Beyoğlu and, farther on, Beşiktaş and Şişli. The main street of Pera has become, since the republic, Istiklâl (Independence) Street. Together with Cumhuriyet Caddesi (Republic Street) and the Harbiye quarter, it forms the shopping center.

In 1854, Sultan Abdul Mecit transferred his court and harem to the gleaming, white-marble Baroque Palace of Dolmabahçe. Stretching along the Bosphorus, the two long wings containing 365 rooms extend from the higher middle section of the enormous throne room—reputedly the largest in the world—in an extraordinary mixture of Hindu, Turkish and Italian styles. Once a year, a state ball takes place in that lavish setting where the apartments of four sultans and the bedroom in which Atatürk died in 1938 are faithfully preserved. Queen Victoria presented a gigantic chandelier and the taste of her period permeates the entire accumulation of ornamental gimcrack, culminating in a verdantique bath and crystal railings on the staircases. Once the Prophet's ban on the representative arts was violated, there was no holding back, and the walls are overloaded with innumerable pictures of dubious artistic value. The palace mosque and ornamental gates are in keeping with this oriental folly.

Other sights in Galata are the old French Embassy; the *tekké* of the Whirling Dervishes; the black lead domes of the Tophane

Camii, and the fine fountain of the same name; a five-storied house all in wood but for the ground floor, near the Park Hotel.

The most moving sight of all is the cemeteries, in Eyüp, in Karaca Ahmet on the Asian shore, everywhere and of all creeds, whether Moslem, Jewish, or Armenian Christian, the fallen tombstones and moss-grown graves wind-blown and forsaken.

The Princes' Islands

Outside of Çamlıca, the townspeople of Istanbul find fresh air, trees and quiet in the islands: the Adalar, which westerners call the Princes' Islands because they were a place of exile for the members of the imperial Byzantine dynasties. Ferry-boats ply back and forth all day long. The longest crossing takes an hour and a half to the biggest island: Büyük Ada. The others are Kinali, Burgaz, and Heybeli. Sivri and Kasık are uninhabited.

A wonderful peace awaits you there. Very wisely, no cars are allowed, outside of police jeeps. You are back in the good old days at their best, even to the long-forgotten smell of horse dung. For the only way to get around is on horseback, on a donkey, or on a bicycle. The old word for carriage, *araba*, nowadays means a motorcar; the horse-and-buggy awaiting the traveler here is called a *fayton*, the Turkish version of an old French word.

Most of the wooden houses were built at the turn of the century. Much of the land on Büyük Ada is not for sale, another wise law to keep the island unspoilt. Time has been set back a hundred years, allowing you to slow down and rest.

Towards the Black Sea

The shores of the Bosphorus, so unlike any landscape anywhere, have one thing in common with riverbanks in every large city— they are crowded with cafés, restaurants, and outdoor taverns, in an unbroken seven-mile front between Istanbul and the outlet to the Black Sea. The small villages on the European shore have merged and been submerged along the all too narrow coastal road, thronged with cars and buses.

Yet in summer the numerous hotels offer still the most agreeable accommodation close to the capital. The outdoor eating-places are always crowded with Turks, who drive out of town in the

cool of the evening to drink a *raki* with *mezes*, or a glass of tea: *çay*. These cheerful villages have the easygoing atmosphere of a suburb and the restfulness of a watering-place. There is Ortaköy and its docks at Kuruçeşme. There is Arnavutköy (you will have understood by now that the word *köy* means village; as for Arnavut, it means Albanian). There is Bebek, with its unbelievably beautiful view. Opposite Ortaköy the Beylerbeyi Palace, built in 1865, housed Napoleon III's Empress Eugenie during her visit to Istanbul. Abdul Hamid II was confined here till his death in 1913. Sultan Abdul Aziz built this dream of Hollywood come true, with the ornamental fountain in the main drawing room, white marble painted an inexplicable blue in another, costly furniture of no recognizable style, innumerable Sèvres vases and gilded clocks. The entrance from the road tunnel is difficult to find and very unprepossessing, but seen from the Bosphorus, the white marble façade has a definite grandeur.

Afterwards, take a look at the fortress of Rumeli Hisar. It was built in 1452, one year before the fall of Constantinople, by Mehmet the Conqueror, together with other fortifications preparing the siege of the city. It has since served as a watchtower at the very place where the narrowing of the Bosphorus makes it almost impossible to force a way into the strait. Shakespeare's plays are expertly performed in the vast courtyard in summer.

Just opposite, you can make out the few remaining towers of Anadolu Hisar, a yet older stronghold, built over fifty years earlier by Bayezit. As we know, the Turks call the European part of their country Rumelia, and the Asiatic part Anatolia. It is said to be here that Darius passed from Asia into Europe, in the sixth century B.C. Here too, in all likelihood, the Crusaders invaded Asia at the end of the eleventh century.

Other names, other beautiful places: Emirgân and its magnificent cypress trees; Istinye around its small and pretty bay, unfortunately spoilt by a naval repairs dock; Yeniköy, a boom town; Tarabya and its brand-new big hotel, admirably placed; Büyükdere, too beautiful for words; Sariyer, where we branch off towards the wonderful beach of Kilyos; Yenimahalle, end of the line.

To end the chapter on outings, two delightful place-names: the Sweet Waters of Europe, a charming spot formed by two small valleys at the far end of the Golden Horn, after Eyüp; and the Sweet Waters of Asia, near Anadolu Hisar.

The Neighboring Beaches

One last word on the beaches: those in Europe and Asia, on the Black Sea or on the Sea of Marmara.

On the European shore of the Sea of Marmara, there is Ataköy, near Bakirköy, Florya, near Yeşilköy—where the airport is, and where was signed, in 1878, the peace treaty of San Stefano, after the Balkan War. A little farther along the shore is Küçükçeşmece, with an inland lake for fishing, and a renowned grill restaurant, *Beyti*, with its wonderful döner kebab. There is also a bathing establishment, reserved—more or less—for the President of the Republic.

On the southern Asiatic shore, we have already been to the Islands of Princes, full of beaches for those who like a long stretch of sea with flat sands, and of creeks for those who prefer the wild beauty of rocks and upflung spray. There are several beaches across the way on the Anatolian shore—Göztepe, Erenköy, Suadiye, and Kartal, the last a starting-place for the Yalova ferry.

Remains the Black Sea. To the west, there is Kilyos. Starting out from Büyükdere, you cut across the forest of Belgrade (so called because Suleiman deported there his Serbian prisoners in the sixteenth century), admiring on the way the dam and aqueduct built by Mahmud I, as well as the Valide dam, built at the end of the eighteenth century by order of Sultan Selim III's mother.

One last word about all these villages and small towns. Nearly all built on the site of ancient cities, they are wonderful hunting-ground for amateur archeologists and historians, or simply for those interested in looking at the remains of ancient Greece and Rome, of Byzantium and the Ottoman Empire.

Illustration at head of this chapter: Jesus Christ between Constantine IX Monomachos and the Empress Zoë (11th-century mosaic in St. Sophia, Istanbul).

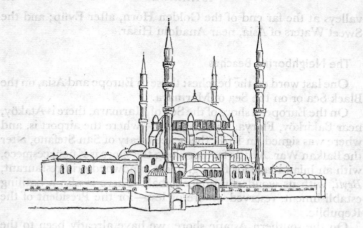

THRACE
Turkey's European Gateway

The huge red star poised on top of the tower at Kapitan Andreevo, right at the Bulgarian border, also looks out toward the nearby Turkish frontier post of Kapikule. At night it is lit up and can be seen all the way from the Turkish motel, looming up like a Communist challenge to the Western world. The paradox begins here, for "the West", lying just across the way, is the town of Kapikule, itself a part of the East. This fact will be confirmed some ten miles farther on by the sight of Edirne's splendid domes and minarets that look as if they are bubbling up on the horizon. Travelers coming in by the shortest route (E 97), via Bulgaria, will at least follow this particular itinerary.

Those driving in from Greece along the Salonika highway (E 5) will, after reaching Kipi, cross over the long Ipsala bridge spanning the deltas of the Maritza River (the Greek Evros, called Meriç by the Turks). The line of demarcation of the frontier falls right in the middle of the bridge. The personnel here have learned to get along with one another in a spirit of mutual comprehension. You won't be surprised to find the Greek frontier guard playing cards with his Turkish opposite number, but don't make too much fuss over this particular form of pacific coexistence, as it is by no means an official diplomatic venture.

One might say that here a gap has been bridged, both literally and figuratively.

Should you decide to veer off in the direction of Edirne, decidedly worth the detour, just continue driving on a short way beyond the Turkish frontier station and then turn left at the Keşan crossroads on to Route 6. However, you may be dissuaded from your purpose not just by the sentry on duty at the crossroads (Thrace is a military zone) but also by the condition of the road. It's more advisable, if you want to see Edirne at all and are entering Turkey from Greece, to drive along the Greek highway leading north via Didimotichon to the Kastanea-Pazarkule frontier post right up to the gateway to Edirne.

Miles before reaching the provincial capital, the minarets of Sultan Selim's mosque are fingering the sky. It is at this distance that the improbable legend becomes more plausible—enemy artillery never damaged its graceful towers. So judiciously are they posted that whichever angle the gunners took their aim from, the four minarets appeared always as one.

Edirne (Hadrianopolis on Greek road-signs, Adrianople in English) is the capital of one of Thrace's three provinces, or *vilayets*. The two other provinces are Kirklareli and Tekirdağ. The climate here is harsh and dry—there is no handy sea to temper either the sizzling summer heat or winter's icy depths. Edirne was the second capital of the Ottoman Empire, after Bursa. Founded in the second century by Emperor Hadrian, who gave the city its name, it was subsequently occupied by the Avars, and the Crusaders laid siege to it several times in the 12th century. It was here that Mehmet the Conqueror prepared his strategy for the fall of Constantinople in 1453.

Practical Information for Thrace

GETTING THERE BY CAR. The highway from Edirne to Istanbul (E5N and E5) has a rough surface, making a good grip for tires; it passes through a rolling plain that foreshadows the barren tableland of Anatolia, and allows the driver an average speed of 60 miles an hour. He may be slowed down by soldiers on the march, for Thrace is a military zone; but, unlike the drive through Bulgaria, he will not be stopped at the many white and red sentry-boxes.

Beginning at the long border bridge in Ipsala (Greece), the rough asphalt road of E5 is in good condition, and nearly deserted. It passes through only one town, Tekirdağ, and joins up with the Edirne highway 48 miles before Istanbul. These two main roads are by far the best in Thrace, in addition to a good road (E24) that leads from the straits at Eceabat, opposite Çanakkale, and links up at Keşan with the Ipsala-Istanbul highway. At Eceabat, cars are ferried across the straits toward Izmir or Bursa.

Boats also ply to the four islands, Marmara and Avşa, in the Sea of Marmara, and to Imroz and Bozcaada, placed at the mouth of the straits. These pine-wooded islands may one day become fashionable beach resorts; so far, the hotels are altogether below par. A filling-station for yachts is at Imroz.

There is no lack of filling stations in Thrace. Long before Istanbul, the road follows the sea, and the countless camping grounds, motels, boarding houses and hotels, either built or under way, bear witness to Turkey's effort to lodge travelers who, when they come by car, nearly all drive through this border.

BY TRAIN. The Munich-Istanbul *Tauern Orient Express* runs on the track coming out of Bulgaria and into Greece at Ormenion; the track then passes through Turkey to stop at Edirne, winds back into Greece where it links up with the railroad from Salonika at Pythion, and back to Turkey at Uzunköprü. (These borderline zigzags are due to the changing of national boundaries after the building of the railroad.) From Edirne to Istanbul, the highway is 144 miles long, while the railroad track is over 186 miles; and the train journey, by fast rail-car called *motorlü tren*, takes from 5 to 6 hours.

Hotels and Restaurants

ABIDE. *Abyde,* the most comfortable motel on the Dardanelles.

BABAESKI. *Park,* 26 rooms (6 with shower).

ÇORLU. The *Marmara Tur Hotel* (3), 12 double rooms, and *Marmara Tur Motel,* 40 double rooms, slightly cheaper, both full board only. *Alp Motel,* 13 rooms; all on the beach.

ECEABAT. At the ferry terminal, *ECE,* 20 rooms; *Park,* 7 rooms, none with shower. Better try the *Dardanel,* 16 rooms, 11 showers, about a mile west at Kilitbahir.

EDIRNE. *Kervan* (2), Talat Paşa Asfalti, 46 rooms, restaurant; *Yeşil* (3), Hürriyet Meydani, 23 rooms, 5 showers; *Rende Palas,* Eski Istanbul Yolu Cad.; *Pension Ar,* Arif Paşa 36.

In 1967, the *Inn of Rustem Paşa* (1), a 16th-century caravanserai restored and brought up to date, was opened, the first of its kind in Turkey.

Several restaurants of the *lokanta* or tavern type: *Çinar,* Daraçlar Cad. 109; *Şehir Külübü,* on Hürriyet Meydani Square; and *Meriç Lokantası,* in Karağaç, open only in summer. *Kırkpınar,* on the island of the same name.

IPSALA. A motel, slightly over a mile from the border bridge.

KAPIKULE. *Bosfor Motel* (2), 30 rooms, well-run; *Kapıkule Motel,* 32 rooms.

KEŞAN. *Belen* (3), 16 rooms, adequate for tired travelers. Restaurant.

KIRKLARELI. *Ipek Palas,* 22 rooms (none with bath).

TEKIRDAG. *Değirmen* (4), 24 rooms; *Gören Motel* (4), Değirmenalti, 12 rooms; *Tuna Palas*, 22 rooms (6 with bath or shower); *Olympiat*.

UZUNKÖPRÜ. The *Edirne*, 25 rooms (none with bath or shower), is passable.

CAMPING GROUNDS. Edirne: *Mocamp* is best, less than half a mile to the south of Edirne, and *Söğütlük Kampi*, not quite as good. Ipsala: *Mocamp*, near the Greek border. Marmaraereğlisi: three camping grounds, all below par, on the E5 highway (Ipsala-Istanbul).

USEFUL ADDRESSES. *Tourist Offices:* in Ipsala, the tourist office is in the Customs House; in Edirne, to the left (coming from Bulgaria), on Londra Asfalti. Sign in Turkish: *Enformasyon*. Another office in Kapikule.

Exploring Thrace

Edirne is truly the Gateway to the East. Although you are geographically in Europe, the transition-less change strikes you here, particularly if you have come in from Bulgaria. (Edirne has yielded its western and southern hinterlands to Bulgaria and Greece, which lost no time eradicating all the reminders of an earlier Turkish past.) As you first step into the little streets of the old part of the city, you notice only outdoor stalls—cobblers, blacksmiths, artisans and craftsmen of all kinds work in the open air, at least when the weather permits. The local marketplace provides a lively and diverting spectacle. The minarets and domes of the mosques largely account for your physical sensation of having been transferred into a completely different world, and your impression is further confirmed by the appearance of the dusty streets, which are covered with rough cobblestones or dirt surfaces.

Your first visit in Edirne should be to the masterpiece of the architect Sinan, Sultan Selim's mosque, or the Selimiye Cami (pronounced *djami*) which was built during the reign of Selim II (1569–1579). The unwary tourist approaching this building for the first time is usually so overwhelmed that he misses the main entrance and its slipper-attendant, and goes in by a side door. No matter—just remove your shoes, leave them at the entrance, and go on inside to feast your eyes. When you find yourself in the interior, you are struck by the strange feeling that the central dome is being held in place by exactly nothing at all. Right below it is the muezzin's loft. The beautiful *mimber*, or pulpit, stands to the right of the main entrance, and slightly to the left is the *mihrap*, the niche that points toward Mecca. The sultan's private loge is also on the left. The mosque's interior lighting, a masterpiece of effect in its own right, further enhances the impression of airiness and weightlessness. Legend has it that the architect wanted to put in a thousand windows, but Sultan Selim objected: "One thousand", he said, "is not an interesting number. Let's have 999 windows—there's a figure that people will remember." The grounds around the mosque include a library, a courtyard, and colonnades covered by 18 domes (the summer mosque), plus a fountain for the members of the faith to perform their ablutions. The nearby school, or *medrese*, houses a museum of ethnography.

In addition to Selim's mosque, there are others that deserve more than a passing visit. See the Bayezit mosque, with its single dome supported by four walls. It was built between 1484 and 1488, and contains a marble *mihrap*. Also visit the Yıldırım mosque, an ancient church, the Eski Cami (*eski* means "old"), probably the earliest Ottoman monument in the city; and the Üç Şerefeli Cami, the mosque with the three galleries. All these buildings date from the 15th century. Of course, don't miss the Maritza (or Meriç) Bridge and the Tunca Bridge. The fortress dates from Hadrian's reign. There are also two caravanserai, or inns. One of them, the Rüstem Paşa, has been restored and renovated to resemble a 16th-century Turkish hostelry.

A short way out of Edirne, a road (Route 20) branches off to the left toward Kırklareli. This is a so-called "stabilized" road, bumps and dust for 31 miles, so better continue on the E5N to Babaeski and take the paved E95 north to Kırklareli which lies in a mountainous area, where agriculture does poorly. The appearance of the landscape in the Turkish part of Thrace is a foretaste of what to expect in the high plateaux of Anatolia, by contrast with the bosky wooded copses in neighboring Greece and the fertile Bulgarian hills. The city has suffered from a long history of invasions and unrest. Long before the Christian era, Asian tribes were in Thrace, not so intent on settling down as on assuring themselves of a passageway to more temperate climes. Still later, the Turks, who were laying siege to Byzantium, established themselves in the area. The local monuments here include eight or nine mosques.

The main highway to Istanbul (E5N) runs on through a somewhat monotonous subdesert region highlighted by only one locality of any importance, Lüleburgaz, with its remnants of Turkish splendor—mosques, mausoleums, and a caravanseray. A triangular intersection beyond Çorlu marks the turnoff to the highway coming in from Greece via Tekirdağ (E5S).

By backtracking a short way west along E5S, then heading south on E 24 from Keşan, you can proceed toward Gelibolu (Gallipoli) and the Dardanelles, and reach Eceabat. A car-ferry plies between Eceabat and Çanakkale, on the opposite shore, near Truva (Troy). It's also possible to take a boat trip to the two islands, Imroz and Bozcaada, guarding the western entrance to the straits. Plans are under way for these pinetree-covered islands to be built up with the hotel and beach resort facilities that their sites call for.

The 60-mile-long Gelibolu (Gallipoli) promontory is of considerable historical importance. When the British and French troops were stationed in the region during the Crimean War (1854–56), a cholera epidemic broke out. This was the occasion for Florence Nightingale to perform her prodigious feat of nursing. Later, at the Eceabat bottleneck on March 18, 1915, British and French warships vainly strove to break through the Dardanelles Straits—thus did the abortive Gallipoli campaign begin. Many Franco-British monuments and cemeteries lie near the village of Seddülbahir, at the tip of the peninsula.

Back on E5S, Tekirdağ, former Rhodestos of ancient times, is the only town of any interest. The road glides down to the sea, forming a pleasant, wide thoroughfare planted with flower beds, where the local inhabitants enjoy their evening strolls. Sinan also built a mosque here, the Rüstem Paşa Cami (Rüstem Paşa was the son-in-law of Suleiman the Magnificent).

It is interesting to note that Tekirdağ was at one time the refuge of the famous Hungarian patriot, Rákoczy, who found a haven here after a series of harrowing adventures. Acting as an ally of Louis XIV and the Turks, Rákoczy had mustered an army of peasants to fight against the Hapsburgs. When the court of Versailles offered him the crown of Poland, Prince Francis II Rákoczy refused. Deserted by all, he went into exile in Turkey. In Tekirdağ, you can visit the house, now a museum, in which he lived until his death in 1735. Do many music lovers listening to *The Damnation of Faust* realize that the *Rákoczy March* which Berlioz inserted into his score is none other than the battle hymn Rákoczy's troops used to sing before going forth into battle?

Some visitors find the adjoining area attractive—there are Marmara Ereğlisi (excellent beaches), Saray, and Mürefte (treat yourself to a bottle of the local wine!).

Beyond Tekirdağ the road hugs closely to the seashore, rejoining the main Edirne-Istanbul highway at the triangle mentioned above. From here on, you become more aware of the presence of man. The concentration of houses, motels, and camp sites increases on the sea side of the road, and traffic becomes thicker. After passing Florya Beach on the right, the road widens out into four lanes, eventually becoming a six-lane highway. Shortly past Istanbul's Yeşilköy Airport, with the first big apartment houses of Ataköy on the right, you find yourself in the outskirts of Istanbul. In a few minutes, there's the trolleybus terminus, and now the old Byzantine ramparts of the great city stretch out ahead.

Illustration at head of this chapter: Selimiye Cami, at Edirne.

The oracles of the Temple of Apollo at Didymus were once as revered as those of Delphi.
Photo by Sonia Halliday

*Typical of the modern facilities along Turkey's Aegean shore are
the Imbat Hotel at Kuşadasi and the Club Méditerranée at Foça.*
Photo by Sonia Halliday

AROUND THE SEA OF MARMARA

Iznik, Bursa and Troy

Like two hulking mammoths coveting the same waters, Asia and Europe stand poised as if one of them were defying the other to dip first into the Straits of the Bosphorus. To the west, as far as Edirne, stretches Thrace. To the east lies the province of Kocaeli (once known as Bithynia). Bithynia, tucked in between the Black Sea and the Sea of Marmara, was the refuge for Hannibal in 184 B.C., following his defeat at the hands of the Romans.

You struck up a nodding acquaintanceship with this area during your stay in Istanbul, a highly cosmopolitan metropolis bearing the unmistakable imprint of the Turks. Now you're about to discover something quite different—Anatolia, whose distinctive aspects will grow more so as you proceed toward the interior. Travelers new to the region never cease to marvel at the prevalence of enduring reminders of its early occupants, the Greeks of the pre-Christian era. It is not an overstatement to say that the Hellenic heritage in Turkey is fully as abundant, as rich, and as interesting as it is in Greece itself. The explanation lies in the fact that Turkey became Hellenized at two separate times and under two sets of circumstances—through colonization in earliest antiquity, and through a cultural substitution under Byzantium in the Eastern Roman Empire. The Turks didn't arrive on the scene until the 11th century. Actually, Anatolia became Turkish long before Constantinople did. The Seljuk and Ottoman empires had ample time to succeed one another before the fall of the former capital.

The average visitor is ill-prepared for this particular aspect of Turkey, and finds himself caught unawares by what appears to be a miracle of successful co-existence between the present, past, and future. He is bemused at the sight of peasants still tilling the soil with an ancient model plough that dates back 50 generations. But he is quickly reassured by the bulky silhouettes of tractors looming up on the horizon, even if they happen to have been converted into vehicles for public transportation waddling casually along the main roads! He may feel distressed by the obvious signs of poverty in Turkish villages, but if he pauses for a few minutes he will soon find himself surrounded by good-hearted peasants serving him coffee and offering him the cigarette that they can't afford for themselves. What emerges out of all this is the "feeling of the archipelago". To the newcomer's unaccustomed eye, the stray evidences of 20th-century existence scattered hither and yon stand out like so many island dots cast down by the heavens to float over the ocean of the past.

Yet despite the vastness of the land, with its extraordinary air of other-worldliness, the people's exotic costumes and customs, their strange-sounding language, and the feeling of perhaps being an intruder, the traveler may often feel at ease, thanks to the straightforward simplicity of the people he meets, and their spontaneous hospitality.

This is the very special little patch of the planet in which, by a kind of osmosis, Eastern ideas, customs, and concepts were transmitted to the Western world as we today know it. On this spot, two continents combined to cook up, as it were, the porridge of an evolution, with all the goings and comings, the mixtures, mergings, acts of faith and of violence that had as their end result the formation of 20th century humanity.

Practical Information for Marmara

HOW TO GET THERE? By *T.H.Y. Airlines*, if you're in a rush. Istanbul-Bursa, ½ hour flight, 3 flights daily; Istanbul-Bandirma-Balikesir, 80 min., one flight daily. *By bus:* Excursion tours organized by various Istanbul travel agencies. If you're driving a car, see section below on *Motoring. Auto-ferries* ply between Kartal and Yalova. Frequent crossings scheduled by the *Denizyollari* shipping line, including the following itineraries: Istanbul-Gemlik-Mudanya; Istanbul-Island of Marmara; Istanbul-Gelibolu (Gallipoli)-Çanakkale-Imroz Islands, and Bozcaada-Karabiga-Erdek-Bandirma, etc. The Eceabat-Çanakkale car-ferry across the Dardenelles makes 8 crossings daily. There are 3 runs weekly by the Marmara diesel train, going from Izmir to Bandirma and connecting with the Bandirma-Istanbul boat.

MOTORING. Most of the roadways around the Sea of Marmara have been recently improved. The car-ferry running from Sirkeci to Kadıköy assigns priority to trucks and buses: private cars are accepted on a space-available basis. Better try the usual crossing starting in front of Dolmabahçe, via Kabataş-Üsküdar. Despite appearances to the contrary, the ferry service runs very efficiently. From 1 to 5 boats go into service depending on the time of day and the demand. Vendors sell tickets from car to car.

The highway begins at Kadıköy and passes a factory area, with a view out over Istanbul and its minarets in the distance. From the double-carriage six-lane Route 1 (E5) which follows the coast to Izmet, branch off to the right for Kartal to get the ferry for Yalova. The ferry trip lops some 150 km. (94 miles) off the distance to Bursa (Brusa). Drive on down to the little town and the railway tracks and join the line of waiting cars. Space is allotted in the order of cars' arrivals. Tea, coffee, and sandwiches sold by itinerant vendors. The crossing takes about 2 hours. The boat passes near the Princes' Islands (on the right).

On the left, the scenery is marred by great clouds of smoke from local cement works. Off the ferry, take a left turn at Yalova onto the paved Route 40 to Bursa (Brusa) via Gemlik. Bursa merits a full day's trip. If you're driving, the best deal is to catch the 8 : 10 a.m. ferry at Kartal and return by the one that leaves Yalova at 6 : 20 p.m. (This means leaving Bursa by 4 : 45 p.m. at the latest, to allow at least half-hour's wait for the ferry.) If necessary, get out of the car to purchase (1) a numbered space reservation ticket and (2) trip tickets for car and passengers, at the window in front of the ferry-slip. (Space reservation for car and tickets may also now be bought at the entrance to Yalova town (coming from Bursa), on the left side of the road.) The line of waiting cars can be pretty long: a bend in the road makes it hard to see just how far you are from the embarkation point. The important thing is to reserve your space first and then buy the tickets. Reservations are also available from itinerant vendors.

Weekends or holidays one might have to wait for several hours and it is quicker then to make the detour via Izmit on the new highway.

WHAT TO SEE? The big local attraction is the ancient city of Bursa itself, a garden city basking in the splendor of the finest works of Ottoman architecture. Your visit will be enhanced by a side trip to nearby Mount Ulu (Uludag). In July, Bursa is host to a Turkish folk-dance festival. Plan a stop also in Iznik (Nicaea) to see the ramparts of this city that fell successively under Roman and Byzantine domination. West of Bursa is the Karacabey Hara, a government-run stud farm for thoroughbred horse. You'll be made welcome here in the warmest Turkish tradition of hospitality. Other pleasant spots are the resorts of Gemlik, Mudanya and Yalova as well as Yalova Spa. Archeological sites dot the entire area, the most famous one being Troy, some 200 miles from Bursa. It's hard to think of the Dardanelles Straits without conjuring up the fierce World War I battles, but there are also fine beaches stretching invitingly along the whole shore of the inland Sea of Marmara.

Hotels and Restaurants

ADAPAZARI. *Beyazit Motel, Dilmen* (3); latter has 55 rooms (28 with shower).

BALIKESIR. *Kervansary* (4), 57 rooms (12 with shower); *Çiçek Palas,* 16 rooms, 2 showers; *Şehir Palas,* 34 rooms, 2 showers.

BANDIRMA. *Özdil* (4), 36 rooms (16 with showers); *Gar,* 24 rooms.

BILECIK. *Gören,* 20 rooms.

BURSA. *Çelik Palas* (2), 29 Çekirge Cad., 134 rooms (119 rooms with bath or shower); swimming pool with natural warm water, restaurant. *Diyar* (3), Çekirge Cad., 40 rooms with bath or shower; the *Kent* (3), Atatürk Cad., in city center, 50 rooms with bath or shower; *Ada Palas* (3), Murat Cad., at Çekirge, 39 rooms (12 with shower); *Gönlüferah* (3), Murat Cad., 54 rooms (48 with shower), restaurant. *Çekirge Palas,* Murat Cad., 27 rooms; *Park,* Murat Cad., 45 rooms, (8 with shower); *Ilman,* Kültürpark Karşısı 17/2, 32 rooms (6 with shower).

Restaurants: *Iskender,* Atatürk Cad., roof dining terrace. Other quite acceptable eating places near the Atatürk Monument: *Romans,* etc.

ÇAN. *Ilica* (4), 17 rooms (6 with shower).

ÇANAKKALE. *Aras,* 13 rooms; *Dogan,* 15 rooms, 2 showers; *Kordon,* 13 rooms.

DARICA. *Bayramoğlu* (2), 133 rooms with shower; *Motel Bekir,* 17 rooms with shower. Both have restaurants, private beach.

ERDEK. *Pınar* (2), 78 rooms with bath or shower; *Gül Plâj* (2), 38 rooms with shower; *Yat* (3), 55 rooms (21 with shower); *Motel Alevok,* 76 rooms with shower; *Türel,* 15 rooms (10 with shower). The first four have restaurants.

GEMLIK. *Tibel* (3), 28 rooms with shower; on a good beach. *Terme,* 31 rooms (16 with shower).

GÖNEN. *Park* (3), 54 rooms with shower; *Derman* and *Yeşil,* all (4). *Denizkent Motel* (3), 78 rooms with shower, restaurant.

HEREKE. On the Istanbul-Izmit highway, *Pina Motel* (3).

INEGÖL. *Oylat Motel,* 24 rooms with shower.

IZMIT. The *Saray Palas*, 30 rooms.

IZNIK (NICAEA). *Belediye Motel*, minute, modest. *Iznik Motel*, 12 rooms with shower.

MARMARA ISLAND. *Mermer Palas* (4), 28 rooms with shower; *Sarigöl* (4), 22 rooms with shower. An unspoilt island halfway between Europe and Asia.

On the much smaller **AVŞA ISLAND,** *Çinar*, 24 rooms, very simple.

MUDANYA. *Köksal Motel*, 40 rooms with shower. *Palas*, 12 rooms.

TRUVA (TROY). About 20 km. (12 mi.) north of Troy, on the Çanak-kale road, *Tusan-Truva Motel* (2), 24 rooms with shower, private beach.

ULUDAĞ. In the mountains near Bursa: *Büyük Oberj* (Inn), 78 rooms (12 with bath or shower), restaurant. Another inn, *Fahri Kinav*, 61 rooms with shower, is also good. In Kirazlıyayla: *Kirazlıyayla* (4), a small out-country hotel next to sanatorium.

YALOVA. Hot springs resort facilities at Yalova Spa, six tree-lined miles from the ferry terminal. *Gör Pansiyon*, 10 comfortable rooms with shower. At Çinarcik on the sea, *3 Reis Motel*, 23 rooms with shower. *Termal* (2), swimming pool. *Güney* (2), *Büyük* (3), *Çinar*, *Küçük*, and *Tas* (4).

CAMPING GROUNDS. Akmeşe: Quite good motel and camp. Bursa & environs: *Kumluk Mocamp*, 6 km. (4 mi.) n. of Bursa (Yalova road), pool; *Güzel Yali Kampi*, near Mudanya; *Çamlik Deniz Kampi*, Gemlik, north of Bursa; *Altay Turizm Deniz Kampi*, Küçük Kumla, near Gemlik; *Altinkum Kampi*, Gemlik, grounds and beach. *Station BP*, at Küplü, near Bilecik. İntepe Çamliği: *Tavus Kamp*. Erdek: *Dinlenme Kampi*. Inegöl: *Inegöl Dinlenme Kampi*, 45 km (28 mi.) east of Bursa. Kepez: Troy: *Sen Kamping*. *Sabit Turistik Kamp*, at the locality called Çamlik, near Troy. Tuzla: *Dinlenme Kampi*, 42 km (26 mi.) south of Istanbul, beach. Yalova: *Dinlenme Kampi*.

SKIING. Uludağ, 21 miles southwest of Bursa, is Turkey's up-and- coming ski area, with a season from November to April. There are 5 chair lifts and 3-T-bars, some après-ski activity.

But as this is only a developing area, it would be as well to check in advance regarding amenities and opening dates of hotels if you plan a winter vacation.

SHOPPING can be fun in this region, and profitable, as the Bazaar in Bursa, vast and attractive, is much cheaper for all items than that of Istanbul, with the sole exception of leather clothing.

USEFUL ADDRESSES. Tourist offices or tourist information: Bursa, Atatürk Cad., tel. 23-59; Çanakkale, Iskele Karşisi, near the embarcadero; Edremit, ask for the *Turizm Bürosu. Türk Hava Yollari Airlines:* Bursa, Atatürk Cad. 90; Balikesir, Kuvetler Cad., 2; Bandirma, Cumhuriyet Meydani 2; *Denizyollari* Shipping Lines: Bandirma; Çanakkale; Gelibolu; Karabiga. On Bozcaada Island, ask for Mr. Orhan Yunatçi: on Imroz Island, contact Mr. Tahsin Özsöz.

Exploring the Marmara Area

From Üsküdar to the capital, Ankara, the distance is 445 km. (276 miles). After you've driven 20 km. (12 miles), you must decide whether to continue on E 5 to Izmit and then turn right for Yalova, or to take the ferry. (You can also take the ferry from Istanbul, but not with a car.) Since your immediate destination is Bursa, it's up to you to decide whether you feel like giving a passing nod to Izmit.

Izmit is a city of 70,000, less than 100 km. (62 miles) from Istanbul (Üsküdar). It was originally called Olbia at the time of its founding in the eighth century B.C., and was completely destroyed by Lysimachus following the death of his master, Alexander the Great. Nicomedes I rebuilt it a century later, calling it Nicomedia. In those days, Izmit enjoyed a certain prominence as the capital of Bithynia. Nicomedes III died without an heir in 74 B.C. bequeathing the city to Rome. Rebuilt by Diocletian after the Gothic raid of 259, Nicomedia became rapidly the fourth city of the Roman Empire and for a short, glorious moment was capital of the eastern half. Accusing the Christians of having set fire to his palace, Diocletian instituted their most violent persecution till he abdicated in 305 near Nicomedia.

It was here that the Seljuks first reached the shores of the Marmara. Not long after, in 1086, Byzantium recaptured Nicomedia and kept it until the 14th century. The Ottomans again changed its name, calling it Iznikmit. Since Nicaea, a short distance to the south, had likewise changed its name, to become Iznik, Iznikmit was contracted to Izmit, to prevent confusion.

See its ancient walls, originally Greek, rebuilt by the Romans and the Byzantines. The Roman aqueduct is fairly well preserved. Ruins of a second-century fountain (*nymphaion*), which must have been quite lovely, are here, too. Need we remind you that the beaches are excellent everywhere here? Sun-worshippers will sense this intuitively!

If you have a few hours to spare, carry on along E 5 as far as Adapazari (35 km., 21 miles), which suffered so very badly in the 1967 earthquake. The natural scenery hereabouts, including the Dikmen Tepesi, slightly over a mile high, is perhaps more impressive than the local historical relics, the most important of which is a 1,400-foot-long stone bridge built by Emperor Justinian. The return trip via Sapanca, along the south shore of Lake Sapanca, is highly recommended, especially for fishermen and water-sports fans. Lovelier still is the drive south from Adapazari up the Sakarya valley and across the mountains to Iznik and thence to Bursa, to return via Yalova, making thus a complete roundtrip.

Iznik (Nicaea)

Though there are numerous prehistoric sites round the twenty-mile long Lake Iznik, the city was only founded in 316 B.C. and six years later conquered by Lysimachus and renamed Nikaea in honor of his wife. Bythinia's rival capital was the site of two ecumenical councils during the Byzantine era. A Nicene Council in 325 rejected Aryanism (the theory that Christ was to be considered as human, not divine); denied the idea of the Holy Trinity; and condemned the doctrine of the consubstantiality of the Word and the Godhead. The second Nicene Council, in 787, denounced iconoclasm. In 362, in between these two councils, Julian the Apostate attempted to reinstate the pagan cult, but the gods of antiquity failed to measure up to the new ideals of monotheism.

Near the end of the 11th century, as the result of an ill-timed appeal made to the Turkish troops by a pretender to Byzantium's throne—Melik Shah captured the city and held it under his sway, changing its name to Iznik. His successor, Kiliç Arslan ("Sword's Lion"), put up a strong defense against the impending Western invasion.

It was right here on these plains that the First Crusade came to an end, and not a day too soon. This expedition had been intended as a sort of dress rehearsal for what was to follow; in reality, it was a distressing "crusade of the poor". Its members were a host of stray souls, utterly destitute, who had been dispatched hastily to handle the emergency until the professional crusaders could get properly organized. The First Crusade deteriorated rapidly into a series of forays by highway robbers and cut-throats on the rampage, constituting a serious menace. Led by Peter the Hermit and the Penniless, they cut a bloody swath across Europe, and soon began strewing their path with the bodies of their own members, as the result of dissension in the ranks. Epidemics helped to decimate their numbers. At the news of their approach, Constantinople became terror-stricken, and simply barricaded itself within its walls to let them go by. It was the sultan of Nicaea who took it upon himself to exterminate every last one of them.

The First Crusade of the Barons reconquered Nicaea with the help of the imperial fleet, transported on rollers from the Sea of Marmara across the mountains to the Lake of Nicaea. Handed back to the Byzantines, it became their capital during the occupation of Constantinople by the Latins. After a long siege, the Turks returned under Sultan Orhan in 1331, and though plundered by Tamerlane's Mongols, Iznik became the center for the manufacture of the lovely tiles which decorate so many mosques and palaces throughout Turkey. Decline set in with the transfer of that thriving industry to the Tekfur Sarayi in Istanbul in the 18th century.

A good part of the Roman and Byzantine ramparts is still visible, complete with half-moon-shaped turrets. You can readily detect the successive stages in their construction, each one marking the advent of a new defender. At a certain period, it was common practice to "import" building materials, principally marble, from ancient ruins. The conquerors' cause was abetted no end by a series of convenient earthquakes at the end of the fourth century, three of them occuring during one ten-year period alone. Men went on rebuilding unceasingly, and towers that had once been semi-circular occasionally were turned into square ones.

The vestiges of four different epochs are still clearly discernible. The Romans relics include, first, the so-called Istanbul Gate, incorporating a triumphal arch of Vespasian. Nearby is a second-century tomb in the form of a pyramid. The Lefke Gate on the east was built in honor of Hadrian's visit in A.D. 120. Perhaps the handsomest of all is the Yenişehir Gate on the south, built under Claudius II. Since invading attacks came mainly from the south, this last gate has had to undergo frequent restorations. The ruined Lake Gate (Göl Kapisi) leads to the blue waters of the large lake, on whose shores a solitary tree and a few stones mark the site of Constantine's palace, now mostly submerged. Here the emperor convoked the stormy Second Ecumenical Council in 325. Pliny the Younger, who was a governor of the region and also left his stamp on Bursa, built the Gymnasium Theater in the southwestern part of the city. A large, remarkably well-preserved fifth-century tomb, with glowing murals depicting peacocks, flowers and abstract designs, was discovered under a hill in 1967. (The museum guardian has the key to this tomb.)

The Seventh Ecumenical Council was held in Nicaea's main monument, the St. Sophia Basilica. This building subsequently became identified with the third, or Seljuk, epoch, and later on with the fourth epoch—the Ottoman—when it was restored by the famous Turkish architect Sinan. (The Seventh Council condemned iconoclasm.) Recent excavations in the city have unearthed traces of mosaics and frescoes.

Two other churches date from this same period, the Koimesis (Dormition of the Virgin, 11th century) and Aghios Triphon. You can see aqueducts that were the work of Justinian, and which were repaired by Orhan; they are still in use today.

The only outstanding souvenir of the Seljuk interlude is the Ismail Bey Hamam (bath) near the First Gate. The Ottoman period, which was the last one, displayed greater activity. It is of more than passing interest to note that a Jewish community was probably established at Nicaea, from the evidence of the reused stones in the well of the Böcek Ayazmasi (this underground room can be visited only with the permission of the archeological muscum). A Hebrew inscription is recognizable on the well-curb, along with a design of the *menorah*, the seven pronged candelabrum that is the emblem of Judaism.

During the Turkish period, Suleiman the Magnificent (1520–1566) outdid himself beautifying ancient Nicaea, which by then had become Iznik. The art and production of ceramics soared to unprecedented heights. Although Turkish architecture has conserved a blend of characteristics from all four periods, it is obvious that it had not yet become completely crystallized and that it was still groping toward a definitive form of expression. As proof of this, note for example the *türbe* of Haci Camasas and that of Yakup Çelebi, both of them from the 14th century and hence predating Suleiman's constructions. The Yeşil Cami, or Green Mosque (near the Lefke Gate), is still more outstandingly typical, and foreshadows Bursa the Green.

There are numerous fascinating monuments of this "Golden Age", during which the artists' and architects' preoccupations with new form prevented them from giving in to conformism. Examples are the *medrese* (school) of Suleiman Paşa, the mosques of Mahmud Çelebi, Haci Hamza, and Haci Özbek. (*Haci*, or *Hadj* in Arabic, is the word used to designate those who have made the pilgrimage to Mecca.) Toward the end of the 14th century, Sultan Murad I built an *imaret* in honor of his mother, Nilüfer Hatun. (An *imaret* is a building constructed in the public interest.) The local museum is installed here.

If you can spend more time, you'd be well advised to continue on to Yenişehir (south) to see Sinan Paşa's 14th-century mosque.

Halfway between Yalova and Bursa, the Gulf of Gemlik and the city of the same name, once known as the Pirates' Hideout, invite you to a swim on the sandy beach. The road rises, the view extends and Bursa, the brightly-glowing jewel of Turkish art is then only 30 km. (19 miles) distant.

Bursa (Brusa)

"*Prusa ad Olympium*, big town in Asian Turkey at the foot of Mount Olympus. Fortified castle in the center of town. Partly enclosed by walls. Extremely narrow streets even for an Asian town, with many houses standing backed up against the mountain, their upper storeys letting out onto gardens. About 70 mosques, largely in ruins. A short distance from the walls there are seven hot-spring baths, known since earliest antiquity. Immense warehouse for raw silk, trade in which commodity is carried on by caravans from Smyrna and Aleppo. Bursa is believed to have been founded by Prusias, king of Bithynia. Following the splitting up of the Roman Empire, the Eastern Emperors controlled the town until 1325, when it was captured by Orhan, who made it the seat of his own empire. After being set fire to by Tamerlane following his victory over Bayezit, razed by Isa (the son of the latter), and rebuilt by Mohammed I, the town was besieged and captured by Suleiman; it was burned again in 1415 during the civil war between Mohammed I and Musa. Estimated population 50,000."

The foregoing extract is taken from a guidebook written some 150 years ago. Returned travelers have been heard to state that

BURSA
(NOT TO SCALE)

1 Ulu Camii
2 Orhan Camii
3 Yeşil Camii & Museum
4 Yeşil Türbé
5 Emir Sultan Camii
6 Yıldırım Bayezit Camii
7 Tourist Office
8 Muradiye Camii

🕌 Mosques 🕌 Türbé

although Istanbul may have disappointed them, Bursa never has. The main explanation is that Bursa (with a current population of 150,000) is completely lacking in any dual nature. It is Turkish in all respects and nothing but Turkish. There's no problem about monuments being pre-Christian, Christian, or Islamic. Another explanation lies in the overall predominance of one single color, yeşil, green.

This is the venerable green of Islam, a deep, changeable sea-green hue, iridescent with patina. The Turks refer to Yeşil Bursa in much the same way that Westerners refer to the green of Erin. (However, to the Moslem mind, green is not necessarily the color of hope that it represents to some cultures.) Let yourself relax for a few minutes at a sidewalk café near the Yeşil Cami with the city spreading out at your feet. You will observe an age-old serenity undisturbed by modern factories, though Bursa is still the center of a flourishing silk industry, beside producing attractive towels. But modern structures are encroaching on the homogeneity of this lovely city.

As noted above, the city's name is derived from that of Prusias II, king of Bithynia in the third century B.C. Prior traces point to earlier occupation of the region by Phrygians, Lydians, and Mysians. After defeating Croesus of Sardis (to the south) in the sixth century B.C., Cyrus the Persian controlled the area. Luck must have been with Bursa from the outset—at any rate, it has no known history of really dire catastrophes. During the Roman occupation, it enjoyed the prestige of being governed by a distinguished personage, Pliny the Younger. The Seljuks strove for a long time to wrest it away from Byzantium and the Crusaders. After a bitter siege it fell to Orhan, in 1326, but immediately became the Ottoman capital until imperial expansion necessitated transfer to Edirne (in Europe) in 1413. As the capital, Bursa naturally witnessed the first flowering of Ottoman architecture, interrupted temporarily by the defeat at Ankara (1402), but even the Mongol hordes of Tamerlane, perhaps because they had sated their blood lust elsewhere, occupied Bursa without inflicting any serious depredations.

Bursa's lessened political significance in no way interfered with its importance as a trading-post on the east-west caravan route. As a matter of fact, the ensuing years of its history are singularly lacking in excitement, and it's just as well. At the end of World War I, there was a short-lived invasion by Greek forces in 1920. In 1922, the Turkish victory was followed by an exchange of people—Bursa's Greek residents departed and were replaced by Turks returning from Greece.

It's a good idea to begin your visit with the Great Mosque, Ulu Cami, at the eastern gate of the fortifications, begun by Murat I in 1379, completed in the reign of Mehmet I in 1421, and extensively restored in 1967 after recent earthquakes. The distinctive thrust of its silhouette, topped by a cluster of 20 domes, provides a spectacle that is unique in all of Turkey. In the interior the domes are supported (in groups of four) by five naves, the latter in turn separated by twelve pillars. The central dome has a window covered by a grillwork through which the daylight filters. Directly beneath is the *şadırvan*, or fountain for ablutions, in the middle of the prayer room.

It isn't necessary to be able to decipher Arabic in order to revel in the exquisiteness of the embellishments, which consist, (as usual) in quotations from the Koran. The Turks are fond of saying, and understandably so, that Bursa's Great Mosque is a museum of calligraphy. See the manuscript copy of the Koran ornamented with gold thread work and dated in the year 770 of the Hegira. Alas, the *mihrap* (prayer niche), which was originally decorated with ceramics, has now been daubed over with paint. The cedarwood *mimber* (pulpit and staircase) has been preserved intact.

The Orhan Cami, or Mosque of Orhan, Bursa's conqueror, is another of the most ancient Ottoman mosques (1417). Continue eastward across the Gökdere River and you will come upon two wonderful sights—the Yeşil Cami and the Yeşil Türbe, both built early in the 15th century by Mehmet I Çelebi. They face each other across Green Street, above the Archeological Museum in the former *medrese*, the theological school, which contains interesting Bythinian, Hellenistic and Roman finds, besides lovely hand-written Korans.

Like the exception that proves the rule, the Green Mosque testifies to the success of a series of restorations. One century ago, a Frenchman named Parvillée brought to light the magnificent ceramics to which the building owes its name. An earthquake at the end of the 19th century wrought considerable havoc, and the mosque's minarets suffered particular damage; the Turkish architect Asim Bey did a remarkable job of repairing and restoring the wrecked parts. The loggias superimposed above the main entrance are the *divan* (or lecturehall) and the *mahfil* (lounge) of Sultan Mehmet I Çelebi. The *mihrap* stands over 50 feet high.

The Green Mausoleum dates from 1421 and is the last resting-place of Mehmet I Çelebi. Rich ceramics decorate the interior of the octogonal edifice crowned by a cone-shaped roof. The *mihrap* here is every bit as handsome as the one in the mosque.

Two more mosques lie farther east—the Mosque of Emir Sultan, Bayezit I's son-in-law, and the Yildirim Bayezit Mosque, completed in 1403, which is an outstanding specimen of Ottoman art. The former fell victim to an earthquake at the end of the 18th century. Although immediately rebuilt by Selim III, it suffered further damage from a new quake in 1855 and had to be even more extensively restored. If you're equipped with a movie-camera, or even if you aren't, you'll enjoy the marvelous view from all directions at the top of the hill south of the mosque. The convenient nearby funicular will get you safely to the mountain.

The center of Bursa is called the *Hisar*, or citadel. Murat II's mosque, the Muradiye, lies to the west. It was built in the 15th century to serve simultaneously as both mosque and *medrese*. The overall use of ribbed arches is a distinguishing feature of its interior, which has a handsome *şadırvan* and fine ceramics.

This mosque is surrounded by *türbes*. Sultan Murat's own *türbe* is notable for its open dome, its ceramics, and its columns with Corinthian capitals. In addition, there are the *türbes* of Hevletşah Hatun (the wife of Bayezit I); of the latter's son Musa, distinguished by a blend of green tiles; of Prince Cem, the son of Mehmet the Conqueror (red ceramics); of Prince Mustafa, son of Suleiman the Magnificent; and of Şehzade Mahmut, where the coffins of four imperial princes are surrounded by a uniquely beautiful pattern of light and dark blue tiles. The 11 *türbes* grouped round a fountain are surely some of the world's most serene resting places. Equally peaceful is the atmosphere in the so-called House of Murat II, nearby, which preserves the dignity but also the discomfort of upper-class domesticity in the 17th century.

The record proves that Osman Gazi failed to capture Bursa, but his wish was to be buried there. In pious fulfilment of this desire, his son Orhan erected a *türbe* for his father between the *Hisar* and Tophane, on the site of the ancient basilica of St. Elijah, which had been converted into a mosque. Orhan himself reposes nearby, in the mausoleum of Orhan Gazi, its square dome resting on four pillars. The tombs of both father and son were made of silver.

Don't miss Bursa's most ancient building, Emir Han, the caravanseray, admirably restored within the completely reconstructed large covered bazaar.

Also be sure to attend at least one performance of the "sword and shield" dance, the *kiliç kalkan*, a basic form of local folk-dancing. You'll scarcely know what to thrill to the most—the costumes, the dancers' agility, or their impeccable rhythm (accomplished without the benefit of any musical instruments), which is struck by the measured beat of metal clicking against metal.

And above all else, don't leave Bursa until you've worn yourself to an absolute frazzle just poking around in it. But you'll be too fascinated by the absorbing drama of the passing scene in the little back streets, the old houses, and the open-work wooden balconies, to even think about such a banal thing as fatigue.

In Çekirge (buses leave from the Yeşil Cami), the principal monument is Murat I's mosque. Its originality resides in the nationality of its architect, who was a 14th-century Italian prisoner. The sultan's tomb, opposite, is a restoration—another earthquake centered here. The *hamam* of Eskikaplica, probably the oldest bath in continuous use, dates from the 14th century and incorporates vestiges of Justinian's imperial baths. The three 16th and 17th-century baths near the Çelik Palas Hotel are also very interesting.

Mysia's Mount Olympus, the Uludağ, is only 35 km. (21 miles) southwest of Bursa. People nowadays use it as a winter ski resort. The Romans and Byzantines enjoyed it as a summer retreat, besides letting it supply the snow which cooled wine and fruit in the palaces of Constantinople. In case you're mildly astonished at stumbling upon Mount Olympus in Asia Minor, all this Turkish atmosphere may have made you momentarily overlook the fact that the Greeks hung around these parts for quite a while. The Uludağ, or <u>Great Mountain, was given another name</u> by the Turks, who called it Keşişdağı, or <u>the mountain of the monks.</u> Back in the eighth century, there was a monastery here. It served as an underground refuge for persecuted priests during the war of the icons.

Inegöl, 44 km. (27 miles) east, contains rupestrian tombs and a 15th-century mosque, the Ishak Pasha Cami. Nearby lie the ruins of the Ortaköy caravanseray.

Toward the Sea of Marmara

Heading northwest from Bursa, you approach the shores of the Marmara. The port of Bursa, <u>Mudanya,</u> was called Myrlea in ancient times; the armistice that consecrated Turkey's victorious War of Independence was signed here in 1922.

Farther to the west on Route 2 lies Bandirma, whose name is a corruption of the earlier Pandermo, or Panormos, meaning "harbor of confidence". The Sea of Marmara can be pretty rough around these parts, except in September, and sailors are grateful for shelter here. Virtually no ancient ruins can be seen, but there are Seljuk and Ottoman monuments. Lake Manyas, to the south, is a bird sanctuary.

All the above is in Balikesir province, which provides a foretaste of the country's fantastic storehouse of archeological treasures. Moreover, this is one of the loveliest parts of Asia Minor. It's hard to know just where to begin and in what order to continue with the scenery, the sites, and the beaches. Erdek, north of Bandirma and one of the most attractive ports on the Sea of Marmara, is blessed with only the gentlest southern breezes. Vineyards, olive groves, and fruit orchards surround it, and there's plenty of historical sightseeing to be done in the vicinity. Kyzikos, where Alcibiades won his great victory over the Spartans in the Peloponnesian War, is here, as are Demir-Kapi, Sulubodur and Kocakilise (temple of Hadrian, the agora, and a fortress). For archeology fans there are also Balya, Edremit, Burhaniye, and Dursunbey. If you're thinking of taking a cure, there's an abundance of mineral spas, including Gönen (rheumatism), Susurluk (skin afflictions), and Kazdaği (which is the Mount Ida of ancient times—its hot sulphur springs bubble forth at a temperature of 158° F!). For sportsmen, the mountain game hunting in the forests of this mythological peak (north of Edremit) includes boars, deer, and bears.

The road (Route 2) follows the sea coast (more or less) via Gönen and Biga. Your destination is Troy. Before leaving the Sea of Marmara, remember that its beaches are so numerous and so varied that you can't help finding at least one that's just the ticket. (When the Turkish government gets around to completing its road building and tourist accommodation facilities, Asia Minor should be in a position to provide ideal vacation spots for an endless stream of visitors.)

The Dardanelles

The way to Troy is through the town of Çanakkale. The road (Route 2) lies in a mountainous region slashed with deep valleys. Scrub, undergrowth, and forests are everywhere. *Çanak* means saucer, which is to say that dishware is produced in this fortress (*kale*). Because of the town's location, in the ideal spot for controlling the Dardanelles, it was coveted by assorted conquerors. The Venetians who set themselves up here were followed by the Byzantines, and lastly by the Turks. Çanakkale got into the news again during World War I, as Gallipoli lies across the straits. One Turkish general managed to foil all the Allies' thrusts in a series of bloody battles—this was Mustafa Kemal, who hadn't yet acquired the surname of Atatürk. His victory is commemorated by a great monument (135 feet tall) rising along the shores of the peninsula, just across the straits. The French and British cemeteries are at the tip of the peninsula.

Again in 1922, Mustafa Kemal played the boldest hand in the whole poker game of his extraordinary career. Izmir had been recaptured, but the Greeks were mustering a new army in Thrace. These troops were going to have to be stamped out before they could even get a crack at Turkey, which at that point wasn't yet entirely liberated. Kemal had no fleet. He dispatched his troops overland toward Europe. A British contingent blocked the way at Çanakkale.

Although Britain sympathized with Greece in the fray, the British hadn't yet actually gone into action. The Tommies were waiting in their firmly entrenched positions. The situation was so confused politically that Sir Charles Harrington, the Commander-in-Chief of the Allied Forces, wasn't quite sure whether or not London would approve him in case he had to fight in accordance with previous instructions. Kemal, by forcing his way through, was running the risk of thrusting Great Britain—plus France and Italy—over into the opposite camp. The substantial gains already won in his War of Independence would be wiped out overnight. It was imperative for him to get through and equally important for British neutrality to be preserved.

The Turks proceeded. When the British summoned them to halt, they kept on advancing. But without firing a shot. It was a colossal bluff by both sides. If a single nervewracked soldier had let fly a bullet in the unbearably tense atmosphere, the powder-barrel would have blown up. The British officer ordered his men to take aim. The Turks just kept marching with their rifles slung over their shoulders. No fighting took place that day at Çanakkale.

The Trojan War

Disregard all the possibly well-intentioned individuals who may try to dissuade you from going to Troy on the grounds that it's a pointless trip to see nothing but a vast heap of rubble. Troy is a site that almost literally calls out to you and stirs up childhood dreams. For after all, what really matters is the scenes that are aroused in your imagination; the present state of the actual surroundings is of little importance.

Maybe Troy today is but a series of trenches, and maybe Çanakkale, the "citadel of the saucers", is only an unprepossessing town. All right. The recorded truth remains that right on this spot is where a lot of early people, whose names have now become legend, lived, clashed, fought and got killed—Priam, Hector, Andromacus, Astyanax—the three generations of Trojans—Agamemnon, Menelaus, Ulysses, Achilles, both the Ajaxes, and Patroclus, the self-sacrificing victim, among others. Perched high above the warriors' struggle, the gods on Olympus championed the cause of one side or another and waged their war on these desiccated plains. The story goes that Troy was destroyed and rebuilt nine times, rather like a cat with nine lives. For centuries, people had ceased to believe that any of it had ever really existed, until at last, one fine day, there came an amateur archeologist, one of a particularly stubborn breed, and everything began all over again. (And anyway, you can't just discard that gorgeous Helen!)

But it's necessary to delve even further back behind the scenes to history's very first beauty contest, held on Mount Ida, with a single judge, and with an apple as its prize. That's really how it began. The story is famous because of the scandal that ensued and because of the war celebrated by Homer. A brief recapitulation is in order:

Everybody, including gods and mortal guests, was having a gay time at the wedding of the nereid Thetis and Peleus, King of the Myrmidons. Suddenly, without even an invitation, Eris, the enraged Goddess of Discord crashed the gate, and tossed a golden apple onto the banquet table with the challenging cry, "For the most beautiful girl of all!" Right away, Aphrodite, Hera, and Athena (the three goddesses symbolizing love, wedded fidelity, and virginity) began to argue over the apple. When they called on Zeus to settle the dispute, he cautiously disclaimed all competence, and appointed an arbiter, a shepherd named Paris, who was a mortal unaware of his own royal descent. At his birth, Paris's father and mother, Priam and Hecuba, had been duly forewarned that their newborn progeny was doomed to cause the downfall of his native land. He had hence been exiled forthwith to the slopes of Mount Ida to watch over flocks. The child was ignorant of his true circumstances, and his father didn't know that the boy hadn't been slain as ordered. (His life had been spared through a quite understandable bit of maternal trickery on the part of Hecuba.)

And now here was the young shepherd surrounded by the three proud beauties, called upon to judge them, his hesitation rendered all the more acute by the fact that all three of them, including the chaste Athena, had stripped to win. No wonder the poor country lad's head was whirling! He was torn between smiles, majesty, gravity, ardor, modesty, and wisdom. Legend has it that he made love to each goddess separately, and of course, each goddess made him lavish promises. Hera promised him greatness; Athena promised wisdom; and the shrewd Aphrodite gave him the address of the most beautiful of mortals, Helen, the daughter of Leda and wife of Menelaus, King of Sparta.

Maybe it was this latter prospect that prejudiced the young

shepherd's judgment, or perhaps it was the fact that the goddess of love had made a point of assuring Paris that he was as handsome as a god. Whatever the real reason, she got the edge over her rivals and carried off the apple, to the immense chagrin of the other two ladies, who were never to forgive.

The rest is history. Under Aphrodite's protection, Paris hied himself to the Spartan court and instantly captivated Helen. The two lovers fled home to father and mother in Troy, and to Paris's big brother, Hector. Menelaus, the deserted spouse, was beside himself with rage. He also had a big brother, named Agamemnon, to whom he sounded the alarm. Agamemnon called out the regulars and the reserves, and everybody who was anybody in Greece got ready to set sail, except young Achilles, whom only crafty Odysseus could recognize in his maidenly disguise.

War was declared. The fortunes of battle varied depending on which goddess's day it happened to be. When Achilles refused to fight and sulked in his tent, the besiegers suffered a setback for lack of a leader, and the Trojans licked their lips for joy. But came the day when Hector slew Patroclus. Achilles's vengeance was as swift as his grief was boundless. It was only natural for Hector to flee to save his skin, because Achilles was utterly fearless—at his birth, his mother, Thetis, had dipped him into the waters of the Styx, thereby rendering him invulnerable. The only spot on which he might be attacked was the heel by which his mother had held him. And the inevitable came to pass when Achilles killed Hector.

Now it was Paris's turn to avenge his brother. Poised on the ramparts, the erstwhile shepherd, who was also a crack shot, let fly a poisoned arrow that found its mark straight to Achilles's heel. The hero was dead and Troy's walls were intact. The war was dragging on futilely and might still be continuing if finally Odysseus hadn't had an idea. There was a big to-do about getting the ships ready to leave, and sailing off with not a soul left on the shore. The only thing that remained behind was a last offering to the gods, an immense wooden horse. The Trojans proceeded to haul the horse into the city, amid much singing and laughter. They celebrated their victory all through the night. Came the dawn's cold light, and all of Troy's warriors were out equally cold, dead drunk, some of them in their own beds or their neighbors', others sprawled where they had fallen. The time was ripe for the Trojan horse's belly to spring open and release all of Greece's ace swordsmen. While a few of them stole out to unlock the city gates for their returned comrades, the rest launched the massacre. Not a brick was left standing in Troy. The only record we have of all this is the epic masterpiece written by the blind poet, some 500 years later. The *Iliad* is the poetic equivalent of the retrospective covering of a battle by the world's first war correspondent.

THE TROY OF HOMER
(13th Century B.C.-6th Layer)

The particular city of Troy in which the events recounted above took place was the sixth of the total of nine layers that have been excavated. But that's another story:

As late as the beginning of the 19th century, Troy was commonly held to be a figment of man's imagination, a myth. But there just happened to be someone in Germany, the son of a Protestant minister from Mecklenburg, who had come to have faith in all this rubbish and clung steadfastly to his convictions. His name was Heinrich Schliemann, and he was a grocery clerk. He took advantage of a long illness to study English, French, and Italian. Later on he tackled Arabic, Latin, and Russian, but throughout his adventurous and restless life he didn't dare to take up Greek, for fear of "not being able to resist the call of the ancient world". In 1863, having amassed a fortune in the California goldrush, he gave up everything to devote himself to his consuming passion, which was to prove that a blind bard had sung of a true story, not a myth.

The few courageous scholars who wistfully admitted that Troy (Ilion) might actually have existed believed it to have been located near the village of Bunarbaşi, because of the two nearby springs that corresponded with those in the Twelfth Canto of the *Iliad*. Using ordinary common sense, Schliemann decided that the Greeks, who had to go back and forth from their ships to the city walls, couldn't have managed at this site, which was a full three hours' march from the sea. Prying about and sifting through all the bits of evidence, he found that Hisarlik fitted in much better with the circumstances. He began digging in the spring of 1870. For years, Schliemann paid about one hundred laborers and helpers out of his own pocket, while the scientific world, with few exceptions, looked disdainfully down on the efforts of this self-taught archeologist. If the miracle hadn't finally come to pass, Schliemann would have been forgotten long ago. He discovered seven separate cities stacked one on top of the other, plus two other layers. All of these were Troy.

Exploring Truva (Troy)

From the excavation site, you can discern the first foothills of Mount Ida, where the award of the golden apple of discord was made. When you climb the sprawling mound of rubble and become aware of the various well-marked layers, it turns out to be intensely fascinating. Its nine "floors" have certainly yielded up more treasures than even Schliemann imagined.

At the very bottom of the heap is Troy I, a vestige of some 3,500 years ago. It was a small fort built on rock. The complete layout hasn't yet been dug out. However, a *megaron*-type house can be seen, with a large rectangular room containing a central hearth. The city's founders had presumably come in from the west. The second stratum, which dates back to 2600–2300 B.C., shows a city enclosed by walls. It led Schliemann to make a miscalculation. He discovered a hoard of jewels there that he wrongly attributed to Priam. (This treasure in turn aroused lively arguments, and was spirited by Schliemann out of Turkey and worn by his Greek wife on festive occasions in Athens. After keeping the museums of the world in suspense for 20 years, German patriotism proved stronger than the justice of the Turkish claim and the emotional Greek appeal; the treasure was bequeathed to Berlin, where it stayed until 1945. The victorious Russians confiscated it, and today it is in the U.S.S.R.) Schliemann concluded that Troy II was undoubtedly the city described in the *Iliad*. The existence of wide gates equipped with ramps for chariots seemed to bear out his theory. Despite careful excavating the third, fourth, and fifth levels, ranging from 2300 to 1900 B.C., haven't yet provided much in the way of new finds. It's just barely possible to make out where one ends and the other begins.

Troy VI dates from 1900 to 1300 B.C. If you're feeling indulgent, you might possibly concede that the walls are pretty much intact. Priam is presumed to have been born here. For purposes of classification, Troy VII has been divided into two parts, "A" (1300–1200 B.C.) and "B" (1200–900 B.C.). Authentification was possible through the identifying of pottery from the Mycenian period. Troy VII-"A" is the city that was rebuilt after an earthquake. The Greeks seized and sacked it around 1200 B.C.; after they had left, the Trojans rolled up their sleeves and began rebuilding. The result was Troy VII-"B".

Although they don't all agree on the matter of the distribution of the various strata, scholars are in accord as concerns the sequence of events. Opinions differ with regard to chronology. Some authorities are inclined to identify Troy VI as Homer's city and Troy VII as a postwar city occupied by a new group of people. Troy VIII and IX are unquestionably postwar. The Aeolians invaded it around 700 B.C. In the following century it was the Persians' turn. The Greek influence persisted nevertheless—there are a temple of Athena, an Odeon (south of the gate of Troy VI) and a theater on the east side. Alexander the Great got rid of the Persians. Lysimachus inherited Troy, which became New Ilion. The Romans arrived and started rebuilding. Julius Caesar paid a visit to Troy, which continued to exist until 400 A.D.

A brief tour: To the right of the entrance, a small museum displays a few specimens of Greek pottery of the classical period. Just follow the arrows: they bring you first to the ancient ramparts and a bit of the enclosure wall of Seventh Level Troy (Troy of the

Homeric heroes), with the foundations of one square tower still visible. This was a redoubtable wall not unlike that of Mycenae, forming an oval some 2,000 feet in circumference. A 16-foot-high wall made of rough-hewn stones and unbaked brick formed the top part, which was built up over a base 25 feet high and 16 feet thick. It contained at least three entrance gates and a postern.

The tour leads you through the east gate of Fifth Level Troy, the only remains of which are a few unprepossessing fragments of a jumble of residential buildings. Turn around and walk back to an esplanade, from which you have a view out over the coastal plains and the sea. Proceed north for a look at the ruins of the Temple of Athena, which was rebuilt by the Romans.

Along the northern ramparts lie scattered bits bequeathed by the divers epochs. Be sure to walk the length of the paved ramp (third millenium) leading up to the city, one of the most vivid reminders of what Troy must at one time have looked like. Continue on to a trench containing a partially restored shrine from Eighth Level Troy, including a sacrificial altar near two wells. On the south, the most interesting sight is that of the ruins of a Roman theater and the fragments of a mosaic paving.

An ancient gate of Sixth Level Troy brings you to the center of the site. This was the acropolis, where the main public buildings doubtless stood—the Romans did a pretty thorough job of levelling them. Retrace your steps and take leave of the illustrious city by way of the *bouleuterion* (assembly building), designed along the same lines as the theater.

A ruined city, a somewhat desolate site, a signpost reading "TRUVA" near the village of Hisarlik, a "hole in the ground" .... This is all that remains of history's most famed military expedition. If Homer hadn't composed the *Iliad*, would we even have known that Troy had existed? Who would hold a thought for the world's dead warriors if the poets didn't immortalize their exploits?

There are Greek, Roman, and Byzantine vestiges at Behramkale (Assos), aqueducts and an amphitheater at Troas (Alexandria or Kestanbol), and at Neandreia, on Mount Çiğridaği (near Ezine), there are ruins of a temple from the sixth and seventh centuries B.C. In addition, Çanakkale has a "Trojan" museum, and Çardak and Lapseki both contain Turkish monuments, although of no particular interest. Lapseki was the ancient Lampsacus, birthplace of the philosopher Anaxagoras, whose revolutionary theories about the universe scandalized the fifth century B.C. The shores of the straits are guarded by ancient and modern fortifications, flanked by Crimean War and World War I memorials.

Illustration at head of this chapter: A general view of Istanbul.

IZMIR

Seaport for Holidays and Commerce

The seafaring traveler will catch his first sight of the town at the far end of a square inlet, one side of which is open to the sea. The town itself, backed and half enclosed by Mount Pagos, faces westward. A ferryboat cuts across the bay to the suburb of Karşıyaka, which can also be reached by car, the long way, on the road that skirts the outline of the harbor. Far away and above, the 'velvet' fortress of Kadifekale overlooks Izmir and the Aegean Sea.

Legend attributes the first settlement at Tepekule near Bayrakli in the hollow of the bay to Smyrna, a queen of the Amazons, or to the Leleges, a roving piratical tribe. Aeolians took over in the 11th century B.C., to be replaced by the Ionians some 400 years later. Around 600 B.C., Alyattes III, King of Lydia, put the town to fire and sword. It was to be rebuilt two hundred years later by Alexander the Great near a sanctuary of Nemesis on the slopes of Mount Pagos, according to the advice of the goddess in a dream.

At his death, the town fell to the lot of Lysimachus. For a time, Smyrna belonged to the kingdom of Pergamum, until it was taken over by the Romans. Rebuilt by the Emperor Aurelius after the earthquake of 178 (Smyrna is exceptionally destruction-prone even for Asia Minor) the prosperous town became the site of one of the Seven Churches of the Apocalypse in Anatolia. The Arabs made several attempts to capture it, but the town held out, to fall at last, in the eleventh century, before the onslaught of the Seljuk Turks.

From 1097 on, Smyrna became a battlefield in the Crusades, passing back and forth between the forces of Islam and Christendom. Destroyed and restored successively by Byzantines and Seljuks, Smyrna was held by the Knights of Rhodes when Tamerlane sacked the town and slaughtered its inhabitants in 1402. Thirteen years later Sultan Mehmet I Çelebi incorporated it in the Ottoman Empire.

Towards the end of the fifteenth century, the Jews, driven from Spain, went to Smyrna and settled here, forming a lasting Sephardim community. But the Greeks still were in the majority, though from the age of Queen Elizabeth on, English traders as well as Dutch and French had formed an important foreign colony, mostly engaged in the lucrative tobacco trade. Despite repeated destructive earthquakes, especially in 1688 and 1778, Smyrna remained prosperous, the most important trading port on the coast.

At the end of the First World War the Greeks occupied the town. The Treaty of Sèvres in 1920 provided for Greek administration of the entire Aegean coast, but the Turkish revival under Mustafa Kemal soon led to a bloody struggle. In one last blow, he crushed the invader at Dumlupinar. After appalling losses the remnants of the Greek forces fell back on Smyrna and were together with the Christian townspeople evacuated across the Aegean. (Aristotle Onassis was one of those who escaped.)

On the 9th of September 1922, he whom his people called the Gazi made a wildly-cheered entry into the liberated port. The joy of the crowds was shortlived; the outbreak of a fire caught everybody, civilians and soldiers, friend and foe alike, in the blaze. The wind, benign Aeolus of the ancient Greeks, made a last stand for its routed countrymen by blowing on the flames. The wooden houses burned like matches, while hidden stores of munitions exploded. It was, in Mustafa Kemal's own words, "the end of an era". The liberation of Smyrna—from now on known by its Turkish name, Izmir—marked a twofold independence:

from the enemy after defeat in the World War, and from the defeated rulers of the Ottoman Empire.

Practical Information for Izmir

WHEN TO COME? The mild weather of April and May is the best for travel to Izmir and its outskirts. It is fairly pleasant in June and September, but July and August are hot months, in spite of the sea breezes.

HOW TO GET THERE? See *Practical Information* in the following chapter, *The Aegean Provinces*.

 WHAT TO SEE? The fire of 1922 destroyed almost all of the old town, only sparing the colorful sprawl of houses on the hillside at whose foot the main antique remains, including the 2nd-century Roman agora; the fortress of Kadifekale, on Mount Pagos, with its beautiful view over the bay of Izmir; the Archeological Museum in the Kültürpark; and the old inns (caravanserai). Opposite the Clock Tower, built in the beginning of the century, it is well worth taking a look at the small mosque of Konak, with its fine glazed tiles.

For a rest from sight-seeing, we recommend, for a quick swim, the beach at Inciralti, about seven miles out of town, towards Çeşme. A pleasant outing: the ferry-boat across the bay, towards Karşikaya.

Hotels

BÜYÜK EFES (L), Cumhuriyet Meydanı, is in itself alone worth a stay in Izmir. Set in a park in the heart of town, it at least equals more expensive *Hilton* in Istanbul. 300 air-conditioned rooms with bath, and all with balconies with wonderful views over the hillside or the sea; 24 suites. Roof and terrace restaurants, *Meyhane* nightclub (suppers and dancing). Five bars, tea-dances from October to June. A splendid swimming pool. (Büyük means "Grand".)

TANER (1), Cumhuriyet Bulvarı, 127 well-equipped rooms.

KISMET (2), 1377 Sok, near the Büyük Efes, 68 rooms, is less modern and cheaper. Airconditioned restaurant.

AN-BA (2), on Cumhuriyet Bulvarı, 51 rooms, airconditioned restaurant, is good value for the price.

Facing the sea, on Atatürk Caddesi, is the **Kilim** (2), 89 rooms. Restaurant.

In category (3), inexpensive, are the *Billur*, 70 rooms (60 with bath or shower) and the *Kaya*, 36 rooms with bath or shower. The former is on Basmahane Meyd., the latter on Gaziosmanpaşa Boulevard. *Kaya* has a restaurant.

Among the category (4), rock-bottom, hotels, the *Babadan*, Çankaya, 45 rooms (25 with shower), *Deniz*, Güzelbahçe Sehitler Cad., 17 rooms, and *Kabadayi*, Fevzi Paşa Bul., 72 rooms (30 with shower) are best.

Also-rans are the *Atlantik Palas*, Gazi Bulvari 126, *Karaoğlu*, on the same street, and the *Atlas*, Şair Eşref Bulvarı 1.

For camping near Izmir, see *Practical Information for the Aegean*, in the next chapter.

RESTAURANTS. Classical: Hotel *Büyük Efes* roof. Interest ng: *Yengeç*, seafood of superb caliber, as well as good service, Atatürk Caddesi 250; a few doors down, at 286, the *Abdullah*, with a Turkish setting; still on the same street, almost at the top corner of the Alsancak, the *Şafak*. *Ada* is a Turkish-style restaurant in the Kültür Parki, as is the *Şükran*, in a courtyard of the bazaar, 60 Anafartalar Caddesi. Near the landing wharf in the Konak Square, the *Deniz Lokantasi* is inexpensive. If you go out of town to Karşikaya, you can lunch reasonably and fairly well at *Tilla*, near the wharf.

Good food, fine view, a little on the "touristy" side: *Şato*, Eşrefpaşa Caddesi; the specialty of *Kale Gazinosu*, at the far end of Kadifekale, is *çipura* fish; on the waterfront, *Ülker Lokantasi* and *Imbat*, Atatürk Caddesi, near the Hotel Büyük Efes, are good.

NIGHT LIFE. Oriental dances at the nightclub of the Hotel *Büyük Efes;* in the Kültür Parki, dinner and dancing at the *Kübana;* floor show and dancing at the *Göl Gazinosu.*

OUTING TO ÇEŞME. Fifty-three miles of good asphalt road will take you to Çeşme, where the land juts out to sea, facing the Greek island of Chios. Leaving Izmir through the suburb of Karataş, you pass the *Mocamp* camping grounds, and very soon come to Inciralti, with its so-so beach. Fourteen miles later, turn to the left towards Seferhisar and Siğacik, a small port with a Genoese fortress and a nearby beach with a restaurant. Near the former are the ruins of the ancient Ionian city of Teos, where Anacreon sang the praise of wine, love and boys some 400 years before the erection of the famous Hellenistic temple of Dionysos.

After Urla, back on the road to Çeşme, you notice to your right the ruins of the flourishing Aeolian port of Clazomenai before the branch to the Karaburum peninsula and the remains of Ionian Erythraea, built during the Trojan War. Past the fine sand of Ilica, where hot sulphur springs bubble on the shore and in the sea, Çeşme, where a stronghold built by the Genoese overlooks the town from a height. The beach is wonderful, and there are good hotels (see *Hotels* in the Aegean chapter. Also re ferry to Chios). Nearby are the up-and-coming beaches of Alaçati, Çiftlik, Dalyan and Şifne.

USEFUL ADDRESSES. *Tourist information:* Offices of the Ministry of Tourism, Atatürk Caddesi 126 (tel. 22-026); Aegean Tourist Federation, Belediye İş Hani, Gazi Bulvari. *Consulates:* British and American. *Airlines:* THY, Hotel Büyük Efes; Swissair, Emlak Is Hani Building 106, Cumhuriyet Caddesi: Olympic Airways, Cumhuriyet Bulvari 137. *Turkish Maritime Lines (Denizyollari):* Atatürk Caddesi 128. *Post Office:* Atatürk Caddesi. *Travel Agencies:* Van der Zee Travel Service, Atatürk Caddesi 134; Egetur, Atatürk Caddesi 126; Doktoroglu, Hotel Büyük Efes. *Bus* for the Inciralti beach (in summer only), departure from Konak Square. *Motor coaches* to all points (Aydin, etc.), Santral Garaji, Bashamane.

Discovering Izmir

If today's Izmir is largely a modern town, it owes its newness to the great fire, which laid waste the old. Its newness means, says the well-known refrain of old-timers, that it is lacking in character. Yet Smyrna compares favorably with most Mediterranean ports, as the large new apartment houses are well constructed (a necessary precaution against the recurrent earthquakes) shining white or painted pleasing pastel shades. There is a Kültür-Park, a large oasis of green round an artificial lake, accomodating several museums besides the usual recreation centers, restaurants, and a yearly international fair.

The town, with its 420,000 inhabitants, has kept its old renown; it is still known as Güzel Izmir, "beautiful Smyrna". Nowadays, however, the beauty lies more in the sea and hills than in the houses on the side of Mount Pagos; it lies in the curving bay, in the moving greens and blues of the water, and in the *imbat*, the soft breeze that cools the harsh summer heat. Every afternoon, it ruffles the waves that beat more strongly against the stones of the wharf, dying down again at the hour when all Turks sit down at café tables for tea.

Izmir is the NATO headquarters for the southeast sector, and the large number of foreign military personnel adds to the modern international atmosphere. The solid frontage of tall blocks of flats is only broken at Cumhuriyet square with its statue of Atatürk and in the very center by Konak square, socalled after the large administrative building in the background and distinguished by a moorish clock tower—all the rage in the reign of Sultan Abdul Hamid II—which faces the delicate Yahli Cami, the Seaside Mosque, dating from the 18th century. Behind stretches the bazaar, a maze of narrow alleys not particularly interesting but the liveliest quarter.

Izmir is the second town in Turkey, after Istanbul, both as a port and as a center of industry; though it ranks first in export trade. (The annual Fair from 20 August to 20 September is the most important in the Eastern Mediterranean.) If the former Constantinople is a main stopover for passengers on cruise steamships, most cargo boats go to Izmir. Modern warehouses allow the fast storage of perishable goods in the well-equipped deepwater port at Alsancak.

What with earthquakes and fires, however, there is little left of historical interest outside of the Agora and Kadifekale.

To the ancient Greeks, the *agora* was both a public square and a marketplace. That of Izmir has the imposing remains of what was once a two-storied marble basilica, 525 feet long, the flagstones surrounded by a colonnade upholding the upper stories (which fell in when the colonnade itself slowly crumbled in the rain and wind of centuries). The reconstruction undertaken by the Romans in the time of Marcus Aurelius was necessitated by the devastating earthquake of the year 178.

Today, the word basilica calls to mind a church. In antiquity, it meant an indoor meeting place for merchants and bankers, politicians and statesmen, who gathered there to talk business and discuss policy. It was a sort of town hall and stock exchange, and, being the center of city life, had its market and temple, sometimes several.

At the far end of the alley, a far-sighted city council has built a glass frame to protect the valuable remains of three carefully restored statues: one of Poseidon-Neptune (one of whose arms and a bit of whose left foot are missing), one of Demeter-Ceres (recognizable as such), and one of Artemis-Diana (less recognizable).

Kadifekale, the "velvet fortress", overlooks the town from the top of Mount Pagos. It was originally part of the fortified wall of Smyrna, and a Roman road connected it to the *agora*. Why "velvet"? One of the reasons given, discounted by scholars but pleasing to the romantic-minded traveler, is the very look of the place. Seen from below, these bare walls that have withstood all weathers, blended their red stone with the grey rock to assume the changing sheen of rubbed velvet. The imposing fortifications were enlarged and strengthened by successive conquerors, till they enclosed two and a half acres of land. The round towers show Byzantine workmanship on Hellenistic foundations. It is a windy place, with a giddy view over the town, the harbor, the rounding bay, the sea, and, on the farther side, the mountain belt that protected Smyrna from the invasion of inland forces.

If the traveler has time to spare, there are, of course, other sights to see. First of all, the mosques—16th-century Hisar and Kemeralti, 18th-century Şadirvan, all heavily restored in the

19th. Near the first is the Mirkelam Han, now used as a covered bazaar, and like the other caravanserais, Kizlarağasi and Çaka-loglu, models of Ottoman architecture. There are still a few traces of the Acropolis of the original settlement at Tepecule; at the foot of the steep hill is a round edifice, supposedly the tomb of the legendary king Tantalus; three Roman aqueducts, restored by Byzantines and Turks, span the Melez stream; the Baths of Artemis are at Halkapinar, and those of Agamemnon near Inciralti; and above all there is the Archeological Museum in the Kültür-Park, which houses finds from the whole Aegean coast, including a superb bronze statue of Demeter, fished from the sea at Bodrum.

All outings are near at hand, on the outskirts of town. Seaside cafés, casino, and a beach are at Inciralti, little more than half an hour away; Karşiyaka, a wealthy suburb is on the other side of the bay—the ferry crossing takes 15 minutes, the drive around the bay on the road to Çanakkale slightly longer.

Büyük Yamanlar is a delightful mountain resort. Those suffering from kidney trouble or rheumatism can take a cure at the Baths of Agamemnon, half an hour away; the watering-place in Urla is even nearer. There are beaches with soft sand at Akkum and Inciralti, and another, poorer one, at Kilizman. For those who love the sea, it is worth going the 53 miles to Çeşme, and its many excellent beaches.

Izmir's numerous adequate hotels, including one of the best in Turkey, make it a natural center for excursions along the Aegean coast, especially the three great archeological sites of Pergamum, Ephesus and Sardis.

Illustration at head of this chapter: The port of Izmir.

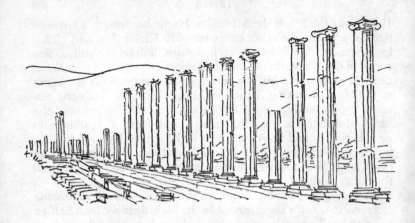

THE AEGEAN PROVINCES

Fabled Antiquities, Glorious Sun

Driven from European Greece by the Dorian invaders of the 12th century B.C., Aeolians and Ionians found a refuge on the hospitable islands and eastern shores of the Aegean. It was here that the slow awakening of the human spirit was transformed by the epic and lyric poets of genius some 500 years later. Inspired by Homer, Sappho and Anacreon (to name but the best known), philosophers, mathematicians, architects and sculptors in the glorious sixth century B.C. laid the foundations of western thought and art. Withdrawing temporarily before the alien Persian conqueror across the sea, Greek civilization returned triumphantly with Alexander the Great 200 years later, not only to the coastal towns where it originated, but spreading all over Western Asia. And thanks to the wealth and liberality of art-loving Hellenistic kings, temples, palaces and monuments of astonishing beauty and size multiplied in town and country alike.

The traveler is thereby warned not to be taken unawares by the sight of Greek temples and theaters, by the wonderful world of mythology that makes whole every broken stone. Although Hellas is today Greece, it once spread out through Anatolia, as every timeworm stone bears dumb witness.

So, the length of the coastline of the Aegean Sea, we shall travel a part of the ancient country of Mysia and the town of Pergamum, through Ionia and Lydia with Ephesus and Sardis, through Caria and its Halicarnassus, and down into Lycia, where Fethiye is located.

Practical Information for the Aegean Provinces

HOW TO GET THERE? By *THY Airline:* Istanbul-Izmir in 75 min., 5 flights a day; Ankara-Izmir in 100 min., twice daily. *By train:* the *Marmara* mototrain makes the run between Bandirma (Istanbul steamer) and Izmir 3 times a week; the Ankara-Izmir Express 3 times a week; the *Aegean* mototrain from Ankara to Izmir every day. *By ship:* the Izmir Express meets the *Kadeş* steamer, which takes 24 hours for the Istanbul-Izmir route. Other ships stop over at Kuşadasi, Bodrum, Marmaris, and Fethiye.

Transportation to Pergamum (Bergama), by bus leaving from Izmir; for Ephesus (Efes), by train from Izmir-Alsancak to Selçuk, and from the Selçuk railway station by bus; to Sardis (Sardes) by both bus and train from Izmir.

MOTORING. The coastal road from the Dardanelles to Bodrum and Marmaris as well as the roads between the main towns and places of interest are paved, though often winding and narrow. The road from Muğla to Fethiye is stabilized and possible, but the tracks to some archeological sites, such as Heraclea ad Latmos and Xanthos are not easy going. On leaving Turkey, for drivers in the neighborhood of Izmir who wish to bypass Istanbul or Çanakkale on the way home, there are boats in Çeşme, 53 miles west of Izmir, that ferry cars to the nearby Greek island of Chios (Sakiz in Turkish). From there, a Greek line ships them to Piraeus, making in all a short cut of 500 miles. Make inquiries on the spot, for the Çeşme-Chios timetable tends to be vague. Like the Bodrum-Kos and the Marmaris-Rhodes crossing, this is only for travelers who enjoy the unforeseen and are not put out by delays or slight mishaps. On the other hand, the Dikili-Mythilene crossing is easygoing for the worst-tempered traveler.

WHAT TO SEE? A member of the Confederation of Ionian Cities, Izmir (the old Smyrna) is a beautifully situated town, still with a few Greco-Roman remains. There are several small villages to the west, with very fine beaches; the best is Inciralti, with its restaurants and dance floors. If you are settled in Izmir, you will wish to travel through the northern part of the Aegean. You will see Pergamum (now called Bergama), one of the most wonderful classical sites near the coast. Sardis, the capital of the legendary Croesus, placed farther inland, is also worth a visit, as is Manisa, the old Magnesia.

South of Izmir, you must see Ephesus, near Selçuk, without fail. A good plan would be to stop over a few days in Kuşadasi before visiting Priene, Miletus,

Didyma and Milâs, and ending the rounds with a visit to Bodrum, the old Halicarnassus, site of one of the seven wonders of the ancient world (the tomb of King Mausolus).

THE SEVEN CHURCHES OF ASIA MINOR. (Biblical reference Revelations II through VIII.) Of special interest to Christians and students, the sites of the seven Asian churches where St. Paul preached are of special interest to Christians and students of history. Any travel agent can arrange a tour of the seven, taking about 3 days and using Izmir as a base. (Cost: about $330 for first person in a car, $40 for each additional person ... £91.65 and £16.65, respectively.) The seven churches:

1. Pergamum (modern Bergama). Like the other cities, visited by Paul during his third journey (Acts XVIII, 23 to XX, 3), when he lived in Ephesus for two years. The place where, wrote St. John to the Church of Pergamum, ',Satan's throne is sited".

2. Thyatira (modern Akhisar). Least important of the 7 cities.

3. Smyrna (modern Izmir). Recipient of a letter from Paul praising the early believers for their faithfulness, and warning of future persecution.

4. Sardis (modern Salihli). The Lydian capital, where Croesus minted the first coins.

5. Philadelphia (modern Alaşehir). The youngest of the 7 churches. Part of the city wall and some remains of an early church still standing.

6. Laodicea (modern Denizli). A crossroads of the ancient world, with recently-excavated theater and church. Near Hierapolis (10 miles), home of Philip the Evangelist, and Colossae (13 miles), to whose citizens (and those of Laodicea) Paul wrote the Epistles, emphasizing the union of Christians in the mystical body of Christ. See Colossians I, 24–29; II, 12–15 and II, 20 to III, 4, the best-known passages.

7. Ephesus (modern Selçuk). "Is there a greater city than Ephesus?" asked Paul, continuing, "Is there a more beautiful city?". Visited briefly by Paul on his second journey, and then his home for two years on his third, Ephesus was also visited by St. John and Paul's disciple, Timothy. In the great amphitheater, when Paul preached that "there are no gods made with hands", the local silversmiths, led by Demetrius, one of their number, rioted against him for two hours, shouting "Great is Diana of the Ephesians" until the town clerk prevailed upon them to go home. Capital of the Roman Province of Asia, Ephesus was the site of the Temple of Diana, one of the Seven Wonders of the Ancient World. To the Christians of Ephesus, around A.D. 60, Paul is said to have written his Epistle to the Ephesians from captivity in Rome. This chapter of the New Testament is concerned with the doctrine of the mystical body of Christ and is famous for its metaphor of the Christian as a pure soldier.

Paul is thought to have written some of his Epistles here, and John may have written his Gospel here in A.D. 95 From Ephesus, indeed, where St. John brought Mary in fulfillment of his pledge to Jesus to protect her, she is believed to have been taken into heaven.

A pilgrim objective longer than any other site in Christendom, Ephesus built the first basilica, and was the scene of the second Ecumenical Council in 431, during which Mary was proclaimed the Mother of God.

Hotels and Restaurants

(Rooms in hotels and motels have at least shower, unless otherwise indicated.)

AKÇAY-EDREMIT. Four motels: *Akçay* (3), 36 rooms; *Beyaz Saray* (4), 26 rooms; *Dogan* (4), 36 rooms; *Öge* (4), 30 rooms. *Günen Pension* (4), 20 rooms. *Akçay Bungalows*, 123 bungalows.

ALTINULUK. *Akçam Motel* (3), 36 rooms; on the Gulf of Edremit.

AYVALIK. Four motels: *Aytaş* (2), 47 rooms; *Aziz* (2), 38 rooms; *Arci* (3), 28 rooms; *Murat Reis* (4), 30 rooms. Hotels: *Berk*, 62 rooms and *Tunç*, 26 rooms, both (4). *Çadir Pension*, 13 rooms.

BERGAMA. *Tusan Motel* (3), 24 rooms, two miles out of town. *Bergama* (4), 10 rooms (6 with shower).

BODRUM. Pensions *Halikarnas* (3) and *Herodot* (4) in town; *Artemis*, *Karaada* and *Hotel Cactus* (4), on beach 7 miles out.

ÇAMLIK, near Ayvalık. Small hotels *Aral*, *Komili*, *Koşcar*, *Yanyalılar*, all (4).

ÇESME. Motels *Motes* (3), 44 rooms, and *Turtes* (4), 106 rooms. Hotels *Akdeniz*, *Imren*. At the thermal beach of Ilica: *Çeşme* (1), best in the region. Motels *Balin*, *Harem*, *Hüsam* (all 3–4). Also 6 modest hotels with thermal establishments and 3 pensions. At Cliftlik, motel and camping *Tursite*.

ÇINE. Try the *Çine Palas*, 15 rooms.

DIDYMA. *Didim Motel* (4), 16 rooms; *Güksu Hotel*, on the beach of Altinkum Plaji, 2 miles from the temple ruins.

EPHESUS. (*Selçuk*). Motel *Tusan* (2), 12 rooms, restaurant, near the ancient city. *Belediye Motel* (3), 20 rooms.

FETHIYE. *Motel Belceğiz; Pension Telmesses.*

FOÇA. Club Méditerranée village (see Holiday Camps in *Planning your Trip*.)

GÜMÜLDÜR. Motels *Paşa* (3), 106 rooms; *Sultan* (3), 110 rooms, on excellent beach.

KUŞADASI. *Tusan* (1), own beach and pool, 100 rooms; *Imbat* (1), 70 rooms, own beach, one of the best. Next, the *Marti*, though only (4). *Kismet* (2), 60 rooms; *Bellevue* (3), even nearer, across main road. *Emkas Palas*, 43 rooms (3 with shower).

In the village: *Akdeniz*, *Alkis*, *Atlantik* (all 4 or below).

Two holiday villages: the elaborate *Club Européen de Tourisme*, on its own secluded promontory; the much simpler and rather crowded *Kuş Tur*.

The *Caravansaray* is only for Club Méditerranée parties.

Restaurants: *Lâle*, *Ada*, *Terminal* (European and Turkish dishes), and *Toros* (seafood). *Van Gogh*, in island castle; discothèque.

MANISA (MAGNESIA). *Mesir* (4), 20 rooms, restaurant; *Atlas*, 20 rooms (8 with shower); *Gündüz Palas*, 11 rooms (2 with shower); *Güven*, 9 rooms (3 with shower).

Restaurants: *Şehir* and *Sipil*.

MARMARIS. *Altinişik* (2); *Lidya* (3), 57 rooms in self-contained resort on good beach; *Martur Motel* (4); *Pension Balci*.

MILAS. *Oğuz*, 10 rooms; *Park* and *Yeni*.

MUĞLA. *Çınar*, very simple, 16 rooms, restaurant.

ÖREN. Four motels: *Artemis* (2), 55 rooms, *Ada* (3), 20 rooms, *Erkali* (4) and *Örtur* (4), 50 rooms.

SÖKE. *Erol Palas* (3), 43 rooms (6 with shower), restaurant.

URLA. *Motel International* (3), 50 rooms.

YENIFOÇA. *Kavala Moteli* (3), 100 rooms, 50 with shower.

 OFFICIAL CAMPING GROUND. Ayvalik: *Sarimsakli Dinlenme Kampi*. Didyma: *Altinkum Plaji*, three and a half miles south of Didyma. Edremit: *Akçay, Güneş Motel, Kamp ve Campingi, Edremit*. Izmir: *Inciralti Mocamp*, two miles south, on the Çeşme highway; *Ilica, Ardiç Campingi*. Çeşme. *Kuşadasi Dinlenme Kampı. Kuşadasi Mocamp*. Burhaniye: *Ören Altin Kamp*, with beach.

 OFFSHORE ISLANDS. You may wish to visit the Greek islands off Turkey's coastline while in this area, or you may enter Turkey via mainland Greece and a trip across the Aegean. From May to October, there are daily small boats between Kuşadasi and Samos, Bodrum and Kos, Marmaris and Rhodes, and less frequently between Bodrum and Rhodes.

Finally, you can charter a small boat in Marmaris, Bodrum, Rhodes or Kos, paying from $25 to $75 (£10.40 to £31.25), depending on the size. This is of particular interest to a group traveling together, needless to say, as the scheduled services are much cheaper (about $5, £2.10) on average.

 USEFUL ADDRESSES. Tourist Offices (*Turizm Bürosu*) in Bodrum, Kuşadasi; Izmir, Atatürk Bulvari 126, Cumhuriyet Bulvari 125; Marmaris. *Turkish Maritime Lines* (*Denizyollari*) branches in Bodrum, Fethiye; (for Izmir, see *Useful Addresses* in chapter on Izmir); Kuşadasi, Akdeniz Turizm; Marmaris, Mr. Hüseyin Güven.

Discovering the Aegean Provinces

Though an obvious stronghold since prehistoric times, it was left to Alexander's general Lysimachus to exploit the strategic potentialities of the great rock on which he built a fortress to guard his fabulous treasure. His local commander Philaretos refused to surrender the treasure to the victorious Antiochus, and in 281 B.C., he headed an uprising of the troops, took over the town, and his nephew Eumenes I founded the kingdom of Pergamon, which under his successors extended from the Hellespont to the southern slope of the Taurus mountains, today Antalya. In 133 B.C. the last king, Attalus III, died, leaving his country to Rome. From then on, the history of Pergamum is that of all the Roman provinces in Asia. It is spoken of again but to bewail its loss, when burned to the ground by the Arabs raiding Anatolia. Rebuilt in the 14th century by the Seljuk Turks, it was in fee to the powerful Karaosmanoğlu family, beholden to the sultan in name only, until the beginning of the 19th century.

Though favored later by several Roman emperors, Pergamon owes its glory chiefly to the Attalid dynasty (214—133 B.C.), staunch allies of Rome, which made Eumenes II the arbiter of Asia Minor and intervened repeatedly in favor of his son Attalus II. Then, all of a sudden, Attalus III, thinking that Attalus II, at 82 had both lived and reigned too long, murdered his uncle by poison. His brief outburst over, he retired from public life and spent his time gardening and pottering with alchemy. At his death, he left a will giving Rome "the furnishings of his palace" which, so the old texts say, the wily "republic took to mean his kingdom".

In the meantime, it seems that Pergamum had experienced trading troubles with Egypt. The library of Pergamum having fast become world renowed, Egypt, not wishing to have its library of Alexandria put in the shade, stopped the exportation of papyrus. As it turned out, it was all to the good—at a loss for paper, Pergamum invented parchment, *charta pergamena*.

Pergamum, the homeland of the renowned doctor and surgeon Gallen, was the center of the cult of Aesculapius, god of medicine. In his honor, the town built the *Asklepieion*, a temple with a medical library and a theater holding 3,500 spectators. The remains are still an impressive sight. Did Asklepios (Aesculapius), the founder of medicine, really exist? To the Greeks, he is a god, the son of Apollo and the nymph Coronis. According to Ovid, Apollo, on learning that his love was faithless, killed her with an arrow and took from her body his unborn child, giving him into the care of the centaur Chiron, whose task it was to raise the motherless babies of the Olympian gods. Chiron taught the arts of healing to young Asklepios who, elated by his own powers, went too far. He annoyed Zeus by bringing his enemy Hippolytus back to life, maddened Pluto by cheating Hades of the dead. To be well rid of him, Zeus struck him dead with a thunderbolt; then, to show that he bore no grudge, put him in the sky among the immortals, his physician's staff etched in stars.

The words carved over the doorway of the Asklepieion still bear witness to the boundless pride of the healer: "In the name of the gods, Death may not enter here". In Roman times, both Marcus Aurelius and Caracalla came here to be healed. It was, in a way, a watering place, of which the one remaining trace is the "Beauty Bath".

It is thought that the building of the Asklepieion of Pergamon was undertaken by a prince, Archias, who had gone to heal his wounds in Greece, at the then best-renowned temple of Asklepios in Epidaurus. Grateful for his recovery, he brought home with him a few doctor-priests, and built a temple in his own town. Like churches throughout the Middle Ages, the Asklepieion had right of sanctuary: "Death may not enter here". (Alone to violate this sacred law, Mithridates VI, king of Pontus, put to the sword the Romans who had fled for refuge to such a temple.)

The theater and the library were added by the Romans under Antoninus Pius (A.D. 138—161) and the Consul Lucius Rufinus. An earthquake in 175 destroyed most of the buildings, but they were at once rebuilt. The earthquake merely shook three Greek temples, safely built on lower ground—that of Telesphorus, son of Asklepios and himself a great physician; that of his eldest daughter Hygiea, patroness of health (his younger daughter, Panacea, was patroness of medicines); and that of Asklepios himself, circular in construction like the first.

Until the beginning of the 20th century, all of lower Pergamum, among the most impressive ruins of the ancient world, was as yet unearthed. It then seemed only what in fact it then was, a tobacco field.

The Remains of Pergamum

Modern Bergama lies on a plain, and its most interesting sight is the Basilica, or Red Court. To the north stands a high hill on which the Greeks had built the first Pergamum: the Acropolis or high town. To the southwest, on a slight swell, stands the Asklepieion, reached by a left-hand turn on the road from Izmir, slightly over half a mile before the town.

At the Asklepieion, you cross a small courtyard, once lined on three sides by a row of Corinthian porticoes; in the middle stands a marble altar engraved with a serpent, symbol of Aesculapius. You then pass through the propylaea or entrance halls, and go down the 12 steps leading to the big inner courtyard. To the right are the remains of the second-century library, with its mosaic pavements, broken marble shelves, and a few remaining facings of colored marble. To the north of the courtyard a portico (many of whose fallen columns have been set upright) leads into the wide sweep of the theater, which seats around 3,500 people, and which is still in use during the Bergama Festival, in May. To the west, another portico led to the toilets. To the south, a two-storied portico makes up for a drop in the land. In the courtyard itself are traces of the sacred basins and the sacred spring of healing waters. Near the spring, a stairway goes downwards to a sacred tunnel, which the supplicants ran through after visiting the spring, while priests shouted words of encouragement from holes in the tunnel's roof. As they ran, they were told that the healing powers of the temple were taking effect, and that by the time they arrived at the round temple of Telesphorus, the god of cure-revealing dreams, they would be well again. To the north of the latter temple stands the round temple of Aesculapius, built in the second century; to enter it, you walked from the courtyard up a stairway and through a monumental hall. It was covered by a dome, and stood on a base 75 feet wide.

The Asklepieion was connected to Pergamum by a sacred way, now partly excavated, which ended in a gate today in ruins, the Viran Kapı. From here, you can go west across the fields to see the remains of a Roman theater, with a fine view over modern Bergama. Farther to the north is an amphitheater astride the Tellidoros, a stream feeding the Bergama Çayı. The arena, part of which rested on archways, could be flooded with river water to make a lake for the combats of gladiators against crocodiles and hippopotami. It seated 50,000 spectators.

Back to Bergama, by the main street. To the left, you have two museums: the archeological, which houses fragments unearthed from the ruins, statues, bas-reliefs, mosaics, and so on; and the ethnographic. After the last, you can cut off to the left, and walk down a street that leads to a 14th-century Seljuk minaret, in brick, and emblazoned with glazed earthenware tiles; then, after a maze of alleys, cross the river to your right to visit the big mosque, the Ulu Cami.

The way to the Ulu Cami is impassable by car, but the 250 yards on foot are not without interest. The uneven cobbles are mostly as old as the very old houses; the slopes of the surrounding hillsides are full of unexplored holes, ancient remains, and barrows, all to be digging sites some day. A strong gale of wind toppled the minaret of this mosque, built by Bayezit; today's minaret is fairly new. The surrounding walls belong to pagan times and a few of the stones, which still bear the sign of Demeter, show that the building materials were brought from the nearby ruins. Such looting was common in the old days, and did much to undo the beauty of the past. The Küplü Hamam, baths built in 1427, are still in use; they are named after a marble jar, once on the biggest pool, which rests today in the Paris Louvre.

By skirting the bank downstream, you will come upon the Basilica, whose red brick has given it the name of Kızılavlu, the Red Courtyard. According to some scholars, it was originally a temple built sometime in the second or third century A.D. to the Egyptian god of medicine, Serapis, whose cult had spread throughout Greece and Rome. According to Mansel, the name Serapis is a Greek merger of the god Osiris and the sacred ox Apis, a shortening of Osiriapis into Serapis. His cult, established in Egypt in the third century B.C. under Ptolomeus I, later spread to Asia Minor, Greece, and Italy. Here, the original Greek temple was enlarged by the Romans in honor of Hadrian. The Christian altar is Byzantine. Transformed into a basilica by the Byzantines, it was then divided into three naves by two rows of columns. The building was 188 feet by 84, and 81 feet high. You can still clearly see the curve of the naves, though the wall fell down in the eighth century, after a fire started by the Arabs back from the siege of Constantinople. To the east lies a vast courtyard, once surrounded by porticoes, under which the Bergama Çayı (Selinos) flows through two tunnels. To the north and to the south stand two squat round towers, maybe old chapels. The north tower is restored, and is today a mosque.

Across the stream flowing by the basilica is a beautiful Roman bridge with three arches. It spans several centuries, from the time of Byzantium to that of Islam.

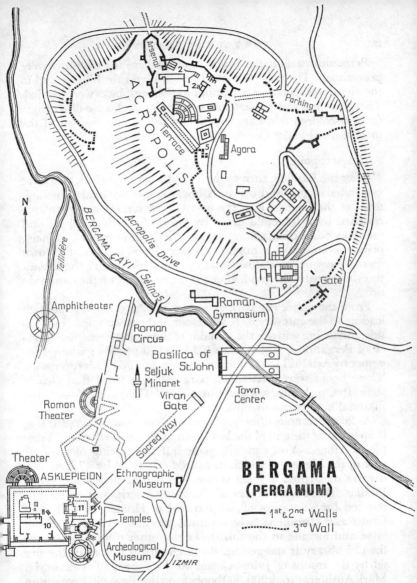

BERGAMA
(PERGAMUM)

— 1st & 2nd Walls
···· 3rd Wall

1. Temple of Trajan. 2. Royal Palace. 2a. Library. 3. Temple of Athena. 4. Temple of Dionysus (later of Caracalla) and Theater. 5. Temple of Zeus. 6. Temple of Demeter. 7. Gymnasium. 8. Temple of Hera. 9. Lower Agora. 10. Sacred Tunnel. 11. Altar of Aesculapius.

Pergamum also had a lower Agora, where the city laws were proclaimed. The growth of the town, both on the hillside and in the plain, was such that two public gathering-places were needed. The great interest for art lovers here lies in the use of trachyte (a light-colored feldspar, rougher to the touch) instead of the marble usual to the Greek and Roman periods.

The Acropolis

After the Basilica, turn to the left—by car if possible, you have two miles to go—and upwards towards the Acropolis, the high town of the Greeks, and the first Pergamum. It was then surrounded by a threefold defensive wall, of which there are still many awe-inspiring traces, and covered with temples, palaces, private houses and gymnasia. In later Roman times, the town spread outwards and downwards to the plain, where the Byzantines later settled for good, after a short-term stay on the mountain side.

From the upper car park you enter the Acropolis by the path leading to the gateway or Royal Door of the town's first wall. Inside and facing you are the remains of the world-renowned library of Pergamum, which once held 200,000 books gathered together by Attalus I in the third century B.C., and by his successors. These books were written on parchment, a word that clearly shows its Greek root, *pergamene*, meaning "of Pergamon"—writing material made from sheepskin.

As for the famous library, a team of German archeologists dug it up towards the end of the last century, to the north of the Temple of Athena. You can still make out the tracing of the four rooms, the biggest of which measured nearly 54 by 47 feet. The diggers unearthed a great statue of Athena, clearly a copy of Phidias. There were others, as shown by inscriptions on the uncovered bases: statues of Sappho and of Homer, as well as of Crates and Hirodicus (who invented parchment, thereby giving fame and fortune to the town). The number of manuscripts in the old library is staggering. Plutarch writes that after the fire set by the troops of Julius Caesar to the library of Alexandria, Mark Anthony "took 200,000 books from the library in Pergamum as a gift to Cleopatra", to make up for her loss. It was a handsome but unlucky gesture, for the library of Alexandra was to go up in flames again four hundred years later in the wars between Arabs and Christians, and every last book was lost forever. Among the known scholars of Pergamum were the Greek philosophers Parmenides and Zenon.

Following the traces of the first wall (nothing is left but a few foundation stones) you come to a pillar and a cistern on the threshold of the royal palace of Eumenes II, built in the second century B.C., today a broken stone skeleton under the timeless sun. To the north juts out a vast embankment used by the Romans as a storehouse for arms and food. A fine view and, on the slope below, the awesome remains of the first wall. Retracing your footsteps, follow that wall upwards to the very top of the Acropolis and the temple of Trajan. Facing south, it was built on a terrace over archways upheld by a strong wall. To the southeast, the temple of Athena, dating from the fourth century B.C., was in the sixth A.D. converted into a church by Justinian. Nothing is left but a flagged courtyard, bright with weeds, and a few broken porticoes. The water in the cistern, if no longer held sacred, is still pure.

To leave behind the first wall and get to the lower levels of the Acropolis, you walk down the steps leading from the temple of Athena towards the theater, backed by the steep westward slope of the hillside (about 161 feet from the top steps down to the pit). The royal box is placed in the lower middle of the stone steps. The acoustics are as good as ever. The most remarkable monument on the Acropolis, its 80 rows of seats held 15,000 spectators. Archeologists are in doubt as to its date, anywhere between the fourth and second centuries B.C. The stage, which was in wood, marks the transition from the classic Greek of the Roman theater. The onlooker is struck by the steep slope of the seats, allowing every spectator an unhampered view of the stage.

Level with the stage, a 677-foot terrace leads to the Temple of Caracalla (A.D. 211–217). It was this Roman emperor who declared Pergamum to be *Neocorus* or guardian of the Imperial cult.

The temple was originally dedicated to Dionysus. It was preceded by an impressive ionian portico and a stairway of 25 steps between the altar and the temple.

The Altar of Zeus

On the east side of the terrace, on top of a slope, are the ruins of a vast altar to Zeus, separated by the first wall from the temple of Athena on its own ledge, 78 feet higher up. The altar stood on an embankment 1,800 square feet in size, at a height of 39 feet. Its base is still standing, eight and a half feet above the remains of five stone steps. According to the plaster model in Berlin (it was mostly Germans who unearthed the ruins of Pergamum), the altar was 117 feet by 110, and was formed by a large portico open to the west on top of a monumental stairway, and by two smaller porticoes placed at right angles to the north and to the south. Both inner and outer walls were embellished with friezes; the votive altar itself was in an inner courtyard, behind the west portico. There is nothing left but a few broken stones half-hidden by the blown grass, an empty place forsaken by a long-dead god.

The altar of Zeus, or what is left of it, is in the middle of the second terrace. Sparing nothing but the foundations, German archeologists sent every unearthed stone to the Pergamon Museum in (East) Berlin. There, the altar was put together, complete with the splendid 375ft-long frieze depicting the battle of the gods against the giants, though some scholars take it to be the warfare between Pergamum and the Galatians.

To the south of the altar of Zeus, there are vestiges of another small temple of Dionysus. On the other side of the ancient road that once led down from the Royal Gate, now barely traceable by a few slabs of worn stone, is the empty site of the upper agora, the oldest marketplace in Pergamum. A right turn in the street leads to the temple of Demeter; the south portico was once 291 feet long, and was upheld by strong foundation walls. The people sat on the north steps to watch the religious rites. To the east of the temple of Demeter are vestiges of the temple of Hera, with an altar. Nearby to the south, stand the ruins of the three-storied Gymnasium, an establishment for both the training of the body and the schooling of the mind. The upper story, for boys between 16 and 18, had a palaestra or courtyard for wrestling and other sports, surrounded by porticoes; beyond that lay the classrooms and a chapel for the cult of the emperor. To the northeast are the remains of a small theater. At the east end, parts of the walls of a bathing establishment are still standing; both they

and the gymnasium are bounded to the south by a stadium 684
feet long. The middle story was the gymnasium for the boys from
ten to fifteen. A long corridor below the stadium, the middle
terrace was bounded to the south by the city's second wall and
the old road, reached, together with the children's gymnasium,
by a vaulted stairway to the left of a Byzantine tower. Farther
down the length of the old road, are ruins of Roman houses—
among which is that of the consul Attalus—and the lower agora,
once surrounded by porticoes and shops. The heap of stone balls
come from the storehouse of the Acropolis, and served to arm
the catapults.

You find yourself at last at the door of the third wall, where the
old road began, and near the lower car park.

Before leaving Bergama, you should take a walk through the
small streets and byways of this very Turkish village, if only to
compare it later to the inland villages. For, in the east as in the
west, closeness to the sea marks both men and towns. An outdoor
café is somehow different beneath the Aegean breeze than
beneath the burning or freezing winds of inner Anatolia.

The traveler who happens to be in this part of the country
between the 20th and the 22nd of May is in luck—he can go to
Bergama for the big yearly festival or *Kermes*. There he will see
Turkish folklore: songs and dances of sword and shield, of horseback and hunting, and, of course, the time-honored shadowplays or Karagöz.

Larisa, Foça and Ayvalik

If you have come from Izmir, skirting the bay to Karşiyaka,
you might have stopped at the remains of pre-Hellenic Larisa
near the village of Buruncuk or branched 17 miles west to Foça,
ancient Phocaea, the northernmost Ionian settlement, from which
Marseille was colonized in about 600 B.C. and which in a modern
invasion-in-reverse from France has become the main center of
the Club Mediterranée in Turkey with the establishment of a
self-contained holiday village. You can rejoin the main road
via Yenifoça, a Genoese foundation on the south shore of a wide
gulf, followed by the ruins of Kyme, the center of the Aeolian
confederacy, whose stones were used in the construction of
Aliağa village three miles north, now a budding summer resort.

Thence about thirty miles north through green hills with occasional glimpses of the sea to Bergama.

Scenically even more rewarding is the return along the gulfs of Ayvalik and Edremit, always in view of the noble outline of the Greek island of Lesbos across the blue water. Don't by-pass Ayvalik, the Place of Quinces which abound indeed but whose blossoms are more attractive than its fruit. It is perhaps the prettiest village on the coast, while from Çamlik beach you might ascend Şeytan Sofrasi, the Devil's Dining Table, which offers a marvellous view over the gulf and the Alibey Islands to Mount Ida towering behind Troy. A series of short branch roads take you to the beach resorts of Ören, Akçay and Altinoluk, or to the even more numerous Greek ruins, like Assos where Aristotle lay philosophy aside and got married, and through pine forests tumbling down the mountainside to the shore to the most famous ruin of all, Troy. Then at Çanakkale you might cross the Dardanelles into Europe or continue to the beaches of the Marmara.

The traveler who happens to be in this part of the country between the 20th and the 22nd of May is in luck—he can go to Bergama for the big yearly festival or *Kermes*. There he will see Turkish folklore: songs and dances of sword and shield, of horseback and hunting, and, of course, the time-honored shadowplays or Karagöz.

Sart (Sardis)

Of the three great sites around Izmir—Pergamum, Ephesus, and Sardis—the last is the least important. Nonetheless, Sardis has a lasting place in the minds of men as the city of Croesus, last king of Lydia and the richest man in the world, whose very name has come to mean great wealth.

Sardis lies inland, about 62 miles east of Izmir. It was built on a river, the Pactolus, whose gold-flecked sand bottom made it known as the river of riches—the panning of the riverbed was indeed in all likelihood the source of the rulers' wealth, which enabled Queen Omphale to buy Herakles (Hercules) as a slave from Hermes, using him not exclusively for labors, but to found the Heraklid dynasty. But according to Herodotus some other of Herakles' numerous sons ventured inland after the fall of Troy and seized Sardis. Traces of their presence, as well as those of the Lydians (six centuries later), have been revealed by a Harvard-Cornell team of archeologists. Their discovery of a prototype bazaar credits the Lydians with the introduction of organized retail trade.

The troubles of King Candaules have become legendary. He belonged to the Heraklid dynasty which by then had ruled for some 500 years. Candaules had a very beautiful wife called Nyssia, in whom he took great pride, boasting of her beauty to one and all. One day, however, overstepping the bounds of good taste, he showed her off naked in her bath. Outraged, the queen urged a minister, Gyges, to avenge her honor. The minister, only too willing to please a woman with both beauty and a throne, killed Candaules, married the widow, and was crowned king, thereby founding, in the seventh century B.C., the Mermnad dynasty. He was a great king, for the Lydians anyway, conquering and ruling the coast from Troy to Colophon.

The kingdom reached its height under the fourth king, Croesus (563–546 B.C.). The court of Sardis was a meeting place for philosophers, for the king "spent his time wisely between warfare, pleasure, and the arts". Solon, the Athenian lawgiver to whom he was showing off his riches, said witheringly: "No man can be called happy before his death". These words, however blighting at the time, were later to save Croesus's life. Misinterpreting a Delphic oracle, which predicted that if he crossed the River Halys he would destroy a great empire—it turned out to be his own—he attacked and was defeated by Cyrus at the battle of Thymbreos, and thrown back on Sardis; the town was besieged by the Persian armies, and fell. On his way to the stake, Croesus, remembering the words, cried out "Oh Solon! Solon!" When asked what he meant, he told the story, and Cyrus, reminded of the uncertainty of royal glory, spared his defeated enemy's life.

Nonetheless, Lydia's power was over. Sardis, under Persia's rule, was taken by Alexander the Great. After his death, it fell to the lot of his lieutenant, Antigonus. Defeated at Ipsos in 301 by Seleucus, Antigonus was killed in battle at the age of 84! Around the year 260, Sardis became part of the kingdom of Pergamum whose fate it shared. Under its walls, Brutus and Cassius quarreled before marching to Philippi and their death in the final defeat of republican Rome. It became the seat of one of the Seven Churches of Asia Minor. It underwent everything—invasion, sack, plunder, fire, and earthquake, but ever rising from its ruins. It was laid waste at last in 1402 by the crippled Mongol, Tamerlane, leaving only the immense walls of a Byzantine palace joined to a basilica and market.

The road from Izmir winds up the Kavaklidere valley, which has given its name to Turkey's most popular wine, to the Belkave Pass where Kemal Atatürk planned the final attack on Izmir in September 1922, putting an end to the Greek occupation. At ancient Nymphaeum, renamed Kemalpaşa in honor of the victor, are the ruins of a Byzantine palace in which the Emperor John III Ducas died in 1254. At Turgutlu, renowned for its cherry festival in June, the road enters the wide Gediz valley, one vast orchard and vineyard, but with fewer villages, and with every passing mile a greater outcrop of barren rock, as you near the stark and lonely Anatolian steppes.

So far, you have driven mostly through orchards; the countryside around Izmir is renowned for its fruit, much of which is dried and shipped abroad. Nearing Sardis, the road is lined with poppy fields, under government control. You are coming into the kingdom of haşhaş (hashish), the opium of Asia Minor. Westerners first met with the drug, smoked through a nargile or waterpipe, during the Crusades. Tough as the Crusaders were, they dreaded these drug-happy hipsters who tore open tents to stab the sleepers to death. The few Crusaders who fought off these onslaughts told blood-curdling tales of the hashasin or, as they pronounced the word, "assassins".

On the outskirts of Sardis, you are struck by the unending rubble of ancient remains—bits of wall, stumps of columns, broken capitals, litter the ground. There is no town at all, only the evidence of reconstruction work (on the walls of the marble court of the gymnasion facing the palaestra) now in progress. At first sight, the place looks like a graveyard of old stones, carefully placed in rows on the grass, and used on summer days as tables and chairs for picnics.

Between the remains of the ancient gymnasium and the palaestra, you can still make out the marble-paved avenue, once lined by shops. A closer look at the deep foundations made by long-dead architects makes you feel they will last forever. They are made of huge round stones, placed one on top of the other; the finished shaft was fluted by specialists, and coated over to hide the joints. Sun and rain have stripped them of the coating, and the worn joints are bared; the capital is often held in place by balance alone, and may so remain another thousand years. It is not unlikely that, here as elsewhere, these old stones have a more moving beauty in ruin than in the new unbroken rows of slick gilded marble.

The walls (those of the palaestra, or boxing and wrestling school, were built in the third century by the emperors Caracalla and Geta) are made of huge flat rectangles of time-defying stone.

A mile or so away stood the famous temple of Artemis on a hill overlooking the Pactolus valley. After the destruction of Croesus' temple during the Ionian Revolt in 498 B.C., Alexander the Great ordered the construction of a splendid new sanctuary, whose grandiose proportions can still be understood from the east side's eight Ionian columns, two of which are intact. There were twenty on each of the long sides.

In spite of the beautiful view from the top, few travelers will undertake the tiring climb to the Acropolis, a place of glaring sun and no shade. The soft rock has crumbled away, so that only two walls remain of the original Lydian citadel beside some Byzantine reconstruction.

On the way back to Izmir, take the longer road by Manisa (Magnesia) shortly past Turgutlu, following the Gediz valley to precipitous Manisa Dağı, ancient Mount Sipylus.

There is yet another road, for reckless drivers who like beautiful landscapes: the Sardis-Izmir road through Birgi, Ödemiş, and Tire. Here, we are in the country of the emirs of Aydın, unwilling underlords of the first Ottoman sultans. The charming village of Birgi boasts a 14th-century mosque, the Ulu Cami, built mostly with old stones from a Greco-Roman town, Hypapea, today altogether disappeared. The nearby *türbe* is that of a few rulers of Aydın. Beyond Ödemiş, you follow the course of the Küçük Menderes river for a long time until, having crossed it, you come to Tire, once an important Byzantine town. Look at the many wooden houses, and visit the mosque of Yahşi Bey, now a regional museum.

On the highway, Torbalı is linked to the name of Lamartine. Embittered by politics, the French poet had thought for a time of settling hereabouts on a big farm or *çiflik*, visited in 1850, and later offered him as a gift by the Sultan.

Manisa (Magnesia ad Sipylus)

At the confines of a fertile alluvial plain, below steep Manisa Dağı, extends neat and clean Manisa with its modern governmental buildings. This outstandingly pleasing provincial capital is bordered on both sides by military camps, and overlooked by the Sandik hill, crowned by a triple Byzantine wall, of which the uppermost rests on the foundations of the antique Acropolis. Halfway up stands the Ulu Cami (Big Mosque), together with a charming outdoor café with a wonderful view over the surrounding countryside. Here you see again the framework of doors and windows painted in blue, a good luck charm to ward off the evil eye and flies, met with in all countries where the Arabs have passed. Lastly, the town boasts of a modern hospital, built by a Turk who emigrated to the U.S.A.

A small town, Magnesia comes to full size in history and legend. To begin with history. So far, we have come across a few traces of the Hittites who had united Anatolia; here, we are in the very heart of the old kingdom. Manisa was once an important stopover on the "royal road" leading to Izmir. At the crossroads of two valleys, the Kum and the Gediz (ancient Hermos), it was to become a key stronghold. Thessalian Magnesia had dutifully contributed a contingent to Agamemnon's army before Troy, but the adventurous band refused to return, and founded a new Magnesia in the well-watered plain of the Gediz River and soon afterwards yet another Magnesia, on the Meander, further south. Subdued by Gyges in about 670 B.C., Magnesia shared the fate of the Lydian kingdom, was hotly disputed by the successors of Alexander the Great, loyally supported the Seleucids in their struggle against Rome and Pergamum, to which it was finally awarded after Cornelius Scipio's victory in 190 B.C. Rebuilt by the Emperor Tiberius after the devastating earthquake of the year 17, Magnesia became the capital of the Byzantine Empire from 1222 till the reconquest of Constantinople from the Latins in 1261. The impressive fortifications of the Sandik hill date from that period of ephemeral hegemony. Occupied in 1313 by the Turkish Emir Saruhan, it served once more as capital, though only of the emirate or principality of the Saruhanoğulları family. In 1390, it was taken by Bayezit I. The Greco-Turkish war of 1920-1922 gave rise to bloody fighting, laying waste much of the countryside around the town, as many monuments today bear witness.

Going back in time, the old historians tell of two remarkable mosques. The first was the Ulu Cami, not as *ulu* (*big*) as all that. Though its Byzantine foundations date from the eighth century, the mosque was constructed between 1368 and 1377 by the Emir Ishak Çelebi, a member of the Saruhanoğulları family. The mosque was placed under the protection of the fortress originally built by the Magnesians, and was both damaged and restored by subsequent invaders.

An unusual feature are the two places of prayer, one roofless for good weather, the other covered for rainy days. Some of the columns have Corinthian capitals with the acanthus leaf design, the Turks having taken stones from the surrounding ruins. A few capitals are simply imitations of the classic style; others are Islamic. The wooden *mimber* is splendid. The minaret is faced with glazed tiles, in the Seljuk style. Nearby is the *türbe* of the founder and a *medrese* or school. The way to the ruined fortress is a short but stiff climb.

The second mosque was built between 1583—6 by the future Sultan Murad III when he was governor of the province. Embellished with very finely worked marble, glazed tiles, and gilding the Muradiye is yet another masterpiece of the great architect Sinan. The *medrese* today shelters the town's Archeological Museum.

Across the road is the fine Sultan Cami, built in 1522 in the classical Ottoman style by Ayse Hafize, wife of Sultan Selim I, mother of Suleiman the Magnificent. Though somewhat neglected, it has remained the center of the annual Merkez Efendi festival on the 15th and 23rd April, when you can gain a year's good health by catching a piece of sweetmeat containing forty-one different spices, thrown from the minaret. Open umbrellas held upside down assist wondrously in the preservation of health. While strolling through the bazaar, you will come across yet another beautiful 15th-century mosque, the Hatuniye, named after Bayezit's wife, Hatun.

Like everywhere in this region, history is complemented, though not always pleasantly, by mythology. Three and a half miles or so out of town, on the road to Karaköy, is a small and delightful wood deep in sun-dappled grass and wild flowers, with a noisy brook that flows over and around stones and through the trees, splashing down in small waterfalls. From the top of a climbing footpath, you will see a reddish rock clearly outlined against the sky. Whether weatherbeaten or hewn by man into the rough likeness of a human form, it is said to be Niobe, a woman turned to stone.

Niobe was the daughter of Tantalus and the wife of Amphion, king of Thebes. Her overweening pride in her 14 children—seven boys and seven girls—got badly on the nerves of Leto, herself a boastful mother. She ordered her own son and daughter, Apollo and Artemis, to go forth with bow and arrow and kill all Niobe's children, though some say that two girls were spared. Nothing was left to Niobe but her tears, and Zeus, moved to pity, changed her into unfeeling stone. Even so, the very stone wept, drops of water forever seeping from the rock, and when the wind blows the rock makes a wailing sound, for neither the hand of God nor the passing of time can lessen a mother's sorrow at the loss of a child.

To the east of the town is another rock bearing undoubted traces of man's handiwork, if almost obliterated by time and weather. A Hittite, Phrygian or Lydian sculptor has cut into a niche a gigantic seated vaguely female figure, perhaps Niobe again or, as the Romans chose to believe, Cybele, the Mother Goddess of Asia Minor. In the plain, beyond the modern swimming pool and picnic gardens, the Romans defeated in one of the decisive historic battles the 82,000 men of the Seleucid ruler Antiochus III the Great and Hannibal in October 190 B.C. The end of the Hellenistic and the beginning of Roman pre-eminence in Asia was ascribed to the intercession of Cybele, whose main cult statue had recently been taken to Rome.

Manisa lies on the shortest road from Izmir to Bandirma on the Marmara (or to Istanbul), via Balikesir through wooded mountainous country, leaving the bird sanctuary of Lake Kuş to the west, but following the northern shore of Lake Ulubat to Bursa and the Yalova ferry.

The time has now come for the traveler to go south. It will spare both time and trouble to lodge somewhere near Ephesus, preferably in the small earthly paradise of Kuşadası, the "island of birds".

The Gulf of Kuşadası

After emerging from Izmir's sprawling suburbs, the first branch right (west) off the main road leads to the beach of Gümüldür near the vestiges of ancient Lebedos, and further south to three scattered ruins: Colophon below a conspicuous acropolis; its dependancy Claros, a renowned oracle of Apollo, whose Doric temple was felled by an earthquake; and the better preserved port of Notion, which took the place of the mothertown after Lysimachus populated rebuilt Ephesus by the forced transplantation of Colophon's population, though it had given birth to Apelles, the outstanding Greek painter and favorite of Alexander the Great.

The main road south continues through gently undulating fertile hills to the plain of Selçuk, once an arm of the sea that carried shipping to Ephesus, but was silted up by the Kaystros. Though there is a small Tusan motel near the ruins and accommodation at Selçuk, it is preferable to continue another 12 miles to Kuşadasi, an ideal center for exploring these parts.

The superb sweep of the landlocked gulf of Kuşadasi—its northern headland separating it from the gulf of Izmir, and stretching within a few miles of the Greek island of Chios, while the southern, ancient Mycale, reaches even closer to Samos island—is broken up by small rocky promontories into several bays fringed by long sandy beaches. The first accessible by road, not yet paved and rather bumpy, is the finest, but so far only enjoyed by campers, as the ground turns marshy in winter.

The Tusan motel stands in a cove of its own, divided by the rock of the Kismet hotel from the village bay, which is followed by an inlet below the Imbat Hotel; then the promontory of the *Club Européen de Tourisme* holiday village, more camps and a yet unexploited wide extense of golden sand beyond Davutlar village, continuing far out below Cape Mycale. In all some fifteen miles of lovely coast, the central sector touristically developed, with a good choice of hotels, holiday villages—answer to a vacationist's prayers or eye sores, according to taste—organized camps, a harbor for cruise ships, a yacht harbor under construction, and a road hugging the sea, not just leading up to isolated beaches.

Tiny Bird Island, Kuşadasi, has given its name to the whole gulf and the village to which it is now linked by a causeway. The village's distinct local color has so far withstood the influx of tourists despite the many gaudy souvenir shops where the suede jackets and trousers are real bargains if you possess the nerve and neck for haggling. The splendid Seljuk caravanseray has been taken over by the Club Mediterrannée, while the equally expertly restored island fortress accommodates a good restaurant.

But in the 16th century the impressive vaulted keep was the retreat of the formidable brothers Barbarossa, Oruç and Hayreddin, Greek converts to Islam, the most notorious freebooters in the Mediterranean, who ruthlessly pillaged the coasts of Spain and Italy, attacked the ships of all Christian nations, and sold passengers and crews into slavery in Algiers or Constantinople. Shipping in the Mediterranean had become so fraught with danger that the Emperor Charles V was forced to lead personally a punitive expedition against Tunis in 1530, where he liberated thousands of Christian slaves and killed the pirate leader.

Unluckily, the leader had a brother, even redder of hair and braver of heart. Appointed Grand Admiral by Suleiman the Magnificent, this legalized pirate conquered the Barbary States and made the Mediterranean a Turkish lake. Late though the season was, Charles V hurriedly launched a new expedition against Algiers, ignoring the warnings of his admiral, the Genoese Doge, Doria. The storms of the equinox as good as destroyed the fleet, and though Algiers was taken by a brilliant feat of arms, it soon had to be evacuated, without a Barbarossa being killed.

Very much alive, the pirate admiral plundered Italy's coast towns, defeated Andrea Doria's Christian fleet in the Gulf of Arta (off the west coast of Greece), won the naval battle of Candia in 1540, made war with the French against Charles V (bringing 7,000 captives back to Constantinople), and died at the age of 70, heaped with honors and riches, in 1546.

Selçuk (Ephesus)

Throughout its long history, the town has been rebuilt so often and has changed so much that it has lost its very name. The blue and white signpost indicates Selçuk, the yellow and black Ephesus.

Mounts Pion and Koressos, Greco-Roman remains, a Byzantine basilica, and a Seljuk mosque constitute a hodgepodge of history. In the village, on the road to the ruins, is the well laid-out museum, whose pride are the two splendidly preserved marble statues, once gilded, of Artemis in the likeness of Cybele, patroness of Ephesus, Greek in name but unmistakably Anatolian in appearance. The triple row of breasts lack nipples and have, therefore, often been held to represent eggs, the universal fertility symbol. Only the archaic smile is Greek, while the headgear, the signs of the zodiac and a strange assortment of monsters on the garments is purely eastern. Nearby is a beautiful Greek mask, made familiar throughout the world through photography and travel posters.

For ancient paganism as for the beginnings of Christianity, Ephesus was an important center, second only to Athens, and later, to Jerusalem. The cult of Artemis changed into the cult of the Virgin Mary, as St. Paul and St. John both preached in the town. Up to the Middle Ages, Ephesus kept its standing, owing in part to its being a well-placed port. The world's first bank—run on the lines of today's banks, that is—opened here.

Ephesus was founded in pre-Ionian times (in the 13th century B.C.) by the Lelegians and the Carians, who, according to Strabo, the ancient Greek geographer, settled in the plain around the temple of "the goddess-mother". Further on in his writings, without giving dates that would seem to lay his former statement open to doubt, he also mentions tribes of Mycenaen origin. Another and later geographer, Pausanias, thinks the first settlers to have been Lydians, as in Sardis and in Manisa.

The 11th century B.C. saw the coming of the Ionians, who founded settlements "without disturbing the people in place", that is to say, not by force of arms but by peaceful immigration. Under the leadership of their ruler, Androcles, the Ionian colony settled on an island, today called Kurutepe, across from the town; over the years, silt from the river Kaystros (today the Küçük

Menderes) bridged the gap of water. When the settlement grew too big for the island, Androcles went for advice to the famous oracle of Delphi, who gave him the usual puzzling answer: "The site of the new town will be shown you by a fish; follow the wild boar". And it came to pass one day, while fishermen were cooking a meal, that the fish leapt off the hot stones into the burning embers and then landed in the brushwood, which caught fire; and a fleeing boar was hunted down and killed. This happened at the foot of Mount Koressos, called by the Turks Bülbül Daği, "nightingale mountain". Androcles at once drove out the people of the place, and settled in the new Ephesus. Time and the river merged the two settlements into one, which slowly grew into a big city.

Riches awake greed—Croesus, king of Lydia, captured Ephesus, and was himself defeated by Cyrus, the town thereby falling under Persian rule. The conquered Ionian cities made a secret alliance, and a widespread revolt broke out in 499 B.C. After initial successes which brought the Greeks to Sardis, a decisive battle near Ephesus heralded the collapse of the rising. Cyrus' successor Darius laid waste the rebel towns, sparing only Ephesus.

The Newer Ephesus

From that time on, Ephesus stayed carefully on the fringe of the endless Median Wars between the Persians and the Greeks, the latter weakened at home by growing strife between Athens and Sparta. Keeping out of a war being no mean feat, then as now, it seems unbelievable that the wily Ephesians even managed to keep on good terms with both sides, winning both ways. True, they took good care not to speak out for peace, wisely giving the goddess Artemis full credit and thanks for keeping the town out of trouble. As a matter of fact, the night Erostratus set fire to her temple, she was busy elsewhere, assisting the wife of Philip, king of Macedonia, who gave birth to a son, Alexander, later the Great. After chasing the Persians from Ephesus in 334 B.C., he reconstructed her sanctuary.

At Alexander's death, his empire was split up among his lieutenants, Ephesus falling to the lot of Lysimachus. By that time, the port was half choked by sand from the Kaystros River. To maintain its political and commercial power, Lysimachus again shifted the site of the town, surrounding it with ramparts.

In the second century B.C., Rome took over Asia Minor. Ephesus, belonging to the kingdom of Pergamum, and so part of Attalus III's doubtful legacy to Rome, became the capital of the Roman provinces of Asia. Under the *pax romana*, the town, containing 200,000 inhabitants, prospered and grew. A crossroads of trade, it fast became a center of culture, attracting the preachers of Christianity, who founded there the first of the Seven Churches of the Apocalypse. In his "Acts of the Apostles", St. Luke, a physician from Antioch (today Antakya), writes at length of the cult of Artemis, known under the Romans by her Latin name, Diana. It was the city's silversmiths who drove St. Paul out of Ephesus, for fear that his preaching would lessen the sale of the "silver shrines for Diana", for "by this craft we have our wealth". When Paul addressed the entire town in the amphitheater, urging them to accept his doctrines, "they were full of wrath, and cried out, saying, "Great is Diana of the Ephesians" (Acts XIX, 24—40). St. John also came to the town, perhaps the first time with the Mother of Jesus between 37 and 48, then again in 95 when he is supposed to have died.

In the fourth century, the balance of power of the known world swung the other way. Constantine made of Rome the seat of the Church, and of Byzantium the seat of the Empire. The pagan temples were plundered for the building of St. Sophia and other Christian churches. In 431, Theodosius II held the Third Ecumenical Council in Ephesus. The Patriarch of Constantinople, Nestorius, who claimed that Jesus was God in man but not God, and who denied the virgin birth, was charged with heresy and cast out of the Church.

About a hundred years later the port was once more choked up with silt. The Ephesians at last abandoned the pursuit of the retreating sea, resettling around the church built by Justinian on a hilltop, over St. John's tomb. The new city was surrounded by ramparts, and a citadel was built. In the year 1000, the Crusaders came from the west, the Turks from the east. Ephesus became known as Hagios Theologos, the "holy word of God", then by the Turkish twist to that name, Ayasuluk. The first Seljuk invaders were fought off in 1090, and the Byzantines held out until 1304. In 1348, Ayasuluk became the capital of the Aydınoğulları emirate.

In the beginning of the 15th century, the town fell under the rule of the Ottoman empire. The greatness of Ephesus was over. Without a port, it lost its trade to Izmir and to Kuşadası. All that 19th-century travelers have to say of the small town of Aia Solouk is that "it has a few classical ruins which lead one to think that it was built on the site of the ancient city of Ephesus, renowned for its famous Temple of Diana". In 1914 it was given the name of Selçuk.

The Cult of Artemis

Who speaks of Ephesus speaks of Artemis, or Diana. Schooled in Greek and Roman mythology, we know her as the daughter of Zeus, or Jupiter, the sister of Apollo, and the goddess of the hunt and of chastity. So chaste, indeed, that overseen bathing in a stream by Actaeon, she changed the young hunter into a stag, torn to pieces by his own hounds. On their farflung travels the tolerant Greeks were prone to identifying their Twelve Olympians with local gods and goddesses in the most incongruous amalgamations. In Anatolia they came across the worship of Cybele, daughter-in-law of Heaven and Earth, and wife of Time, Kronos. She was also known as Ops, the wife of Saturn, god of Nature; as Rhea, mother of Zeus; as Vesta, the Roman goddess of the hearth; and as the "earth mother", symbol of fertility. There are many reasons for this strange-seeming shift to chastity. One, of course, is that on her travels Cybele, like all gods, was made over in the image of her worshippers. Another is that her very relationship to time and to nature made her, following the earth's rhythm, both fruitful and barren according to season. In Ephesus, the goddess of chastity becomes mother nature, Artemis *Polimastros*, with three rows of breasts.

Some say that the worship of Artemis-Cybele, in its Anatolian form, dates back to the Amazons. (According to Strabo it was an Amazon, Smyrna, who founded Izmir.) These women warriors, as we know, were chaste, lying with men once a year, so that the race may not die out; the male children were left to die at birth. This seems a reasonable origin for the chastity cult of the goddess of the hunt, Diana ("Artemis" to the Greeks), always shown as an Amazon, one breast bare, the peplum draped over the right shoulder to hide the scar where the other breast had been cut off to allow full freedom for the bow arm. It also seems to be the origin of the yearly orgies on the feast day of Artemis, in Ephesus. (The sex life of the Amazons being what it was, it is small wonder that the nearby island of Lesbos came to be known for love between women.)

The temple and the statue being, said the priests, a gift of the gods, the Artemision had the right of sanctuary. By Artemision was meant both the temple and the month of the year dedicated to the cult of the goddess. The Ephesians, not unlike the rest of mankind, traded on their faith to make money, and the month of religious rites gave rise to many kinds of entertainment and feasts, sometimes licentious.

A Visit to Ephesus

It takes a whole day to see Ephesus, and is better done by car. In Selçuk itself, see the small 14th-century Seljuk mosque and the remains of the Byzantine aqueduct. Signboards clearly indicate the main sights (tickets required), well-provided with parking space. The fortified town is entered through the Door of Persecution, so called because an 18th-century traveler, Choiseul Gouffier, mistook scenes from the Trojan War, engraved on marble slabs (at that time still on the door) for Christian imagery. Beyond it are the ruins of the basilica, built in the sixth century by Emperor Justinian over the remains of a small church, itself built over the tomb of the apostle John. The tomb is under the altar, whose base is still visible. The basilica, 420 feet long, was once topped by 11 domes upheld by columns, of which the least broken have been set upright. A marble tablet commemorates the visit of Pope Paul VI in 1967. Behind the basilica is the Byzantine citadel, built on the site of the first town, which dates from the 11th century B.C.

Below the basilica stands the vast shell of the mosque of Isa Bey, ruined by an earthquake. A superb stalactite portal and three rows of sculptured windows pierce the unusually high walls, partly built of marble taken from the Greek temples. The mosque was built in 1375 by the architect Ali Damessene. Its outer form differs from the conventional Islamic place of prayer, though the greater part of the square building is reserved as usual to the open inner courtyard around the fountain for ritual washing or *sadirvan*.

Only one minaret remains out of the three; and the missing stones were taken to embellish the mosques in Izmir. On the other hand, the columns of black granite upholding the two domes of the Isa Bey mosque were taken from the ancient baths in the port of Ephesus, together with fallen capitals from the rubble of the Artemision. Waterlogged foundations and a few blocks of marble in a hollow facing the mosque are all that remain of the temple of Artemis, one of the seven wonders of the ancient world. The first temple, with its 127 columns, was plundered and damaged in the seventh century B.C. Repaired—largely by Croesus, the rich king of Lydia—in the sixth century, it was destroyed by fire, and again rebuilt in the fifth century. The story goes that a nobody called Herostratus, wishing to make a name in history, set fire to the temple on the night Alexander the Great was born, in 356 B.C. He got his wish; for in spite of a town decree forbidding the use of his name, it became a byword for meaningless destruction. The fourth building was the most beautiful of all, so much so that Nero plundered the Artemision. In the third century A.D., it was destroyed by the Goths. Rebuilt a last time, on a smaller scale, it was to be stripped of its marble for the building of the St. Sophia in Constantinople, and of St. John's basilica in Ephesus itself. But one of Artemis' statues was buried by a last worshipper in the town hall to save it from destruction by Christian fanatics.

Back on the Kuşadası highway, a small road near a motel turns left about two miles from Selçuk, and leads straight into the midst of the Greek and Roman ruins. Skirting the western slope of Mount Pion (Panayır Dağı), it ends in a parking lot near the ruins of the big theater.

The Gymnasium and Stadium

Shortly after turning onto this small road, to the left, is a gymnasium given to the town in the second century by a wealthy citizen, Vedius. Dedicated to Artemis and the Emperor Antoninus Pius, it was a luxurious establishment with hot, cold, and tepid baths (the heating system is still visible) toilets or *lavatoria* in good repair, and a wealth of statues and mosaics.

A little farther along, to the left of the road, is the monumental vaulted doorway of the first-century Stadium, where chariot and horse races were held on a track 742 feet long, and where gladia-

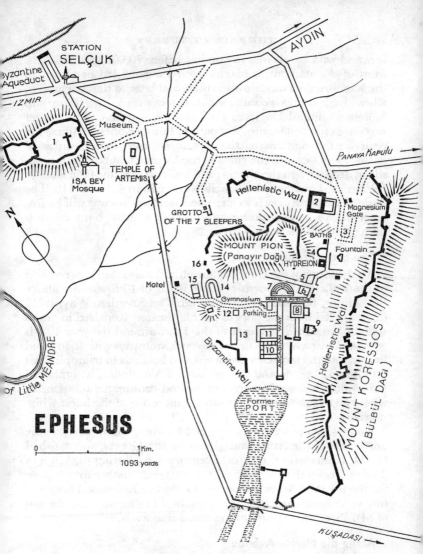

STATION
SELÇUK

Byzantine
Aqueduct

IZMIR

AYDIN

PANAYA KAPULU

Museum

TEMPLE OF
ARTEMIS

ISA BEY
Mosque

N

GROTTO
OF THE 7 SLEEPERS

Hellenistic Wall

2

Magnesium
Gate

3

BATHS

MOUNT PION
(Panayır Dağı)

HYDREION

Fountain

4

16

5

Motel

15

14

6

Gymnasium

MARBLE AVENUE

7

12   Parking

8

13

9

11

10

ARCADIAN WAY

Byzantine Wall

Hellenistic Wall

of Little MÉANDRE

EPHESUS

0   1 Km.

1093 yards

Former
PORT

Byzantine Well

MOUNT KORESSOS
(Bülbül Dağı)

KUŞADASI

1. Citadel and Basilica of St. John. 2. East Gymnasium. 3. Presumed tomb of St.
Luke. 4. Odeon. 5. Fountain of Trajan. 6. Temple of Hadrian and Baths of Scholastica. 7. Theater. 8. Agora and Library of Celsus. 9. Temple of Serapis. 10. Baths of
the Port. 11. Forum of Verulanus. 12. Byzantine Baths. 13. Double Church. 14.
Stadium. 15. Gymnasium of Vedius. 16. Gate of Coressus and of the Acropolis.

tors and wild beasts met in combat before 70,000 spectators. In front of the stadium, a marble-paved avenue led northeast to the Koressos doorway, now in ruins, and later to the Artemision, when Lysimachus rebuilt the town between Mts. Pion and Koressos (Bülbül Daği) in the fourth century B.C. The former was once crowned by the Acropolis of Ionian Ephesus. Across the road lie the remains of the Byzantine baths or "drunkards' baths", and beyond, the ruins of the Double Church. In this basilica, dedicated to the Virgin, and built on the site of the Roman Exchange, Ecumenical Councils were held in 431 and 449. The basin in the baptistery is so large because baptism was still by immersion. A second church was later built nearby, but today it is difficult to tell the ruins apart.

The baths of Constantine

To the south of the Double Church still stand the huge remains of the walls of the fourth-century Baths of Constantine, above the old port now silted up with sand. The Arcadian Way, 1,710 feet long, led from the port to the big theater. Repaired in grand style by Arcadius, Emperor of the East, around the year 400, it was lined by pavements under covered archways with shops, and lit up at night. Here, Cleopatra entered Ephesus in triumph. Past the Roman agora and the portico of Verulanus, a signboard points along a shopping street to the 2nd-century Serapis temple, whose eight massive Corinthian columns are of the finest white marble.

Backed by the western slope of Mt. Pion, the theater, at the north end of the Arcadiana, built by the Greeks, was finished by the Romans in the second century A.D., during the reign of Trajan. Its 66 tiers held 25,000 spectators, whether for plays or for the feasts of Artemis, patron goddess of Ephesus. There is a fine view from the top of the steps. Still higher up, near the top of Mt. Pion, are vestiges of the Byzantine walls.

Along the Marble Avenue

Taking the marble avenue to the right (southeast), you come on the right to the second-century library of Celsus, a remarkable two-storied building with a finely-worked frontage. Crossing the paved courtyard, you go up the wide steps to the reading room, where you can still see the slots for the rolls of papyrus. Also in the wall is a round recess, once an altar for offerings, over a cellar containing the carved marble sarcophagus of Julius Celsus, governor of the Roman province of Asia.

The Library adjoined the Hellenistic agora, a vast 350-foot square once lined by porticoes and shops round a water clock. A brothel stood in the strategic position at the corner of Marble Avenue and the Street of the Kuretes, named after the college of priests whose name was set up in it.

To the right are two monuments to the dead—the first, a block of marble on a rectangular base, was transformed into a fountain; the second shelters, in the hollow of its base, a mortuary chamber which held a sarcophagus. On the slopes beyond, Roman blocks of apartments still partly rise to six storeys high. On the opposite street side is the charming façade of the temple of Hadrian, still in good repair. The steps at the back of the temple lead to the Baths of Scholastica, a second-century lady of Ephesus. Just after the baths, a road has been cleared to the left, leading to a round funeral monument once two stories high, of wich only the base remains. Back on the main street, you come upon the partly restored fountain of Trajan, whose basin was surrounded by two levels of pillars and statues and the sculptured remains of an archway. After a right turn in the street is a square which once held the Prytaneion, the town hall and civic center, as well as the Nymphaion, a small temple decked with fountains where a statue of the goddess of Fortune was found. To the south of the square are vestiges of the temple of Domitian. In the Odeon, over 2,000 spectators could listen to poetry readings and to music. Nearby, to the east, more baths in ruins. Facing the Odeon, on the other side of the street, are vestiges of a fountain and, 644 feet southeast, the so-called tomb of St. Luke, in fact a Greek temple turned into a church.

The street ends at last at the first-century gateway to Manisa (Magnesia) a starting place for the caravan trail and a colonnaded road to the Artemision. This road, following the boundary walls of Lysimachus, skirted, 322 feet to the north, the great Roman Gymnasium of the East, with its still awesome remains. A car just manages the mile to a farmhouse, whence it is a short climb to the grotto of the Seven Sleepers, where, according to legend, seven hunted young Christians went into hiding and slept 200 years, until Christianity became a state religion under Theodosius. When they finally died, they were buried in the grotto and a vast Byzantine necropolis rose round their graves.

If possible, have your pick-up at the Manisa gate, to avoid the long walk back through the ruins to the main entrance. You can then continue to the right (east), passing Mt. Bülbül Daği (Mt. Nightingale), the old Koressos. Its top is crowned by the walls built by Lysimachus around the new Ephesus in the fourth century B.C.; they are still in good repair, now about two and a half miles long, marked by towers, steps, and doorways, and end in the sand-choked port, where a big round tower is said to have been St. Paul's prison.

The road winds up a mountain, affording splendid views over the plain of Selçuk, to Meryemana, the reputed house of the Virgin Mary.

The House of Mary

It all began with a vision. Catherine Emmerich, a cripple, had never left her hometown of Dülmen, in Germany, when she wrote the *Life of the Blessed Virgin Mary*. Two Lazarists, Father Jung and Father Poulain, who knew Ephesus well, were struck by her description of the house where the mother of Jesus is said to have died. In 1891, diggings were undertaken, though only partly (if at all) because of the sick woman's writings. The Basilica of Ephesus had been dedicated to the Virgin Mary, and in those days canon law only allowed a church to be dedicated to saints having lived or died in the place itself. And why else should the Third Ecumenical Council, proclaiming the dogma of "Mary, mother of God", have been held in Ephesus? A few families dating back to the early Christian settlement in Ephesus came down once a year from their mountain village of Kirkinçe to make a pilgrimage to the *Panaya Kapulu* or Doorway of the Virgin, on the Bülbül Daği. To be sure, Islam honors Mary as the mother of a prophet, but why her name there? It can only mean that the Turks also held it to be her dwelling-place. Finally, Pope Benedict XIV (1740–1758) decreed that Mary died in Ephesus, which Pope Paul VI singled out for a visit in 1967.

Catherine Emmerich, of course, had read the Gospels according to which Jesus, on the cross, had entrusted his mother to St. John's care; and it is known that St. John went to Ephesus. Whatever the truth of the matter, it is a startling fact that the ruins unearthed bear out, in detail, the cripple's plan of Mary's house.

But in Jerusalem, on Mount Zion, is a place called the Church of the Dormition, where Mary, so they say, closed her eyes for her last sleep. The faithful who uphold Catherine Emmerich point out that this belief only dates from the seventh century, whereas the tradition of Ephesus goes back to the beginnings of Christianity. The notice at the door of the house says, among other things: "... to escape the persecutions, he (St. John) probably brought her here".

Except on feast days there is no need to leave the car in the wide parking area on top—you may drive down as far as the simple restaurant. A treelined path leads to the undubitably ancient house, tastefully restored in 1951. Inside, there are ex-votos (mostly crutches), a small and very simple altar, with the Room of Sleep to its right, and flowers. Outside, a plane tree seems rooted in the wall. You can still make out the foundations of the ancient chapel, marked by a line on the present walls. Behind the house is another beautiful plane tree. Under the leafy sun-dappled shadows, the house takes on a touching look.

Below the house is the fountain of Our Lady. The sacred spring gushes out of the rock above the densely wooded slopes falling away to the distant sea. Regardless of your beliefs, this truly serene setting leaves an unforgettable impression.

Priene

The second excursion from Kuşadasi leads south into the heartland of the Ionian Union, to two of the most important members of the alliance of twelve cities, and to its oracle at Didyma. The road winds through an idyllic hilly landscape, often in view of the sea and the island of Samos, before reaching the lower Büyük Menderes (ancient Meander) valley. The river is bridged at Söke, founded by the Seljuks in the 14th century to take the place of Magnesia ad Meander, whose ruins are scattered on both sides of the Aydin road 12 miles northeast.

Just beyond Söke you branch right, along the eastern slope of the Mycale promontory for 8 miles and turn up the mountain after a shady village to the parking space below the gate.

But the visit of Priene still necessitates some very steep climbing through the remains of the city laid out by the town planners of King Mausolus of Caria in about 350 B.C. The original Ionian seaport, birthplace of Bias, one of the Seven Sages of Greece, had been razed by the Persians after the suppression of the revolt in 494 B.C. The new Priene regained a certain commercial importance which lasted throughout the Byzantine era, despite the silting up of its two harbours, to succumb finally when its last port Naulochos, some miles distant, was in turn engulfed by alluvial soil which now extends for ten miles between the ruins and the sea.

Marble flagstones, where the gutters for the drainage are still discernible, ascend from the east gate to the theater, which seats some 5,000 spectators, probably the entire free population. The five seats of honor, inserted in the front row in the course of a Roman renovation in the second century, are intact, but the many statues that decked the theater were sent to Germany, before a law was passed forbidding the exportation of Turkey's archeological treasures. (Up to the beginning of the century, foreign archeological teams crated and shipped home the best part of the excavations.)

Remains of a Byzantine church flank an earlier sanctuary, the Temple of Athena, designed by Mausolus' architect Pytheos in the Ionian style, dedicated by Alexander the Great according to an inscription now in the British Musenm and endowed with a colossal statue by the Romans. Five columns have been reerected.

The pine-clad spur of Mount Mycale is crowned by a Hellenistic fortress—as it stands some 1,200 feet high you might well dispense with a visit. Half way up perched the temple of Demeter, goddess of harvest, as always mysteriously remote.

The Athena Temple

To the west is the Temple of Athena, the first in Turkey.

Athena (Minerva), goddess of wisdom, science, and art, shared with Ares (Mars) the godship of war. She was delivered, fully armed, by Hephaistos (Vulcan), with a blow of his axe on the head of her father Zeus (Jupiter): so painful is the birth of wisdom and knowledge and the arts of peace and war, even for the greatest of gods. So we are told by Hesiod in his Theogony: "Then Zeus from his head gave birth to Athena of the gray eyes, weariless waker of battle noise, who delights in war, onslaughts and battles."

Her temple, once very beautiful, was said to be the model of the Ionic style in Asia. Earthquakes have overthrown most of the columns; five have been set upright again with care.

As a backdrop, towering and majestic, is the mountaintop or Acropolis. Below it is the sanctuary of Demeter (Ceres), goddess of the harvest, and of her daughter by Zeus, Persephone (Proserpine), goddess of spring. One day, when Persephone was in the fields picking flowers, she was raped by her uncle Hades (Pluto), who took her down to his underworld kingdom and made her his queen. When Demeter, having looked everywhere in her despair, forbade all trees to bear fruit and all grain to grow, life was threatened with extinction. A compromise was hastily patched up whereby Persephone returned for nine months every year to her mother and descended for the winter to Hades, thus symbolizing the annual death and reawakening of nature. Today, the temple is a pile of rubble, except for the ditch dug long ago to drain the blood of animal sacrifices.

The Agora was in the middle of town. The western wall was engraved with 1,400 lines of writing; near the eastern wall was the Temple of Zeus, encroached upon by the Byzantine citadel. Beneath it was the lower Gymnasium, while the upper backed on the Prytaneion and the well-preserved Bouleuterion (Senate), a rectangular amphitheater once roofed over. Between the Bouleuterion and the Agora the Romans built a splendid Sacred Portico, from which a colonnaded street descended to the western gate opening on the port. Just inside this gate are the insignificant remains of Cybele's Temple, while the Stadium is to the south on a lower level.

Miletus

The direct road from Priene to Miletus is at this writing closed for much needed repairs, so you have to double back to the Söke junction then turn for 17 miles on to the causeway between the rice paddies of the alluvial plain, which was in antiquity an arm of the sea extending inland as far as present Lake Bafa.

Shortly after catching the first glimpse of the lake to the left you turn right to the village of Akköy and back north again to Miletus, visible from afar on a hill in the river bend. But these ruins, somewhat disappointing except for the theater, are not those of the original city which witnessed the birth of Greek philosophy and science in the sixth century B.C. Vestiges of that famous town, going back to Mycenaean origins, crown a cliff some miles to the southwest.

After the arrival of the Ionians in the 11th century B.C., the settlement on the easily defensible promontory gradually assumed preponderance, based as much on sheep breeding, which supplied the raw material for the famous woolen fabrics, as on commerce, which led to the establishment of no less than 75 trading stations from Egypt to the Black Sea.

Economic prosperity, which made Miletus the first Greek city to coin money, reorientated the adventurous spirit from the exploration of the physical environment to the investigation of the mind. Thales, Anaximander and Anaximenes laid the foundations of western philosophy, Cadmus of history, and Hecataeus by drawing the first map of geography. Aristides wrote the *Miletica*, a collection of bawdy tales which inspired Boccacio's *Decameron* some 2,000 years later.

Having retained their independence from the Lydians, Miletus came to an advantageous arrangement with the Persians who contented themselves with the appointment of a friendly chief magistrate. But in 499 B.C., contrary to the advice of the Didyma oracle, Miletus headed an Ionian revolt against the Persians. After initial successes which brought the Greeks to Sardes, the revolt was crushed at a decisive sea battle off the nearby islet of Lades. Miletus was razed to the ground, the male population massacred, women and children sold as slaves.

But a position so favored by nature could not remain unoccupied for long. Hippodamus, the first city planner, was born in the

new settlement, where his ideas of a rectangular lay out were
applied with such succes in the middle of the 5th century B.C.
that Pericles entrusted the architect with the planning of the
port of Piraeus and the colony of Thurii in Italy. His model of
straight streets cut across at right angles to form a chessboard
pattern was followed some 100 years later on the much more
difficult hillside of Priene.

The decline of Miletas

Only under the Romans did the new Miletus regain prosperity, but here too, the encroaching sandbanks of the Meander River, winding around three sides of the town in a slowly narrowing
bottleneck, choked off the port, and with it the livelihood of its
people. It declined under the Byzantines, who called it Castro
Palation after the fortress they erected a top the theater; the
Turks contracted this to Balat, the name or one present tiny
hamlet.

Miletus had two ports, still in use in the 11th century, when the
newly-come Seljuks traded with Venice and the West, until sandbanks shoaled up the harbors and put a stop to shipping. Founded
on water, the town was to founder on sand; its sudden downfall
gave rise to the old saying: "like Miletus, once so great". Of its
past greatness, the splendid 2nd-century Roman theater gives
ample proof. It seated 25,000 spectators and might well do so
again, as the festival habit is spreading in Turkey too. The lower
22 tiers are in excellent condition, the solid arched corridors and
entrances still usable, only the broken sculpture and reliefs from
the ruined stage have been deposited before the immense frontage. A few hillocks in the surrounding plain were once islets
rising from the waters.

The fields are full of forgotten beauty—stones of an old wall,
the broken archway of an aqueduct, are scattered over the countryside; you stumble over priceless capitals as over rocks. This
historic rubble is indeed such that, unlike at Priene, nothing is
left of the city plan. A Byzantine archway, partly made of stones
from the Greek ruins, leads to the Seljuk caravanseray. Next
to the remains of a gymnasium is the magnificent dome of the
mosque of Ilyas Bey, built in 1401 under Bayezit I by the architect Menteşeli Ahmet; the minaret is missing.

The central north-south street ended at the Bay of Lions, where fragments of vast stone lions still guard what used to be the harbor entrance. The town had two agoras, with the town hall, or *bouleuterion*, between. There was a Temple of Athena, a sanctuary of Apollo, and baths (all in a fairly good state of repair) dedicated to the Empress Faustina who, in spite of an unedifying life, was deified according to custom after her death. Fragments of the lavish decorations of the huge cold pool, into which water poured from an earthenware pipe ending in a lion's mouth, the hot baths, dressing rooms and courtyards bear eloquent witness to the opulent life in Asia Minor in the first centuries of our era.

But no matter how sumptuous the profane buildings of antiquity might have been, they never equalled the sacred in nobility of detail and majestic dignity. An outstanding example is close at hand.

Didyma (Didymi)

You only have to return 3 miles to the Akköy crossroad and then to continue 9 miles south to the village of Yenihissar, the New Fortress. It was once Didyma (meaning "twin" in Greek), a town dedicated to Apollo, twin brother of Artemis. The grandeur and beauty of the temple alone justifies the visit to this region. A Sacred Way led from the bay to the temple, whose oracles were as revered as those of Delphi and it still is an awe-inspiring site. Small wonder, as it was some 600 years under construction, from the time Alexander the Great decreed the building of a new sanctuary to replace the archaic temple which had perished at the same time as the first Miletus.

An old Persian lion in marble marks the entrance. The colossal scale of the whole seems made to dwarf man into nothingness. A monumental stairway leads up to a forest of 103 remarkably well-preserved Ionian columns, some still supporting their architraves. The proportions are overwhelming: 389 by 188 feet.

The columns were made of round blocks of marble set one over the other; the finished shaft was then fluted. The few unfluted columns show that the temple itself was never finished. The entrance portico, or *pronaos*, at the top of the stairway, had 12 columns in three ranks of four. A huge slab of marble, 26 feet long by six feet wide and three feet high—68 cubic feet, forty-eight metric tons!—led to the porch where the oracle took his stand to announce the will of the gods to the people.

How was such weight handled by manpower alone? The Greeks slid the blocks of marble along shafts of well-soaped stone, like the wooden logs used today by fishermen to roll boats into the sea.

On both sides of the temple, passages hollowed in the stone sloped up and out into the great hall or *atrium*, from where another flight of stairs led to the sanctuary. The marble walls are still standing, thanks to ancient Greek workmanship and the pouring of lead between the stone slabs. But the fountain in the middle, once fed by a well filled with rain water, is now dry.

Under the courtyard is a network of corridors whose walls, throwing back sound, made of the oracle's voice a deep and ghostly echo which filled the people with religious dread. The oracle or *naiskos* stood in a small marble chamber at the far end, and spoke out of a hole giving on to the maze of echos. There are huge heads of Medusa, and a very small Poseidon and his wife Amphitrite, carved in stone.

You have to be made of marble to withstand the burning sun. Luckily, a small restaurant awaits the traveler under the shade of the palm tree. If you have time to spare, drive on to the "beach of golden sand", Altınkum Plajı, for a swim.

Back on the highway to Bodrum, follow the wooded south shore of Lake Bafa, which maintains the illusion of still being an inlet of the sea as it was until Roman times. The ruins of a walled Byzantine monastery, whose church, tower and water gate rise above the encroaching vegetation, cover most of the nearest islet. Others are scattered to the foot of rugged Mount Latmos, Beşparmak Daği, meaning "of the five fingers". According to legend, it was the birthplace of a handsome young man, Herma-phrodites, son of Hermes and Aphrodite. A nymph, Samakis, having fallen in love with him, he dived into the lake to shake her off; she swam in after him, but he swam faster. Despairing, Sama-kis cried out to Zeus, who, touched by her tears, merged her body with that of her lover. (From what we know of Zeus, it seems more likely that he wished to spite the boy for his lack of manhood.)

From Bafa village a dirt road leads along part of the north shore to Heraklea ad Latmos, whose Hellenistic ramparts rise from the lake up the precipitous rocks. The theater is better preserved than the Temple of Athena, the foundation stones of the Agora and the ancient Town Hall. The castle on the hilltop dates back to the Middle Ages.

Much easier of access and hardly to be missed, thanks to its closeness to the main road two miles past Selimiye, stands Turkey's most romantic ruin. The slender Corinthian columns of an almost intact Roman temple soar above the olive grove which covers most of the old Carian town of Euromos.

Milâs (Mylasa)

Both the Lelegians and the Carians were driven out of this area by the Dorians. The Carians made a comeback, but were conquered by the Persians. At the death of Alexander, his lieutenants and heirs, Antigonus the One-Eyed and Lysimachus (whose dog alone mourned his death) fought over the towns. Then came the Romans, who entrusted the government of the province to Rhodes, but had to send out their legions to quell an uprising against the new rulers. They were followed, beginning in the 11th century A.D., by the Seljuks, then by the Ottomans under Bayezit I. Tamerlane restored the Mentese dynasty, but Murat II finally incorporated Milâs into the Ottoman empire.

The new, like the old town before, rises from the river lined by some exquisite 18th-century mansions to a spur of the mountains encircling a fertile plain. The Roman tomb atop the spur owes its Turkish name Gümüşkesen, the Silver Purse, to the pyramidical roof held by pillars and Corinthian columns above the large stone plinth of the burial chamber. Nearby are remains of a Roman temple, in the lower town those of an older sanctuary of Zeus and antique walls.

Of the three 14th-century mosques, Cazi Ahmet Bey, Haci Ilias and Firuz Bey, the last is the most interesting, being partly built of marble from the old Greek temples. There are a few ruins, among which is an aqueduct, on the outskirts.

Nine miles of very rough road northeast into the mountains take you to Labranda, the first Carian capital and important sanctuary of Zeus, but in this wealth of classical ruins it is hardly worthwhile to jeopardize your car.

Three miles south of Milâs the mighty Byzantine fortress of Peçin Kalesi guards the crossroads to Bodrum southwest, the lovely beach of Ören near ancient Keramos southeast, and Muğla in the east. The road to the first, with a branch-off to the fine beach of Güllük, traverses the Milâs plain, before winding through pine-clad hills which suddenly open up to allow a breathtaking view of Bodrum (45 miles).

Bodrum (Halicarnassus)

Herodotus, known as the Father of History, was born here in 484 B.C. After winning fame in Athens he returned to help in the overthrow of the tyrant Lygdamis. His last journey led him to Thurii, perhaps accompanying its planner Hippodamus of Miletus.

Just as the northern cities of the Aegean had formed the Ionian Union, the southern cities, Halicarnassus among them, had formed the Dorian Union. Though the town had been expelled from the last, it took part in the revolt of the Confederation of Ionian and Dorian Unions against the Persians. The uprising was put down, and Halicarnassus joined Xerxes in his war against the Greeks, thereby losing to Athens when Persia was defeated.

Mausolus, who became King of Caria around 375 B.C., moved his capital from Mylasa to Halicarnassus. He had married his sister Artemisia, who reigned after his death. Seeing a woman on the throne, Rhodes declared war, and lost not only the battle but the island state itself to the enemy. However, the queen's greatest claim to glory was the building of her husband's tomb, the famous Tomb of Halicarnassus, one of the seven wonders of the ancient world. To it we owe the word *mausoleum*.

In 334 B.C. the town fell to Alexander, who razed it to the ground. After his death, the ruins fell to the lot of Antigonus the One-Eyed, then to Lysimachus. They were followed by the Seleucid kings, then by the Romans, who put it under the rule of Rhodes. Ten to eleven centuries later, the Seljuks and the Byzantines fought over it as it passed back and forth between them. The Knights of Rhodes landed here in 1402, rebuilding the ancient fortress already restored by the Turks—both times with the stones of the famous Mausoleum.

Small wonder, therefore, that nothing is left of the tomb but a description in Pliny's *Natural History*, together with a few words written at the end of the 15th century by an Italian traveler, Cepio, the last to have seen its remains. Towards the middle of the 19th century, an English archeological team undertook a thorough excavation on its former site; but little was found beyond the statues of Mausolus and Artemis, now in the British Museum. You can visit the site, today but a hole in the ground behind a small house, not far from the waterfront.

The Petronion or Castle of St. Peter may not be to fortresses what Mausolus' tomb is to mausoleums, yet it is one of the great showpieces of late medieval military architecture. The Knights of Rhodes, founded during the Crusades as the military order of St. John of Jerusalem and still in existence as Knights of Malta, used every known device to strengthen their foothold on the mainland, even installing the latest weapon, the cannon. Thus they resisted victoriously repeated Turkish onslaughts till Rhodes itself fell to Suleiman the Magnificent in 1523.

Below the keep in the center of the immense triple ramparts, which are surrounded by a moat connected with the sea, is the small museum containing statues and amphorae recovered from the sea; the greatest find, however, the superb bronze Demeter, graces the Izmir museum.

Petronion became in Turkish Bodrum, an attractive village now deservedly developing into a popular holiday resort, as the splendid castle is set off by the natural beauty of the bay, beaches and a delightful climate.

The Southern Confines

Though the roads to most points of interest on the coast between Bodrum and Antalya are adequate, it is often necessary to retrace one's steps for considerable distances. The easiest and pleasantest way to see this particular stretch of coast is by boat, the fortnightly roundtrip of the Turkish Maritime Line. This takes you through the spectacular gap in the cliffs screening the wide circular bay of Marmaris, but it means missing the inland sites and the infinitely varied drive through pine-clad hills, lux-

uriant plains and along magnificent bays. For the sake of com-
pleteness we will, therefore, double back from Bodrum to Peçin
Kalesi outside Milâs, then turn east for 38 miles to Muğla via the
village of Yatağan which has given its name to the short Turkish
saber that slashed its way to the gates of Vienna. Muğla, former
capital of the emirate of Mentese, has several mosques, among
which is that of the Three Sages, Üç Erenler Cami.

Nine miles further south route 23 branches to Marmaris (29
miles), picturesquely clustered round and inside the citadel on a
headland jutting out from a lovely beach below densely-wooded
mountains. For the next 80 miles west the road deteriorates but
the scenery, if possible, becomes even more attractive along the
narrow cape of Cnidus, with the sea often visible on both sides of
the ridge.

Cnidus was a famous center of art, birthplace of the architect
Sostratos, who built one of the Seven Wonders of Antiquity, the
lighthouse of Alexandria, and of the mathematician Eudoxus,
the first to measure the earth's circumference. Aphrodite and
Demeter, in a somewhat startling association of the voluptuous
goddess of love with the stern matronly mother goddess, were
equally venerated. Praxiteles' statue of the former so shocked the
great sculptor's patrons at Kos across the sea that the Cnidians
were able to purchase the priceless masterpiece as a tourist attraction. Ships put in to admire the goddess, especially after a back
entrance allowed a rear view. The marble Demeter was no less
perfect in her own way, a Mater Dolorosa which would grace
a cathedral better than the Britisch Museum.

From the road junction south of Muğla stabilized route 6
branches southeast to Fethiye (100 miles). At Köyceğiz hot
springs flow into a lake joined to the sea by a natural channel
on which, near the village of Dalyan lie the ruins of the ancient
Carian city of Caunus, a 20,000-seat theater and rock tombs.

But for the most dazzling display of that particular architectural fantasy you have to skirt the magnificent Gulf of
Fethiye. Magnificent forests of fir trees grow down almost to the
lake-like inner harbor of Fethiye, ancient Telmessos. Some
picturesque old houses on the castle hill have survived the
devastating earthquake of 1958, lower down a prosperous modern
port has risen with remarkable rapidity. The setting between

the rugged peaks of the western Taurus and the wide sweep of
the bay greatly enhances the attractions of the ruins of the
Temple of Kabasbos, a Lycian god identified with Herakles,
the sarcophagi carved out of the rocks and the rock tombs on
the road up to the Byzantine castle.

To the northeast, the most impressive tomb façades were
undercut from the protective cliffs. The 4th-century B.C. Tomb
of Amyntas, two Ionic columns supporting a pedestal topped by
a sun disk above a false door, is typical of these funerary monuments of ancient Lycia all along the coast to Antalya.

At Xanthos, near the village of Kinik a few miles upstream
from the mouth of the Kocaçay, are likewise 6th-century B.C.
sarcophagi on high pedestals among the extensive ruins.

This short survey of the Aegean provinces gives but a faint idea
of the extraordinary archeological riches that abound at every
step of the traveler's way, for the coastline between Istanbul and
Antakya (the old city of Antioch), further east yet, is a veritable
panorama of history and mythology.

Illustration at head of this chapter: Columns of the portico at Asklepieion, Pergamum.

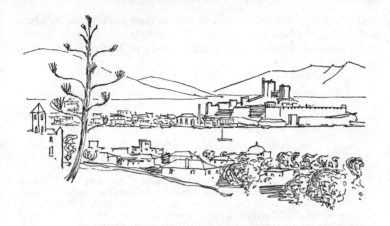

THE BACK COUNTRY

Between Coast and Plateau

The coast is the treasure house of Hellenism, the central plateau is given over to Moslem civilization. The former has been endowed by nature with an incredible variety of scenery, the latter has been denuded by man, who has thus created the majesty of the steppe with its unlimited horizon. But there is a large region between the two, partaking of both, blending these opposed elements and adding, moreover, some distinctively its own.

Roads have reached a sufficient standard to make the whole area accessible, though it may sometimes be a long drive from one comfortable hotel to the next. But some sort of accommodation is available even in the smallest towns.

As there are several alternatives, this guide will not undertake to prescribe any precise itinerary. Rather, it will simply explore on paper the various sights to be seen in the back country. The reader, armed with a map showing the current state of the different highways and byways, can then make up his mind before he sets out. The sequence in which cities, towns, and monuments are listed in the guide may occasionally coincide with your own chosen itinerary. Our principle has been to proceed by regions, taking up the chief places of interest as they occur area by area, and saving the best for the last—Pamukkale and Hierapolis, the most unusual sights that the back country of Turkey has to offer.

Practical Information for the Back Country

HOW TO GET THERE? *By plane:* certain planes on the Istanbul-Antalya flight schedule stop at Afyon. *By train:* Izmir-Denizli-Isparta-Egridir; Izmir-Manisa-Afyon; *By bus:* buses for all destinations from Izmir; *bus station:* the Basmahane Garage.

MOTORING. Route 68 from Izmir via Uşak to Afyon and continuing to Ankara, as well as Route 60 from Eskişehir to Kütahya and then as Route 25 via Isparta to Antalya are asphalted throughout. Route 68 crosses Route 25 six miles west of Afyon at a road junction which connects the former with the eastern sector of Route 80 to Konya, and the latter three miles south of Dinar with the western sector of Route 80 to Denizli-Aydin-Izmir. When traveling north from Antalya, beware of the signposts at Burdur which direct you to Denizli on an atrocious road via Yeşilova near Lake Selda. Instead follow the Dinar sign and turn west on to Route 80 at the Dinar junction. The direct Route 66 from Uşak to Kütahya is but imperfectly stabilized. The 24 miles off Route 80 after Kuyucak to Aphrodisias are asphalted, but not the connection via Tavas with Route 23 north to Denizli and southwest to Muğla.

WHAT TO SEE? The citadel and tiled monuments of Kütahya. The extensive Greco-Roman ruins of Aphrodisias. North of Denizli stands Pamukkale, one of Turkey's most outstanding natural scenic wonders, where calcareous waters have formed lime deposits in the shape of petrified terraces and cascades. This is also the site of Hierapolis, a once splendid Greco-Roman city of the first century A.D., which still has many interesting vestiges. To the north is the awesome Afyon citadel and to the south of Burdur is the chasm of Insuyu Mağarasi. All these lay along the ancient caravan route to the Mediterranean, and along the way are the old inns (*han*), or stopover places, dating from the Seljuk and Ottoman periods, in varying states of preservation.

Hotels

AFYON. *Emek* (3), Ordu Bulvarı, 39 rooms with shower, restaurant; *Sağlam Palas* (3), Bankalar Cad., 40 rooms with shower; *Afyon Palas*.

AYDIN. *Sakim Palas*, *Sükran*, both very simple.

BURDUR. *Kanrıcı*, recent, 25 rooms (3 with bath), on road from Denizli at town's edge. *Cendik Plaj Motel* (4), in Burdur-Tefenni Yolu,

8 rooms with shower; *Ipek Palas*, 16 rooms; *Park*, 23 rooms; *Yalçındağ*, 18 rooms.

DENIZLI. *Koru* (2), 60 rooms with shower, restaurant; *Egemen Palas*, 28 rooms, 2 showers.

EĞRIDIR. *Çinar* (3), 21 rooms (8 with shower), restaurant; *Inci Sinan Palas* (4), 14 rooms; *Göl Palas*, 10 rooms. **At Barla**, on the lake: *Barla Motel* (4), *Gül Oberj* (4).

ESKIŞEHIR. *Gamgam* (3),115 rooms (88 with shower); *Dural* (4), 35 rooms (5 with shower); *Otagar* (4), 45 rooms (12 with shower). Also *Ankara Palas; Divan; Konak.*

ISPARTA. *Isparta* (4), 56 rooms (28 with shower), restaurant; *Konak* (4), 33 rooms, 3 showers; *Kristal*, 24 rooms.

KÜTAHYA. *Erbaylar* (3), Cumhuriyet Cad., 42 rooms with shower, restaurant; *Gül Palas* (4), 24 rooms; *Harlek Motel* (4), 29 rooms with shower; *Benli*, 32 rooms; *Konak*, 18 rooms; *Nizam*, 22 rooms.

NAZILLI. *Toros Palas.*

PAMUKKALE. *Tusan Motel* (2), 24 rooms with shower, sited within old fort ruins with warm water pool overlooking the plain. *Motol Koru* (2), 32 rooms with shower, and a pool; *Motel Pumukkale* (4), 8 rooms with shower; in the former agora, swimming pool. *Belediye* (Municipal) *Motel*, cheap and correspondingly simple, but two large pools.

Kur-Tur, motel and camping, 2 miles beyond ruins.

UŞAK. *Uzcan* (4), 17 rooms (3 with shower).

USEFUL ADDRESSES. *Tourist information:* in Burdur and Denizli, inquire for *Turizm Bürosu. Airlines:* T.H.Y., Afyon, Emek Hotel.

Discovering the Back Country

If you're one of those people who enjoy breaking up the trip occasionally with visits to places slightly off the beaten track, leave Izmir via the west-east highway (68) toward Turgutlu, Sardis, Salihli, Kula, Uşak, and Afyon. You'll be rewarded first by the Kerabel bas-relief, located on a small back road leading south (on the right), about 20 miles from Izmir.

The work depicts a personage known as Eti-Baba, who presumably was of Hittite origin and who was blessed with supernatural powers. Note the hieroglyphic inscription. This bas-relief was admired 2,500 years ago by Herodotus, who claimed that the figure carved by some anonymous sculptor represented the Egyptian conqueror Sesostris. Modern archeologists believe that it is more likely some unidentified Hittite divinity, rather than Eti-Baba himself.

When you get back on the main highway, cross the Pactole River again (before Sardis), but don't take the Sardis turn-off unless you're really keen on seeing it once more. Walls restored by the Ottomans still surround what used to be the famous Roman-Byzantine city of Philadelphia—the site of modern Alaşehir, 30 miles southeast of Salihli on a secondary road. The city succeeded in holding out against the Turks until the end of the 14th century, but today the three main mosques and the covered bazaar are of greater interest than the remains of the antique theater and of the Basilica of St. John, while nothing can be discerned of the temples of the emperors Tiberius, Caligula, and Vespasian.

Uşak was a Hittite city until 1180 B.C., after which it underwent the same fate as Sardis and became successively Phrygian, Lydian, Persian, and finally fell to Alexander. Subsequent to all that, it formed part of the kingdoms of Bithynia and Bergama before falling under Roman domination, to be eventually disputed over by the Byzantines and the Turks.

The city has a "new look" because some of the fiercest fighting in the War of Independence took place here. The vestiges of Flaviopolis near Banaz on the Afyon road are of interest only to archeologists; at Sivasli (Selçikler village), south on Route 23 there are the ruins of a classical theater. There's a carpet factory to visit at Uşak if you're interested.

Afyon, lying some 72 miles from Uşak, is a much bigger place. Among other things, it's a center for the production of narcotics — an opium stronghold! . . . under government supervision, however. (The opium will be used by doctors and hospitals around the world.) Winter can be nasty here, at an altitude of more than 3,000 feet. Afyon's distinguishing landmark is a rock 750 feet high, crowned by the Kara Hisar (Black Fortress), an impressive sight to behold. The view of Afyon from a plane is even more striking. As you approach it from the air, the steppe has something poignant about it, and your overall impression is that the human beings who dwell on it are utterly at the mercy of the hostile elements. The mountain peaks are sprinkled with streaks of snow, minute villages seem to snuggle down at the bottom of the valleys. The rock is sharply silhouetted, jagged and aggressive, until it abruptly relents and smoothes out, a blend of mellow ochres and spinach green colorings. A lone tree, the only one on the whole desolate plain, tentatively thrusts up its branches. Suddenly, Afyon Kara Hisar looms up, jutting forth between the mountains. On the airstrip below, sheep are grazing peacefully.

How much time should you allow for Afyon? A full day, half a day, two hours? You can best decide that for yourself. As you saw from the airplane, the citadel dominates the town. The ramparts are superb. Credit for building the original fortress is given to the Arzawa people, a Hittite tribe. The Phrygians then took over, to be followed by the Lydians, the Macedonians, and so on—there's no need to repeat the sequence of the various conquerors of Asia Minor.

The Ulu Cami dates from 1271. The Imaret Cami, less venerable, is considerably more ornate. Pay a brief visit to the Altıgöz Bridge that spans the Arpa Çay—the inscription commemorates the arrival of the Seljuks. In recent years the town has been further embellished by an arch of triumph (with interesting bas-reliefs) standing on the main square. The arch is in tribute to the 1922 Turkish victory over the Greeks in nearby Dumlupınar. The concern with historical reminders was ushered in with the Turkish Republic and has extended to include the creation of an Archeological Museum. The building itself was formerly the *medrese* of the Ahmet Gedik Paşa mosque, and now houses all the items found at excavations in Kütahya, Isparta, Burdur, and Uşak. (Certain objects go all the way back to the Bronze Age.)

Afyon is a starting point for many different excursions. There are rupestral tombs, caves, and Phrygian monuments in Ayazin, Göynük, Avdolos, Aslan Kaya, Kapi Kayalar, and in Emirdaği; Seljuk and Ottoman vestiges in Bolvadin, Çay, and Sandıklı. If Seljuk art attracts you, you'll find it worth while to thrust on beyond Çay along the Konya road (80) to see the caravanseray in Sultandaği. The mosque, the hamam, and the imaret in Sincanlı (west of Afyon) were designed by the great Sinan. Maden Suyu, 16 miles north, produces Turkey's outstanding mineral water.

Eskişehir and Kütahya

You are now entering the heart of ancient Phrygia, the realm of the famed King Midas. Midas must have been a particularly fanciful fellow. When it fell to him to pass judgment on the matter of the musical rivalry between Apollo and Pan, he decided in favor of the latter's flute, as against the divine lyre of the former. Considerably put out, Apollo caused donkey's ears to sprout from Midas's head. Without being too vain about his appearance, the unfortunate king strove to conceal his deformity. Although he couldn't prevent his barber from discovering it, he swore the man to silence, whereupon the unworthy ancestor of Figaro dug a hole in the ground and whispered his terrible secret to the earth. He filled in the hole, and reeds sprang up on the spot. When the slightest breeze blew, they could be heard murmuring, "King Midas has donkey's ears!"

And that wasn't all. Midas had a spontaneous quality in his pride, which eventually cost him dearly. On an occasion when Dionysus (Bacchus) was his guest, the latter invited Midas to make a wish. The ambitious ruler immediately voiced the desire to have everything he touched transformed into gold. No sooner said than done—and there he was, richer than Croesus, but in what a fix! He couldn't eat—even his food turned to gold, naturally. Dionysus, laughing heartily and derisively, assured the dismayed Midas that he would have to plunge himself into the waters of the Pactolus in order to get rid of his unfortunate "gift". Since that time, the river has flowed with gold, to the joy of the Lydians lower down the river.

The tomb of the legendary king is situated at Midas Şehri (City of Midas) in the wild country 54 miles south of Eskişehir. Some archeologists, however, now discount the theory that this was the vast necropolis of the Phrygians and believe the extraordinary monuments hollowed out of the rocks to be temples. There are interesting Seljuk and Ottoman mosques and tombs at Seyit Gazi, Sivri Hisar, south and east of Eskişehir, as well as in that town itself, which has developed into a prosperous commercial center now, a few miles from ancient Dorylaion, where the barons of the First Crusade decisively defeated the Seljuks in 1097, thereby restoring a great slice of Asia Minor to the Byzantines.

Either every bit of the ancient city of Kotyaion (now Kütahya) has disappeared, or else nothing of it has as yet been unearthed. The Byzantines constructed the inevitable fortress on the dominating hilltop. The local Seljuk rulers enlarged it and piously added two small mosques—the Imaret Mescidi, built by Yakup II in 1440 and now used as a library, the Hıdırlık Mescid, built in 1243 by Ibrahim Dinari—and the Vecidiye Medrese (1314). Bayezit I married the Seljuk heiress, and though Tamerlane established his headquarters for a time at this strategic crossroad, Kütahya prospered in the succeeding two centuries. Mehmet I dedicated the Ulu Cami in 1411 to the memory of his unfortunate father, Bayezit I, who died as Tamerlane's prisoner. The 19th-century restorers replaced the original wooden columns with marble. The Ishak Fakih Mosque dates from 1434 and the Hisarlı Mosque from 1487. The 16th century saw no slackening in religious building, plus seeing the construction of two baths (Küçük and Balik) as well as covered bazaars.

But fame came only with the forced settlement of Persian craftsmen after Selim I's victorious campaign. Kütahya tiles rivalled those of Iznik, but cobalt blue and milky white were predominant till the 18th century, when Iznik green, turqoise, purple and yellow were added. The local production continues.

The little village of Çavdarhisar, 38 miles southwest of Kütahya on the Uşak road (66) lies adjacent to still another famous site of antiquity, Aesani. A noble temple of Zeus ranks among the best-preserved sanctuaries of Anatolia, and there is also a theater, stadium and arched Roman bridge.

The Büyük Menderes Valley

The second road inland starts likewise at Izmir, runs south to Seljuk and then turns east along the Büyük Menderes (Meander River) through Anatolia's most fertile valley, renowned for its grapes, figs, oranges and apricots, to Aydın. Though damaged during the War of Independence, this thriving agricultural town of 43,000 inhabitants possesses several Ottoman monuments, among which is an outstanding example of 18th-century Baroque, the recently restored Cihanoğlu mosque next to the notable twin baths. A statue honors the *efe*, dancer of an old folk dance, chosen for his noble bearing, who wears the traditional costume and stands for the best in Turkish manhood.

On a ridge about a mile north are the agora, theater and gymnasium of ancient Tralles. This Hellenistic center of art developed a technique which reached the height of fashion in the 18th century, *trompe l'oeil*, or trick painting. The Roman architect Vitruvius describes how Hapathourios, wishing to enlarge the setting of the theater, lengthened the rows of marble columns with copies painted on flat ground.

Twenty miles further on, near Sultan Hisar, lie the considerable remains of ancient Nyssa, including the well-preserved amphitheater of the city's senate.

The valley's vineyards and orchards varying with cotton and tobacco fields as well as olive groves can support an unusual number of fair-sized towns. Nazilli's 42,000 inhabitants specialize in cotton fabrics and carpets. Soon after Kuyucak you branch right (south) to Karakasu and the ruins of Aphrodisias.

The City of Aphrodite

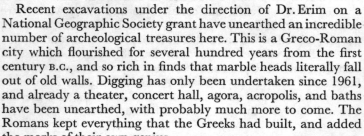

Recent excavations under the direction of Dr. Erim on a National Geographic Society grant have unearthed an incredible number of archeological treasures here. This is a Greco-Roman city which flourished for several hundred years from the first century B.C., and so rich in finds that marble heads literally fall out of old walls. Digging has only been undertaken since 1961, and already a theater, concert hall, agora, acropolis, and baths have been unearthed, with probably much more to come. The Romans kept everything that the Greeks had built, and added the marks of their own genius.

Unless you've come equipped with boots, it is very difficult to walk amid the ruins. But the museum is worth the whole trip—it's something out of this world, a sheer delight in its primitiveness and its rudimentary nature. The building is a kind of shed in which some wary genius has stashed away a hoard of treasures to protect them from the weather. In a big city museum, such riches would be arranged in several display rooms. Here in this barnlike structure, complete with exposed beams, a sort of passageway has simply been left clear in between the heaps of items. If any classification of the contents has ever been attempted, it's the curator's well-guarded secret. The collection includes statues of incalculable worth, carved stones, capitals of columns, fragments of bas-reliefs, all of them lying around in an obviously blithe disregard for chronological order, or any other kind of order. There is something profoundly moving about this bric-à-brac.

A rear section of the barn is partitioned off by a casual wooden barricade. This part contains rows of shelves stacked high, lines of boxes—including cardboard shoeboxes!—odd bits of stone, sundry pieces of sculpture. All this represents a preliminary and tentative approach to an inventory that will eventually entail many years of diligent and painstaking labor. A charming small figure of Aphrodite, even though it's broken in two, gladdens your eyes.

The houses in the adjacent village strike you by their newness. Why? The settlement at Geyre was simply displaced and relocated in order to make room for the excavations! In front of the museum, practically under the nose of the new buildings, a collection of sarcophagi attracts your gaze—there was no more space inside the barn.

Aphrodisias was built against the foothills of the Baba Daği. As in all Greco-Roman settlements, the acropolis dominated this ancient city devoted to the cult of Venus Aphrodite. The city gate and the 12 porticoes surrounding the ruins of the agora are still visible. The temple of the goddess Aphrodite is marked by a cluster of tall Ionic columns adorned with fluted ribbing. To the south is a building with intact blue columns. The Byzantines chose this place to build a basilica practically straddling the temple and the baths. Across the road is the ancient stadium. On a hill to the east lies the theater, in a fairly decrepit state. Notice also the mosaic floors of the Byzantine houses. The city's outer walls are still intact in spots. Try to see the recently-excavated odeon, in white marble, with its dressing rooms intact.

It is just feasible to continue eastwards to Denizli over a stabilized road through pine forests and rugged country to a hidden cultivated plain. A 4,000-ft pass leads through mountains twice as high, before you drop back into the Menderes valley.

If you have returned to the river at Kuyucak, you might try a shorter venture to Buldan, a picturesque settlement clinging to the mountain on the other side of the national highway, north of Sarayköy. This was the former Tripolis of the Meander, adjoining the village of Yenice. According to indications, the city was built before the arrival of the Romans. However, the ruins here don't offer much to the layman. Since you've come this far, you might as well continue on to the rupestral tombs nearby, east of the antique site.

Denizli, several times flattened by earthquakes, is another busy agricultural center of 65,000 inhabitants living along broad, straight avenues. Although the buildings leave much to be desired in the way of esthetic appeal, it's obvious that city planning has entered the picture here. But more interesting is the Seljuk Kale Içi (Citadel Market) dating from the 13th century when Denizli took the place of Laodicaea four miles away. Founded by the Seleucid Antiochus II in the 3rd century B.C. on the site of Ionian Dispolis destroyed by an earthquake, the extensive ruins include a Roman stadium, gymnasium and baths, built by Titus. There are also a theater and aqueducts.

Ak Han is a 13th-century caravanseray only 5 miles east of Denizli, with walls and portico still in a good state of preservation. The façade was originally covered with white marble. Inside stands a small mosque of the same period.

Nine miles further along lived the Colossians to whom St. Paul wrote epistles before their town was levelled by an earthquake in 60 A.D.

At Beycesultan near Çivril, 62 miles northeast at the junction of Routes 23 and 29, recent diggings have disclosed a prehistoric site from the Chalcolithic and the Bronze Ages. So far, 21 separate levels have been discovered, the upmost probably belonging to the capital of the Hittite kingdom of Arzawa. The mighty palace and ramparts were destroyed in the 13th century B.C.

A Stonework Niagara

Nature compensates in the grand manner for the frequent earthquakes by a site not to be missed on any account, the wondrous spot known as Pamukkale. You'll be killing two birds with one stone—in addition to the spectacular natural phenomenon, there are also the ruins of the antique city of Hierapolis. Pamukkale is 14 miles north of Denizli, and its name signifies "cotton fortress". One diehard group of materialists likes to claim that this name is derived from the peculiar chemical properties of its waters, which are excellent for washing sheep's wool and for making it colorfast. We prefer the etymology supplied by the poet who beheld a vision of the Titans' cotton crop spread out to dry on the sheer mountainside.

The mountain is sharply indented by a 300-feet-high cleft forming a circus of white cliffs. Down hurtles the onrushing petrified water, cascading and dripping from basin to basin, crystallized into dazzlingly white stalactites, like some gigantic

organ pipes. The miracle of Pamukkale resides neither in the
cures produced by the medicinal properties of its hot springs
(the ruins of the old baths are still visible) nor in the incredible
resistance of Hierapolis' walls, which have survived two millenia
of destructive earthquakes. The real miracle is the one wrought
by Mother Nature herself, who has more than one trick up her
sleeve in the way of chemistries that mere man could never hope
to duplicate. The water gushes out from everywhere at once, like
teardrops shed by the earth. Fresh drinking water trickles
blithely down the slope, and tiny streams of hot, lime-rich water
glide down, fanning out like veils, carving into the rock, shaping
it into small terraces and great basins that quickly overflow. The
water duly falls down to the next level, hollowing out a new basin
which in turn soon spills over, and so on down to the bottom of the
cliff. On the way down, part of the water has become petrified and
chalky, glistening with the drops that have slid over the bright
white stalactites. This stupendous array forms a staggering
spectacle, a fantastic and completely unexpected stack of terraces
and curtains of solidified liquid suspended in mid-air.

In places, the chalky expanse has the consistency of slightly
damp table salt; in others, it resembles heaps of rock salt; and
everywhere, the perpetually flowing water sprays on a kind of
foam that is transformed into varying shades of green, red, grey,
and yellow by the sun, the passing of time, and the mysteries of
chemistry. Occasional gaps gouged out of the lime carapace
reveal slices of the mountain, like layer-cake, which contrast
acutely by their difference in coloring. Miscellaneous grasses and
plants have thrust up tentative blades and leaves here and there,
but most of them remain drowned, caught in the mass of color;
chameleon-like, they have taken on the many hues of their
environment.

The silence of the mountain at Pamukkale is broken by the
ceaseless murmur of the hot running water that flows along,
forming bubbles which burst along the surface of the hollow
basins. The wind ripples it, the earth drinks it, and it becomes
petrified by its own components. Some of the basins sit empty—
the local peasants have altered the course of the streams in order
to irrigate their fields. Part of this stupendous décor is eroding
away, deteriorating through lack of upkeep. But the part that

subsists—which the Ministry of Tourism is now doing everything to preserve— suffices to make an unforgettable impression on the beholder.

Four motels have been built round large warm-water swimming pools, decidedly pleasant until you emerge into the chilly contrast of the mountain breeze. The walls of an 11th-century Byzantine castle still enclose the Tusan motel, where you might swim right to the edge of the cliff to look over the rim into the vast plain of Denizli to the blue mountains beyond, a wonderful if eery sensation.

Another, somewhat simpler hotel stands a little farther inland. Its swimming pool more than makes up for the modesty of the establishment. The water is exactly as warm and limpid, and the bottom of the tank holds a surprise in the form of ancient columns, steles, and capitals. By taking the elementary precaution not to bark your shins or dive headfirst onto a slab of soaking antique marble, you can enjoy a new adventure in underwater "stalking". And in any case, this initiation into submarine mystery provides the ideal transition for your tour of the ruins lying just the other side of the motel.

Ancient Hierapolis   (Pamukkale)

A terrible earthquake in A.D. 1334 spelled the final doom of Hierapolis. The abandonment of the city is thus an occurrence of relatively recent date. Despite repeated tremors, it had remained a sacred city (*hieron*) up to the time of the Crusades and the Seljuk invasions. Hierapolis was founded in 190 B.C. by Eumenes II, King of Pergamum, and reached its heyday following its reconstruction during the reign of Tiberius (A.D. 14–37). The Christian and Byzantine epoch left extensive traces here.

The area covered by Hierapolis, and notably the size of its necropolis, are astounding. People with ailments came there to take the cure. Some of them died here, and most of them enjoyed the kind of wealth that guaranteed a lavish and durable burial monument. The travertine stone, the glory of Rome, was abundant hereabouts, and no expense was spared to import marble from great distances. Vast expanses of marble can also still be seen near the springs of the local waters, which have a high carbonic salt content. At Cindeliği (Plutonium, or Pluto's realm), poisonous

gases emanate from the soils. The ancients ascribed the asphyx-
iating effect of the gases to the presence of malevolent spirits, and
the place was guarded by priests whose duty consisted in both
warning the passersby and in assuaging their fears. Two great
walls still rise along the main thoroughfare, and empty niches
mark the site where the Hall of Statues once stood.

The theater is an outstandingly handsome structure, extremely
well-preserved, and unrivalled except perhaps by the theater at
Orange, in France, or by the one at Aspendos, on the Mediterranean coast of Turkey. Although the stage has collapsed, the
travertine stone seats are still in perfect condition, and whole
sections of the orchestra have remained intact.

The area opened up for excavation is so vast that it is hard to
see how the archeologists will ever complete their task. Some
Italian archeologists have installed themselves under a huge, intact vault and put up a sign that denotes a singular concern with
the amenities—it forbids entry to persons wearing bathing-suits!
But this incongruous preoccupation with modesty strikes the
visitor less than does the monuments' incredible solidity. A considerable number of magnificent arches have withstood the or-
deals of both time and earthquakes.

The city walls rose up behind the theater, and a few of their
towers are still discernible. Inside the walls, in the northern part
of the city, you'll notice the remains of a Byzantine church. According to one school of thought, this marks the site of St. Philip
the Apostle's martyrdom. To the south, there are the extensive
remnants of another church, one of the earliest Christian ones,
dating back to the first century A.D.

At either end of the column-lined avenue along which you
have just come stand the city gates, still well preserved. The agora
was near the southern gate. The Roman gymnasium has a definitely appealing quality, not on account of its grandiose proportions but because of the babbling brook that frisks through it.

The road to the Kur-Tur camp leads past the 2nd-century
baths transformed into a basilica in the 5th century, through the
vast necropolis that stretches out for nearly a mile. The huge
array of sarcophagi, mausolea, and funerary monuments ranges
from the most sumptuous to the infinitely modest and discreet,
all of them exposed to the mercy of the elements. The custom

was for people to be buried with their jewelry and valuables. Grave-robbers, acutely aware of this fact, were able to operate continuously until the last century. Worse yet, the Seljuks, whose religion forbade the representation of the human figure, in most cases defaced the handsome bas-reliefs that originally adorned the tombs.

Some local peasants possess fine collections of old coins. The simple folk in Anatolia wouldn't dream of trying to palm off phony pieces on foreign visitors so if any of the back country people offer a coin for sale with the story that they themselves retrieved it from the earth, you can generally consider it authentic.

Toward the Lakes

On leaving the Menderes valley shortly after Denizli, the landscape changes abruptly from lush Mediterranean to a foretaste of the stark plateau of Anatolia. Shade is practically non-existent; the forests of antiquity were felled over the centuries of nomad incursions to provide grazing for the Seljuk flocks. Wind and rain have eroded the soil, but the peasants still toil laboriously to wrest grain from the arid fields. The distant mountains rear up ever higher, hostile and ominous. A *yürük* (nomad) camp may be in the vicinity, with its dark grey patched tents with turned-up edges, like those of the Bedouins. Their tenants camp here to be near the tiny rivulet and the few sparse plots of grazing land. As soon as the flocks have devoured the meadow grass, their owners will again fold their tents and steal away in the best time-honored tradition. Animals proceed slowly and majestically across the road, nonchalantly blocking traffic. An independent-looking camel comes to a dead halt in the middle of the highway, utterly indifferent to the irate horns honking. The huge shaggy beasts are often roped from saddle to head into camel-trains by means of colorful woven trappings.

Route 80 crosses from ancient Phrygia into Pisidia in the region of the lakes, along Acigöl and Burdur, allowing for interesting sidetrips to vast Eğridir, Akşehir and Beyşehir, or to the less accessible, smaller but no less picturesque Kovada, Selda and Göllhisar. The landscape is mostly uninviting, with arid, barren stretches of rock broken by gaps that give glimpses into areas of wild beauty, notably along the lake shores. The towns and villages are all unadulterated Turkish, although marked by the typical stubbornness that consists in striving to present the outward appearance of a western style while retaining, on the inside, the ancestral traditions of a type of comfort that remains incomprehensible to us. Examples of this abound—in the Çarşi (market), there is the customary profusion of wares wallowing in the consecrated chaos of the centuries, but housed between modern concrete walls; and there is the decline in picturesque appeal wherever industrially-produced artisanal objects have replaced the personalized craft of the artisan himself. For instance, the çarık, or leather sandals with the pointed upturned toes, which certain habitués of summer resorts would rave over, are no longer to be found in their authentic form. Instead, they are stamped out by machines and made from old tires, with sprightly disregard for the patches.

Forbidding-looking mountain crests bar the horizon—they are those of the Taurus Range (Toros Darı) on the west and the Anti-Taurus on the east, 1,325 km. (830 miles) long. The topmost peak is the Bulgar Dağı, over two miles high. You're traveling at an altitude of over 3,000 feet, yet the daytime is as warm as at the seashore. However, nights become extremely cold, and winters are pitiless. There is mute evidence in the eternal snows on the mountain tops, and in the barrenness of the wastelands on the high plateaus. But suddenly, the land becomes green again, covered with lush vegetation and peacefully grazing sheep, source of both wool and meat. The main crop is tobacco. There are even a few trees. Just as suddenly, you plunge back into a desolate wilderness of bleak slopes covered with gravel, rocks, and moss. The water in the lakes is brownish and brackish. In these parts the nomads are predominantly gypsies, of whom the Turks are not overly fond. They accuse them of "fighting too much, of using language that is as evil as themselves, of being uncouth and ill-bred".

In the old days, this region, which was then the province of Pisidia, was inhabited by a people whom the early records describe as a "wild, uncivilized tribe, probably driven out of the coastal area by the Greek settlers". However boorish and uncultivated they may have been, these people managed to preserve their independence from the Persian and Macedonian conquerors. The Romans succeeded in subjugating them, and made Antioch the capital of Pisidia. The small, picturesque city was later known as Yalvaç. Have a look at the ruins, which lie near the modern town. To the northeast is Akşehir, called Philomenion by the Byzantines, the birthplace of Nasreddin Hoca, one of the first great names in Turkish literature (14th century). You may also enjoy a passing glimpse of the remains of the Taş Medrese, and the türbe of Seyit Mahmut, of incidental interest (13th century).

After following the northern shores of Lake Acigöl with its rugged backdrop of mountains, the road crosses a featureless plain of wheat and barley fields.

At the junction before Dinar, Route 80 veers north to Afyon, providing the best connection with the earlier outlined trip inland. This also takes you the three miles to Dinar's old red-roofed houses rising steeply on an awesome mountain, from which a fierce stream tumbles down among the gardens and trees.

Route 25 turns southeast through orchards whose apples and pears are sold by remarkably unobtrusive children seated on the roadside. Skirting the northern point of 25-mile-long Lake Burdur, you have the equidistant choice to continue south either via Burdur or Isparta, at altitudes of 3,100 ft. and 3,465 ft. respectively. If you decide for the former, branch left seven miles before Burdur to the stalactite cave of Insuyu. The mineral water spring at the entrance flows into an underground river forming nine lakes, whose water is so clear that it is barely visible in the half-light, except in the rippling reflections of the vaults. There is a camping site near the cave.

Burdur (ancient Arcania Limnae, Byzantine Polydorion) is reputed for the architecture of one of its buildings, the Taşoda. Although hardly any bigger than Akşehir (32,000 population), it is an important industrial center for textiles, attar of roses and copper, and famous for cattle-raising. The town is built in a hollow surrounded by low sandy hills. The çarşı (market) features the by-now-familiar but incongruous blend of western progress and eastern conservatism. A visit to the Archeological Museum is as fascinating and rewarding as a stroll through the old streets. The museum collection consists of objects from the diggings in the environs, including, notably, items from the earliest neolithic age. This region was inhabited as far back as the sixth millenary B.C., and the Arzawa Hittites settled here in the second millenary. Some of the museum's treasures come from the nine levels so far unearthed at Hacılar, 15 miles southwest on the rough Tefenni road, which becomes rougher if you venture via Yesilova on Lake Selda (58 Miles) to Denizli, or to Lake Gölhisar (68 miles) with its ruined island castle and the Roman stadium, theater, agora and necropolis at Horzum (Cibyra).

Isparta, once the domain of the Seljuk Hamitoglu, lies to the east of Burdur, and is somewhat larger (40,000 inhabitants). It has a few Turkish buildings and monuments, a ruined fortress, a library crammed with 14,000 manuscripts, and a museum to warm the hearts of numismatists and students of folk art. Redolent with attar of roses and backed by a superb mountain, Isparta is a pleasant base for excursions to the remoter eastern lakes.

After 22 miles the asphalted road drops suddenly to the little town of Eğridir at the southern end of the deep-blue lake which extends for 35 miles at 3,000 feet above sea level. Ruined Byzantine churches rise on the islets, while a minaret tops the castle on the promontory jutting out from the tremendous snow-capped mountains, barren at the shores, but clad with magnificent cedar forests further south. The Çeşnigir Paşa mosque at the attractive village of Barla on the western shore possesses a tiled minaret.

At Anamas, 40 difficult miles east, is a 13th-century mosque, a caravanseray of the same period at Dadil on the better stabilized road to Gelendost, whence either northeast to Yalvaç and Akşehir, or southeast via Şarki Karaagaç with ist fine Seljuk monuments, to Beyşehir, the largest of the lakes, which is, however, easier accessible from Konya.

On Route 25 south Ağlasun (as Sagalassus the second town of Roman Pisidia) boasts of a 12,000-seat theater, rock tombs and a Byzantine castle. Incidere, Suzus, Bujak and, on the way out of the pass, Kirgöz, are Seljuk caravanserays. The gentler landscape heralds Pamphylia. After several turns, you come to another caravanseray, Evdir Han, with the road to ancient Termessos on your right. The Mediterranean isn't far.

Illustration at head of this chapter: General view of Bodrum (Halicarnassus).

THE TURQUOISE COAST

Unexplored Mediterranean Playground

Few areas in the entire Mediterranean region can boast of the wide variety and profusion of the sites offered by the Turquoise Coast. Its two broad, crescent-shaped bays of Antalya and Mersin and the deep waters off Iskenderun, should soon become a familiar sight to discriminating British and American visitors in quest of the ideal vacation sport.

The Turquoise Coast and its valleys, in which thrive an abundance of exotic vegetation, are protected from Central Anatolia's biting winds by the Taurus Range, whose snowcapped peaks tower proudly above. You can swim here through the end of November in the literally turquoise-blue water (which, for some reason, the Turks have chosen to call *Akdeniz*, or white sea.) Discover for yourself the miles upon miles of fine sandy beaches, concealed grottoes, and fragrant pine forests tumbling down the mountain slopes to the red cliffs. An ideal setting for any tourist, especially for the amateur archeologist, since history lurks everywhere in these stones. This part of Turkey is the heart of what the ancients called Lycia, Pamphilia, and Cilicia, and off to the west lies the realm of the small neo-Hittite kingdoms.

Practical Information for the Turquoise Coast

HOW TO GET THERE? *By T.H.Y. plane:* Istanbul-Antalya, 90 min., daily flights in vacation season; twice weekly from Ankara (via Afyon); Istanbul-Ankara-Adana, 2½ hrs., daily flights. *By ship:* Express boats Istanbul-Izmir-Iskenderun (one sailing weekly in summer); stops at Finike, Antalya, Alanya, and Mersin (3 days for Antalya). *By train: Taurus Express,* one trip weekly, Istanbul-Ankara-Gaziantep, with stop at Adana (transfer for Mersin); the *Çukurova* diesel train schedules two weekly trips between Ankara and Adana. *Bus service* from Ankara to the coast.

MOTORING. It is possible to follow stabilized Route 6 from Fethiye along the coast to Finike, but then you definitely have to turn inland to Korkuteli to link up with Route 25. Don't attempt the coastal track labelled Route 30 or even the more direct road via Altinkaya to Antalya. The Antalya-Adana stretch of Route 6, however, is asphalted throughout and between Gazipaşa and Silifke offers some of Turkey's most spectacular scenery. All the way to Mersin and Tarsus, the mountains rise straight up from the shore, leaving room for only a narrow coastal strip, on which bananas grow as one of the principal crops.

East of Adana, the road runs through relatively uninteresting countryside. After Ceyhan, it branches off to the right (Route 1, or E5) toward Iskenderun (Alexandretta), Antakya (Antioch) and the Syrian frontier. You may continue on toward Aleppo on a highway east via the frontier post of Cilvegözü, or south toward Latakia and Beirut via the frontier post of Yayladaği. Beyond the Belen Pass, Beirut is only 230 miles away. This itinerary is usually taken only by travelers en route to Syria or Lebanon. For a stopover, Iskenderun is preferable to Adana.

WHAT TO SEE? Antalya, the ancient city of Attalus II, king of Pergamos, is one of the outstanding places in this region that is lavishly blessed with important sites; from here, St. Paul and St. Mark set out to evangelize Asia Minor. Its historical monuments range from Roman times to those of the Seljuks and Ottoman Turks.

Antalya is the ideal starting point for tours to the outlying Greek cities of Perge, Aspendos, and Side, all of them full of remarkably well-preserved relics of the past. To the west of Antalya, the church of Demre—less easily accessible—contains the sarcophagus of St. Nicholas.

Alanya, further east, was the main fortified port of Alâeddin Keykubat, a 13th-century Seljuk ruler, and in its 700-year-old shipyards, sailing vessels are still being turned out to this day.

Eastward, the coastal landscape between Anamur and Silifke is especially lovely in winter and early spring. If you have a few days in Silifke, see the fortified mountain refuge of the mighty Turkoman emirs of Karaman. In Tarsus, visit the house in which St. Paul was born. And there's a sidetrip to the wilderness gorges farther north, the "Gates of Cilicia". Karatepe, some 90 miles to the northeast of Adana, is an important Hittite site. Antakya, to the south, boasts

St. Peter's Grotto, although its museum of mosaics is more interesting. Further inland, there are other Hittite vestiges at Maraş and at Gaziantep.

Hotels and Restaurants

ADANA. *Ağba* (3), Abidin Paşa Cad., 76 rooms with shower, restaurant; *İpek Palas* (3), Inönü Cad., 84 rooms with shower; *Santral Palas* (3), Abidin Pasa Cad., 58 rooms, 28 showers (rooftop restaurant is good). *Kent* (4), Ticaret Bankası Yanı, 23 rooms, 11 showers; *Erciyas Palas* (4), Özel Cad. 13, 49 rooms, 20 showers; *Kristal Palas* (4), Küçük Saat Karşişı, 32 rooms, 9 showers.

ALANYA. A good choice of modern motels, but only the *Alantur* (1), 75 rooms with shower, private beach, nightclub, 2 miles from town, the *Riviera* (4), *Alâeddin* and *Alanya* below the castle rock, are directly on the sea. All others, though adequate in their class, are across the coastal road: *Banana, Internasyonal* (2); *Merhaba, Panorama, Selan* (3); in town *Baba* (3) and *Alanya Palas* (4) overlooking the port; *Ankara Palas, Çinar, Plâj* of the simplest. Motels *Dinlenme, Turtas, Aspendos, Incekum* on fine beaches 6, 7, 13 and 14 miles respectively west of Alanya.

ANAMUR. Only the *Karan* motel (4), 8 rooms with shower, is on the beach. *Cephe, Saray* in the village.

ANTAKYA. *Atahan* (4), 28 rooms with shower, *Divan* (4) 25 rooms with shower, *Kent*. Better stay at the cooler Harbiye suburb 4 miles out: *Hidro* (3) 20 rooms with shower, but you are not allowed to swim in the large pool; *Cinar, Dephne*.

ANTALYA. *Perge* (2), Park Yanı, 20 rooms with bath, perched on cliffs over private bathing area; some rooms with balcony; *Büyük* (*Grand*) (2), Hastane Cad., 38 rooms with shower; sea views from position above

town harbor; *Villa Park* (4), Karaalioğlu Parkı, 16 rooms and 5 showers; opp. park near edge of town; *Park* (4), 45 rooms, 6 showers; *Divan Oteli* (4), Park içi, 14 rooms, 2 showers; *Hayat* and *Yüksel*, both on Şarampol Cad. and *Yayla Palas*, 45 rooms (21 showers). The *Büyük* and *Perge* have restaurants.

Motels: *Alpay*, 12 rooms with shower; *Antalya*, 20 rooms with shower, overlooking sea; *Derya, Sabo* on Konyaalti beach. Pensions: *Atlas, Olympiyat* and *Nuri* are possible, a few showers.

Restaurants: *Ankara Lokantası*, Hastane Cad. Same street: *Teras Restoran. Kulüp*, Ferner Cad.; *7 Mehmet Lokantasi* (best). Ali Çetinkaya Cad.

ARSUZ. *Arsuz* motel (2), 8 rooms with shower; *Arsuz* hotel (4), 25 rooms with shower.

BELEN. Picturesque village near Iskenderun. Restaurant nearby, motel at Tepebası, 2 hotels at Soğukoluk.

ERDEMLI. *Aile* motel (3), 60 rooms, 20 showers.

ERZIN, near the battlefield of Issos. *Erzin İçmesi*, in an emergency. 19 rooms with shower, restaurant.

FINIKE. *Köşk* (3) on the beach, 15 rooms (7 with shower), restaurant; *Esen Palas*, 7 rooms; *Şirin Palas*, 5 rooms.

GAZIANTEP. *Güney* (3), 32 rooms with bath. *Güzel* (3), 30 rooms with bath or shower; *Fıstık Palas* (4), 44 rooms, 10 showers.

ISKENDERUN. *Güney Palas* (4), 27 rooms (10 with shower), *Atlantik* (4), 32 rooms (11 with shower), both with restaurants, but the *Saray* restaurant on the waterfront is preferable.

KIZKALESI. *Kiskalesi* motel (4).

MANAVGAT. *Sorgun* motel (4), 22 rooms, 12 with shower.

MARAŞ. *Çeltik Palas*, 30 rooms (8 with bath or shower); *Konak*, 18 rooms.

MERSIN. *Toros* (3), Atatürk Cad., 63 rooms with shower; *Türkmen* (4), Bahçelievler, 51 rooms, 36 showers, both with restaurants. *Bonjour* (4); *Ak*, *Kent*.

POZANTI. *Kiper* (4).

REYHANLI. *Göl* (4), 9 rooms, 7 showers. *Reyhanli* motel.

SAMANDAĞ. Beach southwest of Antakya. *Diplomat* (2), new, 32 rooms with shower, restaurant.

SIDE. *Turtel* motel (3); Pension *Pamfylia*.

SILIFKE. *Boğsak* motel (3), 17 rooms, 12 showers.

Good restaurant: *Saray*.

SOĞUKOLUK. Mountain resort about 30 miles from Antakya. *Yeni Turizm* (3), 18 rooms with shower; *Çamlar Oberj* (4), 29 rooms with shower.

TARSUS. *Palas Göz; Palas Berdan.*

VIRANŞEHIR. *Viranşehir Motel*, on the ruins of ancient Pompeiopolis. 12 rooms with shower.

 OFFICIAL CAMPING GROUNDS. Adana: *Küçük Kamp*, 2 miles west of Adana; *Station BP*, Fikircioglu, 8 miles west of Adana. Alanya: *Mocamp*, 13 miles west of Alanya. Anamur: *Altinkum Camping*, Anamur, beach. Antalya: *Sabo Tesisler ve Kampi*, Konyaalti beach. Arsuz: *Iskenderun Dinlenme Kampi*. Side: *Sorgun Kampı*. Silifke: *Silifke Mocamp*, 18 miles east of Silifke and 33 miles from Mersin, near the ruins of Korigos. Mersin: *Boğsak Kampı*.

 USEFUL ADDRESSES. *Tourist Information:* Adana, Ticaret Borsasi; in Alanya, Iskele Cad.; in Antalya, Hastane Cad. 4 (tel. 1747); in Iskenderun, Hürriyet Cad. 1–2; in Mersin, Belediye Binasi (tel. 1265), and at the Toros Hotel; at the frontier posts of Yayladaği and Kilis. The *Türk Hava Yollari Airlines:* in Adana, Atatürk Cad. (Yeni Borsa); in Antalya, Tophane Meydani Posta Sok 11/1; in Gaziantep, Atatürk Bulvari 29/A. *Turkish Maritime Lines (Denizyollari):* Alanya, Antalya, Limaniçi, Iskenderun, Mersin.

To photograph Karatepe, it is necessary to have a permit from the Department of Archeology, obtainable in Istanbul or in Ankara.

Exploring the Turquoise Coast

In Antalya, at last we have a city that truly deserves the adjectives "gentle" and "smiling", descriptions that don't often apply anywhere. Whether it's the newly- and neatly-installed beach promenade, the white houses with their red-tiled roofs, or the infallible Mediterranean genius that performs its reliable miracles wherever it occurs, no matter. The fact remains that Antalya is charming. And yet—there's no doubt about it—Antalya (72,000 population) is in all respects a thoroughly Turkish city. Its identifying landmark is its unusual ribbed minaret, crowning the Yivli Minare Cami, in the center of town. This is an ancient Byzantine church decorated with exquisite blue tiles; the Seljuk Sultan Alâeddin Keykubat (1219–1238) made it into a mosque, and it has now become an archeological museum. (Keykubat was the Great Man of History on this particular bit of the coast—the brilliance of his achievements put all previous ones in the shade.)

The earliest local residents were the Hittites. Greco-Roman colonization led to the founding of the province of Pamphylia. The still extant witnesses to this epoch are the great sites of Side, Aspendos, and Perge. Founded by Greek settlers in about 1000 B.C., these towns increased in importance under the Lydians, Persians and Hellenistic kings as well as in intervals of independance till the 2nd century B.C., when Attalus II of Pergamum, foiled in his attempt to take Side, established a new naval base which he named after himself Attaleia. Known as Satalia to the crusaders who used the port to avoid Seljuk territory, it became Antalya in the 13th century when Alâeddin Keykubat turkified the area.

Antalya's geographical situation deserves a paragraph all to itself. Take a look at the map. The coast stretches along the broad Bay (*Körfez*) of Antalya. To the west rises the Bey's Mountain, and a virtually "perpendicular" shore that provides a magnificent backdrop. Beyond, to the north, the graduated levels of the Taurus mountain peaks thrust up into the sky. Eastward stretches a beautiful length of coastline indented with many streams—the Aksu, Köprüsuyu, Manavgat, and Düden rivers—with waterfalls cascading down into the sea from the heights of the adjacent cliffs. (In spots, this area bears a striking resemblance to parts of Spain's Costa Brava, with its deeply cleft shoreline, and the colors of the rocks, which are so intensely permeated by the turquoise blue waters that they have taken on a coral hue.) A wide variety of crops are grown here, predominantly citrus fruits. The area is further blessed with shady pine forests, lakes, and one of the world's most perfect climates.

The second-century Romans rebuilt the original Greek walls, and the Seljuks made further restorations in their time. Along certain segments, you can clearly discern the contributions made to these walls by successive civilizations. The town has a double set of ramparts—the inner wall defended the port and the other wall protected the city. Needless to say, since the Seljuk era, these walls have continued to undergo many transformations, and today they are in an excellent state of preservation.

Emperor Hadrian honored Attaleia with his visit in A.D. 130 To commemorate the occasion, a splendid portal was built, consisting of three identical arches adorned with columns topped by Corinthian capitals. Since the city has expanded archeologically, you walk down a few steps to reach the earlier level. As you pass under the arches, you're headed toward the typically Turkish center of the city.

An ancient tower, Hıdırlık Kulesi, stands along the edge of the city's flowering park. With its square foundations and cylindrical main structure, it is presumed to have once served as a lighthouse. There is a beach below the park and another called Mermerli close to the port. But the greatest of Antalya's many attractions is the superb view westwards across the gulf to the Lycian mountains where the Twelve Gods held sway. This grandiose landscape can best be enjoyed from the terrace of the Mermerli café above the port, or the square above the museum.

At the other end of the park is the Kesik Minare Cami, a mosque with a truncated minaret. The mutilation of the minaret along the base of its short corolla makes it resemble a candlestick with its candle three-fourths consumed. The building is in a sorry plight today as the result of a fire at the end of the 19th century. The Byzantines transformed this former Roman temple into a triple-naved basilica dedicated to the Panaghia (the Virgin). The Turks consecrated it to Islam. Traces of second-century workmanship are discernible on the stone portal. As for the truncated minarets, expect to see quite a few of them in Turkey.

The Karatay Medresse, recently restored, dates from 1250, and boasts a handsomely decorated portal. Opposite the ribbed minaret stands another medresse, the Seljukid, its squat tower capped by a pointed roof. This building, too, is sadly in need of repairs, and plans for its restoration are currently under way. Nearby is a *mevlevihane*, an establishment which once belonged to the Whirling Dervishes, an order founded by Mevlâna. Unless you feel a particular interest in Turkish monuments, you can afford to skip the remaining mosques—Bali Bey, Müsellim, Paşa, and Murat. On the other hand, the two 13th-century *türbes*, Mehmet Bey and Karataş, are well worth a visit. In the port, see the charming little mosque, Sahildibi Mesciti, in which the fishermen and dockworkers regularly perform their rituals. Lastly, the Archeological Museum, housed in the former Yivli Minare Cami (six domes), deserves your special attention. The mosaics from Xanthos, depicting the infant Achilles being dangled by one heel as his mother dips him into the River Styx; the Greek ceramics; the figurines (including one of Apollo dating from the third century B.C.); the sarcophagi . . . all these objects were retrieved in the course of excavations in the surrounding area, and everything has been arranged and displayed with taste and intelligence.

The Legends

For almost the entire length of the shore, the cliffs plunge sharply down to the water's edge. A guide will point out the place—near the post office—where there is a deep cleft in the rock, with a sheer fall of some 60 feet. This was the outlet for a now dried-up stream, whose bed was deliberately altered. It was called Kadinyari, a kind of Tarpeian rock. From the heights above, unfaithful wives were allegedly hurled to their deaths.

You will undoubtedly be told that a perpetual flame is burning on the wild western shore, atop the Bey's Mountain that looms high above. The most plausible explanation of this phenomenon is that it's a natural gas outlet which catches fire on contact with the air. The fire devouring the mountain has become in local lore "the tongue of the Chimera"—it was right here at Çirali that Bellerophon slew the monster.

The story goes that, as a boy, Bellerophon had inadvertently caused the death of one of his friends, Belleros, whence his surname, meaning "slayer of Belleros". He found refuge at the court of Proetos, King of Argos, and must have been a handsome lad, since Queen Sthenebee tried to seduce him, in the best Potiphar tradition. Proetos, reluctant to complicate his private life, rid himself of Bellerophon by turning him over to Iobates, King of Lycia. The latter, whose explicit instructions were to do away with the youth, couldn't quite bring himself to kill him. Instead, he assigned Bellerophon a mission from which it was believed no one could return alive—the slaying of the Chimera. This creature's peculiarities included a lion's head, a goat's body, a dragon's tail, and a huge gaping mouth from which fire spewed forth.

Bellerophon figured that the successful accomplishment of his assignment would require some sort of airborne operation. At that period in history, the only available air transportation happened to be the winged steed, Pegasus. And the only way to borrow Pegasus was through a petition to the goddess Athena. The latter, touched by Bellerophon's plight, handed over to him the golden reins, the only ones capable of controlling the divine horse. With the aerial problem solved, there still remained the bombing strategy to be worked out. Bellerophon placed a leaden sheathing over his lance blade, which he plunged into the Chimera's maw. The flames belching out of the creature's gullet melted the lead, thereby choking and suffocating the monster. But the flaming tongue somehow stayed put and is continuing to burn to this very day . . .

Not the least of Antalya's attractions, one that makes you want to linger on is the spacious beach of Konyaalti, on the western edge of town. Although it isn't a sand beach, it still issues an invitation to relax. On the other side of Antalya, there's an even better beach, Lara, 8 miles of pleasant driving through luxuriant orchards. There's a fabulous view, and the great waterfall plunging 150 feet down has a guaranteed built-in rainbow, with Lara in the background, thrusting out its prong of sand from the sheltering cove.

West of Antalya

It is only 20 miles to Termessos, but the last mile off the Korkuteli road, ascending a tremendous gorge to 5,000 ft among the wild mountains is hard going. A few tombs lining the edge of the path are the harbingers of your approach to the ancient city. On this rocky site, the most modest attempt at urban expansion required enormous effort. The local residents got around their problem by building terraces. The theater is perched high, and the necropolis begins smack in the middle of the residential area.

The first recorded reference to Termessos, which stands over a mile high, occurs in the chronicle of Alexander's conquests.

When its defenders' heroic resistance prevented him from taking the city, he consoled himself by setting fire to the nearby olive trees. The Romans enhanced the city with many temples, public buildings, and statues. Because of the scarcity of Christian relics here, historians are inclined to set the date of the abandonment of the site at about the fifth century. After the excavations have been completed, more light will have been shed on the history of this place. It sits tucked into a narrow plain between two mountains. If its inhabitants had any of the characteristics of the surrounding landscape, they may well have been of a harsh and uncompromising nature, well able to put up a good fight against Alexander. However, judging from the magnificent remains of the ideally situated theater, it is also logical to conclude that the citizens of Termessos were blessed with extremely good taste.

Most of the public buildings are clustered together in one part of town, thereby facilitating your visit. However, the way in which the ruins lie makes access somewhat tricky. Ladies, wear your flat heels! Remember that all these stones were upheaved by earthquakes, and that the archeologists' task is far from finished.

As you head south, pause for a moment at Elmalı, a picturesque mountain locality (mosque of Ömer Paşa), and also at the village of Tekke, with its ancient dervish settlement (*tekke*). But this area's feature attraction is a natural phenomenon on the outskirts of Elmalı, the Black Lake (Karagöl), whose waters spill out into a yawning chasm, a gigantic slit in the rocky wall bordering the high plain.

Down below at the seashore is Finike (its name derived from Phoenicus), famous for its magnificent tombs sculptured out of the solid rock, and 20 miles farther on, you come to Demre (or Myra), the burial place of a personage dear to the hearts of western children, St. Nicholas (Santa Claus), whose frescoed church has been restored, but the reliquary with some bones of Father Christmas is in the Antalya museum. Most of the ancient town is covered by the Demre river, except the theater. Another one has been cut into the huge rock at Apollonia, a small Lycian township facing Kekova island across the channel.

Lycian sarcophagi are outlined on a ridge and rock tombs are cut everywhere into the cliffs on your way westwards. You zig-zag down a formidable mountain to Kaş (ancient Antiphel-los), the port of the Lycian capital Phellos, further inland. The well-preserved Hellenistic theater commands a superb view over the gulf and the natural breakwater of Meis island.

More rock tombs line the 8 miles north to Kasaba, starting point for an excursion into the vast cedar forests.

The Harpies

Route 30 continues westwards along the coast and past a lake to the Kocacoy (Xanthos River), the border between Lycia and Caria. Near Kinik are the ruins of Xanthos, a flourishing town from the 7th century B.C. till its harbor silted up in Byzantine times. Don't miss the monuments of the Harpies and the Nereids. The Harpies were the monstrous daughters of Poseidon and the Earth, complete with claws, female faces, vultures' bodies, and bears' ears. They probably also had nasty dispositions, since their name is still commonly applied to contemporary untamed shrews. The Nereids were those charming sea nymphs, the daughters of Nereus and Doris, and there were 50 of them, doubtless extremely pleasant to encounter in a bosky clearing. A French team of archeologists has unearthed here a square agora containing a basilica, which was sacked by eight-century Arab pirates. There are also a theater in reasonably good shape and a necropolis whose sarcophagi—alas, like so many others—have suffered the ravages of plunderers of treasure-trove. And there are, of course, still some more Lycian tombs hollowed out of the rock.

After covering the main sites west of Antalya, Route 30 turns inland and at Kemer you have the choice to continue to Fethiye and the Aegean provinces or return northeast to Korkuteli on a very scenic but also very rough road through the mountains.

Before bidding farewell to Antalya the gentle, just one word in passing to remind you that this is one of the rare spots in the world in which you can go skiing in the morning, followed in the afternoon by sailing, scuba-diving, underwater fishing, or just plain swimming and sunbathing. And now we must take regretful leave of this true vacation paradise for the eastern resorts and antique sites to Alanya, 75 miles away. Our road will bring us to three compulsory stopping points, plus two optional ones.

Perge

Perge lies at only a short distance (about 11 miles), from Antalya—take the left turn off Route 6 at Aksu. Although Perge recognized the suzerainty of Lydia, it also enjoyed the status of an independent city-republic up to the time of Alexander the Great's arrival. Under Roman rule the city was further enhanced. Its decline began only with the Byzantine era. During the Hellenistic period, it acquired an exterior wall, strengthened by numerous turrets which still encircle the vast ruins. Two round towers guard the gate and portico at the head of the monumental way which traversed the city. Some 150 feet inside rose a second fortified enclosure. An impressive remnant and one corner of this enclosure are still visible through the entrance arch, as is the Victory Portal. The truncated Acropolis looms in the background—this was the upper city, which was soon outgrown by the citizens, who built the lower part of town out on the plain, toward the south. After you pass the two walls, the two round towers that you saw framing the Victory Portal stand out in all their architectural grace and glory. On the right is the Roman basilica that was converted into a church by the Christians.

Down below on the left, between the first and second enclosure walls, there stands a 30-foot-high building that has held out against all the centuries—the thermal baths. Now turn around and get the full impact of the beauty of the inner surface of the Victory Portal, and of the sweep of the arch where it meets the walls and the niches, placed side by side on two levels. The proportions are truly admirable. The marble plaques that covered the surfaces and the statues adorning the niches have been shattered, and their fragments litter the ground, inextricably mingled with the débris of columns. The agora faces the thermal baths. The best route through these ruins lies along the town's main artery, which begins on the south outside the enclosure wall, at the entrance to the theater, and ends at the Palestra, at the base of the Acropolis. A drainage canal once ran down the middle of this spacious thoroughfare lined with vast porticoes. On either side stood two rows of columns with square shafts, and both the right and the left sidewalks were paved with mosaics, covered with galleries, and lined with shops.

Closer to the Acropolis, a second avenue intersects the first one. The original paving stones are still there, and despite the wear and tear of centuries, the marks of chariot wheels are still visible. In the 13th century, a brief but violent earthquake knocked down all the columns. They have now been placed back in an upright position, and some of them conserve their original capitals. The last four are adorned with figures representing, in the following order as you walk away from the Victory Portal Demeter (Ceres), Zeus (Jupiter), Artemis (Diana), and Apollo (Phoebus). And right here the centuries have spared a precious bit of mosaic that once served as a shop sign. Two other virtually intact columns stand opposite, topped with capitals and their connecting crosspiece. The three letters that you see—B, E, P— are undoubtedly part of a longer inscription, probably "Republic of Perge". At the far end of the main street, on the left, stood the Roman basilica, the one in which St. Paul, coming from Cyprus, met St. Barnabas. The Apostle delivered his very first sermon and won his first converts right here in Perge.

The stadium that lies outside the walls could hold 25,000 people. It is one of the biggest (nearly 800 feet long) and best-preserved stadiums of Roman times. Except for the stage, the restoration of the theater has been completed. The archeologists carefully numbered the stones of the tiered seats that have been put back into place after a bit of cleaning up. A fountain faces the restored arch of the crumbled entrance gate. For the time being, the theater stage is not quite ready for a performance, but should the festival habit spread it could soon be made usable. The theater seated 12,000, culture being fully as important as games and sports. The fine statuary that has been retrieved by the excavators is temporarily enshrined in the local museum.

Twelve miles beyond Aksu a rough track merging into the ancient way leads north (left) to the ruins of Syllion, 750 feet above the plain, near Yanköy. Parts of the high flat rock were split off by an earthquake and a deep chasm cuts through the theater, dividing the stage from the auditorium. Hellenistic, Roman and Byzantine buildings as well as a Seljuk mosque are precariously perched on the remaining southern platform.

Aspendos

The next turn north leads to the best-preserved antique theater, at Aspendos (modern Belkis) 31 miles from Antalya, on the banks of the Eurymedon (Köprüçay). Its excellent state of conservation may be partly due to the quality of the materials used or to the architect's skill, but above all to its conversion—of all the unlikely possibilities—into the palace of a Seljuk sultan.

According to the tale, the daughter of the king of Aspendos was as lovely as only a fairytale princess can be. Many nobles eagerly sought her hand in marriage, but her father, who had his own ideas on the subject, consistently refused all offers. Finally, one day, he issued a proclamation announcing that the princess would be given in marriage to the man who would construct a building contributing to the people's welfare. One contestant came forward and declared: "Aspendos could use more fresh water. I shall construct an aqueduct." Another stated: "Aspendos needs greater entertainment facilities: I shall build a theater." Both architects launched into their undertakings, and each of them urged his workmen on at such a pace that the two projects were completed at the same time. The burning question was to decide which man most deserved to wed the princess.

According to the king, the only solution was to cut the princess in two and give half of her to each of the two suitors. The builder of the aqueduct agreed, but the theater architect said he preferred the poor girl to remain intact, even if it meant his losing her to his rival. And, naturally, it was the builder of the theater who won the fair maiden.

The theater has managed to keep a grandiose air about itself. The acoustics are so fine that performances are put on here without amplifiers or microphones. Turkey's most outstanding acting groups perform ancient Greek plays here (in Turkish) every year, during the drama festival. They also perform the classical repertory, including *Oedipus Rex*, *Julius Caesar*, *Britannicus*, etc. In addition, *karakucak* contests are staged here, this being a Turkish adaptation of Greco-Roman wrestling. The Antalya area is noted for the excellence of its athletes in this particular national sport.

Aspendos lies several miles inland today, but even in ancient times it had no actual seaport. Ships reached it via the Eurymedon River, which in those days was navigable. The river was spanned by a bridge "high enough for a ship to pass under", whence the Turkish name for it (*Köprüçay*: *köprü*, bridge, and *çay*, river).

The first bridge gave up the ghost some six or seven centuries ago. It was replaced by a graceful Seljuk hogback bridge, only high enough to allow the passage of small boats, since the river port in the meantime had become sanded over.

Aspendos at one time enjoyed a thriving commerce, its reputation resting mainly on cattle-breeding. Alexander the Great agreed to spare the city in exchange for a ransom of 4,000 horses. The rest of the local industry was centered around silks, rugs, and miscellaneous luxury items, with particular emphasis on tiny figurines carved out of lemon wood and decorated with ivory, a specialty that might be described as the "high class" souvenir of the times.

Most of the visitors who come to Aspendos seem to limit themselves to admiring the theater. The architect's identity is known —his name was Zenon, and he was a native son of the city (not to be confused with the philosopher who founded Stoicism). The stone he used came from neighboring quarries and possessed an elastic quality that enabled the walls to form a solid block. The cement was a "natural binder blended with water and salt". The edifice has survived in its original state, withstanding all the ravages of 18 centuries of weather, wars, plunderers, and earthquakes. It can be described as virtually intact except for one part of the upper cornice that has become slightly worn away.

In the 13th century, the north wing was threatening to collapse, and the Seljuks reinforced it with bricks, which accounts for the typically Islamic broken arch in the center. A few rows of seats have also been restored. But the theater as a whole has conserved its integrity, an impressive fact when one realizes that the diameter of the amphitheater is some 300 feet. It reportedly sat 20,000 people, but if you allow only one and a half feet per spectator, it's more likely that its total capacity was 15,000. The arches along the upper gallery are also mostly intact—they enabled members of the "promenade" audience to watch the performance while remaining comfortable in the shade. Of course, the wall niches that used to hold the ornamental statuary are now empty, but the raised box seats for guests of honor, on either side of the stage, and the decoratively-carved superstructures over the stage have survived. There are even traces of paint still visible on the south wall. The aisles on both sides of the orchestra are crowned with triple-arched vaulted ceilings, each arch higher than the one that precedes it, the tallest reaching a height of 80 feet! The columns fell prey to the 13th-century quake, but the stone projecting pieces held firm. Various inscriptions are there to remind posterity that the building was financed by two worthy patrons of the arts, Crispinus Arruntianus and Auspicatus Titinnianus, during the reign of Antoninus Pius, between the years A.D. 138 and 161.

Aspendos was built up against two hills, the tallest of them being, of course, the Acropolis. There's no way for cars to go up to the top, and people seem reluctant about making the climb on foot. In any case, the ruins up there are in pretty much of a jumble, and are of real interest to professional archeologists only. They include the basic layout of the agora, with vestiges of the basilica and curia, a wall 115 feet long and 50 feet high that was part of the fountain (or nympheum), and a semi-circular altar in the Odeum, or concert hall. North of the city, extensive segments of the aqueducts that channelled in water over distances of 15 and 20 miles are still visible.

Side

Side (pronounced *See-day*), 49 miles from Antalya, lies to the south (right). Banana plantations vie with orange groves along the roadside, and the vegetation becomes more profuse as you travel east.

From quite a distance, Byzantine ruins herald the proximity of the ancient city, perched on a promontory that is 2,600 feet long and 1,000 feet wide. Finally, the great enclosure wall looms into view. The name of Side comes from a word signifying pomegranate. The exact date of the city's founding and the identity of its founder are not known, although its major development was in the seventh century B.C., under the impetus of Greek colonists from Aeolis. Side was an important port and commercial center, bustling with piracy and a thriving slave trade. However, the Romans deserve the credit for most of its monuments, which date from the dawning centuries of the Christian era. The most prevalently held theory is that the city was devastated by Moslem invasions in the ninth century, and that earthquakes polished off what was left.

The sections of the enclosure wall that protected the more inland part of the city are more or less intact. It's easy to make out the various layers of Greek foundations—and Roman and Byzantine additions. The walls closest to the sea didn't stand up so well. The entrance portal is still flanked by two towers, but the statues that once embellished it are now in the museum. Opposite the entrance, outside the walls, stands what is undoubtedly the most exquisite fountain in all Asia Minor—it has a semicircular façade with three carved niches. Still more fountains are scattered throughout the city itself.

Just inside the entrance, two streets branch off. One is a main thoroughfare leading straight ahead toward the ruins. The other, forming an acute angle with the first one, veers off to the left, and along it stands a Byzantine basilica. The columns lining these two streets, which are bordered by porticoes from 30 to 35 feet wide, were adorned with Corinthian capitals. Note the two clearly discernible houses, separated by a narrow passage, with marble-paved courtyards and a cistern in each courtyard.

A short distance farther on, to your left, the agora spreads out, enclosed on all sides by porticoes, with shops on three sides. The remnants of a circular structure in the center are those of the temple of the goddess Tykhe. It has a central room surrounded by a gallery with 12 Corinthian columns, and a pyramidal twelve-sided dome. In one corner of the square, you'll see a marble-walled building, looking almost like a luxury shop. Guess again! These were the public toilets. Another short street running southeast gives out onto a second agora, where there's still a lot of digging to be done. Among other things is a statue of Nemesis, the goddess of vengeance, the first one we've met so far in Anatolia. The other statues have been removed to the local museum.

The theater stands with its back to the first agora, and is distinctive in that its amphitheater is not set on a hillside. It's larger than those in Perge and Aspendos, and accommodated 25,000 people. The façade curves inward, while that of the theater in Aspendos was straight across. The circular galleries are on a lower level. Although the stage is somewhat the worse for wear, the rows of seats have, as usual, survived relatively well.

At the end of this street lies the old landing dock. This is the farthest point of the promontory. On the right, toward the sea, are what used to be Side's port facilities. History is hovering everywhere—Roman temple casts its shade on a Byzantine fountain; two other temples, on the right, are dedicated to Athena and Apollo; and there's a Byzantine basilica. Still more Byzantine relics along the way include private houses, and public baths, on both sides of the street. The beholder is understandably overwhelmed and perhaps a bit dazzled. Preceding and mixed with the Corinthian style, here come Ionian and Doric columns, and all these distinguishing yet intermingled landmarks left by successive civilizations have become further and inextricably tangled up by the centuries.

Now retrace your steps back toward the agora—the museum rises up straight ahead, housed in the old Roman baths. The statues inside have all been rescued in the course of local excavations, but they had already lost their heads, alas. When St. Paul of Tarsus converted the people of Side to Christianity, the neophytes' overzealous fervor prompted them to decapitate the figures of pagan deities. The capacious hall on the right of the tepidarium, or lounge, features a large collection of detached heads, plus some handsomely-carved sarcophagi, more statues, and capitals. The arch has been restored, but it seems incredible that these walls should have lasted so long.

The adjoining room used to be the *caldarium*—it is now arrayed with showcases and statues. There's Nike, the goddess of victory, who little dreamed that a 20th-century space weapon would be named after her, and here's Hercules, sporting a splendid curly beard, but with only a single leg, impressively muscular. See also the Twelve Labors of Hercules in bas-relief, and the Torment of Ixion, who was changed into a hermaphrodite for having dared to gaze upon Hera (Juno).

As you emerge from the museum, the Taurus Range is visible on the horizon. Popular belief is that its shape resembles Atatürk's death mask. Two fine beaches, a motel, a restaurant, and a few wooden cottages are all that enhance this site, which might well become one of the most flourishing resorts in Asia Minor.

First of the optional stops is at the Manavgat Falls. A few cement footbridges bring you across the many secondary streams. Now, suddenly, you find yourself on a delightful terrace in midstream. The small café serves tea, naturally. It's all extremely primitive and charming. Although the river doesn't rise more than ten feet, the current is powerful, but don't expect to see a second Niagara. Only three miles off Route 6, the falls offer a cool rest even on the hottest days. The second optional is another short turn north, to Alarahan, a 13th-century fortified caravanseray on a precipitous hill overlooking the Alara stream in a lovely wild landscape.

Alanya

From a distance, the 800-foot-high rocky mass of Alanya somewhat resembles a miniature Gibraltar, by a slight stretch of the imagination. Drive right on up for a full view of the countryside. A word of warning: better spare your car this particular ordeal! You can hire a taxi for the excursion. The ancient citadel towers above at the very top. Don't worry if you are bumping up what looks and feels like sheer rock face—the vast panorama that begins to unfold as you climb is an exhilarating spectacle. The car's first halt is merely a pretext to allow a whole swarm of young girls to proffer their silk scarves, which are a local specialty. Ancient Korakesion, high up on the rock, was a haunt of pirates until conquered by the Romans who presented it to Cleopatra. The Byzantines firmly entrenched themselves before Alâeddin Keykubat ousted them in the 13th century. The emir married the daughter of the vanquished governor, and proceeded to call the place Alâiye, a name that eventually became Alanya. Later on, after decline had set in, the Seljuks had to cede the location to the Ottoman Karamanoğullaris, in 1471.

The outer wall is five miles long and required 12 years to build. The existence of some 400 cisterns made it possible to keep enough water on hand to withstand almost any length of siege. Arrows could be rained down on attackers through 108 battlement crenels. When the defenders were finally submerged by the invaders, they withdrew to the ramparts of the second enclosure, and made their last stand in the confines of the third enclosure. The Seljuk city was established inside the first wall, and the

Seljuk shield is emblazoned on the postern gate of the second wall. Inside, there's a high-ceilinged room topped by a vast dome, pierced with loopholes on all sides. The entrance arch is probably of Roman design. A Seljuk-style broken arch adorns the outer façade. The fortress's rather small mosque, Kale Cami, is located between the second and third walls. Although the paint applied by the Moslems and the frescoes that once adorned this ancient church have faded with time, some of the color still manages to gleam through. Its foundations date back to Theodosius, and the restored dome is from the time of Suleiman the Magnificent (1530).

Nearby as you go toward the interior are the remains of the Bedesten, which boasted 26 rooms and vast storage spaces. It was probably a Seljuk caravanseray that housed a storeroom for the castle. Farther on, beyond the reservoirs, stands the small, attractive Aksebe Sultan mosque—its exterior is stone, the inside is red brick. The dome and the minaret—alas, truncated—are also of red brick. Behind the third wall, at the top of the promontory, see the remains of Keykubat's palace, and a Byzantine church with part of its frescoes still visible. This is the highest point of the promontory. The wooden steps of a slightly wayward little staircase pick their way up to the summit of the rock, and from it, with a stiff wind blowing, the view can quite literally take your breath away.

The tiniest detail of the reddish outline of the promontory is sharply etched against the technicolor blue-green of the Mediterranean. Along the base runs the lacy fretwork of the rocks, both above and below the surface of the waves. Boundless expanses of sandy beach bask endlessly in the sunlight. At the entrance to the town, the Red Tower juts up—visit it on the way down—and the jetty and the shipyards sprawl out yonder. Despite the summer heat, the horizon to the rear is sparked with the white touches of the eternal snows of the Taurus, whose foothills glide down to the sea. Densely-planted cultivated land—not one inch goes to waste—edges as close as it can to the sand.

The Red Tower, or Kızıl Kule, which reinforces the low wall at the junction of the north and east walls, served as a watchtower for the yards in which Keykubat's sailing vessels were built and kept shipshape. The caretaker twists an enormous key in the lock of the nail-studded door. This octagonal tower, built in 1225 by Abu Ali of Alep, after the model of the Crusaders' castles, was skilfully restored in 1951. The first two storeys are made of the familiar reddish stone blocks, and the two upper ones are built from great red bricks.

The tremendous hollow central column inside was the cistern. Bricks again, inside, with loopholes conveniently located just about everywhere for the archers to take aim, not to mention the troughs designed to hold the boiling tar and melted lead, which were the special treats in store for the besiegers below. The ceiling, which gives directly onto the lookout gallery, is pierced with holes through which alerts were sounded. A terrace leads to the sentry's path, which wound around the wall and continued all the way to the palace.

Beyond the Red Tower, down along the shore, you can prowl through the 13th-century shipyard. To the casual observer, it looks like an ordinary stone building with brick arches and a dome. It has a marble entrance, a guardroom on the left, and a mosque to the right. The shipyard proper consisted of five compartments, each one 140 by 25 feet.

Something not to be missed is the Grotto of the Weeping Stones—this translation of *Damlataş*, being only an approximate one: a *damla* is a "drop". It offers what may sound like a miraculous cure, but it's recommended by the medical profession. Positive results are guaranteed in 100 hours for sufferers from asthma and respiratory disturbances. The grotto is small, immensely old (between 6,000 and 15,000 years), and extraordinarily beautiful, a wondrous-hued lacy network of stalactites and stalagmites. One of the latter can be said to vaguely resemble a human form, and is identified with that of the Virgin Mary, whom the Moslems honor (the Virgin Myriam appears in the hagiography of Islam).

The success of the "treatment" is presumably due to the humidity, which varies, depending on the season, from 90 to 98 %. The temperature is constant, hovering around 72 to 74° F. It's like a genuine Turkish bath but minus the steam. A soupçon of radio-active elements enters into the picture, apparently just the right amount. The "patients" whom you hear coughing are the beginners.

There are also some fine boat rides, and the shoreline is fairly bristling with coves and inlets—for example, have a go at the Lovers' Grotto on the Dilvarda Peninsula. (Fifteen feet above sea level, within easy walking distance after you land, and don't forget your flashlight!) To the west, see the Blue Grotto, complete with phosphorescent rocks, and the Maidens' Grotto, Kızlar Mağarası, in which the pirates used to keep a harem staffed with their fair captives. And let's not overlook the Green Grotto, just beneath the Alanya lighthouse (Deniz Feneri). If you happen to be spending the night, watch out for the sunset behind the promontory—the last flash of dying rays make the crenels on Alâeddin Keykubat's walls seem to burst into flame.

The next 30 miles to Gazipaşa skirt the sea in the ever narrowing coastal plain. After that colorful fishing village on a fine beach, you enter some of the Mediterranean's most beautiful scenery, reminiscent of the famed Amalfi drive or parts of the Riviera. For 140 miles forests of fragrant umbrella pines—in winter over a carpet of daffodils and anemones—cover the precipitous slopes to the red cliffs or long stretches of fine white sand which fringe the turquoise sea. The few coastal plains contrast with the luxuriant greens of banana plantations and orange groves, often below mighty medieval castles, Byzantine, Armenian, Crusader and Seljuk, while Hellenistic and Roman ruins fit harmoniously into the breathtaking panoramic views.

Kaldiran castle on a towering cliff is of the Byzantine variety, followed by the first of the lush plains walled in by the Taurus mountains at Anamur. Four miles off Route 6 are the Hellenistic ruins of Anamurion, originally a Phoenician colony, on the promontory closest to Cyprus. This proximity induced the island's Lusignan kings to transform the Roman fortress on the beach further on into their main foothold in Cilicia in the 13th century. Protected by the sea, a stream and a moat, the 36 towers of Mamuriye castle project from tremendously strong ramparts which extend to the fourteen-sided keep. The emirs of Karaman added a mosque, bath and fountain. Anamur village lies further inland among gardens and orchards.

Twelve miles on, the pirate castle of Softa rises from the sea; at Kanliviran are the ruins of an Apollo temple and two Byzantine churches, while in the Roman necropolis at Kaya, a short distance before Silifke, are the basilica and tomb of St. Theola

(Aya Tecla), who was St. Paul's first convert, and the very first female Christian martyr. Having resolved to keep her virginity, Thecla broke off her engagement, whereupon her fiancé, who considered himself outraged, promptly denounced her as a Christian. This pure maiden was exhibited naked in the amphitheater but, in the words of the ancient scribes, "since she was clothed in her innocence, the ignominy that was designed to strike her became instead an occasion of glory and triumph". The lions who were unleashed to devour her merely crouched docilely at Thecla's feet, and the flames—the third ordeal—failed to touch her. She finally ended her days peacefully in her retreat at Isauria.

Eighty-five miles beyond Anamur, you come to Silifke (Seleucia ad Calycadnos), which was founded in the third century B.C. by Seleucus 1, some three miles south of the modern town. The Byzantine castle on the hill was transformed by the Knights of Rhodes into a formidable fortress with 23 towers and bastions. The cellars house a cistern whose waters "will never dry up". Bayezit built a mosque within the walls. A Roman bridge spans the Göksu River (Calycadnos) in which Emperor Frederick Barbarossa drowned in 1190, thereby bringing the Third Crusade to a sudden halt.

The ruins of Uzuncaburç (Olba-Diocaesarea), 20 miles north, are noteworthy for the temple of Zeus, the city walls and gates. But it hardly seems worthwhile to make a side trip if the same distance along the coastal road leads to miles upon miles of Hellenistic and Roman ruins superimposed upon a Hittite settlement. Cicero resided in Korykos when he was governor of Cilicia from 52 to 50 B.C. Yet the fallen temples, palace, theater, aqueduct and vast necropolis are overshadowed by the stupendous Armenian twin castles dating from the 13th century. Antique columns are built into the unusually high walls of the huge Land Castle; the Sea Castle on an offshore islet is called the Kiz Kalesı, or Maiden's Tower. Local legend claims that the local suzerain caused his beloved daughter to be confined in the island castle because of a dire prediction, according to which she was to die of snakebite. When one of her admirers sent her a gift of a basket of grapes, a serpent had concealed itself amid the fruit, and thus was the prediction fulfilled.

The ruins of Kanlıdivane (originally Kanytela) near Kız Kalesı belong to a settlement dating back to the Hittites and the Phoenicians. You'll find rupestrian tombs, sarcophagi, and Byzantine churches.

A mile north of Korykos, the two Pits of Heaven and Hell —Cennet ve Cehennem Obruğu—afford the expected contrast; the former a serene orchard in front of a ruined Armenian chapel at a spring issuing from a grotto, and on the lip of the 300 ft.-chasm, the high-walled basilica of Roman Paperon, the latter a frightening narrow hole, accessible with a guide, to which condemned sinners were consigned. On the main road at Narlikuyu, is the mosaic of the Three Nudes that embellished the Roman baths. The water from the fountain was reputed to endow its users with intelligence, beauty, and long life—at least that's what the inscription on the mosaic says.

Excursion into the Mountains

From Silifke Route 35 leads over one of the few passes across the Taurus range to Konya via Mut and Karaman. Mut, lying north of Silifke, is worth a halt. Its ancient name was Claudiopolis, and it has a great 14th-century fortress dominated by four bastions and an imposing turret. There are also a mosque, a caravanseray, and several mausoleums, all of them dating from the reign of the Karaman family. Mavga Castle (10 miles) is partly carved out of the rocks.

On the same highway, some 47 miles farther on, the capital of the Emirs of Karaman continues to bear their name. Along the way roughly 12 miles, take a look at the Alahan Monastery, with its splendid view out over the valley. Here, a few years back, archeologists uncovered the remains of a church dedicated to the Four Evangelists. Another quite well-preserved church stands to the east of the terrace.

It is thought that Karaman was built over the Hittite site of Landa or Laranda. Bitter fighting went on here—Seljuks, Crusaders, Armenians, and Ottomans all had their turns. The Turkomans finally won, and went so far as to occupy Konya. The famous Mevlâna, founder of the Whirling Dervishes, grew up here. Karaman was annexed by the Ottoman Empire in 1466.

The modern city (20,000 population) has conserved obvious

traces of its former prestige. Although the enclosure wall has virtually disappeared, one citadel still remains, and there is also a funerary monument of the Karaman family, as well as two or three mosques, interesting for the richly detailed ornamentation on their doors. The Ak Tekke was a place to which Mevlâna's disciples came to meditate. See the Yeni Hamam, the largest bath from that epoch.

In Cilicia

A host of prominent historical sites dot the area adjacent to Mersin (80,000 population), which is noted for its mild winters. Though the modern town's oldest monument, the Ulu mosque, dates only from the late 19th century, Mersin is a comfortable stopover and thriving port, with broad boulevards leading into vast orange and lemon groves. Yet this is one of the oldest continuously inhabited places in the world. The history of the original settlement Yümüktepe, one mile inland, can be traced back through the Stone Age, the Bronze Age, and the Hittite era—its 32 separate levels are distributed over 12 successive civilizations, and among the sights to see there are the chalcolithic fortifications and pottery from the third millenium B.C.

In the early 5th millenium B.C. the first dwellings were burnt down in a widespread catastrophe which extended inland to Çatalhöyük. In about 4000 B.C. a strong fortress was built above the river and some 2000 years later the Hittites fortified the town against raiders from the sea.

Seven miles west through the luxuriant orchards ablaze with fruit in winter, fragrant with blossoms in early summer, take you to the beach of Viranşehir. As a Rhodian and later Athenian colony it was called Soloi whence the word solecism, immortalizing its inhabitants' flagrant offences against the rules of grammar. Destroyed by the Armenian king Tigranes in 91 B.C., it was rebuilt by Pompey in 63 B.C. and populated with the surviving pirates whose 1,300 ships and hideouts along the coast he had reduced in a brilliant campaign. From this Pompeiopolis date the long row of Corinthian columns which line the Sacred Way to the elliptical mole in the port.

In winter, an unusual sight is added to the local scene—the campsites of the *yürük*, who are nomads of Turkoman origin.

Each year, on schedule, they forsake the icy climes of their back-country mountainous pasturelands and come to pitch their goat skin tents casually among the antique relics hereabouts.

Tarsus, the birthplace of St. Paul, nestles on the Taurus slopes amid cedar groves east of Mersin. The city itself abounds in lush plantations of orange, lemon, banana, fig, date and olive trees. According to Moslem belief, it was founded by one of Adam's sons, Seth, while according to Greek mythology Pegasus injured there his hoof. The fabulous became less nebulous when Tarsus was the setting for Anthony's first meeting with Cleopatra. In Roman days the queen's barge could have sailed right up to the city through a now silted-up lake and the Cydnus river. Cleopatra's Gate is still standing and at the ancient port of Gözlükule, ruins range from the Hittites to the Romans.

The blood-red stones of Şahmeran's Baths enclosed a place of worship of that King of the Snakes. More authentic is the well of the house in which St. Paul was born and it was probably to honor the memory of that illustrious citizen that the Eastern Emperor Arcadius made Tarsus the capital of Cilicia in the year 400. The Ulu mosque complex and the Kirkkaşik were constructed by the Ramazanoğlu dynasty in the 16th century.

Nine miles northwest is another Cave of the Seven Sleepers, only here the Christian neophytes slept for 300 years to escape persecution. On the right bank near the mouth of the Tarsus Çay, the Cydnus of the ancient, the Assyrian King Sardanapal built in the 7th century B.C. the town of Anchiale, while his supposed tomb stands at Dönüktaş.

North of Tarsus Route 1 climbs up via the Gateway of Cilicia, Gülek Pass, to the Namrun plateau, a popular mountain resort below a medieval castle. This is the most awe-inspiring stage of the journey over the mountain pass. The tall peaks stand as if huddled together in the sky, and the sheer drop of their flanks grudgingly leaves a passageway barely wide enough for a road and the roaring Cydnus in whose ice-cold rapids Alexander the Great caught a severe chill. Pines and junipers carpet the top of the cliff overhanging the road, its menacing sides rearing up to giddy heights. At the end of the pass, note the rough-hewn stone tablet, covered with Roman inscriptions. This area was fortified by the Egyptian invader of Turkey, Mehmet Ali, who occupied the Cilician frontier until 1840.

We leave the vilayet of İçel, whose administrative seat is Mersin, for the vilayet of Seyhan, the administrative seat of which is Adana. The distance from Tarsus to Adana on Route 6 is 26 miles.

Adana

Adana, with over 300,000 inhabitants, is Turkey's fourth-largest city and the center of its cotton industry. Various different personages have been credited with its founding—the two sons of Uranus (Sarus and Adanus); the Hittite King Asitawandas, and some authorities associate it with the Hittite empire of Kizzuwatna, the capital of which was Danunaş. This provides a wide range of choice for the layman, who is apt to find himself already floundering somewhat in this epoch. The Assyrians are also supposed to have had a finger in the pie. In more recent times, Adana was occupied by the French, in the wake of World War I (December, 1918). On January 5, 1922, it regained its status as a Turkish city, which it had been in reality ever since 1517.

Adana is situated on the banks of the Seyhan River. In the second century, Emperor Hadrian gave the city a bridge, the Taşköprü, which was restored by Justinian in the sixth century. Take a good look at this massive structure—it's over 1,000 feet long, and 14 of its original 21 arches are still in place. The bridge also possesses considerable historical significance—it was the sole passageway towards Syria and Palestine. Godefroy of Bouillon and his Crusaders crossed it on the way to Antioch.

The ruling family of the Ramazanoğlu left the most lasting mark on the city. They built the Akça Mesçit (lovely doorway and pulpit), the Küçük Mesçit, the Ulu Cami, and the Eski Cami (the latter's minaret was recently restored). All except the last two of these mosques are post-16th century.

Like Istanbul, Adana boasts an ancient covered market, the Kapalı Çarşı. The Bazar Hamam dates from the 16th century as does also the Irmak Hamam. Include a visit to the Archeological Museum, which has on display all sorts of objects—neolithic, chalcolithic, Hittite, etc.—from the excavations at Yümüktepe and Gözlükule. At the end of the 19th century, clock towers were all the rage in Turkey—Adana's is from 1882.

Adana is the capital of Seyhan province which includes the fertile plain of Cilicia, now called Cukurova. The construction of the Seyhan dam, 10 miles north of the city, has formed a vast artificial lake, a favorite picnic area, and made possible intensive cultivation through irrigation. The main crops are early vegetables, citrus fruit, bananas, tobacco, sesame and flax, but above all cotton, of which over 70,000 tons are produced annually. Although industrial development is in full swing, the area is afflicted by what economists term "diminished productiveness", because of the intense heat.

For Hittite-lovers, the trip to Karatepe, via Kadirli (92 miles to the northeast), is a "must". In the eighth century B.C. King Asitawandas built a palace on a hill in the wooded country overlooking the Ceyhan valley. The city itself was founded five centuries earlier. Karatepe's bilingual inscriptions, in both Phoenician and Hittite, have provided scholars with invaluable assistance in the deciphering of Hittite hieroglyphics. Opposite, at Domuztepe, visit the recently discovered ruins of the fortress from the same period. Twenty miles northwest of Kadirli, on a steep hill within the town of Kozan rises the fortress in which Guy de Lusignan, lord of Cyprus, as well as Leo VI, received the Armenian crown shortly before Cilicia was conquered by the Egyptian Mameluks in 1375. The bastions are topped by 44 towers, secret passages lead to scary dungeons and huge cisterns provided for prolonged sieges.

Other crusader castles are at Dumlu, Feke, Kurtlar, Milvan; easiest of access is Cem castle near Kadirli, Flaviopolis of antiquity. Here, archeologists discovered the bronze statue of Hadrian that you may have noticed at the Istanbul Museum. And have a look at the Ala Cami—this admirable former church combines the best features of Roman, Byzantine, and Turkish architectural genius. While you're in the neighborhood, don't overlook Anazarbe (Anavarza), near the turn-off between Kozan and Kadirli. It was founded by the Assyrians at the dawn of the last millenium B.C., and has a Byzantine fortress built with Roman materials. The arch of triumph flanked by six Corinthian columns harks back to the third century A.D. The church hollowd out of the rock, Kayakilisesi, predates the earthquake of 526 after which Justinian reconstructed the town. The Church of the Apostles has fallen into a sad state of disrepair.

Two large lagoons frame Karataş, the beach of Adana, 31 miles south. The present fishing village stands on the site of antique Hagarsus.

Misis (Mopsuestia), 17 miles along the road to Ceyhan, was originally a Hittite settlement, developed by the Romans and the Byzantines, eventually becoming part of the Ottoman Empire in 1515. The ruins of its Temple of Apollo and the baths are still in a sort of jigsaw puzzle jumble, but the local museum houses some beautiful Roman mosaics. Take more than a passing glance at the fourth-century bridge restored by Justinian, that tireless construction engineer who was so happily addicted to improving communications.

The eight towers of 13th-century Yilanlikale (Castle of the Snakes) dominate the plain to Ceyhan, 4 miles east. From that small industrial town on the Ceyhan river it is 18 miles due south to the seaside castle of Yumurtalik, rebuilt by Suleiman the Magnificent above Ayas, one of the oldest Cilician settlements.

There are, of course, lesser sites for the traveler with plenty of time on his hands. But there is so much more of greater interest further on. So 15 miles beyond Ceyhan, turn off from the Osmaniye-Gaziantep road and head due south.

South to Antakya (Antioch)

Just past the crossroad you may drive up to the entrance of the medieval Armenian fortress of Toprakkale. But only the hardiest driver should venture on the track by the side of the Roman aqueduct to the plain of Issos where the armies of Alexander and Darius clashed in 333 B.C. Alexander's overwhelming victory opened the way for the Macedonian occupation of Syria.

The next turn off to the right (west) to Payas is badly marked but only one paved mile to a uniquely complete 16th-century Turkish architectural complex; a huge caravanseray, mosque, theological school, hamam and covered market round spacious courtyards, connected by a bridge over the moat with a strong sea castle, the Cin (Demon) Tower. Built by order of Selim II in 1574, the splendid layout is ascribed to the great architect

Sinan. Expertly restored, Payas owes its preservation to the shifting of the village away from the sea to the main road.

Densely-wooded rugged mountains impel Route 1 ever closer to the sea for the next 15 miles to the busy port of Alexandretta, now Iskenderun. This foundation of Alexander was in antiquity completely overshadowed by the natural outlet of Antioch on the mouth of the Orontes, Seleucia ad Pieria. Destroyed by the Persian Sassanids in 260, Alexandretta's rise dates from the Arab conquest in the 7th century. Ever since it has shared the fate of Antioch, even giving its name to the whole province, the Sandjak of Alexandretta, which was incorporated in the French mandate over Syria after the First World War and only re-turned to Turkey a few months before the outbreak of the Second. It is a pleasant provincial town with an attractive waterfront, greatly preferable to Antakya for a stay of any length.

Nineteen miles southwest is the fishing village of Arsuz on an excellent beach. Nearby are the ruins of Hellenistic Rhosus; the view from the Crusader castle in the Hinzir foothills, 9 miles further on, is particularly splendid.

The 36 miles from Iskenderun to Antakya begin with a steep climb through the Belen Pass, the Syrian Gates in the Amanus mountains. Belen is an attractive village, becoming popular as a summer resort and renowned for its curative water. From the height of the pass you enjoy a staggering view over the Orontes valley, owing to its fertility one of the oldest regions of human habitation as testified by numerous mounds.

Don't miss the first branch off in the plain, 2 paved miles to the romantic Crusader castle of Bakras, built on the foundations of a Hellenistic fortress.

Traces left by successive local occupants of Antioch go back as far as the fourth millenium B.C. It was one of Alexander's successors, Seleucus, who founded the town in memory of his illustrious father, Antiochus, in 300 B.C. Constantly enlarged by subsequent Seleucids, Antioch under the Romans became the third city of the empire, with 500,000 inhabitants. Famed for its luxury and notorious for its depravity, it was chosen by St. Peter for his first mission to the gentiles and for the creation of the first ecclesiastical organization (Acts VIII: 1,15).

Paganism made its last counter-attack from Antioch some 300

years later, when Julian the Apostate attempted to revive the ancient gods before his disastrous Persian campaign. Though the senior Orthodox patriarchate, Antioch's predilection for Arianism and later heresies gravely endangered the unity of the empire. Rising from the ravages of repeated invasions and earthquakes, disputed for hundreds of years by Byzantines and Arabs, Antioch fell in 1098 to the Crusaders. Under the Norman prince Bohemund and his successors, it became the most powerful of the Latin principalities of the ill-fated Kingdom of Jerusalem, doomed to extinction in less than two centuries. In 1268 Antioch was occupied by the Mameluks of Egypt, and in 1516 Selim the Bold made it part of the Ottoman Empire. But Antioch has failed to follow the resurrection of its antique rivals, Rome and Alexandria. Even the Patriarch has left the town whose name he still bears, as with the restoration of Antioch to Turkey in 1939 he was parted from his flock in Syria where he now resides.

Reduced to some 60,000 inhabitants it is today an undistinguished oriental city despite a few modern apartment blocks on the west bank of the Orontes (Asi River). Diocletian's proud bridge was replaced by reinforced concrete in 1970 because the Roman brickwork could not withstand the strong current created by the construction of the dam higher up. Several arches of Trajan's aqueduct (Memikli) span a ravine between the hospital and Mount Silpius. The great fortress that crowned this mountain from Byzantine times onward was the setting for the most splendid Latin court in the Levant, and was last occupied by Egyptian troops from 1831 to 1840, but only sad broken ramparts extending over several miles remain. However, it certainly is worthwhile to drive to the top, though the last mile is very rough going, for the superb view over the town and the Orontes plain from the café.

In the outskirts on the east (left) bank the white façade of St. Peter's Church stands out against the background of the reddish rock from which it was hollowed. The Apostle delivered his sermons here to his converts, the first to be called Christians (Acts 11:26). In 1967, Pope Paul VI declared a plenary indulgence for pilgrims, though only the feast of St. Peter is celebrated in the simple bare grotto on 29 June. The nearby Bath of the Sinners features some reliefs.

The Habib Neccar Cami in Kurtuluş Caddesi was originally a church, while the Ulu Cami is an Ottoman construction from the 16th century. There are a number of mosques in the bazaar quarter, which has remained genuine down to the open drains in the middle of the narrow lanes.

What has been preserved from the ancient glory is now in the Hatay Archeological Museum. In addition to items from the various excavations in the surrounding area, it also contains a collection of magnificent second- and third-century Roman mosaics.

Most of them once graced the sumptuous villas scattered over the idyllic vale five miles to the south. In the cool woods the nymph Daphne was changed into a myrtle bush to escape the amorous advances of Apollo. Even in its present untidy state Daphne (Harbiye) remains a favorite picnic ground, but in antiquity it was the fabulous pleasure resort of the Seleucid kings, where waterfalls and bosky copses surrounded Aphrodite's famous sanctuary with its thousand dedicated prostitutes.

The next 31 miles wind through barren hills to Yayladag, the frontier post into Syria on the way to Tripoli and Beyrut. All tourist pamphlets mention the formidable Crusader castle of Kürsat, ten miles along, but there is no indication anywhere of how to reach it.

The Romans are especially remembered for the attention they lavished on the problem of piping in fresh water. For this purpose, they bored the Titus Tunnel, near Samandağ, which is also blessed with a splendid beach on the mouth of the Orontes (18 miles southwest of Antakya). The ruins of Antioch's port, Seleucia ad Pieria (Süvediye) now lie some two miles inland near the village of Mağaracik. In the precipitous cliffs of the Musadağ are numerous rupestral tombs.

On the Trail of the Hittites

The frontier town of Reyhanli, 20 miles along the Aleppo road, is the center for a visit to the 183 mounds covering settlements as far back as 3400 B.C. The plain round artificial Lake Amik, which submerged prehistoric pastures and fields when a dam was built across the Orontes, is literally swarming with tumuli, many of which have yet to be explored. Teams have been excavating already at Tel El Cüdeyde, Telaçana, and Tel Tainat.

It is possible to return from Antakya or even directly from Reyhanli on inland Route 55 via Kirikhan and the castle of Trapaesa to the region watered by the Sögütlü and the Hurmas, the two streams eventually merging to form the Ceyhan River.

Maraş, whose crowning glory is a fortress with Hittite foundations, claims to possess the densest concentration of mosques in Turkey per square mile. Its boast may well be true if we include those in ruins. When work finally begins in earnest here, the task facing the architects, archeologists, and restorers will be gigantic. Hittite objects that are on display in the local museum provide us with an inkling of what treasures are still to be unearthed.

Gaziantep, on Routes 6 or 59 south of Maraş, is an industrial center busy with cotton, threads, and oils, and it also has its local artisans, who do copperwork. Among other things, pistachio nuts from here find their way as exports all over the world. The wooden mosque of Ahmet Çelebi dates from 1672; the Ömeriye looks somewhat more Arabic in origin, and belongs to the 11th century. The former Seljuk *medrese* houses the town's museum, which contains objects from the sites of Zincirli, Sakçagözü, and Kargamiş, plus a remarkable collection of Hittite seals. The fortress that Justinian built here in the sixth century was considerably retouched by the Seljuks, and other Seljuk strongholds abound in the vicinity.

Zincirli, the site of an ancient Hittite principality that flourished from the 12th to the eighth century B.C., lies some ten km. (six miles) east of the little town of Islahiye. Its only remains consist of a few scattered foundations. The most interesting items unearthed during the excavations are displayed at the museums in Ankara and Berlin.

Another important site, Kargamiş, stands near the frontier opposite the Syrian city of Djerablus. Sometime around 1200 B.C., following the collapse of the Hittite empire of Anatolia (Boğazköy), the rulers of Kargamiş regained their independence and managed to hold on to it until they finally lost out to the Assyrians, four centuries later. The bas-reliefs from Kargamiş in the Ankara Museum betray a marked Assyrian influence.

Illustration at head of this chapter: The Hunt, bas relief. Archeological Museum, Ankara.

ANKARA

From Old Angora to Modern Capital

At the dawn of the 15th century, the Turks occupied nearly all of Asia Minor, as well as most of Thrace in Europe. Turkey was then what is now called a "world power". The Crusaders' kingdoms had been overthrown, the last Christian soldier driven out of the East. Sultan Bayezit I was preparing to lay siege to Constantinople, the last Byzantine stronghold, when the cry of alarm rang out: "Tamerlane is coming!"

This dreaded warrior, a descendant of Genghis Khan, galloped through history like a horseman of the Apocalypse. His real name is unknown: we know him only as Timour Lengh, the cripple. Limping and one-armed, he murdered his way to power as Khan of the Mongols. In 1370, he rode out with his soldiers to conquer the world. His feats were beyond belief: he subjugated all Asia east of the Caspian Sea, invaded Persia, laid waste the Kirghiz Plain, marched on Russia, turned south and attacked India, drove the Egyptians from Syria, and destroyed Baghdad. In the course of 30 years, he wrought havoc throughout the East, leaving a trail of blood and tears in his wake.

It was this savage conqueror who now threatened Asia Minor,

and Bayezit I was up in arms. An able soldier, the sultan was called Yıldırım, "the Thunderbolt". He was by now the master of Asia Minor. In Europe, he had wrested Bulgaria, Macedonia, and Thessaly from the Christian emperors. In 1396, at the battle of Nicopolis on the Danube, he had slaughtered an army of Crusaders, including Polish, Hungarian, and French troops.

Faced with the invincible cripple, the Thunderbolt rightly felt that his honor was at stake. Giving up the siege of Constantinople, he marched at the head of a huge army against the Mongol enemy, riding headlong against him with an equally large contingent. The clash took place in July, 1402, in the plain below the small town of Ancyra, Engüriye to the Seljuks, which was rendered as Angora by the Europeans who applied the name to the breeding-place of long-haired goats from Tibet.

Much has been written about the defeated, broken-hearted sultan (the poets of Islam sing readily of those forsaken by Allah, who waste away and die). It is known that the Thunderbolt was taken prisoner, and alleged that the ruthless Tamerlane took pleasure in humiliating him, both in body and soul. "He shut him in an iron cage, where Bayezit beat his brains out against the bars." Most authorities, however, agree that the prisoner was treated with the regard due his rank. Be that as it may, the poets go on to say that Bayezit "died of a stroke after eight months of captivity".

His death was followed by one of the most baffling mysteries of all time. With Bayezit out of the way, the door to the West was left wide open to Tamerlane. While Europe waited in dread, Tamerlane moodily turned his horse around and rode back with his men to the Mongol plains. He was never heard of again.

Defeated, the Turks were not long overcome. Half a century later, in 1453, Constantinople fell to Mehmet II, and for 400 years, the Ottoman Empire was a great world power.

Practical Information for Ankara

WHEN TO GO? Placed on a high tableland, Ankara is dry in winter as in summer; but it can be bitterly cold in winter, and excessively hot in summer. The best times of the year to go to Ankara and the surrounding countryside are spring and autumn.

HOW TO GO? *By air* from Istanbul, Izmir, Adana, New York, London, Paris, Beirut, etc. Very good *highway* from Istanbul to Ankara. The day *train* from Istanbul is about 12 hours. However, by taking the *Anadolu Express* night train, with sleeping car, you gain a whole day on your holidays. A daily motor train links Izmir to Ankara, and the *Izmir Express* has a thrice-weekly run; about fifteen hours. Several *motor coach* companies ply back and forth between Istanbul and Ankara; the bus stops in Ankara are in Ulus Square and Kizilay Square, and the bus fares are very cheap.

WHAT TO SEE? The unique Hittite Museum, first and foremost. The Ankara citadel or Hisar, founded by the Galatians, is still a fine sight with its many towers, added by the Seljuks. Among the Roman monuments, the Temple of Augustus is well worth a visit, while the Column of Julian the Apostate, though nothing remarkable in itself, is delightfully topped by a stork's nest. Caracalla, who seems to have dearly loved a bath, not only built his renowned Baths in Rome, but even in far-off Ancyra, in what is today the Çankiri Caddesi.

But Ankara is first and foremost a modern city, and its greatest monument, the Atatürk Mausoleum in the Maltepe quarter, was built in honor of the founder of modern Turkey and its new capital. At the far end of the Atatürk Bulvarı and on the hill of Cankaya the modern embassies are well worth seeing.

Hotels

LUXURIOUS

BÜYÜK ANKARA, Atatürk Bulvarı 315, leads the list. In a fashionable quarter of town, it is a large (210 rooms), modern, fully airconditioned hotel under Swiss management. There are 14 luxury suites. The Büyük ("Grand") has three restaurants—the rooftop *Grill*, the *Başkent*, and the *Snack Bar*, which serves light meals. Heated swimming pool, and garage.

MARMARA, equally modern, is intimate, with only 51 rooms, but large public facilities. Operated by the same management as the *Büyük Efes* in Izmir, it is an excellent place to stay. Located at the Atatürk Orman Çiftliği Farm, just outside the city.

FIRST CLASS

KENT, Mithatpaşa Caddesi 4, is a recent hotel in the busiest part of town. 114 rooms with bath. After lunch in its excellent restaurant, go to its *Oriental Salon* for coffee and *keyif*, meaning rest and peace.

DEDEMAN, Akay Caddesi, 119 rooms with bath. Rooftop nightclub, restaurant.

BULVAR PALAS, on Atatürk Blvd. has 150 rooms (140 with bath or shower), good restaurant.

BALIN, Izmir Caddesi 35, is more up-to-date. 91 rooms with bath, restaurant.

MODERATE

Also in the middle of town, the *Barıkan* (2), Izmir Cad., lately done over and comfortable, is good. 68 rooms (56 with bath), restaurant.

The *Modern Palas* (3), Ziya Gökalp Caddesi, has 56 rooms (34 with bath). Restaurant.

In the Ulus quarter in old Ankara, not far from the citadel, try *Berlin* (4), Hisar Park Caddesi, 67 rooms (24 with bath), followed by the *Belvü Palas* (4), Istiklâl Câd. Çapa Sok. 5, 59 rooms (35 with bath). Both have restaurants.

Cad. 5 is with 221 rooms (159 showers) and a restaurant the largest; *Elhamra*, 51 rooms (33 showers), *Emperyal*, 50 rooms (30 showers), *Kennedy*, 48 rooms (24 showers), *Namaldi*, 48 rooms with shower, *Turist*, 116 rooms (100 showers) all hover in the 4th category in Çankiri Cad; *Gönç*, Rüzgârlı Sok., 55 rooms (16 with shower), and *Hitit*, Hisar Parkı Cad., 44 rooms with shower.

INEXPENSIVE

This includes hotels in the third and fourth class and even slightly below. In mid-town: *Monako* (3), Meneşe Sok., 30 rooms with shower; *Sultan* (3), 40 rooms with shower, *Apaydin* (4), 50 rooms with shower, *Gül Palas* (4), 42 rooms (28 with shower), all in Bayindir Sok; *Pinar* (3), Cemâl Gürsel Cad., 35 rooms with shower; *Yüksel Palas* (3), Atatürk Bul. 51, 53 rooms (19 showers); *Yükseliş* (4), Necatibey Cad. 49, 41 rooms (12 showers), all except the last with restaurants.

In Ulus: *Cihan Palas* (3), Sanayi

ROCK BOTTOM

There are a few fairly well-kept rock-bottom hotels, such as the *Ayko*, Cihan Sok. 22, 31 rooms (11 showers); *Uzun*, Yildirim Beyazit Meydani, 95 rooms (21 showers); *Çelik Palas* and *Yenişehir Palaş*, both in Çankiri Cad.

ENVIRONS

Outside Ankara, on E5, 40 miles north, the *Toleyis* (3) is a convenient stopover en route to the Black Sea or Istanbul. 39 rooms with shower.

There is a camping ground 14 miles from Ankara on the Istanbul highway: *Susuzköy Mocamp*.

 RESTAURANTS. Outside of the restaurants of a few hotels (see above), the most fashionable restaurants in Ankara are the following: Among the best, the *Washington*, Bayindir Sok., run by nine brothers, several of whom took turns as chef at the Turkish Embassy in the American capital. It has a Hittite setting, Turkish food, and a few American and French dishes. *Set* has a restaurant and cafeteria on the 3rd floor of the department store. Its large outside terrace is especially pleasant. On the heights of Çankaya, the *Kazan*, Ahmetağacğlu Caddesi 28/1, serves both Turkish and western food in, of all things, a Swiss chalet setting. If you like Russian *borscht*, go to *Bekir*, in Tuna Caddesi, near Atatürk Bulvari.

The two best places for the world-renowned Turkish *kebab*, meat broiled on a skewer, are on Atatürk Bulvari: the *Kebapçi Yesil Bursa* and the *Kebapçi Bursa Iskender*, whose specialty is the "Bursa Kebab", a mixed grill served on flat unleavened bread called *pide* and garnished with grilled tomatoes and green peppers, the whole topped with yoğurt.

For a light snack, go to the *Piknik* cafeteria in Tuna Caddesi, near Atatürk Bulvari or to the *Set*, Gökdelen, Kizilay.

In the village of Atatürk (Atatürk Orman Çiftligi), the Turkish food at the *Lokanta Merkez* is fairly good. Dancing in summer.

SHOW BUSINESS. There are eight theaters in Ankara, among which are the *Büyük* (big) *Tiyatro* and the *Küçük* (small) *Tiyatro*, for straight plays; the *Üçüncü Tiyatro* often puts on musical comedies, where not understanding Turkish is less of a handicap. You may also go to a concert by the Presidential Symphony at the *Concert Hall*, on Talat-paşa Bulvari, not far from the main railway station. Operas and ballets are performed at the *Büyük Tiyatro*.

NIGHTCLUBS. Nightlife in Ankara is fairly lively at the *Pavillon* in the Balin Hotel, Izmir Caddesi, and at the Railway Casino, *Gar Gazinosu*, which also serves late suppers. Also at the *Playboy*, behind the Büyük Ankara Hotel, and the *Klüp Bulvar*, in the Bulvar Palas Hotel. Dinner and dancing at the *Intim*, Meşrutiyet Cad. 19; *Babilon Gazinosu*, Bestekar Sok. Dancing only, to an orchestra, at *La Bohême*, Serçe Sokak 51/B; and the *Külüp Dervis*, Adakale Sokak 20/B. Background piano music only at the *Altan'in Yeri*, Menekşe Sokak, in the Maltepe quarter. At the Kizilay skyscraper is *Gökdelen Club*.

MOSQUES AND MUSEUMS. The 13th-century *Arslanhane Cami*, or mosque, is the biggest in Ankara (see map); the *Alaaddin Cami*, built in 1178, is the oldest. See the Seljuk sculpture on the doors of the *Ahi Elvan Cami*, in Koyunpazari Sokak in Samanpazar, built at the end of the 14th century; a few of its columns have capitals of Roman or Byzantine origin. Other mosques are the 16th-century *Yeni Cami* ascribed to Sinan, the 15th-century *Imaret Cami* and *Haci Bayram Cami*, decorated with tiles some 300 years later. The *Maltepe Cami* is a fine example of modern Moslem architecture.

The *Archeological Museum*, also known as the Hittite Museum, is near the citadel, housed in two 15th-century buildings: a covered bazaar or *bedesten*, and a highway inn or caravanseray. It contains the world's biggest and finest collection of Hittite and pre-Hittite art; closed on Mondays. The *Ethnographic Museum* has a rich collection of Turkish art and folklore; closed on Mondays. The *Anit Kabir Museum* in the arcaded wings of the Atatürk Mausoleum is dedicated to mementos of the War of Independence and Atatürk, including numerous personal belongings.

TRANSPORTATION. *Buses:* all lines end in Ulus Square. Yeni-şehir is a starting place for the many buses and trolleybuses that go down Atatürk Bulvari towards Ulus, and the other ways towards Çankaya or Kavaklidere. Bus fares in town are from 70 to 90 kuruş. The *dolmuş* taxis drive everywhere along specified routes with 5 or more passengers who share the cost, from 1 to 2 TL a head. Private taxis ask from 8 to 10 TL within the town, and from 50 to 70 TL to the airport.

SHOPPING. In Ankara, there is no big covered Bazaar as in Istanbul, and the shops selling souvenirs and gifts are scattered throughout the town. The nearest thing to a bazaar is the *Büyük Çarşi*, in the basement of the Büyük Cinema in Kızılay, with its many shops. Among the best are *Safir*, jeweler and silversmith, with an owner who speaks several foreign languages; *Gülistan*, with its wide range of artcraft: Turkish slippers, dolls, brasses, etc. The *Gima Department Store*, in the skyscraper at Kızılay, has many souvenirs and gifts.

You will find wooden sculpture on sale at the *Exhibition of the Ministry of Rural Handcraft* sells handmade embroidery, *kilims*, etc. In the Büyük Ankara Hotel, *Sim* has a wide range of brasses, *kilims*, and so on. If you want to buy jewels, old or new, go to *Hodja*, Meşrutiyet Caddesi 19; for brasses and antiques, *Moda Model*, Ulus Iş Hani. *Antikite*, Anafartalar Caddesi, is the most important antiquity shop in town.

 SPORTS. Turks in general, and the townspeople of Ankara in particular, are great lovers of horse races. Races are held at the hippodrome near the stadium, from the middle of May to the middle of June, and for three weeks in September-October. For information as to dates, booking tickets, etc., throughout all Turkey, go to the *Jockey Club of Turkey*, Atatürk Bulvari 169/2, opposite the Parliament. *Football* (soccer) matches at the stadium. *Tennis* Club in Kavaklidere. *Mountain climbing*, Türkiye Tabiatini Koruma Cemiyeti, Bayindir Sok. 43; Yenişehir or Elmadağ Spor Klübü, Sakarya Caddesi. *Hunting and shooting*, Türkiye Avcilar ve Atıcılar Klübü, Tuna Caddesi. *Swimming*. Gölbaşi Beach, 16 miles southwest of Ankara, in the lake of Mogan; swimming pool in the Hotel Büyük Ankara; and at Karadeniz, not far from Atatürk's Farm, driving out from Konya Yolu Avenue.

USEFUL ADDRESSES. *Tourist Offices:* Mithat Paşa Caddesi 20 and Milli Mudafaa Caddesi (tel. 17-44-04). *Airlines*: THY (Türk Hava Yollari), Zafer Meydani; BEA, Zafer Meydani, Yenişehir; KLM, Atatürk 67/A, Yenişehir; Air France, Emer Ishani Bldg. (the skyscraper); Sabena, Atatürk Bulvari 88/B; Swissair, Atatürk Blvd. at Bakankiklar; Pan Am, 53 Atatürk Bulvari.

Travel Agencies (excursions to Boğazköy, Cappadoccia, etc.): *Vanderzee* Travel Service, Atatürk Bulvari 68/B. *Train travel* (to book sleeping car on night trains): Wagon-Lits/Cook, Ziya Gökalp Cad. 20/A. *Embassies*: United States of America, Kavaklidere Cad. 221, Çankaya. Great Britain, Çankaya.

Religious services: French Catholic Church, Mass on Sundays at 10 and 11 o'clock. Protestant Church, Kizillrmak Cad. 20; service on Sundays at 11 o'clock. Synagogue, Birlik Sokak, near Ulus Anafartalar Cad.

Useful phone numbers: Traffic police, 11-64-69. Ambulance, 11-77-29. Railway Station Information, 11-06-20. Esenboğa Airport Information, 10-52-06. Ministry of Tourism Information, 12-57-98. Department of Highways (state of roads), 12-53-03.

Discovering Ankara

It is no overstatement to say that Ankara is the work of Atatürk. In 1935, it was a town peopled by 75,000 Anatolians; it is a capital city of nearly one million today. Yet despite the ultra-modern appearance, Ankara's history can be traced back some 3,000 years. Legend attributes its foundation to the redoubtable Amazons, but archeologists have decided on a Phrygian origin at the time of the Trojan War, though recent excavations have brought to light even earlier Hittite traces in the citadel.

The usual succession of Lydian, Persian and Macedonian conquerors was rudely interrupted by barbaric Gallic tribes. In 278 B.C. Nicodemus I, King of Bithynia, gave the Galatians a gift of land with Ankyra as capital. Defeated by Attalus I of Pergamon in 229 B.C., the reduced Galatian kingdom subsisted under varying overlords till final annexation by Augustus in 25 B.C.

The derivation of the name is as problematic as the rendering —Ancyra, Engüriye, Angora, Ankara. Perhaps it is Phrygian for "ravine", or Greek for "anchor" (an Egyptian anchor captured in battle featured for some time on the city's coins).

All Turkey is haunted by the presence of Kemal Atatürk, but it is in Ankara, the town he made his city, that it is most strongly felt. Why did he choose far-off Ankara as the capital of "his" republic, in spite of lack of water, the marshland, the poor communications; and the sparse population? One of his reasons was doubtless sentimental: the Constantinople of the sultans and of Enver Pasha had scorned him. On a higher political level, he wished a clean break with the disastrous Ottoman past. And lastly, the soldier always alert in the statesman rightly saw that where Constantinople was highly vulnerable, Ankara was guarded by its very remoteness.

In answer to his call, tens of thousands of homeless and jobless Turks streamed into the town, mostly on foot, to undertake the building of the new capital. This peaceful army set to work, laid out streets, built houses and, sometimes, lived in them, whenever growing earnings allowed. Slowly, with unshakeable steadfastness and patience, Atatürk shifted the weight of the old and discredited empire on to the new republic, and the country's center of gravity from Istanbul to Ankara. All the while, he went on planning and imposing—by force if need be—revolutionary reforms that would have cost any other reformer his following.

To foreigners who have but vaguely heard of Atatürk, Ankara is a revelation of what one man alone can achieve in a short span of time. A grateful people erected many monuments in his honor, more statues in his likeness, and countless streets in his name. Yet the people of Turkey need no reminder to remember him; since his death in 1938, the country is governed in his name, and nothing has been done since without invoking him. The full force of this is nowhere clearer than in Ankara. The traveler may never get to understand the Turkey of today unless he undertakes this pilgrimage. If the foreigner barely knows this folk hero by his first name, that of Mustafa, he will now hear the names given him for all time by his grateful countrymen: Kemal, the perfect; Atatürk, the father of the Turks; and Gazi, the conqueror.

If the above lines sound like a song of praise, it is the man more than the town that stirs the imagination. Ankara is a rather pleasant city of government offices and white-collar workers who have, to the outsider, little of the colorful charm of the old-time Turks. Traffic, as crowded as in Istanbul, is less tangled, the straight new thoroughfares and streets were made for cars. Of course, there is the usual traffic jam of big cities at the rush hours, greater in Turkey than elsewhere because of the stop-and-go dolmuş. An outstanding feature of the crowd: it is young, like the town itself. Only the ruins of the Temple of Augustus, Julian's Column, the untidy remains of the Roman Baths and Palestra, but above all the Citadel witness that modern Ankara adjoins ancient Ancyra.

The mosques are a reminder of yet another past. The Turk's respect for the house of God is the same in the country as in the towns, except in Istanbul. Seeing a devout old man deep in his prayer book, you will understand how important religion is to the people. Storks in Ankara are ubiquitous and are allowed to break the tiles—they are a sign of prosperity.

Whereas old Istanbul has learnt through the centuries to make room for new customs, Ankara, itself new, has still to find a way of life. Many of the townspeople, whenever Atatürk's iron hand allowed, tended to go back to the old ways; now, they think some harmless backsliding can no longer disappoint him.

Another Kemal touch is the greenery. The Anatolians have had few trees, but the Gazi loved them; he planted them everywhere, surrounded the town with a green belt, and built on the outskirts a model farm where the townspeople go for a breath of fresh air, ice cream, or a meal—the restaurant serves very good food. The farm has a dairy, renowned for its yoğurt and its buttermilk (*ayran*). In Ankara itself, Kemal laid out a park for young people, and a zoo; he urged the town-dwellers to grow flowers on the house balconies. That, too, is the mark of a whole man.

Together with its modern building units, matchbox style, and the skyscraper on Atatürk Boulevard, Ankara has a hill covered with a sad huddle of shacks, the Gecekondu or shanty-town of all Turkish cities. In Ankara, the wooden planks and tin roofs have given way to slabs of cement, topped however by the sign of the times—a television aerial.

The Atatürk Mausoleum is indeed stately. Designed by Emin Onat and Orhan Arda, it is strictly modern, but in a style not untouched by Turkish art. On a hilltop, it is reached by the marble-paved Lions' Path. To each side are pavilions with remarkable bas-relief carvings. At the far end is a square hemmed in by a colonnade, and in the middle, a towering mast with the Turkish flag floating red and white in the breeze. At the entrance are carved the words: "Beyond all doubt, government belongs to the people". Sailors in white duck and soldiers in olive drab mount the guard. A monumental stairway leads up to the golden-colored mausoleum, a vast soaring hall lined with brilliant gold mosaics and marble, pierced by seven tall windows. The immensely impressive solitary marble sarcophagus is symbolical, as Atatürk's actual remains rest in the vault below. In the wings of the mausoleum are many objects associated with his life, from library books to motorcars.

The Citadel (Hisar)

The hill opposite the Mausoleum is topped by the citadel, Anatolia's mightiest stronghold. The often repaired walls enclose the Roman Agora and a warren of narrow lanes in which an ancient way of life is stubbornly perpetuated though it has long disappeared outside the Double Gate.

In the formidable walls, as in the lowliest hovel, you will make out broken stones and stumps of columns taken from the Roman ruins. A small and charming column of flawless white marble upholds two sides of a ramshackle wall that has, makeshift as it is, withstood the passing of centuries. In a wretchedly poor courtyard, broken chapters of marble columns are used as seats around the table, a touch of elegance few elsewhere are rich enough to afford.

There are fountains, a blessing from heaven not given to all. The broken paving is as old as the town. The doors to the small courtyards are all open in summer, to make cool draughts, and you hear the voices of the housewives preparing the evening meal. A poor seller of cheap candy, covered with a sheet of plastic to keep off the dust and flies, squats by his wares on a chair. Surrounded by ragged children who look longingly at the sweets, he will not shoo them away; they have the right to look, if not the money to buy, and sometimes he tells them stories. A woman at a window will stop beating her carpet to let visitors pass. Here, none is so poor that he is mannerless, and thus is never so bereft as the slum-dweller of more industrialized nations.

The Galatians built the double walls, later strengthened by the Romans and afterwards by the Seljuk Turks. They were once flanked by 20 towers, of which 15 are still standing. The inner wall surrounding the town is roughly heart-shaped; facing inward are four levels built of stone and basalt, pierced by two gateways. Most people pass through the one called the Hisar Kapisi, topped by a carved inscription dating back to the Ilhanli, and by a modern clock. The second wall, near the gate called Parmak Kapisi, is the most remarkable part of the fortifications.

The Hittite Museum

At the end of the garden terrace below the citadel's outer rampart is the very fine Archeological, or Hittite, Museum. It is housed in two 15th-century buildings, skilfully fitted together to form a whole—one a caravanseray or overnight stopping-place for caravans, the other a *bedesten* or covered market. On display are many archeological findings, prehistoric, Phrygian, and Urartu (Assyrian name for the country later known as Armenia). Among the latter are 35,000 tablets inscribed with cuneiform, or wedge-shaped, writing. But the museum's outstanding asset is its collection, the biggest and finest in the world, of Hittite art and crafts, dating back to the sixth millenium B.C. The Turkish cultural authorities mean to add to the collection as more findings are unearthed, the surrounding countryside still being a rich mine for archeologists. As it is, however, it is an amazing sight. We are taken by the formal beauty of an art passed down to us by a hitherto unknown people, whose powerful empire vanished overnight at the time of the fall of Troy, to come back to light in our own lifetime.

We shall not weary the reader with a list of countless objects, which the visitor can see for himself by wandering through the rooms. Outstanding pieces to look for include a bronze statuette of a bull (c. 2400 B.C.), a limestone Cappadocian idol with two heads (third millenium), a ram's head vase (19th cent. B.C.), a large bull's head cauldron, a threefaced jar (seventh cent. B.C.), and the wreathed portrait bust of Emperor Trajan (second cent.).

What elegance in the brittle antelope, what beauty in the rough rock with its cave paintings! A bit forged nearly 2,000 years B.C. is all the more interesting when we remember that the horse was then a new and wild animal, broken in on the Anatolian plains. Looking at it, we are moved again by the closing lines of Homer's *Iliad:* "And thus were held the funeral rites of Hector, tamer of horses." And there is another huge cauldron with lovely clean lines, upheld by four figures with a hint of the Egyptian—it was found in Gordion, where Alexander the Great cut the legendary knot before his march on Ankara. There are small statues, jewels worked in gold and iron, combs and needles. There are, above all, the wonderful bas-relief carvings in stone. While the workmanship of the objects of daily use shows a feeling for proportion and harmony, it is in the higher art of sculpture that we see the Hittite mastery of movement. It is best shown in a small bas-relief whose warriors, brandishing lances under cover of their shields, still bear faint traces of color. Another bas-relief pictures the legend of Gilgamesh, the Babylonian version of the Deluge. Look also at the statue of an emperor, intact but for part of a hand and a chip in the beard, finely curled in the Babylonian fashion.

Whatever you do, do not miss the Hittite Museum!

Ankara also has its Atatürk Museum, with a display of his

personal belongings and gifts received; a house in which he lived
during the War of Independence, now open to visitors; and an
Ethnographic Museum, which houses a collection of musical
instruments, weapons, tools, household objects, costumes—all
you may wish to see of Turkish folklore.

Mosques and Roman Remains

On the eastern limits of the old town Suleiman's Grand Vizir
Cenabi Ahmet Paşa built the Yeni Cami (New Mosque) in dark
red porphyry, the stone of Ankara; though said to be by Sinan,
it is more likely by one of his disciples. The 16th century *mimber*
and *mihrap* are in white marble. The Imaret Cami near the
Kilektepe Park was built by Karaca Bey in 1428 on a T-shaped
plan; it has a rather thick minaret, striped in colored glazed
tiles. Here, even more than elsewhere, much use was made of
the stone from the nearby Roman ruins. There is a magnificent
carved door, untouched by clumsy repairs. *Sancta simplicitas*—a
small stove is placed in the middle of the hall of prayer. Nearby
is the tomb, or *türbe*, of the founder, together with the 15th-cen-
tury Baths, the Çifte Hamam.

Among the mosques to the southeast of the citadel are the
14th-century Ahi Elvan and the 13th-century Arslanhane, the
Lionhouse Mosque, the biggest in Ankara and the oldest except
for the small Alâeddin Cami, built in 1178 within the citadel.
Either the lion reliefs on a wall in front or a Roman stone lion,
now vanished, gave the Arslanhane its name. Indeed stones from
the ruins are scattered throughout the building—in the base
of the minaret, Roman and Byzantine chapters in the hall of
prayer, and even broken blocks in the walls of the old houses
surrounding the mosque, itself a wooden structure, however.

The modern Maltepe mosque is the newest in Ankara, and
very handsome. Its tall minaret is as fine as a needle above the
large dome plated with brass. The Haci Bayram mosque is of
yellow stone and brick; built in the early 15th century, the glazed
Kütahya tiles on the inside walls were added three hundred years
later. The door of the fine *türbe* is in the Ethnographic Museum.
As is often the case, loud-speakers spoil the clean lines of the
minarets. The tiled roof is odd and unusual.

The mosque is backed by the remains of the Temple of Augustus. Built in the second century B.C. as a shrine to Cybele, nature goddess of Asia Minor, it passed on to the worship of Diana. When a law was passed in Rome deifying dead emperors, the Galatians of Ancyra, wishing to show their gratitude for the lenient Roman rule, dedicated the temple to Augustus. Later, the Byzantines turned it into a Christian church. It is now a ruin among many others, but it has a tale worth telling.

Augustus, heir of Caesar (whose name was adopted as an imperial title), left a testament, a model of clarity and conciseness. In few but telling words, he summed up the achievements of his rule. Both politically and historically, this document was priceless. The emperor's contemporaries mourned his death, revered his memory, and engraved his testament on two bronze tablets meant for his mausoleum, "that all may know". So wrote the Roman historian Suetonius; but the testament itself had disappeared, forever—or so it seemed, lost to the world.

One fine day in January, 1555, a gentleman of Flanders, entrusted with a mission by Ferdinand I, youngest brother of Charles V, arrived in Constantinople. His name, Ghislain de Busbecq, would in all likelihood be known to fellow scholars only if the sultan, Suleiman I, had not happened to be away in Amasya. On his way to Amasya, the diplomat stopped over in Angora. It may well be that the learned gentleman, looking at the Roman ruins of Ancyra, did not recognize as such the wording of the testament of Augustus; but he understood the importance of the long inscription, and copied it from what was left of the wall in the old temple once dedicated to the emperor. At that time, nearly all of it was still legible. Scholars have so far listed 350,000 Latin texts inscribed in stone; of them all, the *Monumentum Ancyranum* is the longest, and by far the most important.

Though time has crumbled the stone and worn away most of the writing, a Latin scholar can still make out a few words here and there, sometimes a whole line. The less learned traveler, lingering by the old wall, can read in it what he will of the passing of time, and the death of gods and Caesars, and man's eternal wish to live forever.

The Romans have left two other important remains in Ankara: The Column of Julian commemorates the Emperor's visit in 362; not quite fifty feet high, the 15 fluted drums are topped by a Byzantine capital with acanthus leaves. Ankarans also call this column "the minaret of the Queen of Sheba".

Facing Julian's Column is a typical Turkish building, formerly the Ministry of Finance. It is white, with pointed arches, and blue glazed tiles above the big windows. The small square between the two would be lifeless without the charming little fountain in the middle.

Of the Baths of Caracalla, built in the third century A.D., nothing is left but the brick foundations. With an effort of will you can make out the plan, most clearly the Palestra and the swimming pool.

You can also take a walk through the Youth Park, Gençlik Parkı, with its artificial lake, its fair booths, swings and roundabouts, and its casino. Nearby are the stadium and the hippodrome. (See map on page 313.)

Barely two miles west of town on the road to Istanbul is Ak Köprü, a 13th-century Seljuk bridge with arches, partly built o marble from the Roman ruins of Ancyra.

For an outing, we have already mentioned Atatürk's Farm, Atatürk Çiftliği, four miles to the southwest; it is a meetingplace for picnics, the Turk's favorite outdoor sport. Some may like to see the Çubuk Dam, eight miles to the north; or go to Göl Başı, a lake 16 miles to the southwest, with a beach and a casino. If you are a Kemal fan, you may wish to see, in Söğütözü, the house where he settled his mother; it is now a museum. Elmadağ, 12 miles to the north, is a winter sports resort. You can also ski on Huseyin Gazi, eight miles away, near Arapköyü; and on Çal Dagı, near Dikmen.

Illustration at head of this chapter: Bases of Hittite columns (c. 1100 B.C.). Istanbul, Archeological Museum.

CENTRAL ANATOLIA

Triangular Tour of Wonders

Anatolia shows up on the map like some outsized rectangle, but its central portion may be likened to an upside-down triangle, almost equilateral, propped up on one of its three angles. To the north, as the crow flies, it's practically one straight line from Eskişehir to Tokat passing above Ankara. On the west: Eskişehir-Konya-Karaman; on the east: Sivas-Kayseri-Karaman. In the northern part, the climate tends to extremes of temperature, while the south enjoys warm, dry weather. For miles and miles, as far as the eye can see, there's the steppe, sometimes an arid plain, mountainous on all sides, poised high on a plateau 3,500 feet high. Anatolia is dotted with modern metropolises like Ankara, centers of tradition like Kayseri, and strongholds of religion like Konya. Among other points of interest, it contains famous burial places—those of Turkey's most illustrious 20th-century native son, Kemal Atatürk, of Turkish literature's most beloved and renowned storyteller, Nasreddin Hoca (whose tomb is in Akşehir), and of Islam's most eminent philosopher, ranking second only to the Prophet himself, Mevlâna (in Konya). Over and above all this, Anatolia is also the cradle of one of the world's most ancient civilizations, that of the Hittites.

History with a capital "H" didn't begin here until about one millenium after things had started happening in Mesopotamia. Boundary lines between regions were nebulous, and the people were in the throes of the transition from their nomadic state to a more settled way of life. There were no frontiers, nations, or empires in the political sense as we know them today. The basic differences between peoples lay in the rudimentary elements of culture—language (meaning dialects), pottery, and religious beliefs. In these respects, Asia Minor, including neighboring Assyria and Babylon, was to play a role of prime importance. Here, man designed his first written symbols, the cuneiform characters which were used for expressing the earliest known recorded human thoughts, and which were discovered on the tablets at Kültepe.

When the Hittites emerged from the outlying regions to settle here, they brought with them their own Indo-European tongue. These early arrivals also introduced a new type of hieroglyphic writing totally unrelated to its Egyptian counterpart, which they expressed by means of ideographs rather than by letters. The newcomers, quick to grasp the practical advantages of cuneiform transcription, lost no time in adopting the latter.

This minute nucleus of civilization gradually began having contacts (not always peaceful) with both the eastern peoples, who were nomads roving from one pastureland to another, and the westerners, the bulk of whom had already settled and were developing their own personal culture. This civilization also experienced the determined thrust of dawning imperialism reaching out from Egypt and from Assyria to the south. In a pinch, the only point of support upon which it could fall back was its northern province on the shores of the Black Sea.

The last Asiatic center, Troy, which by then had become deeply Hellenized, was destroyed as the result of an Achaean coalition. The straggling remnants of the victorious forces dug themselves in and set up housekeeping in the heart of Anatolia, bringing with them miscellaneous reminders of the Greek and Aegean civilizations. After numerous clashes, a *modus vivendi* was eventually reached with the southern peoples, and an equilibrium was established among all these populations of roughly equal might. But destruction was in the offing, at the hands of the "Sea People", whom the Greeks called Phrygians, or "free men".

Ankara's modern architecture ranges from the sombre grandeur of Ataturk's Mausoleum to the slick efficiency of its Kizilay Square.
Photos by Sonia Halliday

The Medrese at Sivas, in central Anatolia, was a masterpiece of Seljuk architecture. Built in 1271, only its façade remains, however.

They literally stepped into the Hittites' sandals and took over.

The Phrygians must have turned up sometime around the second half of the second millenary B.C., since the record shows that they were furnishing King Priam with military assistance against the Achaean invasion, in about 1200 B.C. Prior to that, the Trojan king had lent *them* a helping hand in their scuffles with the Hittites. These Phrygians entrenched themselves in a kingdom that managed to put up a pretty stiff resistance for some time against ensuing waves of would-be conquerors. The big turmoil set in some six centuries later, and ended only with the founding of the Ottoman Empire, in the 13th century. First came the Medes and the Persians, who met their fate at the hands of Alexander the Great; the Romans trundled along, and then the Byzantines; later on, it was the turn of the Arabs, the Mongols, and the Seljuk Turks, and finally the latters' cousins, the Ottoman Turks.

Phrygia succeeded in hanging on for a while longer, but was dealt a death-blow in the seventh century B.C. by the Cimmerians, a people who eventually got lost in the shuffle. The watching neighboring country of Lydia promptly pounced on this ready-made prey and proceeded to swallow it up. In the third century B.C., the Galatians began trailing in from the west, to settle in the region of Ankyra. When the last king of Pergamum died in 133 B.C., he left a will bequeathing his kingdom to the Romans—a testament that, needless to say, was hotly contested. The name of Phrygia lingered on for a while as the name of a province, but its people were no longer free. In A.D. 300, Emperor Diocletian divided it into two parts, *prima* and *secunda*. Byzantium simply wiped it out with one stroke of the quill, and these days the adjective Phrygian is applied only to a highly special item of headgear ... thanks to the French Revolution, whose protagonists adopted the Phrygian bonnet as the emblem of freedom.

In the meantime, both the Galatians and the Phrygians had contrived to build quite a respectable assortment of cities, including notably Ankyra and Iconion, which were capital cities. Iconion became Konya, and two of its Seljuk rulers, Kiliç Arslan and Alâeddin Keykubat, bestowed some remarkable monuments upon posterity. The 13th century also produced an inspired theologian, Mevlâna, who back in those early times was already busy preaching the principle of the equality of all mankind. And at last, in the 20th century, there came a man who put his finger on the true pulse of Turkey and felt its heartbeat throbbing in Central Anatolia—Kemal Atatürk.

Practical Information for Central Anatolia

HOW TO GET THERE? *T.H.Y. planes:* Istanbul-Ankara, twelve flights daily, DC-9 jets, Fokker and Viscount turbo jets (about 1 hr.). Ankara-Kayseri, 3 flights weekly, 1hr. 10 min. *Trains:* Daily between Istanbul and Ankara (*Bogazici Ekspresi*). *Anatolia Express*, same trip, night train, Pullmans. Additional train service: Ankara-Kayseri (8 hrs.). Ankara-Konya (the long way round; shorter by bus). Daily *bus service* between Ankara and Nevsehir; *taxis* from Nevsehir. Daily buses from Kayseri to Nevsehir. Taxis at Ürgüp.

MOTORING. (See also section on Motoring in *Sea of Marmara* chapter, p. 179.) From Istanbul to Ankara (273 miles): from the Asian ferry terminals the double-carriage six-lane Route E5 approaches the Bay of Izmit past the Kartal junction, but the fine view across the sea is all too often marred by factories belching forth what seems a disproportionate amount of acrid smoke; traffic usually heavy. Beyond Izmit the air pollution ceases, but Route E5 turns into a modest two-lane way through a fertile plain, skirts Lake Sapanca and climbs through the magnificent forests round Bolu (155 miles) to the barren Anatolian Plateau. Conveniently located service stations. West of Ankara, the highway approach skirts the city, using modern clover-leaf highway structures. *Return trip:* Recommended itinerary is Ankara-Eskişehir-Bursa-Yalova (car ferry)-Istanbul. (Routes 68, 60, 2 and 4-0.) Road conditions slightly inferior to those on the main Ankara-Istanbul highway but there is less traffic.

To Boğazköy and East: Owing to the lack of signposts inside Ankara, by far the easiest exit is by Çankiri Cad., the continuation of Atatürk Bulvarı. This is the road to the Esenboğa airport, but the branch off right to the Çorum-Samsun road is clearly marked. Other possibilities are turning right from Atatürk Bul., either into Cemal Gürsel Cad., or lower down into Talat Paşa Bul. All three branches merge at the outskirts into Route 2 (E23), the central artery east, which crosses the broad valley of the Kızılirmak to the intersection before Delice (78 miles), where Route 41 branches left (northeast). Just past Sungurlu (33 miles), a stabilized road leads right (southwest) to Boğazköy (18 miles) and another branch to Alacahöyük (25 miles).

From the Sungurlu intersection, paved Route 41 continues for 42 miles to Çorum where it becomes Route 43 but remains blissfully paved till it ends as Route 45 at Samsun (104 miles) on the Black Sea.

Route 20 following the coast east to Trabzon, then striking inland on Routes 65 and 40 (E100) to Erzurum to link up with Route 2 (E23) is the recommended (because mostly paved) itinerary to the Persian frontier (see chapter *The Eastern Provinces*, p. 376), though considerably longer than following Route 2 all the way.

That main artery runs southeast from the Delice intersection through the Delice Irmak valley to Yerköy (38 miles) where it parts company with the railway to Kayseri to veer northeast to Yozgat (24 miles). If you are young in heart and car you might undertake Boğazköy from there too, a mere 20 miles north on a sort of road. Route 2 continues due east to Sivas (142 miles), but soon afterwards the asphalt gives out and there remain 302 gruesome miles through clouds, of dust and over washboard ruts to Erzurum.

The Ankara-Adana Highway: The way lies through a few hundred miles of barren steppe ungraced by a single tree. Although road conditions are excellent, the landscape can grate on your nerves. By summer's end, the road is covered with a thick ochre dust. The scattered brownish patches are low-lying settlements some distance from the road. Service stations and restaurants are few and far between on the 304 miles of Route I (E5) to Adana, unless you go via Konya (163 miles from Ankara on Route 35), a mid-desert oasis, from which Route 35 continues to the coast at Silifke (158 miles) via Karaman and Mut; while 57 stabilized miles lead to Beyşehir on the vast lake at an altitude of some 3,500 feet; 125 miles on Route 80 bring you back to Route I.

Some 80 miles almost due south of Ankara Route I skirts for 30 miles the immense expanse of the Tuz Gölü salt lake, almost dry in summer but a seemingly limitless sheet of shallow water after the winter rains. At Aksaray (141 miles from Ankara) you cut Route 73, leading right (southwest) over 93 horribly dusty or muddy miles to Konya; or excellently paved 62 miles to the left toward the fantastic universe of Göreme and Ürgüp. A visit to this wonderland will usually include Kayseri some 50 miles northeast and 204 miles from Ankara.

Although there's nothing remotely resembling a decent eating place along the way, there are plenty of service stations, so don't worry about gas. But do bring a picnic lunch from Ankara: don't expect even a halfway acceptable restaurant or hotel before Adana.

The peaks of the Taurus Range break the monotony of the scenery, and the road beyond Ulukışla passes through mountainous country before continuing down the Gülek Pass (Gates of Cilicia) toward the Mediterranean area. It's a narrow, extremely winding road—careful around the curves! Cars emerging from around a bend not infrequently find themselves face to face with a big truck whose driver may have only the sketchiest notion of where the right side of the road should be.

The Eastern Plateau: There's a road (Route 55) leading up from Ordu on the Black Sea via Ulubey and the Gürgentepe Pass (altitude 4,200 ft.) to Koyulhisar, in the valley of the Kelkit (a tributary of the Yeşil Irmak, or Green River); this brings you to Sivas via Suşehri (on E23) and the Karabayir Pass (altitude 6,352 ft.). The route is spectacularly scenic, especially along the first part of the way, and sharply points up the transition from the lush vegetation of the Black Sea region to the barrenness of the Central Anatolian plateau. It is mostly "stabilized", i.e., bad, and certain portions aren't even that good, so you can count on dust in the summertime and mud in the rainy season. Gas stations are rather far apart. However, if you've plenty of time, a sturdy automobile, and sharp eyesight, the adventure is more than worth it. It's often necessary to inch along at 25 or even 20 miles an hour, so deflate the tires a little.

WHAT TO SEE? Central Anatolia is the heart of the ancient Hittite and Turkish civilizations. A visit to the Archeological Museum in Ankara provides an excellent background for the one-day trip to Boğazköy and Alacahöyük. Arrange with an agent before arrival in Ankara for visits to Boğazköy or Göreme. Amasya is a typical Turkish settlement. You can revel in Seljuk architecture in Sivas and Kayseri. And before continuing on to Konya, don't fail to catch a glimpse of one of Turkey's most unique sights, in Cappadocia, the land of the "fairy chimneys" (Ürgüp-Göreme area). Konya was once a Seljuk capital, and is still replete with stunning mementoes of the past, plus an excellent and unusual museum dedicated to Mevlâna, the great 13th-century poet and philosopher. If you're keen on archeology, you'll also want to see Çatal Höyük, Turkey's most important prehistoric site.

Hotels and Restaurants

ABANT GÖLU. (Lake of Abant). *Abant* (2), 47 rooms with bath. Full board only. Detached cottages available. *Piknik Dağevleri*, modest, small.

AKŞEHIR. *Dağ* (3), 16 rooms with shower; *Ilgin Motel*, 91 rooms with shower.

AMASYA. *Apaydin*, 23 rooms (8 showers); *Şehir Palas*, 20 rooms (5 showers).

BEYŞEHIR. *Bademli Motel*, 8 rooms with shower.

BOĞAZKALE (Boğazköy). *Hattusas Motel*; in an emergency, the small *Turist*.

BOLU. The one recommended stopover on the Istanbul-Ankara highway. Three comfortable motels in the environs: *Çizmecioğlu*, 30 rooms (20 showers); *Emniyet*, 35 rooms (25 showers); *Koru*, 28 rooms with shower.

In town: *Menekşe* (4), 28 rooms with shower; rock bottom *Turist*, 20 rooms; *Itimat*, 24 rooms; *Yeni*, 30 rooms.

ÇANKIRI. *Emniyet*, 35 rooms.

CIHANBEYLI. *Ağabeyli Çeşmebası Motel*, half way between Ankara and Konya.

ÇORUM. *Konak*, 36 rooms; *Emniyet*, 32 rooms; *Yayla Palas*, 21 rooms;

Evsan Motel; Yeni Konak, 25 rooms.

HAYMANA. *Cimcime* (3), 34 rooms with shower.

KAYSERI. *Turan* (2), 55 rooms, most with shower, restaurant; *Turist*, 30 rooms (6 with shower), restaurant. Also possible: *Divan, Ipek Palas, Kent, Mimar Sinan, Posta*.

Restaurant: *Cumhuriyet*, Mayis Caddesi 27.

KIRŞEHIR. *Konak Palas*, 20 rooms (6 with shower).

KONYA. *Saray* (3), 40 rooms (31 showers); *Başak Palas* (4), 40 rooms (12 showers); *Şahin* (4), 45 rooms (22 showers), all convenient on Hükümet Mydanı, the central square. *Yayla* (4), Babalik Sok., 27 rooms (18 showers); *Ipek Palas* and *Şehir*, Karaman Cad., *Olgun Palas*, Alâeddin Bulvarı.

Restaurants: *Konak Lokantası, Merkez, Saray*. All three are located near Hükümet Meydanı Square. Try the local specialties: *tandır kebab, etli pide* (meat pizza), *peynirlipide* (cheese pizza).

MERZIFON. *Tore Palas*, 17 rooms.

MUCUR. *Meydan*, 15 rooms (10 with shower).

NEVŞEHIR. *Tusan* (2), 80 rooms with shower, restaurant, the best hotel in the Göreme region; less so the *Koç Palas* and *Şehir Palas*.

Restaurant: *Lâle*.

NIĞDE. *Merkez Turist Oteli* (2), 32 rooms with shower; *Ciçek Palas*, 14 rooms, 2 showers; *Turing Palas*, 39 rooms (9 with shower).

ORTAHISAR. *Belidiye*, primitive but clean.

PINARBASI. On junction of Routes 60 and 55 east of Kayseri, *Melik Gazi Motel*, 13 rooms (5 showers).

POLATLI. *Gordion* (4), 24 rooms (4 showers).

SIVAS. *Koşk* (3), 52 rooms with shower; *Belediye* (4), Cumhuriyet Cad.; 60 rooms (24 with shower), restaurant; *Özden Palas* (4), Cumhu-

riyet Cad., 44 rooms (2 with shower), restaurant.

Restaurant: *Çiçek*.

SUNGURLU. If you really must: *Imren Palas*.

TOKAT. *Belediye*, 14 rooms (4 with shower).

UÇHISAR. *Güvercinlik*, but accommodation only through the Club Mediterranée.

ÜRGÜP. *Tusan* (2), 50 rooms (32 showers), restaurant, lovely view; *Peri*, 16 rooms (10 showers), and on the same simple but clean level, 5 pensions: *Efes, Europa, Göreme, Tepe* and *Turist*, most rooms with shower.

YOZGAT. *Saraylar*, 33 rooms with shower; *Şehir*, 34 room s, 4 showers.

 CAMPING GROUNDS include: Abant: *Camping* and *Motel*, 21 miles west of Bolu. Ankara: *Mocamp Susuzköy*, 15 miles west on the Istanbul highway, near the military airport Nevşehir: Two *Mocamps*, each one mile from the town, respectively on the Ankara and Göreme road. Silvas: *Station BP*, 3 miles on the Ankara highway. Ürgüp: *Çimenli Tepesi Camping*, with big swimming pool, just outside the town.

 USEFUL ADDRESSES. *Tourist Offices* (*Turizm Bürosu*). Konya, 21 Mevlâna Cad. (tel. 1074); Niğde, Vakif Iş Hani (tel. 261); offices also in Kayseri, Nevşehir, Hacibektaş, and Ürgüp. *Türk Hava Yollari Airlines* (T.H.Y.): Kayseri, Cumhuriyet Mah. 41/A Yeni Carsi Cad.; Sivas, Bankalar Caddesi 1.

Discovering Central Anatolia

The great sites of the Hittite empire are contained within the Boğazköy-Alacahöyük-Yazılıkaya triangle, just east of Sungurlu. It's also possible to go via Yozgat, on the Sivas road (Route 2) if you don't mind driving your car over a washboard.

Boğazköy, officially designated as Boğazkale, is the topic of endless discussions and controversy. And even the most eminent scholars have the grace to admit that they still don't know very much about what was once a great civilization. The fact is that, although there arc many points of reference on which to fall back, there are still numerous gaps in the documentation, and much remains yet to be filled in.

The Old Testament lists the Hittites among the people whom the Hebrews found already on the scene when they reached the Promised Land (Genesis: xv, 19–21); both Esau and Solomon had Hittite wives (1 Kings: xi, 1), and Solomon even supplied horses to the Hittites (11 Chronicles: I,17). But nowhere in the Bible is there anything to indicate that the Hittites represented more of a culture than a nation, nor, more particularly, that they had left such extensive traces of their culture. An inscription on the walls of the temple of Karnak in Egypt refers to the battle of Kadesh, in which the Egyptians fought against the people of Kheda, but research had failed to establish any apparent connection. In 1812, a German traveler named Burckhardt found at Hamath, in Syria, a stone tablet bearing hieroglyphics different from the Egyptian ones. Much later on, additional stone tablets were found on the same site. In 1839, a Frenchman, Charles Texier, finally stumbled upon the ruins of Boğazköy, its stone carvings and bas-reliefs. Other archeologists have hied themselves to Boğazköy, and mention should be made of Davis, Wright, Hamilton, Hogarth, Chantre, Perrot, Langlois, and Winckler, among many others.

It soon became obvious that there were two kinds of writing. The cuneiform types in the Akkadian language, related to the Babylonian and Assyrian dialects—were gradually deciphered. The hieroglyphic inscriptions still guard their secrets, but after two decades of research, it was clear that there had once been a civilization whose existence hadn't even been suspected—a powerful kingdom (or more exactly, a federation of kingdoms) and its empire had extended all the way from the Black Sea to Palestine. The capital was Hattuşaş, the humble Boğazkale of today, where the Hittite state archives were discovered in 1906.

Most of the artifacts and art treasures that have been brought to light here are now in the Ankara Museum. A visit there is an indispensable background preparation for your trip to the ruins of the memorable site at which they were discovered. Once you are actually in Boğazköy, you will be stunned by the arresting sight of the great walls and the exquisite carvings. These are described in more detail in the section entitled *The Hittite Sites at Boğazköy*. Right now, let us concern ourselves with the Hittite people as such.

Where were they from? Had they come from Assyria, from Babylon, from beyond the Caucasus? The Assyrian hypothesis is favored by many scholars because of the language the Hittites used, and also because of the distinctive nature of their artistic expression. However, one thing appears certain—they were not a sharply defined group in the sense in which we generally conceive of a single, unified people or tribe that conquers a territory and proceeds to settle in it. The Hittites were not a nation as we think of such political entities today; rather, they were more of an aristocracy, which began infiltrating early in the second millenium B.C. Within a few centuries, these overlords had subjugated the indigenous populations, and between 1500 and 1200 B.C., expanded their territory, until their empire reached into Syria.

The civilization that resulted was inevitably a blend of the Hittite influence with the cultures of the peoples whom they had overrun. The overall political structure was Indo-European, enhanced by a smattering of Semitic influences (Babylonian, Syrian), plus contributions from Interior Asia, which was in all probability the Hittites' original homebase.

The Sea People, who, as the many ancient records show, were the Phrygians, succeeded in overthrowing this empire sometime around 1200 B.C. However, the civilization itself was perpetuated both in Cilicia (the southern coast of modern Turkey) and in Syria. On the basis of the evidence available so far, it must have vanished in about 600 B.C. The sands of time, as is their wont, took over and buried this great culture with all its stupendous monuments until two and a half millenia later, when they were disinterred by man's curiosity.

The citadel, or Büyükkale, looms sharply up against the Hattuşaş hillside. The postern gate slices abruptly through the citadel wall, and gives off on an underground gallery that was of immense strategic significance—during sieges, the Hattusians would sneak through this passageway and rush out to stage surprise attacks on their unsuspecting enemies.

There is no question that the Hittites were crafty and fearsome warriors. And, judging from other evidence, they were also fun-loving and charmingly child-like in their fondness for animals and in the importance assigned to entertainment in their lives. They were also perfectly capable of abandoning an uncompleted enterprise midway in order to launch a new and more interesting one. Although of small physical stature—probably under five feet —the Hittites were muscular and strongly-built. Their diet included bread, honey, cheese, vegetables, and fruit, but this didn't mean that they were necessarily vegetarians at heart. The Hittite kings and nobility had the privilege of eating both fish and meat, and this distinction may well have been one of the ways of pointing up the difference between the Hittites and the indigenous population. Their society was sharply divided into free men and serfs, and the sovereign who ruled over the federation of principalities was also its spiritual leader.

Their religious beliefs provided for considerable elasticity and tolerance, and the Hittite Pantheon appears to have welcomed plenty of local divinities with no questions asked. The temptations of etymology lure us on to discover further connections. The mythologies that have come down to us may have derived their symbolism from the Hittite set of creeds. For example. there were Runda, the god of hunting, and Tarhund, the god of the tempest. Compare these with the Etruscan Tarchuna, and with the Taraxippus of the Greeks, who set up statues of this god right at the starting-line in stadium chariot races. Then, too, there were the Universal Mother, who eventually became Cybele, and Kupapa, the god of victory, whose attributes are reflected in those of his Hellenic female counterpart, the goddess Nike. And there may well be many points in common between the mischief-making god Telepinu, the perpetrator of all manner of joyous tricks—he specialized in banquets for the gods—and Dionysus, whose practical jokes set his Mount Olympus colleagues' teeth gnashing.

In today's terminology, the Hittite might well be described as the "outdoor type". Among other things, he enjoyed open-air religious rituals. The Hittite sculptor and stone-carver, once confronted with a mass of rock, seemed to lose all sense of restraint and became literally intoxicated with his work. Look at that marvelous procession of warriors on the rock face at Yazılıkaya. And Hittite art attained its summit in the stylization of animal bodies. See, at the Ankara Museum, the emblematic deer, with its antlers an ingenious pretext for multiple transformations.

The site of Yazılıkaya, carved right out of the sheer cliff, lies quite near Boğazkale. A properly overwhelming array of gods and goddesses stand in line high overhead, decorating the open-air galleries. Once again the beholder is struck by the infallible rigor of the theme and the hieratic pose that characterize this art.

Alacahöyük isn't far off, but to reach it you must retrace your steps and take a different road (for some 23 miles), that represents a solid hour of driving. But it's an hour well spent. The bas-reliefs here are wholly as astonishing, particularly the one depicting a royal couple in adoration before the bull. This was a city that flourished during the copper age (2500 to 2000 B.C.), before the earliest Hittite colonization. Fourteen tombs from that period have been brought to light on this site. The Gate of the Sphinxes, where a god is resting on a two-headed eagle, elicits gasps of admiration from the most blasé art experts.

The Hittite Sites at Boğazköy

The ancient sites of the Hittite civilization abound, from Anatolia to the Euphrates. However, it isn't often that you can squeeze in three different ones on a single excursion, as you can in the case of the ruins of Hattuşaş, the Yazılıkaya rupestrian shrine, and the excavations at Alacahöyük. (It's only fair to point out that this trip can be of real interest only to the genuine archeology enthusiast—all others had better desist!)

If you do not wish to take the organized tour from Ankara, then plan to use Boğazköy village as your base. Hotel accommodation here is strictly local in style—in other words, definitely primitive, and in limited supply. You can also use Sungurlu or Çorum as your point of departure. To reach Boğazköy from Sungurlu, start off along the Çorum road (Route 41) and, one mile farther on, turn right onto the Yozgat road. At *Boğazköy* village (Boğazkale), leave this road, cross the bridge, and start climbing up toward the citadel.

This particular site appears to have been occupied as early as the third millenary B.C. by pre-Hittite peoples. The city of Hatti, subsequently called Hattuşaş, dates from the reign of one of the first known Hittite kings, probably Anittas (beginning of the second millenium).Labarnas II transformed the place into the capital of his empire; he proceeded to take the name of Hattusilis I and the city became known as Hattuşaş. After being frequently besieged by invading neighbors, it was destroyed toward the 14th century B.C. Following the abrupt end of the Hittite empire at the beginning of the 12th century B.C., the city was burned by the Phrygians, who built a new one, which was eventually occupied by the Persians in their turn.

The tour of the ruins can be exhausting; save your strength for the most important places. When you've gone round the ramparts of the lower city, the first ruins to the right as you go up toward the citadel are those of Temple I. Hattuşaş had five temples, all patterned on an identical model. Like the Babylonian temples, they consisted of small rooms arranged around a paved courtyard roughly 700 to 1700 feet square. The only difference between the temples lay in the means of access to the sanctuary in which the statue of the divinity was enshrined. (In Babylon, the people were allowed to contemplate the statue from a courtyard through the small open gates of an intermediary chapel. Hittite temples were designed so that it was necessary to run a sort of obstacle course to reach the sanctuary, and the god's statue was not placed facing the entrance—rather, it stood to one side. It is therefore reasonable to conclude that the Hittites regarded religion as something reserved for only a select few, who were admitted into the innermost shrine, and that the people had a right only to an indirect form of participation in religious rites or ceremonies.)

The rooms opening out from the courtyard were doubtless administrative offices and archives at least in Temple I. It is more difficult to reconstitute the exact circumstances for the other four temples. Temple I stands on a terrace overlooking some of the public buildings; to the north and east of it lay private residential buildings, parts of which have been dug out. They were occupied by a thriving colony of Assyrian merchants and traders.

The second most important ruins are those of the citadel, or Büyükkale (something of a climb up from Temple I). This was the residence of the kings who built those remarkable fortifications. They lived in constant fear of invasion, and rightly so, since one eventually destroyed their empire in 1200 B.C. The citadel's outbuildings include storage rooms where the archives were kept; here, in 1906, thousands of stone tablets were found, mute but eloquent survivors of the plundering Phrygians, who hadn't ferreted out this particular hiding-place.

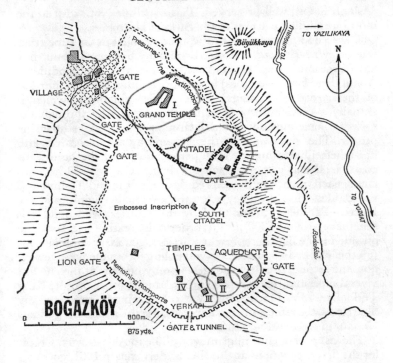

Continuing up the hill, you come first to the eastern side of the fortified wall of the upper city, with its Royal Gate (Kral Kapisi). It is here, and also on the south, that the ramparts are most impressive. They consist of two parallel walls connected by the two main gates, the latter in themselves being formidable bastions. The overall concept of this defense set-up, plus the other military installations at Hattuşaş, prove that the Hittites had attained a higher level of perfection in warlike, political, legislative, and judicial matters than in art, literature, and religion.

Now follow along the ramparts. The ruins of Temples V, II, and III lie to your left. Beyond is the entrance to a tunnel (Yerkapı) leading to the base of the wall outside. The ruins of Temple IV are to the north. Beyond, at the end of the pathway that runs the length of the ramparts, rises the Gate of the Lions

(Aslanli Kapi), well preserved. This concludes your visit to the most outstanding features of the ruins of Hattuşaş.

The second part of your tour can be devoted to the rupestrian sanctuary at *Yazılıkaya*. Leave Boğazköy, backtrack about five km. (three miles), and take the road to the right (in bad condition). About three km. (two miles) farther on, another road (to the right of the caretaker's cottage) leads to the sanctuary, which is actually a crevice forming a narrow passageway through the rocks and emerging onto a small circular open space—the shrine proper. The rocky walls of the passageway are decorated with bas-reliefs illustrating various personages, and the figures increase in size as you approach the shrine. On the wall beyond, facing each other, are the carved figures of the god Teshub and the goddess Hepatu. They were the two main divinities of the Hurrite Pantheon, assimilated by the Hittites, who built this sanctuary around 1300 B.C. In order of increasing size, from the outside in, the figures represent warriors, genies, and minor gods (on the left) and goddesses. As you emerge from the passageway, note the second, smaller passageway on your left: at the end are several more bas-reliefs representing, among other people, King Tudhaliyas IV (13th century B.C.), probably protected by Sharruma, the same god who appears directly behind the goddess Hepatu in the main sanctuary.

The last part of your pilgrimage will be to Alacahöyük. Credit for the first excavations at this site, undertaken in 1861, goes to a French archeologist, Georges Perrot, who was 29 years old at the time. To reach Alacahöyük, go back to the Boğazköy road, turn right, and continue on to the Yozgat (Via Alaca) road, where you turn right at the village of Boğazköy. Shortly after, turn off this road, to the left, toward Alacahöyük. Just before the village, turn left for the excavation site. Although the prize finds from these diggings have been placed in the Hittite Museum in Ankara, the local museum also contains some interesting items, including an assortment of objects from the third millenium B.C., Hittite bas-reliefs, and Roman and Byzantine tombstones.

Many scholars believe that, in the fourth millenium B.C., this was the site of the city of Kussara, occupied by the Hittites, who were already in Cappadocia before the Indo-Europeans got there. The latter—who also happened to be Hittites—may have used Kussara as their first capital, prior to Hattuşaş, toward the end of the third millenium, though this theory is contested. The two-headed eagle on the bas-relief is a frequently recurring motif in Hittite art, as are the altars shaped like animals.

From Alacahöyük you can get directly onto the Ankara-Amasya road back near Sungurlu.

You are truly reluctant to have to leave these places. You find yourself wishing that you had lived back in those ancient days when there was more time for everything, perhaps even envying the passing peasant slowly ambling along behind his plodding oxen. The chariot that his animals are drawing is a replica of those used by the Hittites, down to the minutest detail, including its solid wood wheels. These wheels, which have continued to be used for at least 3,000 years now, are in evidence in the most impoverished areas of eastern and southern Anatolia. Who can gainsay Atatürk's statement that the Hittites were the real ancestors of the Turks?

It goes without saying that a civilization as vigorous as that of the Hittites was not going to confine itself to the three sites of Boğazköy-Yazılıkaya and Alacahöyük alone.

Thirty-two miles east of Alacahöyük, at Pazarli there are, in addition to Hittite vestiges, strata from the bronze age and remnants of the Phrygian, Hellenic, Roman, and Byzantine epochs. Its most important building is a Phrygian citadel. A mere ten miles north of Alacahöyük lies Büyük Göllücek (closest village is Keltepe), with excavations revealing strata going back to the chalcolithic age, and a Phrygian citadel.

Yozgat (116 miles east of Ankara), which you did not go through on your way to Boğazkale, was another important Hittite city already in existence in the bronze age and even as far back as the chalcolithic era, before the Hittites had arrived. Excavations at Alisar (Ankuva), 41 miles east, have yielded hoards of pottery, ceramics, and weapons. Farther away are even more Hittite sites. While visiting the Çubuk Dam, you have already stopped at Etiyokuşu (the Hittite hill) to see the ruins of a settlement dating back to prehistoric times and including a Hittite period. At Gavur Kalesi, the "Fortress of the Infidels", 42 miles southwest of Ankara, still another bas-relief immortalizes the glorious days of Hatti.

Amasya

Modern Çorum, on Route 41, some 42 miles northeast of Sungurlu, on the site of antique Niconia, possesses several Ottoman monuments, especially the Ali Paşa Hamam; the 13th-century Ulu Cami was restored during the 19th century; the Inayet Cami is of more recent construction. Amasya, 54 unpaved miles to the east, is a more interesting and picturesque place. Under its original name of Amaseia, it was a settlement clustered around the ancient fortress built high on a rock overlooking the valley of the Yeşil Irmak. Amasya served as the capital city of the Pontic kingdom described in the chapter dealing with the Black Sea. According to the historian Strabo, who was born here, the city had been founded by the Amazon queen, Amasis. The Seljuks moved in fairly early, in 1071, following their victory over Byzantium, and the Mongol hordes found their way there, too, in the 13th century. At the dawn of the 15th century, Bayezit I conquered the place for the Ottoman Empire. On the right bank of the Yeşil Irmak, a palace, the Saray Düzü, was built for the heirs to the throne, who often acted as governors and even retained the office after their accession. Only the outer walls and baths remain.

The local *türbe* of Törümtay, dating from 1266, is characteristic of the Seljuk style. The nearby Gök Medrese Cami is completely blue-colored, as its Turkish name implies, but no longer in use. It was built as a mosque and Koranic school ten years after the *türbe*, and by the same gentleman, Törümtay, who was the governor of Amasya. The angles of the portal are supported by cylindrical abutments. In the little street opposite stands a mosque (1430) bearing the name of its builder, Mehmet I's vizir, Yörgüç Paşa.

Amasya's local dignitaries appear to have been deeply concerned over their own final resting places. Both sides of the town's main street are lined with *türbes* containing the mortal remains of such dignitaries as Prince Şehzad, Halifet Gazi, Mehmet Paşa, and Sultan Mesut. These *mescit*, or little mosques add a note of tranquility to the neighborhood.

The Sultan Bayezit Cami is a much bigger mosque, built in 1486. It stands out on a terrace shaded by plane trees along the banks of the Yeşil Irmak. Its *mimber* and *mihrap* are made of marble, and the blue tiles have quotations from the Koran exquisitely inscribed in white.

The venerable Burmali Minare Cami (1242) is perhaps a bit over-restored. One of its outstanding features is its fluted minaret that, despite the restorations, has managed to retain a distinctive air of originality. The Fethiye Cami, a ruin standing close by, also has an ancient history—it was built first as a Byzantine church and became a mosque in 1116. And these are by no means all that Amasya has to offer in the way of mosques. The Timarhane hospital dates from 1309, and the local museum merits a visit, if you don't feel that you're already up to your ears in Hittite civilization. In any case, take a stroll around the town just to see the wonderful old bridges. Near the Bayezit Cami, there's the sultan's bridge reposing at the bottom of the river. The Alçak Köprü bridge has spruced itself up with a new span, but still proudly rests on its genuine original arches. The Kuş Köprü has a poetic name meaning "Bridge of the Birds". In your meanderings, you will have seen, at least from the outside, the Kapı Ağasi Medrese (1488), now the School of Arts and Crafts. At the citadel, the inevitable *kale* of every townsite that has had to withstand the centuries of warring attacks, only a few bits of wall remain upright. In the vicinity of Amasya, to the south, is Kaya Mezarlari, with rupestral tombs, more of which can also be seen at Aynali Mağara (north, on the left bank of the Yeşil Irmak): its name signifies "mirror grotto", because it literally shines in the rays of the sun.

Halfway between Amasya and Tokat, at Turhal, take the road to the right leading to the walled city of Zile, from where you can gaze out on the scene of Caesar's victory over the Pontic king. This was the battle that inspired Caesar's celebrated and terse message to the Roman Senate: "*Veni, vidi, vici*" ("I came, I saw, I conquered"). Although perhaps never actually uttered by Caesar, these words were contained in a letter that he wrote to his friend Amintius, describing his victory in Asia over Pharnaces, the son of Mithridates.

The first written records mentioning Tokat (50,000 population; 72 miles southeast of Amasya) date from the time of the vast Persian sweep in the sixth century B.C., followed, in the fourth century B.C., by the reverse sweep of Alexander and his

Macedonians. Byzantium succeeded Rome, which installed itself in Asia Minor between the years 190 (Antiochus III's defeat at Magnesia of Sipylus) and 133 B.C., which saw the completion of the conquest. Tokat became Comana Pontica before being occupied first by the Arabs, next by the Seljuks, and finally joining the Ottoman Empire in the 14th century.

You may find that by now hilltop fortresses over the Anatolian countryside have become a pretty familiar sight, but their fascination never palls. Tokat's 28 towers date from the Middle Ages, and the fortress looks robust even now. The most characteristically Seljuk building, the Gök Medrese, is now a museum —it is full of tiles, Byzantine frescoes and geometrical designs. The mausolea are likewise of Seljuk origin—look for those of Elbükasim and Halef Gazi, Açikbaş, Nurettin Şentimur, and Sümbül Bab. The Hatuniye, a school and mosque dating from 1485, was built in memory of Bayezit II's mother. The Ali Paşa Cami is of more recent construction. Niksar (a contraction of Neo-Caesarea), 36 miles northeast, possesses two 12th-century monuments, the Ulu Cami and the Yağibasan Medrese within the imposing Byzantine-Ottoman citadel.

Sivas

From Tokat, it is 67 dusty miles to Sivas (100,000 inhabitants) where wide modern boulevards surround the old quarter. Probably a Hittite foundation, it became as Sebasteia an important trading center under the Romans, a position it only regained with the construction of the Anatolian rail line. An Armenian principality for 350 years, it passed for several centuries between Seljuk and Danişment sultans, Mongols and Ottomans, and suffered badly from Tamerlane's hordes in 1400. Sivas was the setting for the congress convened by Atatürk in September, 1919, which decided the liberation of Turkey, then still partly occupied. Today the meeting hall and the room in which Atatürk lived constitute the Inkilâp Museum ("Museum of the Revolution").

Photographs on one of the Turkish Ministry of Tourism posters feature a beautifully-carved portal topped by two intricately-wrought, open-work brick and tile minarets. The picture was taken right here in Sivas, and the building is the Çifte Minare,

Cappadocia, in central Anatolia, was host to a colony of Byzantine hermits, who carved rooms in the cones and pyramids of soft stone.
Photo by Sonia Halliday

The tenth-century Aktamar Basilica, on an island in Lake Van, is an excellent example of eastern Turkey's Armenian heritage.

the former medrese. The centuries have wrought their havoc, and nothing remains of this once splendid Seljuk monument except the façade, but the portal itself is a sheer masterpiece. The medrese was built in 1271 by the vizir Şemsettin Mehmet. It may have touched off a rash of competition, because in the same year another vizir, Muzaffer Bürucirci, had a Koranic school built, which bears his name. Of the two buildings, the latter has more successfully withstood the ravages of time; it houses its founder's mausoleum. A third vizir, Sahip Ata, constructed a third school, the Gök Medrese.

The Şifaiye started life in 1217 as a hospital, back in the days when portals and their adornment were a matter of supreme importance. This one is a particularly handsome example, and the mosaics in the interior are also exquisite. The Sultan Keykâvus *türbe*, in the Şifaiye, is truly a symphony in faience. The mosques in Sivas are of much later construction, dating from the Ottoman period. The Ulu Cami is the only 12th-century mosque, but its minaret, with its ribbon of enamelled tile-work, dates from the 14th century. The Yeni Cami, or New Mosque, has been recently restored. The façade of the Güdük Minare is made of marble, a material conspicuous for its scarcity in Asia.

The city has a *han* named after its founder, Behram Paşa, and a *hamam* that bears the name of the lead roofing that covers it— Kurşunlu. This about takes care of the main points of interest in Sivas, but the place still has much more to offer to the leisurely stroller. Just be careful not to wander too far astray in the maze of tangled little streets.

Southeast of Ankara

Çankırı, north of Ankara on Route 39, is another interesting stop; there is a traditional array of historical edifices, including a Byzantine fortress, or *kale*, duly restored by the Turks.

The busy Seljuk whom you've already encountered in the south, Alâeddin Keykubat, also managed to find time in 1235 to put up a hospital here, the Tasmescidi. And of course there's the strikingly situated Ulu Cami, designed by the great Sinan himself (1522—1558).

As for local color, if you should happen to stumble across a flock of sheep, try to edge up close enough for a good look at the cloak worn by the shepherd (*çoban*). It's a solid cylinder of hand-woven raw wool, with no openings except for the head. Also look for the *sadouf*, used for dipping water from wells—it is a straight stick with a shaft to which the dipper is attached, and a counter-weight at the other end of the shaft.

Take the southern route (E 5, Route 1) out of the capital. This time your destination is Kayseri to the southeast and Konya to the south. Your trip to Turkey can't be complete without at least a stopover in these two all-important places.

A few miles outside of Ankara, past the green belt with which Atatürk endowed the city, you are once more confronted with the taunting grey starkness of the bare mountains and their rocky slopes, sparsely patched with bits of shy moss and reluctant clumps of brush. Occasionally, a ridge or peak may stand out from the others by its sharply indented overlayer of colored rock, shading from ochre through lavender to red, reminiscent of the hues in a coxcomb.

After twenty miles turn left on to Route 60, paved all the 204 miles to Kayseri, through the grandly desolate sweep of the steppe, punctuated by an occasional dwelling or a cultivated field. A huge grain silo, Anatolia's new architecture, dominates the village of Bala at an altitude of 4,500 feet. The road drops to the Seljuk bridge over the Kızılırmak river, ancient Halys, which King Croesus so rashly crossed somewhere near here.

Sixteen miles of stabilized road to the right lead to the Hirfanli dam which has formed a vast artificial lake. The distances between settlements grow greater and greater, and the occasional squat houses made of hard materials look rather incongruous. They seem somehow less sturdy than the buildings constructed of sun-baked, mud-covered brick. Kırşehir is an important agricultural center, the usual provincial blend of modern buildings, picturesque monuments and hovels. Part of Turkey's history happened here, between the 14th century and the 18th, when the place was the center for a religious sect, the Ahis, who gained considerable influence.

As everywhere else in Turkey, you'll be most richly rewarded by strolling about, letting your wandering footsteps follow your fancy. You'll feel as if they were your very own discoveries when you casually come upon the Cacabey mosque (which started life as an observatory), the mosque of Alâeddin Keykubat (yes, again!), and the mausolea of the great poet Aşik Paşa, of Muhterem Hatun, and of Ahierevan.

Beyond Mucur, Route 41 branches right (south) the shortest (42 miles) but also roughest road to Nevşehir. After 12 dusty and bumpy miles you arrive at Hacibektaş, a place that deserves some attention. A religious sect was founded here by Haci Baktaş Veli in the early 16th century. His teachings were based on a synthesis of Sunnism and Shiism blended with an admixture of Christianity. The dervishes of this sect also acted as almoners for the Janissaries, and gradually came to exert considerable political power. In fact, their influence survived the liquidation of the Janissaries in the 19th century, but was finally eradicated by Atatürk. The monastery that belonged to Haci Baktaş's disciples is still standing, and he is buried in a türbe here.

Back on Route 60 you recross the Kızılırmak and soon see the great volcanic cone of Mount Erciyas rising above Kayseri.

Kayseri

The name Kayseri is the Turkish equivalent of Caesarea, as the former Eusebia became known when the Emperor Tiberius took over Cappadocia in A.D. 17. In the fourth century Saint Basil, founder of Eastern monasticism established a monastery in his native town round which the Byzantine settlement developed. Arabs, Armenians, Danişment and Seljuk Turks, Mongols and Mameluks held ephemeral sway till annexation to the Ottoman Empire in 1515 finally put an end to long unrest.

The citadel walls on the north side are still in excellent shape, complete with storks' nests, even though they date from Byzantine Emperor Justinian's reign. The fortress was strengthened by Sultan Alâeddin Keykubat and later again by the Ottomans, so that you can still make a complete circuit of the mighty ramparts and towers round the open bazaar. Everywhere you look there are reminders of ancient history, juxtaposed with modern trucks! The trucks seem to be concentrated on the new esplanade, Cumhuriyet Meydani. Some of them have been suitably adorned with propitiatory inscriptions that are actually prayers for the safekeeping of the drivers on the highways.

Southward lie the eternal snows of the Erciyas Dağı (13,000

feet), which was the Mt. Argeus of the ancients. Everything in Kayseri might best be described as an inextricable tangle of the antique, the recent, and what passes for modern. The most unobtrusive-seeming vacant lot is bound to contain a venerable arch, an assortment of steles, portions of ancient walls overlooked by passing time, side by side with a big, late model car parked near an ox-cart. Kayseri is a center for goldsmiths and rug-weavers. In a somewhat different vein, it also produces a garlic-redolent veal sausage called *pastırma*, which, to counterfeit a metaphor, could win hands down over any other competitor the world over. We dare you to sample it.

The Ulu Cami, built by a Danişment ruler in 1335, faces away from the Roman baths. Its tall, brick and marble minaret, cylindrical in shape, looks somehow less slender than others you have seen. The interior is beautifully proportioned and lovingly cared for, glowing with handsome rugs. What commands admiration in any mosque is its austerity of design, the absence of all superfluous decoration, the quiet gravity of the people at prayer and these qualities are nowhere more evident than in the Grand Mosque at Kayseri.

The main *hamam* is a huge square room surmounted by a brick dome. A pool occupies the center, and on all sides stand wood-burning ovens for heating the water. The back part of the baths has been restored and is being used today.

The covered bazaar (*Bedesten*), swarms with the traditional milling crush of customers and vendors. Sometime around May 19th, the narrow market streets are festively decked out with decorations festooning the space between the stalls. Kayseri still boasts many skilled artisans and craftsmen, but most of them do work only on order—otherwise the risk is too great. Already most of them are forced to sell industrially-produced wares in order to eke out a living.

One of Kayseri's greatest curiosities is the Döner Kümbet, or "turning" mausoleum (by now, you've already seen and sampled, we hope, the Döner Kebab, lamb on a rotating spit). This mausoleum is a superb testimonial to 13th-century art, a low-set structure with 12 intricately carved stone facets, with tiny plants growing amid the interstices. The mausoleum rests on a specially-designed pedestal and is roofed with a conical dome. It rises on a small square to the right of the avenue that continues to the new museum with its miscellany of exhibits ranging from the Hittites to the Ottomans.

The Ahmet Paşa Mosque (1584), known as Kurşunlu (like so many others throughout the country) because of its lead dome, is another of the great Sinan's achievements. However, in this case, it's sometimes difficult to recognize the art of the master architect despite its detached position in Atatürk park. The Güllük Cami is one of the most ancient, hailing from 1205—it has a faience-decorated *mihrap*. By far the most impressive group of buildings is the Honat Hatun mosque and medrese dating from 1237. Designed as an architectural whole along with the *türbe* of Honat Hatun (none other than the wife of Alâeddin Keykubat) it has a beautiful portal and double arches. The geometrically-adorned mausoleum is octagonal in shape and contains three sarcophagi, that of the sultana—who eventually became the queen mother, and founded the mosque—is of white marble. Connoisseurs will appreciate the rare beauty of the Arabic inscriptions, considered a masterpiece of calligraphy. But confined within a narrow court it is difficult to view, best from the entrance corridor to the mosque which belongs to the basilica type favored by the Seljuks.

In 1249, the vizir Abdul Gazi erected the mosque and medrese dedicated to Haci Kılıç, notable for their handsomely wrought portals. The 13th century in Kayseri was outstanding for its profusion of Seljuk mosques and Koranic schools. The year 1267 witnessed the construction of the Sahabiye medrese, with its distinctive geometrical ornamentation, more perfect here than anywhere else... if that is possible. The black-domed Mosque of Industry, completed in 1967, provides with its handsome fretwork portals a pleasing proof of the vigor of religious architecture.

Kayseri has several more *Kümbet*, or mausolea. Without wishing either to encourage or discourage the traveler, we propose you visit—Kasbek (the oldest: 1281); Sirçali (cylindrical, with faience); Çifte (meaning "double"). with twin domes.

Kayseri is also the home of the first Turkish school of medicine, Giyasiye Şifahiye, built in 1205. It consists of two buildings with an inner connecting passageway. Here are extraordinary embellishments on the portal. There are more *hamams*, too—Sultan (1205), Cafer Bey (1151), Kadi (1548), and Selâhattin (1590).

The Environs of Kayseri

Three famous *hans* can be visited near Kayseri. The Sultan Hani, 30 miles along Route 45 to Fivas, was built by Keykubat and is one of the handsomest in the entire Middle East. The Karatay caravanseray, near Bünyan, 25 miles on the Malatya road (Route 60), is also Seljuk. The Kara Mustafa caravanseray at Incesu, 23 miles along Route 45 to Niğde, belongs to the Ottoman period, 1660. Partly restored, this vast complex is intended to revert to its original purpose of providing rest to the weary travelers.

The ancient city of Kaneş, 14 miles northeast of Kayseri, at Kültepe (off Route 45), harks back to Hittite and Assyrian times. Diggings here have yielded up artifacts and vestiges from the copper and the bronze age, plus objects from the Hittite, Phrygian, and Roman periods. Another important site, Karum, lies outside the ramparts. In this former Assyrian colony, the archeologists have identified four separate strata of antique civilizations. Among other things, they have excavated priceless Phoenician stone tablets, and objects from the first Hittite epoch, including seals, ceramics, and idols. The finds from these digs are on display in the Kayseri Regional Museum and the Ankara Archeology Museum.

More Hittite remains are to be found at Fraktin, 48 miles south, via Develi with its several Seljuk monuments. This trip takes you round towering snow-covered Mount Erciyas, one of the highest peaks of the Anatolian plateau and the best ski run so far south.

Yet a greater spectacle than this mighty extinct volcano lies 54 miles southwest, a lunar landscape without parallel on this planet, perhaps more intriguing than the moon itself because here man's ingenuity has triumphed for almost two thousand years over nature, bending the hostile surrounding to his own ends.

To reach this wonderland, retrace your steps west on Route 60 to the junction with Route 45 (E 98) on which you turn left (south) towards Niğde. Eleven miles after Incesu, turn right for Ürgüp and Göreme.

Göreme (Cappadocia)

With the horizon virtually sealed off on all sides by soaring mountainous heights, the landscape immediately takes on a special aspect. The houses are spaced farther apart, but unexpected and luxuriant vegetation forms an abrupt contrast with the aridity of the valley. The rock itself is covered with a greenish moss that imparts a glossy patina, making a smooth blending between stone and fields.

You reach a structure made of heaped-up stones, with a great stone block for a roof—it's a night shelter for the harvest workers. Beyond, the sandy desert resumes, dotted with protruding rocky crests. A storytale village sits perched in a rocky cleft. Life is precarious here at an altitude of almost one mile. The sheep graze listlessly, the donkeys look depressed. The cliff does its best to pretend it's a fortress. It's riddled with holes along the base, and an occasional anachronistic troglodyte may still be seen gaping at the cars as they whizz past in a cloud of dust. In front of some of the residences, perhaps those of the better-off families, masonry walls have been added to enlarge the living quarters. These cliff settlements are too small to have their own mosques. But the Moslem religion doesn't require its followers to perform their rites in a regulation house of worship. A prayer rug and an abiding faith are all that are needed.

At the bottom of the valley, the mountainous walls grow more widely spaced. Here, also, the slopes are riddled with openings, like so many Cyclopean eyes. You come to a group of twisted cones. The tallest, some 100 feet high, supports at its summit a great flat slab, exactly like a witch's stone. The overall effect is like that of a cemetery of giant tombs in which dead souls have garbed themselves in sand shrouds for a macabre dance.

It is an arresting sight. For miles around, it's as if the winds, the rains, volcanic eruptions, and earthquakes had deliberately pooled their efforts to prove that they could produce an effect weirder than any ever dreamed up by man's wildest imagination. The few scattered examples of similar phenomena found on the North American and European continents pale into insignificance alongside these extraordinary "fairy" chimneys and needles, which are like veritable villages hewn out by the elements. Surrealistic fingers have clutched the sandy soil and modeled it into bizarre shapes, irregular pyramids and cones. Here and there, just for fun, at the top they've stuck an ingeniously balanced extra slab, looking for all the world like a head-piece rakishly pulled down over one eye.

Old Turkish storytellers like to tell children their version of what happened here. According to them, a king from a neighboring country had come to wage war on the defenseless local inhabitants, who had no army. The besieged people offered up prayers to Allah, who was properly stricken by their plight and sufficiently moved to pity to cause the wicked warriors to become petrified right where they stood, clad in full armor and clasping their weapons.

The scientific explanation may sound just about as plausible to the layman. The ground here is fragile tuff-stone, split and fragmented by erosion. In some places, streams, many of them long-since vanished, have hollowed out their beds. The wind has chipped in its bit, and so of course have the rains. Depending on whether the tuff is pure—therefore easily eroded—or blended with more resistant ingredients, the indentations in the landscape have been more or less extensive and violent. Whatever the case, the results are utterly fantastic, far beyond the eeriest moonscape. Salvador Dali would be completely fascinated by these "villages of the realm of the dead".

It was probably soon after Christianity had gained a foothold in Asia Minor that the Byzantine anchorite movement started, and the anchorites, in search of solitude, began settling in Cappadocia. The conflict of the iconoclasts undoubtedly caused a new influx of refugees between the end of the fifth century and continuing up to the ninth century. The first Arab incursions occurred in the seventh century, and in the face of this new danger, the hermits, often men with families, felt a need to stand together and to join forces with a community. Rather than bother to build houses, they found it simpler just to hollow out shelters in the soft rock, the only tool necessary being a stout stick. Since these people were mainly preoccupied with the worship of God, all sorts of underground sanctuaries, chapels, and churches in an ever-increasing number were constantly being consecrated to their cult. And, since the believers understandably experienced the need to express their faith in some other way than by prayer alone, the walls of the artificial grottoes gradually became covered with crosses and the temples acquired more and more illustrations of Biblical scenes. The result was a series of amazing frescoes, whose colors even today sometimes remain fresh and bright, their compositions clear and pure, and rather summary in outline.

Not quite all of these strange churches have been discovered—some are still blocked up. The prevalent belief is that there were 365, enough to enable mass to be said at a different altar every day in the year. (But this figure is probably an exaggeration.) In any event, those that are now open and ready to receive visitors are enough to wear to a frazzle the sturdiest legs and the keenest curiosities, as are also the anchorite cells in the ancient grottoes.

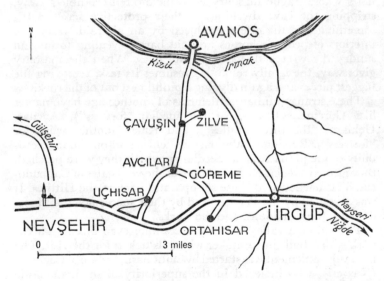

The administrative center for this extraordinary conglomeration is located at Nevşehir, which together with Ürgüp provides the most convenient tourist accommodation in the triangle between these towns and Avanos.

To use a short stay to best advantage it is advisable to hire a guide (about 150 TL for the day). They speak good English and are knowledgeable, but perhaps a little too eager to acquaint you with all the marvels. Yet expert advice is indispensable to choose among the unique sites according to the visitor's time and vigor, the latter being somewhat tried by the difficulty to distinguish between tracks and dry river courses. By all means venture south as far as the underground cities of Kaymakli and Derinkuyu; but resist firmly, at least till the presently excruciating 28 miles have been paved, the temptation of Soğanli, whose churches are simply a duplication of Göreme's, involving more climbing than seems justified to the average tourist.

From the windows of the Ürgüp hotels you look straight into a cataclysmic scenery, a large white cliff riddled with man-made holes whose fragile masonry walls have often crumbled away, stripping the cave dwellings of their protective screens. It's something like the effect produced by an air raid, when the interiors of people's houses are laid bare, revealing to all and sundry the wretchedness of private lives. When the masonry gives way, the family resolutely resumes its task, removing the biggest pieces and again digging a pitiful nest out of the rock.

These strange human settlements of another age have names like Göreme, Ortahisar ("the median fortress"), Avcilar, Uçhisar ("the three castles"), and Kale (another word for "fortress"). Relying on the narrow defiles and on the inaccessibility of the pinnacles and needles on which they were perched, they formed a defensive installation at the very gates of Cappadocia. This particular defense set-up dates back to the Hittites. It was also used by the Persians and by their successors, the Macedonians, the Christians, and the Turks.

The Göreme valley is easily accessible, even boasting a car park with a built-in caretaker who sells tickets for the visit. The monastic settlement was started by Saint Basil, Bishop of Caesarea (Kayseri), who believed in the superiority of small monastic communities over larger establishments as well as over the hermit system. You can see rupestral "houses" (dwellings of three and four storeys, sometimes higher).

Tokalı Kilise is the largest of the Göreme churches, hollowed out of a rock pillar only a few yards from the Ürgüp road. Its frescoes depict the life of Jesus, the Apostles, the Annunciation, and the seizure of Christ by Judas and the Roman soldiers. Tokalı used to boast another proud possession, a gold buckle (hence the name), which vanished in 1929.

The guides are fond of stating that the iconographic paintings are in a perfect state of preservation, but their statement is a relative one. The guides may be right in the sense that the frescoes are indeed in good shape considering the climatic conditions and the passage of time. The fact nonetheless remains that they are heavily deteriorated, and all the more admirable for it.

Certain frescoes go back as far as the fifth century. There is a kind of pathos in this great concern with adornment, and also something infinitely touching in the clumsiness of the decoration of the arches. It's easy to imagine the struggling artists wielding their metal-pointed sticks and attacking from either side the columns that provided the surface for their compositions. Once the designs had reached the upper part of the columns, the lines occasionally just didn't meet the way they were intended to. But God in his boundless loving wisdom has somehow made it all seem quite right. Not infrequently, a painter who had run out of space casually daubed right over some predecessor's work, and now that a few hundred years have passed, all the superimposed colors have begun to show through, with the same tones predominating—ochre, golden yellow, and red, with sporadic touches of a sprightly green.

The Karanlık Kilise, or Dark Church (karanlık = dark, kilise = church—bring a flashlight!), contains frescoes illustrating the Nativity and the Wise Men. In the Çarıklı ("Sandal") Church, there are scenes of the Crucifixion and the Ascension, plus the Evangelists. Yılanlı ("Serpent") Kilise specializes in saints—St. George, St. Theodosius, and Emperor Constantine and his wife Helen, who are shown surrounding Christ. The frescoes in Elmalı ("Apple") Kilise are the "newest"—they date only from the 13th century. And you haven't even begun to see all the churches—Saklı (St. John), Aziz Theodore (angels and saints praying), and Kılıçlar (prophets and saints). That total of 360 might not be so far off after all!

Four miles west of Ürgüp, the gigantic rocky needle of Ortahisar thrusts up, bearing a citadel hewn out of its sugarloaf point which you may climb to the railed-in top, though the cave dwellers have been removed to ordinary houses on the safer ground below.

Another four miles west, the serrated honeycombed escarpment of Uchisar dominates the northern horizon. It is an extraordinary setting—the village is still inhabited, and if picturesqueness is what you're after, this is it—plus a magnificent view from the citadel out over the countryside.

In Avcılar you experience a renewed feeling of enchantment. The shapes of the some of the chimneys and needles put you in mind of figures in old prints. Kale has two citadels, big and little—the larger one rises off the summit of a 130-foot-high needle, and the small one rests on a flat terrace, both strongholds of feudal chiefs in the Middle Ages.

And everywhere are vast numbers of pigeons, whose dung fertilizes the vineyards (which produce excellent grapes and a pleasant white wine) and fields. In a constant fight with the tourist authorities, the peasants have blocked up again many of the lesser churches to make dovecotes, perhaps in the end a satisfactory move all round, as the exclusion of fanatics, children and daylight might help to preserve the frescoes.

The road to Avanos, the northernmost point of this triangle of supermarvels, holds more surprises. At Özkonak a subterranean town of supposedly 60,000 inhabitants has been hailed as the eighth wonder of the world.

On the way you pass the semicircular cliff of Çavuşin, the Sergeant's Cave, almost pitted through with crumbling dwellings and the chapel and the chapel of St. John the Baptist.

The branch right (east) leads to Zilve where the central ridge divided the valley into a Christian and a Moslem sector, mosque and church hewn out of the same rock back to back. The Christians were expelled in 1922, but the Moslems did not remain long in undisputed possession as several fatal rockfalls necessitated their evacuation in the 1960's.

From Avanos on the north bank of the Kızılırmak it is possible to return directly to Ürgüp (8 miles). A dusty detour east takes in the Seljuk Sari Han, the Yellow Caravanseray, with a fine entrance and courtyard.

Nevşehir and Niğde

As you leave the Göreme valley, the countryside gradually settles down to a more habitual aspect. Part of Nevşehir is ensconced in verdure; the other part clings to a mountainside, with a citadel at the top, as it usually is hereabouts. The buildings are constructed from the creamy white local stone. Two mosques should be seen in the old city: Kaya Cami (Seljuk) and yet another leaden Kurşunlu Cami (Ottoman).

Pink and white mushroom rocks are scattered along Route 41 the 14 miles north to Gülşehir on the Kızılırmak, and beyond to the underground city of Açik Saray and the Tuzka salt mines which supply the whole of Anatolia; nearby Tuzköy boasts a fine 13th-century mosque. More impressive is the rare Ottoman baroque complex of the Kara Vezir Mehmet Paşa mosque, medrese, bath and six fountains at Gülşehir next to some Roman and Byzantine ruins.

The two references to underground cities should have whetted your appetite sufficiently to make you want to explore one. At present the easiest accessible, complete with electric light, is at Kaymaklı, 7 miles south of Nevşehir on Route 41. Here the ingenuity of persecuted humanity has created an underworld with ominous overtones of the shape of things to come. Eight spacious floors, each offering accommodation for 200 people, have been carved into the bowels of the earth. The narrow entrance was uncovered only in the 1950's; a central air shaft assures perfect ventilation all the 250 feet down to the bottom; cooking arrangements existed on every second storey, and the smoke was not allowed to escape for fear of betraying the hideout. Otherwise each floor was self-contained, down to the individual cemetery. A tunnel connects this city to another six miles south at Derinkuyu.

Who were the people who devised these engineering wonders of despair? No matter that history has not yet yielded up the secret of these grim monuments of man's eternal struggle for survival, they present an awesome and apposite warning.

Several interesting caravanserays stand along the 47 paved miles of Route 73 west of Nevşehir, part of the Seljuk empire's main artery; the Oresin and Alay Hans feature the usual handsome portals, but only Alâeddin Keykubat's Ağzikara Han, 10 miles before Aksaray has been restored to a likeness of its former splendor. Even more impressive is another of Keykubat's innumerable foundations, the superb Sultan Han, 25 miles east of Aksaray, but Route 73 has degenerated into such washboard ruts that only the true lovers of Seljuk art will venture.

The Seljuk monuments of Aksaray are sadly decayed, except for the 14th-century Nakkasi mosque with its leaning brick minaret. But the town is an oasis in the baked plain, thanks to the Melendiz, which is dammed to form an artificial lake higher up south and loses itself in the salt marshes of the Tuz Gölü north. A difficult track leads upstream into the Belisirma valley where the fantastic world of Göreme is duplicated with fairy chimneys, frescoed rock churches and cave dwellings.

Either Route I (E5) south from Aksaray or a return to Route 45 at the Incesu junction is preferable to the much shorter but very rough direct Route 41 from Nevşehir to Niğde (52 miles south), though it takes in Kaymakli and Derinkuyu, thus saving considerable time if you limit yourself to the essential sights. The steppe is different here, and the soil is riddled with blisters from extinct volcanoes. Water is in short supply from both heaven and earth—the only river is the Melendiz. But suddenly greenness appears on the horizon, enclosing the town of Niğde, which flourished in the 13th century when Sultan Keykubat built the Alâeddin Cami. It proudly bears its three domes, exquisitely pure in line, but it is more famous for the human figures on the portal. A century later, the Mongol Sungur Bey constructed another mosque here. It's a good question as to how it came by its various Gothic features (rose window, etc). The inevitable fortress looks down from the heights—it's the earliest Seljuk monument, dating from the end of the 11th century. Subtle lacy stone carvings adorn the Hüdavent Hatun *türbe* (1312), and the charming white medrese (Akmedrese, 1409), built by the Karaman princes, is now a small regional museum.

Five miles northwest is the 10th-century church of Eski Gümüş, featuring exceptionally well-preserved frescoes; the adjoining monastery is hollowed out of the rock. Nine miles south along Route 45, the small town of Bor possesses a 16th-century covered bazaar and bath, but more interesting is the Roman aqueduct, pool and hot springs at Tyana nearby, which is now Kemerhisar and was the Hittite's Tuvana.

Route 45 joins Route 1 (E5) and Route 80 in the featureless steppe. The only town west along the latter is Ereğli, ancient Heraklea of Cappadocia, famous as the scene of the Crusaders' crushing defeat in 1101 at the hands of the Turks. (A track leads 10 miles southeast to some Hittite reliefs at Ivriz.) Then it is 90 miles of monotonous steppe to Konya, the only relief afforded by the deep-green uncanny lake of Karapınar in an extinct crater and later on a vast marsh to the south, providing excellent grazing for vast herds of cattle. And straight ahead to the west is the "granary of Turkey".

Konya

Konya is, without doubt, a city of note. At one time, it enjoyed the prestige of being a holy city and was a Seljuk capital, and may well be considered one of Turkey's finest towns. (Altitude 3,400 feet, population 130,000.)

Speculation is rife as to the etymology of Konya's name. One unappetizing version drags in Perseus and the slaying of Medusa, whose severed head he nailed to a pillar, thereby creating an "icon", or image, of sorts, whence the name of Ikonion. But this hair-raising explanation has no real foundation in fact, and most accounts have Perseus stashing the hideous trophy away in his reticule, hauling it out only in order to terrify his enemies.

In any case, Konya is one of the world's most ancient cities. To many archeologists, the excavations in the Alâeddin hill (the former Acropolis) in the center of town are proof of the site's having been occupied as early as the seventh millenium B.C. The Hittites lived here, too, as did the usual succession of conquerors. When St. Paul and St. Barnabus were expelled from Antioch of Pisidia, they made their way to *Claudiconium* (renamed in honor of the Emperor Claudius) and delivered sermons there in the years 47, 50, and 53. It was here that Thecla heard them preach and was converted to Christianity, as a prelude to becoming the most venerated saint in orthodox hagiography. Konya was the host to one of the first church councils, in 235. Over the ensuing years the city of *Kûniye* was overrun in turn by the Arabs and the Seljuks. It was promoted to the rank of capital under Kılıç Arslan I (1097) and under Alâeddin Keykubat, whose lust for power led him on to conquer all the territory between here and Antalya. Next came the Karamanoğlu family, before Mehmet the Conqueror proclaimed Konya an Ottoman city, in 1467.

Mevlâna and the Whirling Dervishes

The scenario is by now fairly familiar. Konya might easily have remained a place of only minor significance if it hadn't happened to be the home of Mevlâna Celâleddin Rumi (1207–1273), a poet, scholar, and philosopher, and the founder of the Order of Whirling Dervishes (*mevlevi*). Thus the city was forever marked with the imprint of one of Islam's greatest mystics. Mevlâna, who had been born in Horasan, made his way to Anatolia after accomplishing the ritual pilgrimage with his father. The name of Rumi denotes his Afghan origin—for the Afghans, Anatolia already represented an Occident inhabited by *rumis*. Mevlâna had had a sound education, and during Keykubat's reign he was invited to join the faculty at the great medrese in Konya. His life appears to have been uneventful for a period of many years, up until the time when he began frequenting a mysterious dervish, Mehmet Şemsettin, a native of Tebriz, with whom he had become acquainted during his young er days in Damascus. Mevlâna was then 37 years old. His contacts with Şemsettin opened up his eyes to what was to be his life's work. He abandoned the teaching profession and gave himself over to profound meditation. In his writings, his own name and Şemsettin's are inextricably mingled. Mevlâna was the author of the *Mesnevi*, a collection of distichs that rank immediately after the Koran and the Hadis in Islami literature. His *Divan El Kebir* is an even longer work, containing 40,380 distichs. Both were originally written in Persian and translated into Turkish.

The basis of Mevlâna's doctrine was the seeking after good in all its positive manifestations, together with the practice of infinite tolerance (love and charity). He condemned slavery and advocated monogamy. He recognized that man must earn his bread by the sweat of his brow, and also that he must strive for beauty and truth while consistently avoiding display (the doctrine of humility). While these moral teachings may appear self-evident to us in the 20th century, things were doubtless quite different in the 13th century.

And the Whirling Dervishes? Mevlâna was a firm believer in the virtues of music and of its corollary, the dance, as a means of abandoning oneself to God's love and freeing oneself from earthly bondage. He considered the whirling pattern of motion as being both the exterior representation of the sphere and the interior representation of the soul's state of agitation. It is of course by this more spectacular external aspect that the world has come to know of the existence of the *mevlevi* dervishes, if not of the theologian himself and his teachings. After Mevlâna's death, one of his disciples, Hüsameddin Çelebi, succeeded him, and when the latter died, Mevlâna's son, Sultan Veled, assumed the leadership. It was in fact the son who actually got the sect into an organized form. Mevlevi is derived from Mevlâna, but also has a connection with the word *tevellû*, which is found in the Koran, and signifies the fact of seeing God's face whichever way one turns.

The *tekke* (monastery) and *türbe* of Mevlâna are situated at one end of Konya's main avenue, Mevlâna Caddesi. A blue band adorned with Arabic inscriptions runs round the conical drum of emerald green glazed tiles, a startling yet pleasing color combination visible from far away. The small lead-stopped domes set over the dervishes' cubicles form an honor guard around the garden with its marble flagstones leading up to the entrance. There are 18 flagstones, the mystic number of the sect.

The huge building complex, which became a museum in 1927, has remained to most visitors a place of worship, especially Mevlâna's tomb, where his body has lain for seven centuries. Everywhere you look there are carved woodwork, gold and silver work, tiles, calligraphic ornamentation, precious rugs, and rich fabrics. Vivid reconstructions illustrate the founder's and the dervishes' way of life in their former cells, while soft piped music contributes to the creation of the right atmosphere.

The square room that you enter first is the Koran reading room. On the walls hang framed examples of distinguished calligraphy, including one specimen executed by a great devotee of this art, Sultan Mahmut himself. The translation of the quotation above the silver door would be: "He who enters incomplete here will leave complete". On the right and left lie the tombs of the most illustrious disciples, those who were closest to Mevlâna,

65 in all. The tomb of his eldest son reposes next to his own.

In one of the showcases containing the manuscripts that the founder dictated as the inspiration came to him are the first 18 verses of his work, written in his own hand. The intricately wrought chandelier has 18 branches. The mausoleum itself dates from the 13th century, while the rest of the monastery was built later.

Mevlâna's enormous tomb rests on a pedestal. At its head are his black turban and the curious cylindrical headgear of the sect. Two silver steps lead up to the platform—they are the sacred stairway. Believers press their faces against it as a sign of devotion. A brocaded cover embroidered with gold thread and weighing 90 pounds covers the biers of Mevlâna and his son. (They used to be covered by the rug that now hangs on the wall in the back.) Sultan Mehmet II was responsible for the extraordinary cover that has replaced the rug. At the foot of the tomb, the coffin of Mevlâna's father stands vertical, his white funerary turban on top. The quotations from the Koran are embedded in the sarcophagus with the exquisite precision and mastery of technique that characterize Seljuk art at its best.

The opulence of the wall decorations defies description. In the music room, the ceiling cross-beam has a chain of marble links hanging from it. Pause to admire the skill of the artist who carved these links out of a single block, but first have a look at the round ball that's attached. It, too, has been wrought with typical Seljuk artistry, plus an added refinement—inside there is a second ball, completely detached, on which the artist carved four of Mevlâna's verses.

The Rite of the Whirling Dervishes

This famous ceremony symbolizes man's love for God—extremely detailed and specific directions govern every slightest pattern and gesture in this ritual dance, the ultimate purpose of which is to effect a mystic union. The instrumentalists and singers sit opposite the floor on which the dancers perform. The Sheik's pole stands at one end, and an imaginary line connecting this pole with the center of the entrance to the room represents the most direct route to union with God (*Vahdet*). This line must never be crossed. The Sheik incarnates Mevlevism, and is the representative of the Islamic faith at the ceremony. The pole is red, which is the color of union and ceremony.

The dervishes' ritual starts with a gathering for prayers and meditation in the room off the music room in the monastery. The narrative portion of the ritual begins when the musicians, the dancers, and the Sheik enter the great hall through the wrought-iron door and have taken their places. The flutes intone a melody expressing the desire for mystic union, and this is the signal for the whirling dances to begin. In the center of the floor the Sheik and the dervishes whirl three times to the rhythm of the music.

The dervishes' costumes are symbolic—the conical hat represents a tombstone, the jacket is the tomb itself, and the skirt is the funerary shroud. The right side of the room represents the known, tangible world; the left is the unknown and invisible part of it.

Each whirling dance consists of three stages—the first is the knowledge of God; the second, the seeing of God; and the third, union with God. At the end of the first stage, the Sheik returns to his pole and the dervishes resume their places. The main part of the ritual now commences. The dervishes remove their jackets, signifying that they are thus shedding earthly ties and escaping from their graves. While this is going on, the Sheik performs certain steps near the pole, and each dancer proceeds to follow him. The leading dervish passes in front of the Sheik and kisses his hand. Each man in turn then presents himself to the Sheik, and a new whirling dance starts up. As they whirl, the dervishes extend their right hands in prayer, while their left hands point toward the floor. The symbolic meaning of these gestures is that "what we receive from God, we give to man; we ourselves possess nothing". As the dervishes whirl, they also rotate around the room like the astral bodies. Their whirling motion is the symbol of the rotation of the universe in the presence of God. It is also the means of attaining that form of ecstasy that leads to the soul's bliss and a full awareness of the divine presence. The leading dervish directs the patterns of the other dancers, who follow the gestures he makes with his feet and head.

In the final part of the dervishes' dance, the Sheik, incarnating Mevlâna, joins the dancers and whirls in their midst. When he finishes, he slowly returns to the pole, and the dances end.

The whirling dervish dance is performed here in early December, on the occasion of the celebrations commemorating Mevlâna, which last two weeks. Two galleries run the length of all four sides of the music room—the lower one is for the men, the upper one reserved for the ladies, who are screened off by a wooden latticework partition. (Plans are presently being made to allow visitors to see a form of the dance outside the place of worship, at various times throughout the year.)

Don't be astonished if you should happen to see more women than men at Mevlâna's *türbe*. As far back as the 13th century, he was staunchly advocating the equality of the sexes, something that Kemal Atatürk was still fighting for in the 20th century.

Nearby stands the Selimiye, the mosque that Selim II started building when he was still only the governor of Konya, in 1558. By the time it was finished he had already ascended to the throne. The style is resolutely Ottoman, reminiscent of the Fatih Mosque in Istanbul, another typical specimen of Turkish architecture. The reminiscence is enhanced once you're inside, because of the well-preserved colors and pillars, the arches soaring to giddy heights, and the windows surrounding the base of the dome.

On the avenue leading from Mevlâna's *tekke* toward the old acropolis, now called Alâeddin Parkı, stands the Şerefettin Mosque, on the righthand side of Hükümet Meydanı (square). The mosque has had a troubled history. Its construction was begun by the Seljuks, but it was completed by the Ottomans. The ravages of time, plus a series of fires, wrought havoc on the building, which was extensively restored in the mid-19th century.

Almost exactly opposite is the recently restored Iplikçi Mosque, or Merchants' Mosque, in some ways evocative of the Arabic style. This is Konya's most ancient structure, dating from 1202. Unfortunately, almost nothing remains of the original mosaics in the interior.

Alâeddin's mosque rises above the park that bears his name—it's our old friend Keykubat, who finished in 1220 the construction started by Sultan Mesut I seventy years earlier. Designed by an architect from Damascus, the mosque is of the Syrian style, unusual for Anatolia. Recent extensive restorations preserved the original magnificence, setting off the lovely 12th-century pulpit against the forest of 42 columns taken from Roman temples. The decagonal *türbe* in the courtyard contains the remains of Kiliç Arslan and seven subsequent Seljuk rulers.

From the top of the rise there's a fine view out over Konya. At the foot of the hill, in the shadow of Alâeddin's mosque, lie what are left of the ruins of the Seljuk *saray*, the palace, corner of two venerable truncated stubs of walls, Konya's "oldest". The city has somehow deemed it expedient to throw an unsightly concrete roof-shelter over them.

Across the way beckons one of the world's most exquisite portals. It belongs to the former Karatay Medrese, the theological seminary founded by Celalettin Karatay in 1251. The beautiful intricacy of the stone carvings leaves one entranced. A ceramics museum now occupies those of the old buildings that have survived. Inside, the dome's surface is entirely covered with tiles, with blue predominating on white, and the effect is one of dazzling brilliance. The frieze is still in an excellent state of preservation, while the hunting scenes on the rare figurine tiles from the royal summer residence show the influence of Persia on Seljuk art.

In the old days, the students lived in this school, where everybody was assigned a small cubicle. For their astronomy courses they had only to scan the heavens through the dome's central opening, which also provided light for the study hall. In the middle of the room, a fountain still murmurs in a pool. The fountain spilled itself into the basin, and "the gentle sound of the water soothed the future scholars' minds and hearts, while the lightly shaded blues of the tiles roundabout were restful to their eyes". Many inscriptions covered the walls as an ever-present reminder of the fragility of human judgment and of the condition of mankind's knowledge. In these halls, students were "entering into wisdom". The end of each quotation is marked by a star. "Are those who seek knowledge more worthy than those who do not?" A small mosque (*mesçit*) stands near the *medrese*, as does the *türbe* of the founder. The west slope holds the Ince Minare Medrese (Slender Minaret Seminary), decapitated by lightning ...like so many others. Consider the infinite patience and loving artistry that went into the ornamentation of the stone, into the harmonization between the colors of the ceramics and the enamel work on the brick. This is the Museum of Stone and Wood

Carvings, featuring amongst others representative bas-reliefs of the Seljuk period.

In the southern outskirts of Konya you will come to another set of buildings dedicated to Sahip Ata, complete with mosque, monastery, mausoleum, and baths, the whole complex dating from the 13th century. Nearby is the new Archeological Museum, containing some splendid sarcophagi. Along the way lies the Sırçalı Medrese, lavishly adorned with faience tiles (*sırçalı*). At the risk of sounding a bit repetitious, we still urge you to contemplate again the endless wonder of the ornate portals and gates. In this building, the Museum of Tombstones displays specimens from Seljuk times.

The small Catholic Church of St. Paul is located between the Sırçalı Medrese and the park. No one is too finicky, and other Christian rites are also regularly celebrated here, including the Protestant and the Greek Orthodox.

If you're bound on performing another esthetic pilgrimage, have a look at the Aziziye Cami, near the bazaar. It's adorned with two short minarets that provide a charming effect—instead of tapering to a point, they are topped off by a sort of open-work loggia, which you would swear to be Florentine if you weren't in Turkey. The essential difference between the Seljuk and Ottoman mosques is in their ornamentation. The Seljuks decorated more; the Ottomans built higher mosques, so had taller minarets. The nice thing about this whole situation is that the Aziziye dates from 1676 and therefore belongs to the Ottoman period.

Additional Seljuk buildings include the Hasbey Darül Hüffazı Cami, the Hatuniye (1213), and the mausoleum of Turgutoğulları. The Kapı Mosque and the Peri Paşa Mosque go back to the Osmanlı era. Of the more contemporary structures, about the only one that hasn't been listed so far is the Atatürk Museum.

People enjoy hunting in the environs of Konya, and there are plenty of good spots, such as Akşehir, Beyşehir, Çavuşçu, and Hotamiş. You'll find wild pigeon, goose, duck, fox, and boar, with no restrictions on the hunting season. Partridge, hare, and snipe can be hunted from September through April.

The Dede Garden at Meram is five miles west; the same distance northwest is Sille with its rock churches and monasteries including St. Helen, supposedly Anatolia's oldest church but heavily restored in the last century; and again 5 miles along the Ankara road is the Horozlu Han with a fine Seljuk portal.

Beyşehir (57 miles west), on the shores of Turkey's third largest lake—on a low plateau in the Taurus mountains—was founded by Alâeddin Keykubat. As an important Seljuk town, it contains the usual great mosque, medrese, covered bazaar and baths. Unusually attractive, however, are the 23 islands, especially the biggest, Moda. In the vicinity is the ruined Seljuk palace of Kubadabad. At Ilgin (60 miles northwest of Konya), Sinan's comprehensive creation of mosque, medrese, caravanseray, bath and harem for Lala Mustafa Paşa is complemented by hot springs whose curative properties for an astounding variety of afflictions have been used for centuries.

If you're bent on archeology, you'll be thrilled by Çatalhöyük, the site of the most ancient city that has been unearthed so far. Expert opinion has concluded that it was founded in the seventh millenium B.C. Twenty-one miles along the Karaman road, turn left toward Çumra and then to the Forked Mound near a stream, altogether 32 miles. The bigger of these two mounds has yielded to British archeologists relics of neolithic buildings, sanctuaries and mural paintings, dating from a period at which cattle-raising was already a going concern.

If you continue on as far as Karaman (66 miles), there's a sidetrip of some 20 miles via the Kilbasan road (bad condition, impassable after rainstorms) to Binbir Kilise (1,001 churches), a valley at the foot of the Karadağı (the Black Mountain). Still more remains here, of a Byzantine city concerning which very little is known so far. The ruins of the churches, mostly in a sad state of disrepair, appear to date from the end of the first millenium of the Christian era.

Other Hittite sites, in addition to the one at Ivriz mentioned in connection with our arrival in Konya, include Eflatun Pinar (14 miles north of the Beyşehir road.)

West of Ankara

Thirteen miles northwest of Polatlı are the remains of Gordion, (Yassihüyük), a large mound of successive towns in a bend of the Sangarius River. This may be an opportune moment to review the timehonored expression, "the severing of the Gordian knot".

There was once a poor Phrygian laborer named Gordios who, literally overnight, found himself king for having unwittingly fulfilled the prophecy of an oracle predicting that the first man to enter the gate of a certain city would become its ruler. The city of Gordion was promptly named after him. Gordios was both painstaking and conscientious. In addition to performing the customary ritual devotions to Zeus, he decided to further express his gratitude by offering the great god a chariot. He tied the chariot's yoke and shaft together with a stout knot, one that indeed looked as if it would resist all efforts by ordinary mortals to undo it. Since oracles in those days never missed a chance to get their word in edgewise, another prophecy promptly predicted that whoever was to rule Asia would first have to untie the knot.

The rest is more history. Alexander happened along at that point, and after watching the others fail with the knot, he decided to try himself. When Alexander decided to have a crack at it, he turned out to be as practical as Gordios had been crafty. It would have been unthinkable for him to miss out on the conquest of Asia just because of a foolish old rope. What Alexander did lack was patience, and with a freshly sharpened sword blade, he merely sliced through the whole problem. Although this may have been a somewhat overly-simplified solution, it worked, and since Alexander was also accompanied by a rather large army, the assembled audience had no choice but to applaud politely.

Gordios' son, Midas, transferred the Phrygian capital to the south (60 miles from Eskişehir), where his monument has already been described (See *The Back Country* chapter).

Illustration at head of this chapter: The "fairy chimneys" of Cappadocia, carved by the wind from soft volcanic stone.

THE BLACK SEA

The Wilder Shore

The time has come to follow the coast upward and eastward, to the border of Soviet Russia.

There is little of historical or archeological interest in these parts. However, both the countryside and the small towns around the Black Sea give the traveler a new and different insight into the daily life of the Turkish people. The wooden houses, nearly all decorated with fretwork and not a few painted in gay colors; the craftsmen's shops; the inward look of the faithful on his prayer-rug; the clothing, the children, and last (but to be honest not least), the scarcity of tourists—all help us towards a better understanding of the people and their culture.

Furthermore, the landscape is, to many eyes, quite beautiful. Altogether, the place is well worth a passing visit, though accommodation is still very simple indeed.

Pontus occupied the shole length of the coastline to the borders of what is today Soviet Russia. Its name came from the Black Sea, known to antiquity as the Pontus Euxinus. After the death of Alexander the Great, Mithridates II, Satrap of Pontus, forced Antigonus, a general of Alexander's and heir to the conquered province, to hand over his rights, and made himself king. Mithridates VII Eupator (120-63 B.C.) extended his rule down to the Bosphorus, in spite of Roman opposition. Rome, of course, got the better of him in the end, and the luckless king was driven to suicide. Pontus was split into two provinces, the western half falling to the lot of Mithridates' son, Pharnacus. An astute statesman, he skillfully used the rivalry between Caesar and Pompey to play one against the other, and for a time succeeded in reuniting Pontus. But Caesar, having defeated Pompey, reconquered the lost half. In any case, the whole was taken over by the Roman Empire under Nero; and from that time on its history of invasions is that of the rest of Asia Minor.

Practical Information for the Black Sea Coast

HOW TO GET THERE? Whether by train or by car, it is hard going to the picturesque towns on the Black Sea, the coastal road being under constant modernization. The best and most pleasant way to travel is by the *Turkish Maritime Lines* (*Denizyollari*), whose comfortable ships will serve as inexpensive floating hotels. The Istanbul-Hopa two-way passage usually takes ten days (*Hopa Express II* run); but you can go by sea on the *Hopa Express I* run, which takes two and a half days, and back by air on the Samsun-Ankara or Trabzon-Ankara flight of the Turkish Airline Company, *THY*; or the other way round. There are also boats that stop at the small ports all along the west coast of the Black Sea, up to Abana and beyond. *By train:* (1) Ankara-Zonguldak; (2) Ankara-Kayseri-Amasya-Samsun, a long roundabout way best avoided and replaced by the Ankara-Samsun *motor coach;* and (3) the *Eastern Express*, Istanbul (Haydarpaşa)-Erzurum-Kars, then a motor coach to the coast.

BY CAR. The Ankara-Çorum road (Routes 2 and 41) winds through the low mountain passes of the Pontic Range. From the mountains, at Mahmurdaği Geçidi, a wonderful view over the Black Sea (Kara Deniz in Turkish) and the town of Samsun. The climate here is much damper, and the trees grow thick and tall, forming almost northern-like forests, which sometimes cover the landscape down to the coast.

Scenically of equal interest and shorter, but mostly unpaved, is the road from Ankara via Çankırı and Kastamonu to Sinop on the Black Sea (Routes 39, 20 and 12). The coastal road (Route 20) east to Samsun through the plain of Bafra is also rewarding, despite some bad stretches.

The highway (Route 20) that follows the coastline from Samsun to Trabzon is beautiful; the road passes through the green countryside at the mouth of the Yeşil Irmak River, and then closely hugs the sea to Surmene. There are plenty of filling stations, but so far little super grade.

Cars may be shipped on the *Denizyollari* boats. Small private craft also make the journey, but getting the car on board may be more than your nerves can take.

THE BLACK SEA 363

Small fishing villages are scattered all along the coastline. The way of life
throughout the region is still very patriarchal; you can move in on anybody,
but everybody moves in on you, or rather in your car: the country people
dearly love a ride. Towards Rize and Hopa the road along the coast goes from
bad to worse; but the discomfort is offset by the subtropical beauty of the hilly
landscape, covered with tea plantations.

 WHAT TO SEE? The Black Sea region has beautiful scenery, fine
beaches for swimming, mountain climbing to the east, and many
historical remains. The traveler can spend pleasant holidays at low
cost in Şile, Akçakoca, Filyos (Hisarönü), Bartin, Amasra, and near
Inebolu. The road from Sinop to Giresun, now in a good state of
repair, allows leisurely outings to Samsun, Ünye, and Ordu, as well
as to many picturesque fishing villages. Trabzon, long one of the biggest and
most thriving ports on the coast, became a Byzantine empire when Alexis
Comnenus fled there from Constantinople in 1204; it grew in power and glory
until the fall of the exiled empire, some 250 year later. Byzantine remains, both
architecture and frescoes, still bear witness to the past greatness of the times.
Rize, a sea port, is the center of a teaplanting region, just below the chain
of high mountains, many of whose tops are as yet unclimbed.

Hotels and Restaurants

ABANA. Near İnebolu. Small
hotels and restaurants.

AKÇAKOCA. Beach resort west of
Zonguldak. *Çinar*, 18 rooms with
bath; also *Belediye* and *Deniz Palas*.

AMASRA. Small harbor and beach
east of Zonguldak. *Paşakaptan* (3) unassuming, 20 rooms (3 with shower);
Belvü Palas, still more unassuming.
In Çakraz, a good beach and two
simple hotels: *Palas* and *Turistik*.

EREĞLI. *Faruk Tanyeli* (4); *Eken*,
24 rooms (12 with shower).

GIRESUN. *Kristal Palas*, 23 rooms
with shower; *Emek Palas*, 22 rooms
with shower.

HOPA. *Çoruh Palas*, anything but a
palace.

INEBOLU. *Deniz*, 30 rooms; *Park*,
12 rooms.

KARABÜK. *Demir Palas*, 29
rooms, 9 showers.

KASTAMONU. *Arslan* (4). 36
rooms (18 with showers); *Koçoğlu
Palas*, 16 rooms; *Şehir*, 18 rooms.

ORDU. *Turist* (3), 26 rooms with
bath or shower; *Orpalas* (4), 18
rooms, 9 showers; *Kervan Palas*, 16
rooms, 4 showers. Also: *Gülistan*, 12
rooms with shower.

RIZE. *Turist* (3), 30 rooms with
bath or shower; *Saray* (4), 18 rooms,
4 showers; *Divan*, 22 rooms; *Kıbrıs
Palas*, 10 rooms.

SAMSUN. *Vidinli* (3), 65 rooms
(40 with shower), adequate. *Atlantik*
(4), 40 rooms, 8 showers; *Sahil Palas*,
17 rooms.

ŞILE. *Kumbaba* (3), 40 rooms, 14
showers; *Değirmen* (4), 32 rooms with
bath or shower; *Deniz* (4), 20 rooms.

SINOP. *Toleyis Turistik* (3), 63
rooms with shower; *Gümüş Palas* (4),
30 rooms, 5 showers; *Sinop Palas* (4),
32 rooms, 4 showers; *Ada Palas*, 19
rooms; *Onur Palas*, 46 rooms, 5
showers.
Restaurant: *Liman Lokantâsı*.

TRABZON. *Horon Oteli* (4), 42
rooms, 22 showers; *Benli Palas* (4),
36 rooms, 3 showers; *Turistik Palas*

(4), 15 rooms (5 with shower); *Ural Palas* (4), 29 rooms, 3 showers; *Kadakal Palas* (4), 20 rooms; *Yeşilkurt*, 22 rooms.

Restaurants: *Emperyal*, Iskele Cad.; *Yeşilkurt*, Taksim; *Gülbahçe*, in the park; *Çinar Lokantası*, Uzun Sokak.

ÜNYE. Half-way between Samsun and Ordu. *Atlantik* and *Deniz* (latter 21 rooms), passable.

ZONGULDAK. *Emniyet Palas*, 47 rooms (10 with shower).

OFFICIAL CAMPING GROUNDS. Abana: *Abana Dinlenme Kampı*, near Inebolu on the Black Sea. Akçakoca: *Dinlenme Camping*. Akçakoca, bungalows. Havza: *Maarif Otel ve Dinlenme Kampı*, motel and camping grounds over 50 miles south of Samsun, on the road to Çorum. Vakfikebir: *BP Station*, 26 miles west of Trabzon, on the sea shore.

USEFUL ADDRESSES. *Tourist Offices* in Samsun; in Trabzon, Bölge Müdürlügü: ask for the *turizm bürosu*. *THY Airlines*: in Samsun, Kâzim Paşa Cad. 11/A; in Trabzon, Belediye Sira Mağazalari 18/A. Agencies of the *Turkish Maritime Lines (Denizyollari)*: in Abana; in Akçakoca; in Giresun; in Inebolu; in Hopa; in Ordu; in Rize; in Samsun; in Sinop; in Trabzon; in Unye; in Zonguldak.

Discovering the Black Sea Coast

On landing in Anatolia from Istanbul we traveled into the countryside towards Adapazari. This time, we shall go further, to Bolu, 72 miles inland on the road (E5) to Ankara. If you fork off towards the Black Sea at Düzce (Route 20), you will come to the archeological site of Üskübü, with the remains of a theater and a Gate of Lions, together with Roman mosaics. Twenty miles or so down the same road is Akçakoca and its long sweeping beach. About 8 miles before Bolu, you turn to the right for a look at the lake of Abant. At a healthy height of 4,500 feet, with good hotels and camping grounds, it makes a pleasant stopover, with boating and fishing in a wonderfully sunny mountain setting.

The province of Bolu bears the name of its capital. Once part of the Hittite Empire, it became, after the death of Alexander the Great, the kingdom of Bithynia, whose capital, Claudiopolis, is today called Bolu. (Mut, in the south between Silifke and Karaman, also went by the name of Claudiopolis.) Within the town, a mosque, the Ulu Cami, and the *hamam*, or Turkish baths, were built by order of the great 14th-century sultan, Bayezit.

Gerede (Esentepe), 32 miles away, with a swimming pool shaped like a small-scale Sea of Marmara, is a pleasant stopover. In Zonguldak, north of Gerede on the coast, Turkey's heavy industry was born. The discovery of coal mines gave rise to the building of the first iron foundry. The second in Ereğli, on the west coast, is the biggest in the Middle East.

The traveler hereabouts will no longer find much that is worth his while, aside from a few traces of ancient Rome in Hisarönü (Filyos), complemented by a Genoese castle at Ereğli, founded as Heraklea of Pontus in 560 B.C. by the Megarians. Through one of the three grottos in the vicinity, Heracles descended to the underworld to accomplish the worst of his labors by fetching Cerberus, Hades' three-headed, hundred-eyed watchdog. The story goes that in Amasra, 62 miles east of Zonguldak, the beaches (the Big Harbor and the Little Harbor) were discovered by Amastris, nephew of the Persian emperor, Darius III. There are the ruins of a Roman temple and baths, and a fortress rebuilt in the 14th century by the Genoese.

In Kastamonu, we are on more familiar ground. This old Byzantine town was of some importance at the time of the Seljuks. Oddly enough, it owes much of its reconstruction, in the early 15th century, to the Mongol hordes led by Tamerlane. Shortly before it became part of the Ottoman Empire, it was the seat of the powerful Isfendiyaroğlu family. The castle, on its low hilltop, still has a few massive towers. There is no shortage of mosques—Atabey, Isfendiyar, Ibn Neccar, Yakup Ağa, and so on. By far the most beautiful is Mehmet Bey Cami, a 14th-century wooden mosque in the nearby village of Kasaba. In town, the traveler may take a pleasant stroll through the Karanlık Bedesten, a 16th-century bazaar which is still going strong. In the building which houses the town museum, Atatürk announced, in 1926, the abolition of the fez.

There were, as we have said, two towns called Claudiopolis. Here, in Taşköprü (on Route 20), we have a second Pompeiopolis. (The first was near Mersin.) An old stone bridge with five arches, the *Köprü*, crosses the river. Two hours away on muleback, at Kale Kapi, there is an interesting cave tomb, with colonnades and a frieze. On the coast is Inebolu, a small coasting harbor, and Abana, a fishing village with long miles of beach.

Sinop, to western ears, has a more familiar ring. It is here that the tobacco fields begin, already crowding out the fields of wheat and corn and flax. Vast forests cover a good third of the province. The sheltered port of Sinop and the nearby fertile plains have both aroused greed since the beginning of time. According to legend, the town was founded by the Amazons (the same is said of Izmir, the old Smyrna). It is a historical fact, however, recorded in Hittite texts, that Queen Sinova, who gave her name to the town, was indeed a living woman. The remains of a Greek temple dedicated to Serapis, the Egyptian god revered in both Greece and Rome, are near the Municipal Park, and confirm the town's antiquity. The citadel was built by the Hittites, though its present outlay dates from the time of Mithridates IV, king of Pontus, who ordered its reconstruction in the first century B.C.

Alâeddin Keykubat, in whose footsteps we have already trod on the shores of the "White Sea", built, in 1214, the mosque that bears his name. The splendid *mihrap* was sent to the Museum of Islamic Art, in Istanbul, after the collapse of the rounded vault The Alâiye Medrese, now a museum, was built in 1262 by the Grand Vizier of Keykubat, Süleyman Pervane. Of interest to the traveler, too, are the tombs of the great families—Isfendiyaroğlu, in the courtyard of the Alâeddin mosque; and Çandaroğlu, at Ibrahim Bey Türbesi. There are also the touchingly small mosques or *mesçit* of Saray and of Fetih Baba, both built in 1339; the Turkish baths or *hamam* of Çifte and Varoş, built in 1332; and a Byzantine church, Balat Kilise, also dating back to the 14th century. Walking through the town, you will come across many small mosques, as well as tombs, *türbe*, and fountains, *çeşme*.

For outings, you can drive to the hilltop of Seyyit Bilal, for the view; to Zeytinlik, for a picnic; to the beaches of Rüya and Ak Liman Koyu, where the forest grows right down to the shores of the island-studded sea.

Tobacco Land

Bafra, Samsun and Merzifon form a triangle that may be called the Turkish tobacco region, although the planting of corn, cattle breeding, and fishing are all thriving industries. Tobacco leaf and cigarettes, farm produce and fish are shipped from

Bafra and Samsun; Merzifon is the crossroads of a network of highways and railways leading inland.

Of the three, Samsun, with its 90,000 inhabitants, is the most important. Founded by the Milesians in the seventh century B.C., it was subject to Hittite rule before falling to later conquerors. Its ancient name, Amisos, was changed by the Turks into Samsun. The old Amisos is two miles from the middle of town.

It is the birthplace of the War of Independence. Mustafa Kemal had set sail from Istanbul, with an army inspection order rashly signed by the Sultan. By the time the hapless monarch was made to see his blunder, it was too late—the dauntless rebel was on the high seas, with the paper that was to open to him the door, of the army. His faith and his powers of persuasion did the rest. To all intents and purposes, the Turkish Republic can be considered to have been born in Samsun, on the 19th of May 1919. (The 19th of May is a national holiday in Turkey.) In honor of its great man, the town put up a monument, opposite the government house; it is one of the finest in the country. The hotel in which he stayed after his landing has become a regional museum; it displays the archeological finds of the countryside (above all at Duhdar) and has an interesting ethnographical section.

The Samsun coastline is one long sweep of beach, with fine white sand.

Bafra, 28 miles to the west, at the mouth of the Kızıl Irmak River, exports caviar as well as tobacco. Those interested in the War of Independence can go to Havza, near Merzifon, where the house which lodged Atatürk has been turned into a museum. The small town also boasts a library containing a few valuable manuscripts, and some cave-tombs nearby, in Kapu Kaya, as well as on the banks of the Kızıl Irmak. Gentlemen with a bent for archeology can visit the excavations at Akalan, near Samsun, and have a look at finds dating from the sixth and seventh centuries B.C. Ladies with a weakness for carpets will go to the looms in Lâdik.

Last but not least, the whole countryside is rich in game—hare, stag, wild boar, fox, and every kind of bird, particularly wild duck, pheasant, and woodcock; a hunting paradise worthy of Nimrod himself.

From Samsun to Trabzon

So far, the traveler has met with no real discomfort. From now on, he will have to rough it until roads improve. To the east of a line, unseen but felt, drawn from Sinop down to Kayseri and Adana, he will have to put up with antiquated notions of comfort and cleanliness. All stopping places, and the means of getting there, will become a question-mark; what was tourism changes into old-time travel, even into adventure. He will find fewer and fewer hotels marked *turist*, that is to say, affording what the Anglo-Saxon has come to think of as basic needs. The smaller roads are barely passable in bad weather; thick summer dust will soon seem a lesser ill. This part of the country is not meant for foreigners; it is, therefore, all the more interesting.

The coast road leading from Samsun to Trabzon (the old Trebizond) is very beautiful; it winds between a calm sea and plains covered with hazelnut bushes, fruit trees, and vast corn-fields bending to a soft wind. Minarets watch over long stretches of beach, big empty spaces for the lonely swimmer. Inland, the mountains rise up and offer wonderful views.

The towns and outskirts of Ordu and Giresun have so much to offer to the sightseer, such an overflow of riches in art and history, known and unknown; of Greek, Roman, and Byzantine remains, of Seljuk and Ottoman mosques, of beautiful beaches—always something to somebody's taste—that we fear to overwhelm the reader. Still, we shall also say in passing that the very look of the land changes, tobacco giving way to tea and to the soyabean, though there are still cornfields and hazelnuts in plenty; and that the coast is lined with fishing villages.

A few facts at random. Outside Ordu, a Greek settlement of the seventh century B.C. has left traces of its passing on the beach at Kotiora, also known as Bozzukale. The best beach for swimming is Güzelyali. At Ünye, the sea-caves called Fokfok are a breeding-place for seals. The old name of Giresun was Karasu, from *kiraz*, the Turkish word for cherry; well-known to all lovers of good food, the Roman general Lucullus brought the cherry back to Europe, and with it the only lasting outcome of his warfare in Asia Minor.

Now, a mere roll-call of interesting sights, not to overtire the would-be traveler.

(1) The ruins of a Pontine citadel in Giresun, together with the tomb of Seyyit Vakkas, whose part in the battle led to the taking of Karasu by the Turks.

(2) The ruins of a temple, said to be of Mars, on the island facing the town.

(3) Rest, sea and sunbathing at Tirebolu and Görele, halfway to Trabzon.

For some time past, the open-eyed traveler has noticed eggshells hanging over the doors and windows of the houses. They have more or less the same meaning as the brass plates of Insurance Companies on western buildings—they ward off the evil eye. The eggshell is airtight—it has no opening to let harm in. Superstition thrives, and old customs are still firmly rooted in all lonely countrysides where man feels helpless before nature.

Trabzon, the Trebizond of old, today has 60,000 inhabitants, and has become the liveliest port of the Turkish coastline on the Black Sea, and the richest, due to its shipments of tobacco and corn.

Historians like to relate that at the sight of Trebizond, Xenophon, himself a historian as well as a soldier, cried out "Thalassa!" ("The sea!"). Every town on the coast, beginning at Şile, near Istanbul, has its own story of the backward march of Xenophon and the Ten Thousand. Seeing the long line of beaches passed through in its flight, we cannot help but wonder why the retreating army should be so glad to catch sight of the sea.

When Persia made a spectacular if ephemeral come-back at the end of the 5th century B.C., the Greeks thought nothing of fighting in the ranks of their former mortal enemies—for a price. In the year 401 B.C., Cyrus the Younger was defeated at Cunaxa, in Mesopotamia, by his brother Artaxerxes II. It so happened that the defeated army had a paid force of 10,000 Greek soldiers, who, though Cyrus had been killed in battle and his generals had laid down arms, refused to surrender. Flushed with victory and in a handsome mood, Artaxerxes offered to let them go, even to give them enough food and water to last them to the Pontus Euxinus, or Black Sea. But the Satrap Tissaphernes, a thrifty soul, thought it less costly to murder the Greek leader, Clearchos, and so force his men to admit defeat. Disheartened, the foreign soldiers were about to give in when a young officer, Xenophon by name, cried out: "March on, boys! We'll make it anyway!"

So 10,000 Greeks set out on the famous march, whose footsteps still sound down the corridors of time. An endless file of wounded and hungry men trudging through deserts and over mountains and around enemy towns, it was at the time—and would scarcely be less so today—a desperate undertaking. After told and untold dangers and hardships, they at last got safely to the Black Sea. On his retirement at Corinth, Xenophon wrote the story of the march in a book, the *Anabasis* or "Inland Journey".

In those days, Trabzon was called Trapezos, named after its shape. It was, in all likelihood, founded by the Arcadians, in the seventh century B.C. The former Pontine province was greatly developed under the Emperor Hadrian. After the fall of Constantinople to the Crusaders, its Emperor, Alexis Comnenus, fled to the Black Sea port, thereon known as Trebizond, and there founded a new, if short-lived, Greco-Byzantine empire. Ten years later, Mehmet the Conqueror swept the token empire off the map of Asia, and put a crescent on the domes and bell-towers, together with a coat of whitewash over the often lovely frescoes.

The best-known Byzantine monument, at the entrance to Trabzon, is the church of St. Sophia, built in the 13th century, and today a museum. Set on a green hill overlooking the bay, it has magnificent frescoes well worth a thorough study. Long hidden, for the most part, under a hard layer of plaster, they have recently been uncovered by a team of Scottish archeologists.

A short distance away, there is a fine 16th-century mosque, the Gülbahar Hatun Cami, with the *türbe* or tomb of its founder, the mother of Sultan Selim I.

The citadel, which has held out against so many sieges, is still imposing. It is divided into three parts, of which the Güzel Saray, built fairly lately, is something of a mistake. The old church of Panaghia Chrysokephalos, the Virgin of the Golden Head, is in the middle part, the Orta Hisar; made over into a mosque, the Fatih Cami, it still has the trace of the old basilical plan, in spite of later tamperings. The Yeni Cuma Cami was originally a church, that of St. Eugene. There, too, the three naves in a row are cut through by an upper nave, to form a Latin cross. Also of interest are two places of Christian worship: the church of St. Anne, in Maras Street, and of St. Blaise, a few steps away.

At the end of the First World War, the Czar of Russia was to pay a visit to Trabzon, occupied by his forces. A palace was built for his reception, in a style "combining Turkish architecture and western decoration". The Republic turned it into a girls' school, which did nothing to improve matters. Luckily, the nearby silver-smiths' bazaar, the Gümüşçüler Çarşi, makes up for the eyesore.

The art-lover should not fail to go to the monastery of the Vir-gin at Sumela, 33 miles or so to the southwest, turning left after Maçka. It is the most important Byzantine monument in the region, but is now abandoned and crumbling away in the hollow of a sheer cliff some 1,000 feet above the valley floor, at an altitude of 3,900 feet. Ninety-three steps ascend to a locked wooden door, the key to which can be obtained at the forest ranger station at the end of the motor road. Founded by Blessed Barnabas to house a miraculous icon of the Virgin painted by St. Luke, the venerated shrine was greatly enlarged by the Comnenes. Alexis III completely rebuilt the monastery where he had been crowned in 1340—as depicted in the frescoes of the main church in the grotto. Tolerant sultans further added to the sanctuary's trea-sures and the frescoes were restored in 1740. Before the expulsion of the Greeks in 1922, the monks hid the icon of the Virgin in a neighboring chapel, and in 1930, the Turkish government allowed the transfer of the relic to the new monastery of Soumela in Greek Macedonia.

The pass of Zigana Geçidi is one of the most remarkable in all Turkey. It is a rift between two different worlds, in look as in way of life. Leaving below the lush damp green of the coastline, the traveler climbs steeply upwards through misty forests to find himself, on the south side, amid the low-lying brushwood and yellow dust of the high and dry Asiatic plains. Here shepherds move with the changing seasons between highland and lowland pastures, dotted with makeshift huts and grazing flocks.

Towards the Soviet Border

We are only two provinces away (about 150 miles) from Soviet Russia. Wooded mountains, a mild but very damp climate and therefore a rich plant life, are the surroundings as well as tea plantations and rice paddies. The traveler will go on at his own risk: lodging is practically non-existent.

A word in passing on the inhabitants, the Lazes. They speak a Turco-Georgian dialect that always leaves, whatever their level of education, the trace of an unmistakeable accent. Outside their own small homeland, they are astonishingly quick-witted and enterprising. Here, carts are not in use, the mountain paths are mostly impassable. Luckily, the weaker sex is at hand to bear the burdens. The old men often wear the turban. The men of Bolu have a well-deserved reputation as cooks; they can be found in hotels, restaurants, and pastry shops all the way to the west, to Istanbul.

In Rize, the driver can take the Ikizdere-Ispir-Erzurum road, if his car is up to it: this is jeep country.

Setting out from Ardeşen, there are mountain walks inland, and unforgettable trout-fishing in the streams of the Çamlihem-şin Valley. Mountain-climbers will have a try at the Kaçkar Dagi (over 12,000 feet), having taken care beforehand to find an interpreter-guide. Nearby Findikli is surrounded by tea plantations.

The last stopover for the liners of the *Denizyollari Steamship Company*, Hopa is a stone's throw from the Soviet border.

The road to Artvin climbs up through thickly-wooded forests to just before Borçka, and has many beautiful views on the winding way down. Overlooking the Çoruh River, the capital of the province—far removed from this world—is in a wild and wonderful setting.

Illustration at head of this chapter: A typical folk dance.

THE EASTERN PROVINCES

Unsung Discoveries for the Adventurous

The big attractions in the eastern part of Turkey are Mount Ararat, the Nemrut Dağı, and Lake Van. With the exception of this last-mentioned place, which through a burst of Turkish effort has developed into a full-fledged resort center, getting to these localities implies a real travel expedition, not just a junket. Tenderfeet stay away! But if a few minor inconveniences don't easily worry you and if there's a spark in your soul that makes you hanker after more than just the dutifully trodden paths blazed by the travel agencies, you'll find the experience enchanting. Now that you've been duly forewarned, we can promise you enjoyment and delight far beyond your wildest dreams, pleasure that will more than compensate for a few rugged moments.

When you were in Anatolia, you saw Roman and Greek ruins, specimens of Turko-Seljukian and Ottoman architecture and ancient Byzantine churches, some converted into mosques and others left intact. The Armenian and Georgian architectural style in Eastern Turkey dates from the ninth to the 12th centuries, and is something quite different. Although this region, located between Byzantium and Iran, underwent the influence of these two countries to a certain extent, it nevertheless remained primarily a breeding-ground for producing highly original and independent architects.

The reason that the nation's great number of important shrines are so widely scattered over various parts of present-day Turkey doubtless lies in the fact that there used to be many independent local monarchs ruling at one time. The basilical floor plan that prevailed in the western part of the country was early abandoned in the eastern part to make way for a central structure featuring domes topped off with the characteristic conical roof. Exteriors are generally simple and solid, in striking contrast with the highly ornate and intricate interiors. The inside niches, secondary rooms, and even the apse itself are built right into the great walls, the very thickness of which conceals the partitioning. The core of the walls is quarry rock, and the interiors and exteriors are covered with carved stone. The outer surfaces are embellished with arcades and occasionally with designs in relief. Although these edifices predate the Gothic style, and are based on different principles, they feature among other things slightly ogival arches with light alveolations.

Brushing up on History

The Armenians are undoubtedly one of the world's most ancient tribes. Their origins allegedly can be traced back to the fistful of survivors who escaped from the deluge by taking shelter in Noah's Ark. Making their way down Mount Ararat's slopes, these people scattered over the land. From 4,000 to 2,000 B.C., numerous Hurri principalities in this area provided an independent racial buffer between the Indo-European Hittites and the Semitic Assyrians from Lake Van to the Mediterranean. After unification by the Mittani, either a Hurri tribe or a dominant Indo-European aristocracy, a Hurri empire held sway over the greater part of Asia Minor for about 300 years, to disintegrate again in the 15th century B.C. before the onslaught of the New Hittite Empire and the Egyptians. The Mittani of the south eventually merged with the Assyrians, but the Urartu of Lake Van maintained a powerful kingdom and their language clearly indicates a Hurrite origin. Christianity supplied an abbreviated version almost a thousand years later: the first Urartu king, Hayq, one of Noah's descendants, gave the name Aram to his

successor—hence the term Armenoid. In the eighth century
B.C., King Rusas I established his capital at Toprakkale, on
the shores of Lake Van. Out of the mixture of sundry influences
from both East and West there gradually emerged an Armenian
language and culture.

According to the information yielded by Assyrian stone tablets, the descendants of Noah and Aram displayed an acute
flair for business, and lost no time in striking up a brisk trade with
Scythia and China. They likewise tackled the job of combatting
the successive yokes of Assyrian, Persian, and Macedonian domination. After allying itself with Rome, Armenia gained a semi-
independent status, but soon the master's rule began to weigh
heavily. King Tigranes and his father-in-law, Mithridates, King
of Pontus, formed their own alliance against Rome. Finally,
Nero recognized Tiridates I as the king of Armenia under Roman
suzerainty (A.D. 66). Rome's authority was eventually replaced
by that of Persia.

In A.D. 303, St. George converted Tiridates III, who decreed
Christianity as the official state religion. A break with Persia
ensued. Rome and Persia settled their conflict in 387 by dividing
Armenia. Nothing daunted, the Armenians proceeded to proclaim their independence, at least in the spiritual realm. In 541,
after refusing to accept the conclusions of the Council of Chalcedon, they broke away from the Roman Church. Then the Arabs
arrived, and by 653, a treaty had been signed with the caliph.

As Byzantium declined and Arab power became dissipated,
the Bagratids who were ruling Armenia consolidated their own
strength. The kingdom was reconstituted with Ani as its capital.
Another kingdom, Vaspurakan, covered what is today the province of Van. Byzantium took a dim view of these brethren who
were worshipping Christ in their own way, and Constantinople
threw this part of Asia Minor open to the invading Turkish
forces.

In 1080, Armenian refugees who had settled in Cilicia (on the
Mediterranean coast) founded a kingdom that aided the
Crusaders in exchange for the latters' assistance in freeing their
country. The upshot of it all was that they got the de Lusignan
family to reign over them, in place of the Bagratids (1320). This
frail monarchy was doomed to early extinction at the hands of

the Seljuks, in 1373. (Leon de Lusignan fled to France, where he lies buried in the basilica of Saint Denis, in the suburbs of Paris.) For centuries, the Armenians' only hope lay in the Christian East, with the Russians. For centuries also, they remained trapped in the relentless vise of iron and fire that was the perpetual conflict between the Turkish and Muscovite empires.

The honor of protecting the Christian minority in Asia was vied for by the great powers in search of expansion: England, France and Russia. (Curiously enough, in 1916, after wresting the Eastern territories from the Turks, Russia refused to permit the Armenians to return to their homeland: she happened to be anxious to install the Cossacks, there.) The Armenians' greatest tragedy arose out of World War I, during which Turkey sided with Germany against the Allies. The majority of the Armenians, who were subjects of the Ottoman Empire, refused to serve in the Turkish Army. Instead, they formed a resistance movement and their irregulars ended up on Mount Moses (Musa Dağı), in the sub-province of Alexandretta. Turkey dispatched an expeditionary force against them—the French fleet picked up the survivors.

Practical Information for the Eastern Provinces

HOW TO GET THERE? By Air: Ankara-Erzurum 1 hr. 10 mins. Ankara-Malatya-Diyarbakir-Van, four hours. **By train:** the *Eastern Express*; daily run between Istanbul (Haydarpaşa)-Erzurum-Kars; also Istanbul (Haydarpaşa)-Muş-Tatvan, and on by ferry to Van; the *Southern Express*, four times a week, Istanbul (Haydarpaşa)-Sivas-Malatya-Kurtalan, and on by motor coach.

BY CAR. The road (E100) that climbs from Trabzon towards Erzurum passes through a wooded landscape and green valleys up to the mountain pass of Zigana, about 6,500 ft. high. A smooth surface, but the steep and winding road makes for slow driving. Beyond the pass, the landscape changes back to high and lonely tablelands. There are few filling stations; check both gas and oil before setting out, and take along a spare can to be on the safe side. From Erzurum to Artvin, the scenery is breathtaking, but the road is dusty in summer, muddy in winter, and bumpy at all times.

The Erzurum-Ağri Route 2 (E23) is mostly paved. It runs through a valley hemmed in by mountains as much as 9,850 ft. high. At Pasinler, a road (Route 75) branches off to the right towards Muş, but is hard going and best by-passed. Farther along Route 2 to the left, a good stabilized road leads from Horasan to Kars. After Kars is Kizilçakçak, the Turkey-USSR border station. The E23 from Erzurum towards Ağri, last major town and stopover before the Iran border, climbs up the mountainside and through the pass of Tahir (8,123 ft.), and downwards into an ever beautiful countryside. At Ağri, a stabilized road (Route 95) branches to the right towards Van and its lake. From Ağri to the border on E23, the macadamized road runs flat and straight beneath the awe-inspiring mountain tops, among which is Mount Ararat, 16,945 ft. high. At Doğubayazit, last village before Iran, a road (Route 40) branches to the left; there is no crossing point into the USSR in this region. At Gürbulak, Turco-Iranian customs; lodgings for travelers on the Iranian side, at Mako.

The road (Route 6) from Van, skirting the southern shores of the lake to Bitlis and then west to Diyarbakır, is only for the adventurous.

Route 60 from Kayseri via Malatya-Elaziğ-Bingöl-Muş to Bitlis on Lake Van is paved throughout as also the Malatya-Elaziğ-Diyarbakır-Mardin highway (E99 and Route 69). A good asphalt road on half the length between Gaziantep and Mardin (E24).

 WHAT TO SEE? Back of the green coastline of the Black Sea lie the vast empty stretches of the tableland of Anatolia. The biggest town of the region is Erzurum, mostly military barracks; however, the *medrese* with its two minarets (Çifte Minare) is worth a stopover. If you like lonely places, visit the many Georgian churches on the way to Artvin, or the Armenian monasteries around the Lake of Van. On the road to Iran, stop at Doğubayazit to gaze at the legendary Mount Ararat (Ağri Dağı), or wander through the ruins of the enchanted palace of Ishak Paşa. To the south, around Hakkâri, countless mountain tops await the climber. To the west, Diyarbakır, on the banks of the Tiger, has black basalt ramparts and interesting monuments. To the south of Urfa is Harran, mentioned in the Bible, a most picturesque village with its already Syrian houses, like ant heaps. And at last, in the middle of nowhere and the eery solitude of the Nemrut Dağı, not far from Adiyaman, you will come upon the extraordinary funeral monument of the Comagenes, 2,000 years old.

 THE CILO AND SAT RANGES. These mountains lie in the southeast spur of Turkey, in the province of Hakkâri, between the borders of Iran and Iraq. They have nearly 20 glaciers and over 100 peaks of different heights, covered with snow all the year round. Icy lakes are scattered among the mountain tops, most of which are over 11,500 ft. high. The most awesome peaks in the Cilo chain are the Resko (13,680 ft.) and the Supan Durik (13,324 ft.). The Sat Mountains, more to the south, are also renowned for their beautiful lakes and nestling valleys. If you carry binoculars, you can follow the movements of the wild goats or ibex of Asia Minor, the forebears of our tame goats; together with sheep, bears, and other wild life.

For mountain climbers without a car, there are regular airline services for passengers from Istanbul and Ankara to Van. Those who would rather go by train can take the Istanbul (Haydarpaşa)-Kurtalan express. At Kurtalan, a bus takes the passengers to Tug, a small port near Tatvan, on the shores of the lake of Van; the journey takes four hours. Tuğ has a hotel. Travelers who spend the night there should go up to the beautiful lake in the crater of Mount

Nemrut (not to be confused with the more famous Nemrut at Malatya); the climb takes three and a half hours. A boat will take you straight from Tuğ to Van in 6 hours; another, by a longer route, takes 9 hours.

In Van, you can take a bus or a truck to Hakkâri, or, better still, to a village called Yüksekova, the starting point for mountain climbers, whether on pony, donkey, or muleback. It will cost you about 40 TL a day for the animal and its owner. On the way south, stop over at Hoşap, dominated by an awesome 16th-century Kurd castle, with a fine gate.

1. *Sat Mountains*. Leaving Yüksekova toward Piskasir, and following the mountain ridges to the village of Bay, you will come to the lake of Bay in 12 to 14 hours, guided by the owner of your beast.

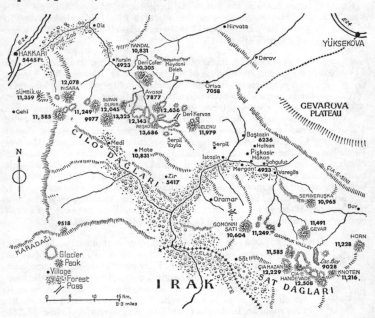

2. *Cilo Mountains*. You can reach the Cilo Mountains through the village of Hirvata, passing by Meydani Belek, Deri Çafer (10,303 ft.), and going down again through the valley of Avaspi. You can also follow the track Derav-Orisa-Deri Kervan. Here, you are on the path that leads to the eastern glacier of Reşko, at 13,680 ft.; and here, if you are a hardy climber, that you undertake to scale the steep mountainside, up to the most majestic glacier in Asia Minor. On the way, you will come across a *yayla*, or seasonal grazing land for the live-stock of Kurd herders, at Serpil. Farther to the south, in the village of Serpil itself, you will find lodgings.

Continuing southeast toward the village of Istazin, you come to the lake of Sat. From there you go down, through the Beraga Pass, towards the village of Oramar (at 4,770 ft.) and the ruins of Zir to your right; after visiting Zir, continue northwest to the village of Medi; then the cleft between Mount Kisara (12,077 ft.) and Mount Sümbül (11,354 ft.), until you reach Hakkâri. This excursion may last a week or more. For information, apply to *Türkiye Tabiatını Koruma Cemiyeti*, Yenişehir, Bayindir Sok. 43, Ankara; to *Elmadağ Spor Klübü*, Sakarya Caddesi, Ankara; to *Belediye Baskanliği*, in Van; or to *Belediye Başkanliği*, in Yüksekova.

THE STONE HEADS OF THE COMAGENES. Southeast of Ankara 250 miles as the crow flies, and to the south of the town of Malatya, the Nemrut Dağı (also spelled Nemruth) towers up in the Anti-Taurus, striking the onlooker by its unnatural symmetry as that of a man-made mountain—and so it is. On the top of a mountain shaped into the form of a cone, at a level of 8,205 ft., Antiochos I Comagenes (69-34 B.C.) built a sepulchral mound some 100 feet high, surrounded by stone statues nearly 30 feet tall.

It is not easy to get there. You must take the road (E99) from Malatya to Gaziantep, then branch off (Route 54) at Gölbaşi to Adiyaman. You can drive your own car as far as Kâhta, then change to a jeep to go to the village of Eski Kâhta; from then on, you ride on muleback. (We recommend that you stay overnight at Kâhta. Your guide will awaken you at 3 a.m. to take you to Eski Kâhta by jeep. Leave the latter between 4 and 5 a.m. by mule, arriving at the summit by 9 a.m. You then descend in the afternoon.) Between Kâhta and Eski Kâhta, you will cross the Roman bridge at Cendere (the ancient Chalcinas); it was built under Septimius Severus and is still in good repair. You can still see a marble column with Latin inscriptions, and another topped by an eagle. To the south of Cendere, at Karakuş, towers the mound built by Antiochos as a burial place for the women of his family. A sandstone eagle, symbol of Zeus, tops a neo-Doric column still standing among the broken remains of 18 columns, once pedestals for statues of the dead.

The ascent of Nemrut Dağı is no child's play. Most of it is on muleback, but in the rougher parts, where the beast stumbles over the loose stones, you will have to dismount and go slowly on foot. The climb takes nearly 4 hours; it is, of course, faster going down, but even so it takes about 3 hours. Near the top, it is almost unbearably hot during the day, and icy cold at night. There is neither shade nor water. Take warm sweaters, drinking water, sunglasses, and some kind of head covering; also sturdy shoes for climbing over the rocks. On no account set out in bad weather.

The mound was surrounded on three sides (north, east, and west) by terraces; the eastern and western terraces, nearly square in shape, were decked with statues whose size and majesty are awesome still, in spite of the havoc wrought by time and weather, lightning and earthquakes. The upward path leads to the east terrace, where you can have a close look at the headless remains of the statues that still stand upright among the tumbledown ruins, among which lie fallen heads some 10 feet high.

Diggings have been undertaken in the hope of finding the tomb of Antiochos I, who, according to some archeologists, was buried in the mound; but it has

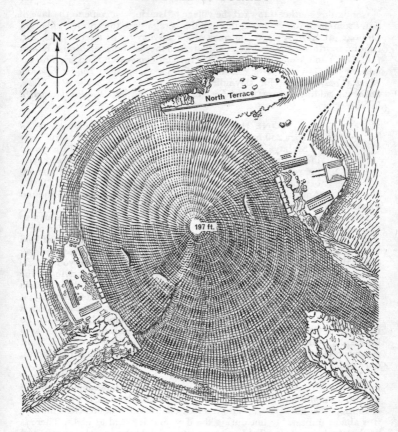

North Terrace

197 ft.

proved impossible to shovel through the bottomless depths of small stones, which fall in and choke up the many tunnels vainly opened. The mystery remains unsolved.

Hotels and Restaurants

ADIYAMAN. *Sümer Palas*, 20 rooms.

AĞRI. *Acar Palas*, 60 rooms (3 with shower). Last stopover on the road to Iran.

ARTVIN. *Erzurum*, 12 very modest rooms.

BINGÖL. *Divan Palas*, 12 rooms.

BITLIS. *Konaklık*, 16 rooms.

DIYARBAKIR. *Tatlicilar* (2), best in the region, all rooms with shower;

Demir (3), 30 rooms with shower; *Turistik Palas* (3), 52 rooms (26 with shower); *Ömür Palas*, 60 rooms, 6 showers.

ELAZIG. *Gülistan Palas*, 33 rooms (9 with shower); *Divan Palas*, 40 rooms; *Emek Palas*, 42 rooms; *Turistik Palas*, 44 rooms.

ERZINCAN. *Kent Palas*, 35 rooms (16 with shower); *Çelik Palas*, 21 rooms, 3 showers.

ERZURUM. *Örnek* (3), Kâzım Karabekir Cad., 56 rooms, 40 showers; *Lâle Palas*, 36 rooms, 3 showers; *Sarıkaya*, 35 rooms; *Temelli Palas*, 41 rooms, 5 showers; *Şehir Palas*, 45 rooms; *Avrupa*, 21 rooms (1 with shower).

GÜMÜŞHANE. *Gürses Palas*, 16 rooms; *Özesen*, 6 rooms.

HAKKARI. *Site*, 21 rooms (17 with shower); *Sümbül Palas*, 8 rooms.

KAHTA. A hotel should be open 1972, as starting point for the ascent of Mount Nemrut.

KARS. *Turistik Bal.*, 37 rooms with shower; *Güngören*, 67 rooms; *Ferah*, 33 rooms.

MALATYA. *Çinar*, 53 rooms (29 showers), *Çoskun*, 20 rooms (12 showers), *Keban*, 21 rooms (4 showers) just make grade 4. *Kanter Palas*, 25 rooms; *Park*, 22 rooms; *Uğur Palas*, 20 rooms.

MARDIN. *Başak Palas*, 11 rooms and *Turistik Palas*, 18 rooms.

MUŞ. *Üzel Idare* (3), 40 rooms with shower; *Turistik*, 30 rooms, some showers; *Belediye*, 17 rooms.

PASINLER. 25 miles east of Erzurum on Route 2: *Kale* (4) 36 rooms with shower.

SIIRT. *Özgen Palas*, 19 rooms (4 with shower).

TATVAN. *Karaman*, 13 rooms, boarding houses and bungalows.

TUG. Small hotel.

TUNCELI. *Turistik Palas*, 24 rooms; *Çelik Palas*, 17 rooms.

URFA. *Altay Palas*, 24 rooms; *Ipek Palas*, 45 rooms.

VAN. *Beşkardeş* (4), 41 rooms (12 showers): *Turistik* (4), 20 rooms with shower; *Nuh Palas* (4), 43 rooms; *Divan*, 13 rooms; *Saydan Palas*, 6 rooms.

USEFUL ADDRESSES. *Tourist Offices:* in Diyarbakir, Erzurum, Hakkâri, Van, Yüksekova (ask for *turizm bürosu*) and when at the Turkey-Iran border station in Gürbulak. *Airlines: Türk Hava Yollari* in Diyarbakir, Inönü Cad., Surpalas; in Erzurum, Cumhuriyet Cad., Kızılöy Iş Hani; in Erzincan, Hükümet Cad.; in Elaziğ, Istasyon Cad. (Post Office); in Malatya, Istasyon Cad. 70; in Urfa, Sarayönü Hazaer Pasaji; in Van, Serefiye Cad. 142/2.

Ferry boats of the *Denizcilik Bankası* (Maritime Bank), carrying cars, cross Lake Van in 2 routes: Tatvan (Tug)-Ahlat-Adilcevaz-Erciş, by the northern shore 9 hours and a half; and Tatvan (Tuğ)-Reşadiye-Van, by the southern shore, 6 hours. For the timetable, apply in Istanbul to the *Denizcilik Bankası*, Denizyolları Işletmesi Salıpazarı; or to the *Acenteliği*, Rıhtım Cad., Karaköy.

Exploring the Eastern Provinces

We advise you to pick out your own itinerary and then check out the road situation on the spot. (Although this book provides a list of likely stopping points, it cannot attempt a day-by-day survey of the state of highways under construction.)

It's quite a way from Sivas to Erzurum, 302 miles on Route 2 (E23), most of it unpaved and very exhausting indeed. Motorists should bear in mind that because of heat (in summer), dust, and sheer travel-weariness, a trip that at home would be just an average lap in a journey can begin to feel like hard labor in Turkey. If you set out from Trabzon (Trebizond), the road is less arduous, much shorter, and definitely more enjoyable. You will cross the Zigana Pass (*Zigana Geçidi*, 6,600 feet) and the Kop Pass (*Kopdaği Geçidi*), at 8,000 feet. Storms can burst here so suddenly that even the most cautious traveler can be caught unaware. The local inhabitants have installed a bell—a relic from an Armenian church in the east—which tolls a warning whenever the wind begins to show signs of blowing up.

There is an alternate route to Erzurum starting from Rize, on the Black Sea, passing via Ispir. This isn't as good a road as the one described above for crossing the Pontic Range, and it emerges onto the plain only a few miles from the city. Lastly, you can drive over a road that begins at Hopa, right near the Russian frontier. It wends its way through dense mountain forests, crosses the Pontic peaks at the Borçka Pass, and comes out at Artvin. This particular itinerary will be described in more detail for the trip from Artvin to Erzurum, later.

Coming back to our first itinerary, the Sivas-Erzurum road (E23), there are two side excursions with which to break the monotony. First, there is Divriği (turn off to the right at Zara), which is the old Byzantine Tephrike. It boasts a 13th-century Seljuk fortress, and an even older mosque within its enclosure walls. The Ulu Cami, or Great Mosque, and the hospital next door to it also date from the 13th century. The northeast portal, or Taç Kapisi, is richly carved. Both of these are exceptionally lovely works of architecture. It is only too bad that Divriği is still so hard to reach, but priority is being given to more urgent work near by, such as the completion of the Zara-Refahiye main road.

Erzincan in the upper Euphrates valley, about halfway between Sivas and Erzurum, is of no particular interest. However, 13 miles further on lie the Altintepe diggings, a necropolis in which Urartean funerary artifacts have been discovered. Turkish archeologists have also unearthed here the remains of a palace and temple.

Erzurum is a big town, at an altitude of 6,500 feet, with 100,000 population. (Beware of winter weather here—it can be bitterly cold.) Under its earlier name of Theodosiopolis, this was one of the eastern bastions of Byzantium at the peak of the latter's prime. After the seventh century, the Byzantines managed to wrest it from the Arabs on recurrent occasions, during the periods of strife that rent the Moslem world asunder—the struggle for the caliphate and the wars between the Ommeyyads and the Abbassids. The Armenians gained a foothold here around the year 1,000, but the city fell to the Seljuks in the famous battle of Malazgirt (1071). The etymology of the city's present name is "Arz", or "world", and "Er Rum" ("of the Roman").

One early 19th-century historian listed Erzurum under its Armenian name of Garen. He described it as having narrow, ill-paved streets, and terrace-roofed houses built of brick, stone, or wood that were all "low, unclean structures". He failed to note any interesting works of architecture aside from the citadel and the Ulu Cami mosque. However, he did admit to being impressed by the amount of brisk trading that was being carried on, and by the warehouse full of goods both on their way from and en route toward India and Persia. This writer's population estimate is also interesting—150 years ago, he counted 100,000 inhabitants, including "2,500 schismatic Armenians, 1,600 Catholics, 400 Greeks, and the remainder Turks". (J. Mac-Carthy, *Dictionnaire de geographie*, Paris, 1841).

The Ulu Cami, built in the latter half of the 12th century, is still standing, complete with its beautiful colonnaded courtyard. Nearby lies the citadel, with its own mosque and minaret, bright with gleaming tilework, its walls intact. We feel much more lenient than Mr. MacCarthy, and urge you to visit the Çifte ("double") Minare Medrese, built in 1253, as well as the truncated minaret of the Yakutiye Medrese, from the early 14th century. The first of these two Koranic colleges— built by Alâeddin Keykubat—is now a museum. The Hatuniye Türbesi, which is the mauso-leum of this great man's daughter, is also located in Erzurum. Among the other mausolea, the most interesting is the circular Emir Sultan Türbesi.

After some fierce fighting in 1916, the Russians occupied Gümüshane, on E100 east of Erzurum, evacuating in it 1918. This is a community that is quite literally on the move—it has progressed over two miles since World War I! The old part of town is now just a mass of virtually uninhabitable ruins. By the time of your visit, the frescoes on the walls of the old Byzantine churches may have been completely uncovered. It seems that the route followed by the Ten Thousand in Xenophon's march to the sea was the Ispir-Bayburt-Gümüshane route. There aren't too many souvenirs of Xenophon cluttering up Bayburt's bazaars (population 13,000). A Seljuk citadel overlooking the town, on E100 midway between Erzurum and Gümüshane, affords a breathtaking view. Satala, near Bayburt, was the site of the Roman Legions' remotest outpost . . . or its nearest one, depend-ing on one's point of view.

Three Ways to Kars

The best, and also the shortest, road from Erzurum to Kars (142 miles), runs through Horasan, mostly parallel to the rail route. At Andereköy, you might just enjoy making your way to Mecinbert castle, and from Karakurt you can take another side-trip off E23 to see the Çangili church. These two venerable relics have come down from the Armenian epoch.

There are two other ways of getting to Kars, but the situation involved is a bit like running away from home—you need a stiff upper lip and a stout conveyance. Your extra time and trouble will be amply rewarded by the sight of the landscape's wild, al-most arrogant beauty, which is virtually untouched, and by the various stops to be made along the way. One of these two alter-nate roads climbs north on Route 75 to Artvin, veers east toward Ardahan, and finally continues southwards on Route 20. This is the longer road (298 miles)—it's advisable to investigate its state of repair before plunging ahead. And don't even give it a thought except in the summertime!

You will gain some idea of the inaccessibility of this entire region by remembering that, throughout history, it was never once "occupied" by conquerors. Although the big bosses did occasionally divide up the country nominally, for all practical purposes the local Armenian prince—mainly David of Tayk—enjoyed complete autonomy, punctuated now and then by punitive expeditions fitfully organized by his overlords. It would be idle to attempt to describe at any length the beautiful Çoruh River basin, the gorges, the peaks, and the meticulously "manicured" fields. About 14 miles beyond Tortum on Route 75, you will enjoy taking the trail off to the left leading to Haho (a two-hour hike), where, in the 10th century, David of Tayk built a Georgian monastery, which is now a mosque.

The purposeful peregrinator who is undaunted by resorting to shank's mare will once again leave his car, this time at Öşk, to walk to Vank for a look at another monastery from this same period. Although local farmers are using it as a storehouse, the building is in a remarkably fine state of preservation. Take time for another halt at the end of Lake Tortum (an exquisite gem), where you can marvel at the Tortum Çay waterfalls from the opposite side of the road. Some fourteen miles farther on, another foot trail (right side of the highway) leads to the village of Işhan. Here you will find the cruciform Church of the Mother of God (10th-century), which was damaged in World War I. Notice the lovely bas-reliefs on its outside walls. From Yusufeli, you can visit two more churches—Dört Kilise (10th-century Georgian) to the southwest, and Parhal, near Sarigöl, to the north.

In the course of your wanderings along the Black Sea, you may have already explored Artvin and either visited or skipped (depending on your energies) the local fortress. The road from Yusufeli to Artvin, which crosses through the Çoruh gorges, may be in poor condition, but that doesn't prevent it from boasting some of the most spectacular views in all Turkey.

The environs are so crammed with other great things to see that you can afford to miss the ruins of Dalis Han. Now you're entering the valley of one of the Çoruh's tributaries, the Imerhevi. Churches, monasteries, and convents abound on all sides. The Opiza Basilica dates from the eighth century. As far as the landscape itself is concerned, there's no need to list its many attractions. Besides, it's more fun to be surprised and enraptured at every turn, and the beauty of the scenery is enough to bring the most blasé motorist to a screeching halt. The forests, peaks, and precipices are unlike anything you've ever beheld elsewhere.

Ardahan is a sturdy garrison town. It was Russian at the beginning of the century, and the Turks didn't regain it until 1921.

But we still haven't reached our destination—there are 62 miles yet to go, your sights are set on Kars, and after all this extra sightseeing, it would be mean to make your passengers stop again.

The Middle Road

And we must explore the middle road from Erzurum, Route 22 (172 miles) long. Although it is frequently in pretty bad shape, repairs are constantly under way. This road shoots off from Route 75, the northern, Artvin, road, after Tortum. Oltu, which we go through next, was the capital of the Tayk princes mentioned a while back. Here stand a castle, a church, and some mosques.

The Lazes aren't the sole inhabitants of the region. From Artvin on, you'll be seeing the Kurds, who are equally deserving of special mention. Their fierce mien and their equally fierce mustaches set them apart. The Kurds, of Semitic origin, live in tribes, and speak a language belonging to the Iranian group. They are Moslems of the Sunnite, or orthodox, branch. The Kurdish race is a hot-blooded one, and has ceaselessly defended its independence against all challengers, including the Russians, Turks, Persians, and Iraqis. Kurdish women are considerably more self-assertive than their Turkish counterparts, and fully as courageous as the men. They have never worn the veil, and they definitely have a say in community matters.

No conqueror ever succeeded in absorbing the Kurds. However, their own petty domestic quarrels have prevented them from becoming a homogeneous force. The Kurds now number some five million people, 1.5 million of whom live in Turkish territory. After centuries of turbulent nomadic existence, they are at last beginning to simmer down, subsequent to a few rather violent clashes with authority, and are engaged in agriculture and stock-breeding. These "mountain Turks" are thus gradually making the transition from nomadic to sedentary living. (In Istanbul, Kurds form the majority of the members of the dock-workers and stevedores' corporation.) The Kurds in northeastern Anatolia are in the process of relinquishing their horses and tents in favor of a more settled existence. In the southeast, however, the evolution is being accomplished more slowly.

Kars

For centuries Kars was the stake over which bitter fighting took place. The town lies in the heart of the area that both Turks and Russians have been vying for over many centuries. To the Russians, Kars represents the key city of Transcaucasia. For the Turks, it is a defense point along the Erzurum road, and a block against potential invasion of Anatolia from the north.

Consequently, the city's history is that of the successive sieges it has withstood. In the 11th century, the Seljuks expelled the Armenian princes from Kars. Tamerlane then proceeded to streak it with his bloody mark. The vicissitudes of the Russo-Turkish wars caused it to fall into the hands of the Czars on three different occasions during the 19th century—in 1828, 1855, and 1877. The irresistible tides of the Turkish war of independence swept it back under Turkish domination in 1921. Kars has its own local tradition of heroism—for five months during the Crimean War, a Turkish garrison of 15,000 men held out here against 40,000 Czarist troops.

Kars is the center of a thriving farming community, noted for its butter and other dairy produce. Men who only yesterday were still roving warriors now spend their time tending flocks or processing milk in great round moulds. The resultant "solid" wheels of excellent cheese are distributed throughout Turkey. To the casual traveler, Kars (population 30,000) may look just a bit forbidding. It's a typical frontier town, cold and greyish, perched at 6,000 feet and at the mercy of the winds. An old Georgian fort overhangs it from a high rocky vantage point, looking for all the world like something out of a comic strip, dangling out over the Kars River that winds around its feet. The heap of grey rock beneath that looks like a millstone is the Armenian church. Its interior is embellished with circular niches representing the Twelve Apostles. Originally dedicated to the Holy Apostles in the tenth century, this church was converted into the Kümbet Cami by the Seljuks, and eventually reconsecrated by the Russians at the end of the 19th century.

The old and new parts of town stretch out on either side of the river, forming its upper and lower levels. The old bridge between them is of Seljuk origin. A weekly train runs from Kars to Kizilçakçak, at which point it is taken in tow by a Soviet locomotive as far as Gümrü-Leninakan, just across the border. There is also a highway open, with Armenian monuments all along the way, including the tenth-century Argina basilica and the Tiknia castle. The frontier post is 49 miles away.

Up to the time of the devastating Mongol invasion, Ani (Aniköy) was a prosperous rival to Kars. These days, it's hard to say which is in a sorrier plight—the town or the road leading there. However, your drive over this dirt track will be worth it, if only for you to gaze on the redoubtable great wall that used to defend the city lying between two deep ravines. Of all its past glories, including the "thousand and one" churches of bygone days, scarcely half a dozen remain standing. What was once a city of 200,000 people is now merely a village. The ruins and the reddish rocks have suffered a further invasion by tall weeds and thistles. The two rivers that wind their boiling black waters around what is virtually the "ghost town" of Ani put one in mind of snakes coiling possessively around a treasure.

Make it a point to visit the remnants of the Georgian Church (early 13th century); the Church of St. Gregory of Gagik, which was built in the year 1,000; the Church of the Holy Apostles (built just a few years later); and the Church of Gregory of Abugamrentz (tenth century). The cathedral was originally Armenian, became a Seljuk mosque in 1064 (50 years after its building), and was restored to Christendom in the 13th century by the Georgians. The Church of St. Gregory of Honentz dates from a slightly later time (1215): note the truly remarkable mural decorations in the interior. Clinging to the heights overlooking the Arpa River, the Menucer Mosque also emphasizes the Armenian influences. Take the climb up to the first citadel, and continue on to the second, at the far edge of town, where the two gorges converge.

Recommended excursions: the Horomotz monastery, 10th century (ten miles northeast); the Bagnaïr monastery, also 10th century, 14 miles west; and the Magasbert fortress. Give the shock-absorbers a rest and stretch your legs for a change. (The trip to Digor is recommended to only the sturdiest hikers in top form.)

Mount Ararat

The name of Büyük ("great") Ağri Dağı probably doesn't ring a bell. You know only that it's a mountain, or *dağı*, and you've noticed on your map the town of Ağri (which is of no particular interest). All this just happens to be Mount Ararat territory. "In the six hundredth year of Noah's life, in the second month, the seventeenth day of the month, the same day were all the fountains of the great deep broken up, and the windows of heaven were opened" (Genesis VII : 11). That was the Deluge. "And God remembered Noah ... and the waters assuaged ... And it came to pass in the six hundredth and first year, in the first month, the first day of the month, the waters were dried up from off the earth; and Noah removed the covering of the ark, and looked, and behold, the face of the ground was dry" (Genesis VIII : 1, 13). The survivors had just landed on top of the Büyük Ağri Dağı. Connoisseurs of wine will also find this a pious pilgrimage, for it was here on the slopes of this mountain that Noah discovered the grapevine.

On either side lie two small settlements. Iğdir can be reached by a climb up the northern slope (the shortest route goes via Aralik, but is fraught with hazards—all but the staunchest alpinists beware!). Doğubeyazıt is to the south, and you can begin your ascension from here, too. The lofty peak of Mount Ararat soars up nearly 17,000 feet. Its spurs thrust out into Russia and Iran, and its hidden roots are steeped in the fragrance of roses and oil.

The mountain itself is an extinct volcano. There is scant likelihood that over a period of 6,000 years whatever fragments of the Ark may once have been there could have survived all the many earthquakes and volcanic eruptions. The two versions of the Book of Genesis (the Yahwist, from the seventh century B.C., and the Sacerdotal, from the sixth century B.C.) both

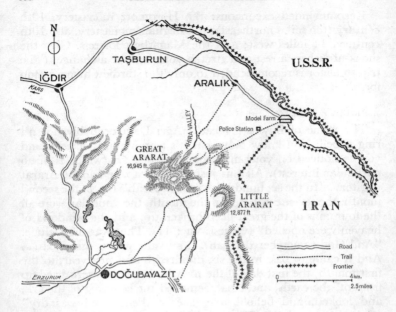

provide a complete and concordant account of the Deluge. A Chaldean priest named Berossus, in the third century B.C., bequeathed to posterity a similar report (based on Eusebius of Caesarea), in which Noah appears as "Xisuthros" and Jehovah is called "Chronos". Tablets deciphered from among those found in Ashurbanipal's library at Nineveh (seventh century B.C.) recount the Epic of Gilgamesh, whose ancestor Utnapishtim (none other than Noah himself) duly constructed an ark when ordered to by the god Ea. The Babylonians likewise have handed down an almost identical version. The tradition—or the legend, unless, of course, all this is historical fact—of the deluge and the ark is known even in China. Scientists agree that during the fourth millenium B.C., a veritable cataclysm may have occurred, accompanied by rains and floods.

It remains to be seen whether Noah's Ark, or its debris, is really still where it is presumed to have landed. A Frenchman, Fernand Navarra, who is an archeologist, historian, and amateur mountain-climber, claims to have actually laid eyes on the Ark. He brought back with him wooden fragments of what is supposedly the Ark. These bits of wood have been conceded by the experts to be at least 5,000 years old. Navarra's book, *J'ai trouvé l'Arche de Noé* (*I Found Noah's Ark*), published in 1955, nonetheless aroused considerable controversy. He writes that, along the bottom of a passageway on a slightly sloping terrain at the top of the mountain, he perceived "through the thickness of ice, some dark and intermingled outlines. These could only be fragments of the Ark . . ." Digging through the ice until he reached water, he "touched with numbed fingers a piece of wood, not just something from a tree-branch, but wood that had been shaped and squared off".

Prior to this adventure, a few Turks, who had climbed the mountain in 1840 to set up anti-avalanche barrages had also noted the "prow of an ancient vessel emerging from a glacier". In 1876, James Bryce, an Englishman, discovered "amid blocks of lava, a piece of wood about four feet long and five inches wide, which had obviously been shaped by means of a tool". Most recently, an elderly American was reported to have abandoned his fifth attempt to find the Ark in the summer of 1967.

It is only fair at this point to warn potential mountain-climbers that their favorite pastime is frowned on here because of the proximity of the Russian frontier. In addition, Turkish authorities decline all responsibility in this connection because of the many risks involved, the difficulties of the ascension, suspicious Kurdish nomads, the danger of avalanches, and divers technical problems. Lately, some Kurds seem to be offering "tourist" accommodation to outsiders in their *yaylas* (transient camps). Whatever the case, the native themselves shun the mountain, either through indifference or superstition, or both. Despite this impressive array of local hindrances, traditional Western stubbornness has managed to prevail, and today, with a bit of luck and pluck, you can hire horses and guides at Iğdir, Aralik, and Doğubayazit. This last-named was moved to a new site in the 1930's; but high above the abandoned earlier village rises the Ishak Paşa Saray, a fairytale castle built by a Kirdish chief in a fantastic mixture of Armenian, Georgian, Persian and Seljuk styles in the 18th century. The magnificent view from this

romantic conglomoration ranges over the valley guarded by a
Genoese fortress to the western spur of Ararat.

Lake Van

The area around the huge body of water called Lake Van is
the only place with a limited number of facilities for accommo-
dating tourists. Every village of any importance boasts at least a
hotel or a pension. The surrounding countryside is magnificent,
and its varied décor contains settings to startle the jaded eyes of
the most blasé cameraman. People who think Lake Geneva looks
like a sea will feel here as if they're standing on the edge of a
boundless ocean—Lake Van is seven times bigger. Although the
presence of water generally connotes the existence of life, Lake
Van's shores are dry and desolate, and few fish live in its surface
waters. (The main catch here is the *darekh*, the "poor man's
herring", which is a staple item in the local diet.) The fact is that
Lake Van contains sulphur springs at a depth of 300 feet
(along the shore) and at 600 feet (in its center), which impart
an excessively high salt content to the water. It's rather like the
Dead Sea, except that the latter lies 1,300 feet below the level of
the Mediterranean, while Lake Van stands at an altitude of
nearly 6,000 feet!

The landscape roundabout is like nothing that most mortals
have ever seen. The scenery is the result of a landslide that occurred sometime in the tertiary epoch, and it looks utterly wild, untouched by human hands. Whatever their reasons may be, local
dwellers have left the land alone, and a true nature-lover occasionally goes so far as to feel a pang of resentment at seeing even the
small boat that plies across the lake. In the wintertime, naviga-
tion is impossible—fierce, unpredictable storms make it too
treacherous. The scattered lakeside settlements are by no means
safe from the water's fury. In the 19th century, a flash flood
completely inundated a number of localities, including Arsis and
Kale, which have remained under water. There is no known
outlet for Lake Van's excess liquid. Within five years, the fluctua-
tions in its water level can vary as much as ten feet. The scheme
of things here is far beyond the merely human scale.

Although Van province was inhabited long before our era,
history's first significant mention of it is with reference to the

creation of an Armenian principality known as the Vannic, in the seventh century. Under Arab sovereignty, this later became the Kingdom of Vaspurakan. The Turkish conquest brought about no changes in the population structure, which continued to be Armenian and Kurdish, two minorities that were sharply differentiated by their languages, religions, and origins. In addition, there were other religious minorities, including the Nestorian (among the Christians) and the Yezidis (among the Moslems).

The town of Van, on the east shore, was the capital of the Urartu kingdom and later on, of the Armenian kingdom of Vaspurakan. It has never fully recovered from the World War I fighting between Turks and Russians that occurred here. Interested visitors will appreciate the Urartean cuneiform inscriptions adorning the citadel hill, ruins of Armenian churches, of Seljuk and Ottoman mosques, and the tombs that are hollowed out of sheer rock. Archeology enthusiasts will enjoy inspecting the Toprakkale mound, three miles east, where various teams of diggers have uncovered the remains of a Urartean city.

If you're not too demanding as far as creature comforts are concerned, you can spend a truly memorable vacation in the Van area. It's the best way to find time for visiting the localities near the lake, notably Erciş in the north, and to make side-trips to the many mausolea of Turkish dignitaries, as well as to the Urartu citadel, repaired, amongst others, by Sinan in the reign of Suleiman the Magnificent at Ahlat. All of these are highly recommended to travelers, including the young and the less young, who have a hankering for the adventurous life with the aid of good camping equipment, or who have a healthy indifference to creature comforts.

Note: You will see the Süphan Dağı (13,750 feet) rising up north and west of the lake with, to the south and west, the Nemrut Dağı. The latter isn't the one you may think it is, and climbing it is a feat that not everybody should undertake. And anyhow, this peak of the extinct volcano (about 10,000 feet high) despite the luxuriant vegetation round the crater lake, doesn't begin to compare with the *real* Nemrut Dağı.

Eastward lies Hakkari province, wedged in like a knife-blade between Iraq and Iran. It has one single road, which passes

Hoşap (39 miles from Van) with an unexpected Genoese castle above the river, and the town of Hakkari. There are excavations of settlements dating from 2,600 B.C. at Resibayn, even older rock carvings in the Gevarik Valley, and some vestiges of a flourishing Urartu principality between 900 and 600 B.C. The main attraction lies, however, in the natural beauty of the Cilo and Sat mountains (see p. 377) and of the Zap Valley, but you proceed at your own risk.

To the south, the road ends at Çukurca, before the Iraqi frontier. The only stray souls you're likely to encounter are a few Kurdish nomads. Don't be dismayed by their wild looks—in all probability, they'll offer to put you up in the shelter of their *yaylas*. The only problem is whether Westerners can take this particular form of hospitality.

This is a miraculously untamed area, wilder even than the appearance of its inhabitants, and it has as yet barely been explored. At one time, it became the refuge of the Nestorian heretics subsequent to their condemnation by the Council of Ephesus in 431. About a thousand years later, they fled there in still greater numbers to escape from Tamerlane. The Nestorians survived the Kurd's animosity, only to succumb finally to the friendship of Czarist Russia, which evacuated them in World War I, thereby spelling the doom of this once-tenacious community.

After Van, the road skirts the southern shore of the lake. The 10th-century monastery of Surp Agop is here. On an island opposite Gevaş (where rowboats are for hire) there stands the Aktamar basilica, also tenth century, one of the most exquisite architectural treats in the vicinity, with its peculiar blend of Christian and Islamic art. The well-preserved exterior reliefs illustrate contemporary history. Tatvan, further west, is a deservedly popular summer resort.

Bitlis (132 miles), in a narrow valley, commands at over 5,000 feet the only gateway to the west among the towering mountains. Countless bridges span the river below the Hellenistic citadel and there is the usual variety of Seljuk and Ottoman mosques. The Kurds in Bitlis did not submit to control until the 19th century. You will see a 16th-century Serefi Cami, and a caravanseray called the Sarafhan.

Malazgirt (north of the lake, to the west of Patnos) has had

too much said about it to be left out. This is the site at which Byzantium was crushed by the first Seljuks, in 1071. Its black stone
wall is still in an excellent state of preservation. Muş (43 miles
northwest) and Siirt (60 miles southwest) both possess all the
required local color in lovely natural setting. Elazig (139 miles
west of Muş), has a Harput fortress.

Diyarbakir, Mardin and Urfa

Southwest of the Eastern Provinces lie three more cities that
merit fuller attention.

The name of Diyarbakir in Arabic signifies the "City of the
tribes of Bakir". These tribes changed for their own benefit the
earlier name of the city, Amida, under which name it was founded
by the Hurri-Mittani. After absorption into the Assyrian empire,
interrupted by a century of Urartu domination, followed by the
now familiar succession of Medes, Persians and Macedonians,
Diyarbakir came under successive domination by Romans,
Sassanids, and Byzantines. Then came the Moslems, including
the Ommeyyades, the Abbassids, and the Marwanids, who
battled with one another for possession of the city, a period that
was punctuated by occasional (temporary) but redoubtable
reoccupations by the Byzantines. Absolutely everybody was
after this place—the Turkomans, the Ortokids, the Eastern and
the Western Seljuks. Next came the Mongolian hordes. Finally,
Selim I made it an Ottoman city and it settled into a relatively
calm period, disturbed only by a few scattered Kurdish incursions
that barely made a dent.

Diyarbakir's triple walls of black basalt, constructed by the
Emperor Constantius in 349, have been kept in a constant state
of good repair by their various occupiers, and are still in excellent
shape along their entire length (close on to three miles) encircling
the city. Be sure to go to the Frankish Gate, Bab El Rumi (also
called the Urfa Gate). And there are also the Great Bastion, or
Ulu Badan; Bab El Tell (the Mardin Gate); Yeni Kapı (or New
Gate); and the Harput Gate—in other words, all the main gateways and defense towers of the city walls. Inside the town, the
most interesting sights in Diyarbakir are its citadel in the elevated
northeast corner, where the tiled walls of the Artukid palace
surround an octagonal pool and the Ulu Cami, dating in its

present form, with Corinthian marble columns, from the 12th century. Numerous mosques and medreses furnish an exhaustive illustration of Moslem religious architecture, complemented by two caravanserays, eight baths and an occasional ruined Byzantine church. The local museum is housed in the Zincirli, a former theological college building; the exhibits cover a period of some 4,000 years.

And, of course, you know that the river flowing nearby is a famous one—it's the Tigris. The most widely-accepted hypothesis has always been that the cradle of humanity lay in the area between the Tigris and the Euphrates (*Dicle* and *Firat*, in Turkish). It is assumed, therefore, that this region witnessed the mutation of *homo sapiens*, with the concomitant rise and fall of his various civilizations. Some scholars boldly claim that this was the site of the earthly paradise, the Garden of Eden. However, the scene as it looks today bears not the remotest resemblance to the one described in the Old Testament, afflicted as it is by drought, dust, and stark stretches of rough country. Whatever primordial lushness may once have existed hereabouts has been replaced by a barren landscape.

The present population of the town of Mardin is 30,000. Its ancestor, Marida, was no less important in the Hurri-Mittani and Assyrian empires, though often threatened by neighboring Amida and Nisibis. The Roman citadel with its 800-yard frontage was reputedly impregnable as neither the Seljuks in the 12th century nor the Mongols in the 13th managed to capture it. The only victor here was Tamerlane, at the tail-end of the 14th century. And when he returned to Mardin in 1401 in an attempt to crush the revolt of his own brother, Isa, this time the citadel resisted even Tamerlane.

England may have had its War of the Two Roses, but the Turks, in the 15th century, had a War of the Two Sheep (the *ak*, white; *kara*, black, war). This particular area served as the chessboard for their rivalry, with Mardin as one of its pawns. Bear this in mind when you visit what is left of its fortress. Also see the Latifiye Cami (built in 1371); the Ulu Cami (with its rectangular minaret dating from the 12th century, restored in the 14th and 15th, disfigured in the 19th); and the Sultan Isa Medrese (1385), remarkable for the exquisite stone carvings and exedra; the stately Kasim Paşa Medrese of the following century; mosques, medreses, türbes (those of Zeynel Mirza and Imam Abdullah are noteworthy for their delicate ornamentation) and the 17th-century covered bazaar.

The road southeast to the Syrian border (42 miles, E24) passes the ruins of Dara and the frontier fortress of Anastasiopolis, founded by the Emperor Anastasius in the sixth century. Road and railway cross into Syria at Nusaybin, ancient Nisibis, mentioned in Assyrian inscriptions some 3,000 years ago, and constantly fought over as witnessed by a Roman triumphal arch, a castle and numerous tombs. The border crossing at Derbesiye, due south, though closer, is less frequented.

The Tur Abdin plateau lying northeast of Mardin, near Savur, was a prominent stronghold of Christianity as early as the fourth century. The Syrian church founded a large number of monasteries here, some of which were occupied up until the early 1900's. The Midyat area farther on contains several interesting churches dating from the eighth to the twelfth centuries—in Salah, the Mar Yakub; near Arnas, the Mar Kyriakos and the Mar Azaziel; in Kakh, El Hadra; and the fifth-century Mar Gabriel monastery, near the village of Kartmen.

To be called Hurri in the second millenium B.C. is sufficient proof of outstanding importance in the Hurri-Mittani empire. But it is under its Macedonian name of Edessa that present-day Urfa became best known in the West, as a romantically forlorn Crusader outpost conquered by Count Baldwin, second king of Jerusalem. Heroism and treachery, reversals of fortune unparalleled even in this turbulent corner are crammed within the 150 years the Latin principality precariously maintained itself among the powerful Moslem territories. Even now Urfa's 40,000 inhabitants are crowded between the 25 towers of the Crusader citadel on a spur of Mount Damlacik and the outer ramparts. The 17th-century mosque of Halil Rahman is particularly attractive with its cupolas and minaret reflected in a large pool, a rare pleasure in this burning land. Local tradition places the birth of Abraham in a cave to the south, while Genesis XI : 31, 32 mentions that the patriarch on his way from Ur to Canaa rested for several years at Charan, present Harran, near the Syrian border station of Akçakale. The countryside is studded with Byzantine and

Crusader castles; the best-preserved are at Harran, Birecik and Siverek.

Malatya and Nemrut Dağı

Malatya lies in a fertile plain at the foot of the Anti-Taurus, a welcome change in the endless steppe extending from Kayseri to Elazig. The prosperous but uninteresting market town of 50,000 inhabitants developed on its present site only after 1838, four miles west of Hittite Milidia (now Arslantepe) and five miles southwest of Roman Melitene (Eski Malatya). Milidia became a Hurri principality, an Assyrian dependency, a vassal of Urartu. Abandoned after the Cimmerian incursion in the seventh century B.C., the excavations at Arslantepe have yielded up precious finds in the way of objects from ancient Hittite settlements, notably bas-reliefs and the foundations of the palace of the eighth-century B.C. Assyrian king, Sargon II. After an interval of some 700 years, the Romans established a legion headquarters at Melitene, which was later fortified by Justinian and promptly taken by the Persians. Occupied by the Arabs in 640, Malatya was plundered and burnt down with monotonous regularity by Byzantines and Moslems till the advent of an Armenian adventurer who was miraculously delivered from his Seljuk besiegers by the opportune arrival of the First Crusade. Then, in 1243, came an incredible switching-over of alliances. When the Mongols laid siege to the city, it was jointly defended by Christians and Moslems! Traces of the double wall of Eski Malatya can still be seen. The Ulu Cami is a handsome edifice of Seljuk origin on which a certain amount of 15th-century repairs managed to wreak not too much havoc.

Last, but certainly not least, there remains one of the most difficult but also uniquely rewarding excursions, almost an expedition, to the Nemrut Dağı. The distance from Urfa is shorter, but the track to all intent and purposes is impracticable. So take the Malatya–Gaziantep road (E99, Route 5) until Gölbaşi (75 miles). From here, branch off to the left (eastwards) onto an even less perfect stretch of track (Route 59) to reach Adiyaman and Kahta, which are, *quite* roughly 42 and an additional 25 miles distant. Leave the car here, hire your mules and guides through the local *muhtar* (head-man), and your adventures have begun!

(Part of the first portion of the ascent can be done in a jeep.)

Approximately six miles ahead, at the base of a hill, stands a splendid column bedecked with the Roman eagle (which has become acephalic, or single-headed, its "other head having been gnawed away by the starving centuries"). Originally there were more columns, all marking the tombs of the queens of Commagene. An authentic Roman bridge conveys you safely over the Cendere Suyu (*suyu* = "water"). A short distance beyond, you are greeted by a medieval citadel, Yeni Kale. And then you reach Eski Kahta (*eski* = old). In 1952, the site of ancient Arsameia was uncovered here, and was found to contain, among other things, the funerary monument erected by Antiochus I, King of Commagene, in memory of his father, Mithridates.

The fun really begins after you've left Eski Kahta. It's no picnic for the mule, either, who's sometimes up to his knees in water. Occasionally his load must be lightened, and you have to dismount entirely. Strictly for good sports! Every least pebble and blade of grass fairly shouts of tragedy. The landscape is grandiose in its sheer desolation. It's a hike of several hours to the point from which the top of the Nemrut Dağı finally looms into sight. As a supreme mockery, Antiochus I selected the highest peak, visible from all around, for the site of his own monument.

At last you reach the top, and what a spectacle awaits you! You'll agree that all the toil and trouble were worth it. Although people promptly proceeded to forget all about Antiochus I, he had wanted them not to, and in this vain hope he had built on the topmost pinnacle a huge tumulus thrusting up 200 feet in the air! It took a series of fortuitous events, aided by the benign virus of archeological fever, for a properly identified Antiochus I to get even a nod from 20th-century historians, despite this proud monarch's elaborate precautions, including invoking the assistance of the divinities, the erecting of colossal statues 25 to 35 feet tall, and the laying out of vast terraces. The inscription reads: "I, Antiochus, caused this monument to be erected in commemoration of my own glory and of that of the gods". It was inevitable that through the centuries such vainglory should fall prey to the forces of erosion, to thunderbolts (unleashed by jealous gods?), to earthquakes, and to the ravages of time itself. The gigantic statues have lost their once lofty heads, which by now have been thoughtfully set upright on the ground and arranged around the incredible tumulus.

There may even be a temple concealed beneath. So far, extensive explorations by experienced and eager archeologists have failed to bring to light any passageway, if indeed one exists. Despite the elaborate precautions observed, all the attempts at excavating have caused cave-ins. The experts hesitate to persist, lest the whole extraordinary monument should collapse. It's something of a feat just to have uncovered the statues and heads. (As recently as 1962, a thunderstorm brought the last one crashing down—ironically enough, it was the head of the goddess Fortuna.)

It is obvious that a veritable army of men, in all likelihood slaves, must have toiled like ants for an inestimable time to heap up this pyramid of small rocks on a mountain top, just to perpetuate the name of a master drunk with his own power. Now, two millennia later (Antiochus died in 34 B.C.), the miracle of discovery has resuscitated the extraordinary array, and the world is at least aware that this man, too, lived and dreamed his dreams of grandeur. The enormity of his wager is somehow stirring, its very naïveté touching.

And no less a miracle is the scope and structure of contemporary tourism, geared to enable the modern traveler to roam where his fancy dictates. These days, for the price of an air ticket, anyone who feels so inclined can go pay his respects to King Antiochus's last monument.

Illustration at head of this chapter: Head of stone figure at Mausoleum of Antiochus, on Nemrut Daǧı.

SUPPLEMENTS

TURKISH-ENGLISH
TOURIST VOCABULARY

For hints on Turkish pronunciation, see the section
Language *in* Turkey: Facts and Figures *at front of book.*

GENERAL

English	Turkish
I don't understand	Anlamiyorum
Is there someone who can speak English (French)?	Ingilizce bilen birisi var mi? ... Fransizca ...?
Do you speak English(French)?	Ingilizce (Fransizca) konuşuyor musunuz?
Yes, No	Evet - Hayir
How do you do?	Memnun oldum
Very well	Çok iyi
Good day	Günaydin
Good evening	Iyi akşamlar
Goodbye	Allaha ismarladik - Gülegüle
Cheers! (Here's to you)	Şerefe
How are you?	Nasilsiniz?
Thanks, thank you very much	Teşekkür - Çok teşekkür ederim
Until tomorrow	Yarin görüşürüz
Until later	Yakinda görüşelim
I beg your pardon	Affedersiniz
If you please	Lûtfen
What do you want?	Ne istiyor sunuz?

AT THE STATION OR AIRPORT

Is there a train for ...?	... ye tren var mi?
... a dining car?	Vagon-restoran ...
... a sleeping car?	Kuşetli ...
... a seat?	Yer var mi?
I would like a ticket for ...	... e bir bilet istiyorum
... a roundtrip (return) ticket	Gidip-gelme bir bilet
... to reserve a seat	Yer tutmak istiyorum
First class	Birinci mevki
Second class	Ikinci mevki
When does the train for ...depart?	... ye tren saat kaçta kalkiyor?
Is it necessary to change (trains)?	Aktarmasi var mi?
Where?	Nerede?
When?	Ne zaman?
Is there an airplane (ship) for ...	... ye uçak (vapur) var mi?
What is the price of the ticket?	Bilet ücreti kaç lira?
Porter	Hamal

AT THE CUSTOMS

English	*Turkish*
Nothing to declare	Beyan edecek bir şeyim yok
For my personal use	Şahsî eşya
How much?	Ne kadar?

IN THE TOWN

What is it called?	Adi ne?
Where is?	Nerede?
Mosque	Cami
Church	Kilise
Museum	Müze
Street	Sokak
Square	Meydan
How do you get to ...?	... ye nasil gidilir?
Is it far?	Uzak mi?
Bank	Banka
Post office	Postahane
Station	Tren istasyonu
Police station	Karakol
City Hall	Belediye Binasi
American (British) consulate	Amerikan (İngiliz) Konsolosluğu
Airport	Hava alani
Theater	Tiyatro

SHOPPING

I want to buy ...	... Satin almak istiyorum
I want to see ...	... yi görmek istiyorum
Show me ... please	Lûtfen gösteriniz
This, that	Bu - öteki
It's too much	Bu çok pahali
I don't like that	Bu hoşuma gitmedi
Cigarettes	Sigara
Cigars	Püro
Tobacco	Tütün
Razor blades	Jilet biçaği
Stamps (postage)	Pul
Envelopes	Zarf
Writing paper	Mektup kâğidi
Postcard	Kartpostal
Souvenir	Hatira
Roll of film	Bir makara film
Cine (movie) film	Sinema filmi
Black and white	Siyah-beyaz
In color	Renkli
Flowers	Çiçek
A map of the city	Şehir plâni

English	*Turkish*
Lower the price	Fiyati daha indiriniz
I'll take it	Aliyorum
Can you wrap it, please	Paket yapar misiniz?

AT THE HOTEL

A good hotel	Iyi bir otel
One bed, two beds	Bir yatakli, iki yatakli
Is there a room available?	Boş odaniz var mi?
With bathroom	Banyolu
One person, two persons	Bir kişilik, iki kişilik
The key	Anahtar
Boy, porter	Garson - Kapici
Bathroom	Banyo
Hot bath	Sicak banyo
Toilet	Tuvalet, helâ
Ladies, gentlemen	Bayanlar - baylar
Blanket, quilt	Battaniye, yorgan
Table napkin	Peçete
Hot water	Sicak su
Chambermaid	Faındöşambr (Odaya bakan kadin)
Laundry	Çamaşir yikanmasi
Dry cleaning	Kuru temizleme
Come in	Giriniz
The bill	Hesap

AT THE RESTAURANT
(See also the chapter, Food and Drink)

Restaurant	Lokanta
I would like to have lunch ... dinner	Oğle yemeği yemek istiyorum
	Akşam ...
Bring me ...	... getiriniz
Give me ...	... veriniz
Drink	Içmek
White wine, red wine	Beyaz, kirmizi şarap
Mineral water	Maden suyu
Beer	Bira
Fruit juice	Meyva suyu
Bread	Ekmek
Butter	Tereyaği
Salt, pepper, mustard	Tuz, biber, hardal
One egg, some eggs, an omelette	Bir yumurta; ... yumurta, Omlet
Soup	Çorba
Fish	Balik
Meat	Et
Beefsteak (rare)	Bir biftek (az pişmiş)
Cheese	Peynir
Tea	Çay

English	Turkish
Coffee with milk	Sütlü kahve
Cakes	Pastalar
Fruits	Meyva

AT THE GARAGE (GARAJ)

English	Turkish
Fuel (petrol, gasolene)	Benzin
Fill it up	Doldurun
I am stranded (broken down) at ...	... de arabam bozuldu
Can you tow us?	Bizi çekebilir misiniz?
Sparkplug	Bir buji
Platinum screws	Plâtinli vida
Carburetor	Karbüratör
Gearbox	Vites kutusu
The spray	Jikle
Throttle	Gaz
Exhaust pipe	Egzos
Windshield (windscreen) wiper	Cam sileceği
Dynamo	Dinamo
Selfstarter	Marş
Brakes	Frenler
Brake linings	Fren aksami
Electric wire	Elektrik kablosu
Clutch	Debreyaj
Brake fluid	Idrolik yaği
Tires	Lâstikler
Puncture	Bir patlak
Headlights	Farlar
Radiator (leak)	Radyatör (su kaçiriyor)
Tank	Benzin deposu
Change of gear	Vites değiştirme
An accident	Bir kaza
Police	Jandarma
Doctor	Bir doktor
Ambulance	Ambülans - Cankurtaran
License	Ehliyet

NUMBERS

English	Turkish	English	Turkish
One	Bir	Eleven	Onbir
Two	Iki	Twelve	On iki
Three	Üç	Thirteen	On üç
Four	Dört	Fourteen	On dört
Five	Beş	Fifteen	On beş
Six	Alti	Sixteen	On alti
Seven	Yedi	Seventeen	On yedi
Eight	Sekiz	Eighteen	On sekiz
Nine	Dokuz	Nineteen	On dokuz
Ten	On	Twenty	Yirmi

Twenty-one	Yirmi bir	Eighty	Seksen
Thirty	Otuz	Ninety	Doksan
Forty	Kirk	One hundred	Yüz
Fifty	Elli	One hundred	
Sixty	Altmiş	and one	Yüz bir
Seventy	Yetmiş	Thousand	Bin

DAYS OF THE WEEK

Sunday	Pazar	Thursday	Perşenbe
Monday	Pazartesi	Friday	Cuma
Tuesday	Sali	Saturday	Cumartesi
Wednesday	Çarşanba		

COLORS

White	Ak	Green	Yeşil
Black	Kara	Yellow	Sari
Red	Kizil	Dark, light	Koyu - Açik
Sky Blue	Gök		
Blue	Mavi		

COMMON PLACE NAMES

City	Şehir	Mountain	Dağ
Village	Köy	Island	Ada
Castle	Hisar	River	Irmak
Tower	Kale	Stream	Çay
Hill	Tepe	Valley	Dere
Small	Küçük	Big	Büyük

GRECO-ROMAN MYTHOLOGY
AND ARCHEOLOGY

In addition to the many other wonders Turkey has to offer, those of the Hellenistic Period are of great importance. For the reader who can't quite remember his school-day lessons in mythology and archeology, we offer this capsulized version of what the ancient Greeks and Romans were up to in arts and religion:

GREEK MYTHOLOGY. The forces of nature that science could not explain at the time appeared to the Greeks as the work of superhuman beings, interpreted into the deeds of man. They set up gods in whom power, wisdom and eternal youth could not perish. They lived, under the rule of Zeus, on Mount Olympus. Rivalries and intrigues existed in their relationships and marriages, and they often associated with mortals, their offspring becoming demi-gods or heroes. The collection of stories about their adventures form the mythology of Greece.

The Romans, influenced by the arts and letters of Greece, often identified their gods with the divinities of Greece, with the result that the Greek gods were given Latin names as well.

The twelve chief gods formed the élite of Olympus. Each represented one of the forces of nature and a human characteristic, interpreted by sculptors in their statues of the gods. The following are the twelve main gods, with their descriptive characteristic.

Name		Natural and human characteristics	Attributes
Greek	*Latin*		
Zeus	Jupiter	sky, supreme god	sceptre, thunder
Hera	Juno	sky queen, marriage	peacock
Athena	Minerva	wisdom	owl, olive
Artemis	Diana	moon, chastity	stag
Aphrodite	Venus	love, beauty	dove
Demeter	Ceres	earth, fecundity	sheaf, sickle
Hestia	Vesta	hearth, domestic virtues	eternal fire
Apollo	Phoebus	sun, music and poetry	bow, lyre
Ares	Mars	tumult, war	spear, helmet
Hephaestus	Vulcan	fire, industry	hammer, anvil
Hermes	Mercury	trade, eloquence	caduceus, wings
Poseidon	Neptune	sea, earthquake	trident

GRECO-ROMAN ARCHEOLOGICAL OUTLINE. Mycenaean civilization at its peak c. 1400 to 1200 B.C., disappeared with the arrival of the Dorians whose architecture was born of a combination of solemn Nordic inspiration, measured Mycenaean outlay and of Oriental influences in decoration. The Doric style (800-500 B.C.) was characterized by severe simplicity; the flowering of the Ionic style lasted until the period of Macedonian hegemony (338 B.C.), branched out into the more florid Corinthian style and fell into decadence from the date of Roman domination (146 B.C.).

Greek sculpture played an important role in the ornamentation of temples but it was also an independent art. The most important periods of its evolution were: the *archaic* (8th to 6th century B.C.), characterized by a column-like rigidity of its subjects; the *classic* period, attaining the summit of corporeal harmony (500 to 300 B.C.). The most outstanding artists of this epoch were Phidias, Praxiteles and Skopas. Alexander the Great and his armies introduced Greek art in the eastern Mediterranean and this era (300 to 150 B.C.), typified by an opulent anatomy and by Asiatic influences, is known as the *hellenistic* period.

The Greek temple, open mainly to priests but sometimes to prominent citizens, was the home of the Divinity, and more often than not it was of small proportions. Rare exception to the oblong, rectangular outlay is the *tholos*, a round temple with circular colonnade. Ictinos, Callicrates and Mnesicles were among the most outstanding architects.

Secular architecture consisted of open-air theaters, stadiums and of the *agora*, the city's commercial and civic center. The *acropolis*, a citadel, usually enclosed all the sanctuaries. The Greek cities were surrounded by ramparts, the walls of which varied with the epoch (cyclopean, pelasgic, trapezoidal, etc.).

Current archeological terms, with their meanings, are:

Amphora vase, jug

Apse semicircular part of an edifice

Basilica rectangular, oblong edifice

Bouleuterion senate house

Capital uppermost part of a column, usually decorated

Caryatid sculpture of maiden, replacing a column

Hieron sacred enclosure

Megaron reception hall in Mycenaean palace

Metope plain or carved panel on temple's frieze

Naos sanctuary of temple

Odeion roofed edifice for artistic performances

Peristyle inner or outer colonnade

Pinacotheca picture gallery

Plinth rectangular base of a column

Pronaos vestibule of sanctuary

Propylae gate to monumental sites

Stele upright, decorated tombstone

Stereobate substructure of a temple

Stoa roofed building, supported by frontal columns, usually a business center

Stylobate foundation platform of a temple

INDEX

This index is based on modern Turkish place names. For a table of classical and historical names, giving their modern equivalents, see page 31.
In this index, H indicates listings for hotels, R for restaurants.

414   INDEX